The Late Voice

The Late Voice

Time, Age and Experience in Popular Music

Richard Elliott

Bloomsbury Academic
An imprint of Bloomsbury Publishing Inc

B L O O M S B U R Y
NEW YORK · LONDON · OXFORD · NEW DELHI · SYDNEY

Bloomsbury Academic

An imprint of Bloomsbury Publishing Inc

1385 Broadway	50 Bedford Square
New York	London
NY 10018	WC1B 3DP
USA	UK

www.bloomsbury.com

BLOOMSBURY and the Diana logo are trademarks of Bloomsbury Publishing Plc

First published 2015
Paperback edition first published 2017

Library of Congress Cataloging-in-Publication Data
A catalog record for this book is available from the Library of Congress.

ISBN: HB: 978-1-6289-2118-2
PB: 978-1-5013-3214-2
ePUB: 978-1-6289-2064-2
ePDF: 978-1-6289-2083-3

Typeset by Newgen Knowledge Works (P) Ltd., Chennai, India

Contents

Preface to the Paperback Edition:
Late Thoughts on Late Singers

There's a line in the first verse of Jerry Jeff Walker's song 'Mr Bojangles' in which the titular figure is described as seeming like 'the eyes of age'. The words capture what it means to recognize the passage of time and experience in another's body, as both evidence of that passage for anyone looking in and as a reminder of what the person behind the eyes has witnessed in the course of their life. The one who observes the eyes of age, who recognizes them as different enough from their own to take note of them, marks a gap in experience, an awareness and an anticipation of what the other knows and of what the self might yet discover. Walker's song gives agency to Bojangles, far more so than the old people described in John Prine's 'Hello in There', a song quoted in the pages of this book and which, on reflection, does not provide the empathetic reading of later life that I once thought I heard in it. Walker's singer-songwriter-storyteller recognizes *himself* (his present down-and-out self and his future self) in his old cellmate and realizes that he too may come to know what it is to know life from the other side of the eyes of age. It's Walker, too, who gives Bojangles a legacy in this popular song that has been performed by countless later singers, from Bob Dylan and Sammy Davis Jr to Nina Simone and Whitney Houston.

I would often think of that line about the eyes of age when I thought of Ralph Stanley, and I'd supplement it with a similar term: 'the voice of age'. Stanley wasn't the first artist to set me to thinking about the late voice, but once I started to develop the ideas into a book project I knew that I wanted to try and write about him. For the reasons I explain in Chapter 2, Stanley epitomized for me, as for many others, an ancient voice in terms of timbre, texture and text, bringing a chilling temporality to both the act and the content of sung words, the enunciation and the enunciated. To witness Stanley singing was to witness age itself, and with it the passage of a life spent communicating messages that were even older than the man expressing them. The voice itself seemed older than its owner, something acknowledged by Stanley himself when he joked, in his eighties, that he would be able to catch up with his voice if he were given a couple more decades. To do that, of course, the voice would have to stay still, to not change. But that was part of what I wanted to try and get at in *The Late Voice* – that the voice *might* change with age, but that lateness might also already reside within it, even from our earliest days. Lateness was not only about later stages of life, but also about an experience of life, or rather a series of experiences that could be recognized at flashpoint moments throughout the life course.

If lateness was to be only partly about later life, it was also only ever partly to be about the lateness of the recently departed. When *The Late Voice* went to press in 2015, I had been researching and writing about late voices that, in the case of all but one of my major case studies, belonged to still living singers. Even when I did consider lateness in relation to the recently lost, I was mainly working with the idea that recorded voices are always dead voices, temporarily reanimated in playback. Now, however, at the start of 2017, I write with the knowledge that two of the major case studies – Ralph Stanley and Leonard Cohen – have died since the publication of the hardback edition in October 2015. The year 2016 also saw the deaths of Merle Haggard and Guy Clark, two artists whose work deeply informed my thinking about the late voice, even if they are only mentioned relatively briefly in the book. These were only four names among many more musicians who died in 2016, a phenomenon that became increasingly discussed in the media as the year wore on. From David Bowie's passing in January to George Michael's in December, it seemed as if each week brought another high-profile obituary, leading to numerous end-of-year reviews under headlines such as 'The Year the Music Died'.

The attention given to musicians who died in 2016 is notable for many reasons, but in terms of its relevance to *The Late Voice* I was interested not only because of the loss of some of those I had written about, but also because the voices of those who reacted to the many losses that year – whether in professional media outlets or on social media – reinforced for me the sense in which music and musicians act as conduits to understandings of time, age and experience. While it may be a commonplace to talk of music, and especially the kind of popular songs I tend to discuss, as 'the soundtrack to our lives', the ways in which those soundtracks reflect, challenge and meld with our lived experience still deserves further philosophical exploration. Many of the responses I read in the wake of the lost musicians of 2016 brought this home to me in narratives whose eloquence, emotion, honesty and sense of collective connection were often overwhelming. In telling the stories of what their favourite musicians had meant to them, thousands of people went beyond the copy-and-paste hackwork of celebrity biography to trace instead the arcs of their own lives. In 2016, pop's audience wrote its autobiography like never before.

As for the recently deceased who make an appearance in this book, their passing does not fundamentally alter what I wanted to say about them originally, though the use of the present tense in the chapters that follow may occasionally seem strange. Death has brought to a close some of the narratives left open in the text, though of course there are still new narratives to add to these artists and their music, new discoveries to be made and new life experiences to be soundtracked by the work they left behind. I offer here a few additional facts and thoughts to supplement the stories told in the book.

Ralph Stanley died on 23 June 2016 at the age of 89. In the final footnote to Chapter 2, I note an announcement given in 2013 that Stanley was to embark on a 'farewell tour' that would run until December 2014. Evidently, retirement did not suit the veteran bluegrass musician and in 2015 further concert dates were announced running into 2016. In the last two years of his life Stanley received an honorary Doctorate of Music degree from Yale University (his second honorary degree – he had been known as 'Dr Ralph' since receiving his first from Lincoln Memorial University in 1976) and was elected a fellow of the American Academy of Arts and Sciences. An addition to the extensive Stanley discography also arrived in 2015 in the form of a series of solo songs and duets (with artists including Elvis Costello, Del McCoury, Buddy Miller, Jim Lauderdale, Robert Plant, Gillian Welch, David Rawlings and Lee Ann Womack) under the appropriate, if inevitable, title of *Man of Constant Sorrow*. Against these foils, Dr Ralph sounded, as ever, like the voice of age.

Leonard Cohen died on 7 November 2016 at the age of 82. He had recently released the album *You Want It Darker*, which, as with so much of his work, dwelled on themes of love, mortality and religion. If he sounded even older and more broken in this record, it was no doubt due to the illness he had endured while making it. Listening to the title track, particularly the parts where Cohen sings 'hineni hineni', I developed the fancy that perhaps the singer would continue to live until his voice became so deep it could no longer be perceived by humans. Cohen would disappear into the depths of his own voice. In the end that wasn't to be, but he got a lot of the way there. Cohen always sounded older than his years, even when, early in his career, the only way he sounded was through the pages of his poetry and prose. Making the move to music in the late 1960s, he was notably older than many of his peers in the singer-songwriter world. He became uniquely gifted at channeling that maturity into songs that showed that wisdom has a place in everyday culture, that lives lived can be lives shared through the medium of popular song. As listeners, we believed him because he seemed so genuine, so human, so attuned to the dialectic of joy and melancholy that constitutes the human experience. When I started to think about trying to communicate my ideas about late voice in book form, I knew I would have to include Cohen. In the end, I decided to place him alongside Frank Sinatra, a connection that worked in my mind but one which I'm not sure others would feel comfortable with. The results can be found in this book and the connection between the poet and the crooner still works for me, though I find myself wondering whether I should have given Cohen a chapter to himself. There is certainly much more to be said about his particular form of lateness.

Guy Clark died on 17 May 2016 at the age of 74. He lived long enough to be able to 'run his fingers through seventy years of living', as he so memorably wrote of the old-timer memorialized in his song 'Desperados Waiting for the Train'. That song, like Walker's 'Mr Bojangles', showed an ability to make connections between youth and old age and to offer the kind of empathetic maturity and anticipated experience that I refer to in the pages of this book as 'early late voice' (Walker, appropriately, wrote the liner notes for Clark's first album and helped to popularize some of his songs). Clark was a fabulous songwriter – for me, one of the very best – and a great singer and guitarist to boot. His writing, singing and playing voices came together in a united front suited brilliantly to the soundtracking of lives, his and those of others. His work sounded forever attuned to the ways that time, age and experience are written into the bodies, words and actions of the people we meet along the way, including those seemingly stable, but really ever-changing selves we see in the mirror, what Proust called that 'sequence of selves which die one after another'.

Merle Haggard died on 6 April 2016 at the age of 79. In a year already rife with notable deaths in the music industry, I felt this one deeply, for reasons both objective and subjective. Objectively, Haggard was a colossal figure in country music, as a singer, songwriter, hitmaker and soundmaker (by which I mean there is particular country sound that is distinctive to him and those who've been influenced by him). Subjectively, I'd been a fan of Haggard's music for around two and a half decades, with a steady rise in my appreciation of his work during that time. But adding to these reasons, and perhaps combining them, Haggard had played an important role in my work as an academic and writer, and I was aware that I hadn't yet managed to repay the debt I owe him by writing about him properly. I'd wanted to do so for many years. I still have extensive notes filed in various places about him and his music that remain undeveloped, waiting for their ideal opportunity. When embarking on writing *The Late Voice*, I thought I'd finally get around to writing about him, for if anyone fitted the bill of a late voice singer-songwriter, it was Haggard. And indeed, my original plan for the book contained a chapter on country music that aimed to discuss Haggard, Willie Nelson, Johnny Cash, Kris Kristofferson, Guy Clark, Townes Van Zandt and Steve Earle. It was always going to be a crowded, and hence potentially lengthy, chapter and perhaps that's why I felt I had to abandon it as the book took shape and I started to worry about cohesion and word count.

But perhaps there were other reasons. Perhaps, even though I continue to deny, against the claims by those who place anti-intellectualism amongst the primary responses to artistic creation, that studying the things you love somehow spoils them, even though I have never believed this, I still have found it difficult to turn that study into writing that communicates what I have heard, learned and felt when listening across the years to particular artists. It wasn't until *The Late Voice* that I attempted to write about Neil Young and Joni Mitchell, two artists who have provided my life's soundtrack since I first started to comprehend, in my late teens, what I later came to refer to as 'anticipated experience'. What I ended up writing about them barely scratches the surface of what I want to say, but it's a start at least. The same goes for Van Morrison, whose work I have started to explore in writing only very recently, since the publication of *The Late Voice*. I still long for, but simultaneously dread, the time I finally try to get down at length what Guy Clark and Townes Van Zandt have meant to me over the years, what they continue to mean to me.

With Haggard, though, it should have been a bit easier. I had the notes and I had written a little about him before. When I decided to write my

Master's thesis on country music and hip-hop, I focused my account on place, race, experience and authenticity; Haggard was one of my main country examples and a major influence on the work more generally. I listened closely to the Legacy CD reissue of his 1981 album *Big City* and was also engrossed in his then-recent album for the Anti label, *If I Could Only Fly*. Songs from these albums became my main examples, songs such as 'My Favorite Memory', 'Big City', 'Are the Good Times Really Over', 'Wishing All These Old Things Were New', 'If I Could Only Fly', 'Bareback', 'Leavin's Getting Harder' and 'Thanks to Uncle John'. Some of the songs were Haggard originals and some, such as his version of Blaze Foley's 'If I Could Only Fly', were brilliant takes on the work of other fascinating singer-songwriters.

As news of Haggard's passing was spreading over the internet, Noah Berlatsky wrote an excellent assessment of *If Could Only Fly* for *The Guardian*, focusing in particular on the album's title track and how this late, sparse version of Foley's song eclipsed earlier versions (Haggard had been performing it since at least the mid-1980s). Where earlier renditions proved that Haggard was more than capable of mastering the song, the 2000 version, for Berlatsky, 'feels as though the grief is clotting around him, and he's trying to dig out'. I agree with Berlatsky's assessment of an album that was so central to my early attempts to write about popular music as an academic. But, for me, the album was also an invitation, at the height of the critical obsession with 'alt. country', to take a retrospective look at Haggard's career and venture into areas of country music that I, along with other fans of alternative or progressive country, had been avoiding for various reasons. The most obvious of these was a lingering sense of unease about some of Haggard's more notorious material, such as 'Okie from Muskogee' and 'The Fightin' Side of Me'. I already knew there was more to Haggard than this and had done since at least the purchase of my first Haggard album, *Serving 190 Proof*. As has often happened in my record-buying career, I hadn't started with the definitive work but with what was available one day when, intrigued at a market stall or car boot sale, I'd taken a plunge on an artist I'd heard of but whose work I didn't know well. As it goes, *Serving 190 Proof* wasn't a bad place to start at all, especially as an introduction to Haggard's late voice. The opening trio of 'Footlights', 'Got Lonely Too Early (This Morning)' and 'Heaven Was a Drink of Wine' are fine examples of Haggard's more melancholy, even self-pitying, side; all contain great lines and vocal performances.

I'd had a generally overlooked but fascinating album as my introduction to Haggard, back around the time I was first getting into Willie Nelson and the 1970s progressive country artists. Later, as I wanted to delve deeper, there was still my resistance to 'Okie' and 'Fightin' Side' to get over. I'm not sure I ever did get over that – and I still tend to avoid playing those songs – but I came to realize that there was so much more to Haggard's story and to his songwriting. I also realized that those songs, regardless of what I might personally think of them, had to be part of that story and could, as in David Cantwell's masterful account in *Merle Haggard: The Running Kind*, be convincingly placed into historical, cultural and personal contexts. But by then those songs had started to stop mattering to me as I discovered the gems to be found across Haggard's massive back catalogue. At some point during the research for *The Late Voice*, Haggard overtook Neil Young to become the most represented artist in my record collection. I have a silly amount of Haggard albums, yet they all seem essential, with each album containing at least a few masterful, ear-catching examples of songwriting or revelatory versions of other people's songs.

Pretty high on the list for me would be one of the many duets Haggard recorded with his running mate Willie Nelson, a leisurely, beautifully paced version of David Lynn Jones's 'When Times Were Good' which the pair included on their 1987 album *Seashores of Old Mexico* (an album that also includes their duet of 'If I Could Only Fly'). It's a critically unloved album, but I've long had a soft spot for it, and 'When Times Were Good' is one of the main reasons. Nelson starts the song wonderfully, with a stark vocal accompanied by minimal guitar. He sets the pace and manages the dramatic development as the band instrumentation gradually builds the song towards a chorus which Nelson attacks in his highest, lonesomest register. For me, though, the standout has always been the moment more than three and a half minutes into the song when, following a relaxed instrumental break, Haggard's voice takes up the narrative. In two drawn-out lines – 'There's a Golden Eagle rollin' out of Memphis / And a country singer still lost between the lines' – we get to ride the rolling slopes of Haggard's voice, its breaking highs and creaking lows, the moments where the voice dips or drops out momentarily, just enough of a catch in the throat for us to get the sense of weariness the singer is carrying, his almost paralyzing burden of memory, loss and nostalgia.

I've tried and failed to write about Haggard on a number of occasions and he only makes very fleeting appearances in the main body of this book. Even the thoughts gathered in this new preface are as much thoughts about me as they are about Haggard or the other musicians I mention. I've been driven once more by my reaction to musicians whose work has moved me and has invited me to supplement my listening with attempts to write about what I have loved and learned, even if that means occasionally losing my way through the corridors of memory. But perhaps that's what our connection with our favourite musicians always brings, an opportunity to learn about ourselves through what we feel they've taught us. That was true of the collective autobiography that accompanied the loss of all those musicians in 2016, and I hope it is true of this book. *The Late Voice* was written as a way of formalizing some of those lessons we learn from popular music. It was also written as a celebration of the living spirit of that music and of the living artists in whose eyes and voices of age we become aware of our changing selves.

Acknowledgements

Many thanks to Ally Jane Grossan at Bloomsbury Academic for commissioning this book and to her and Michelle Chen for working with me on the preparation of the manuscript. I am grateful to the readers of the original proposal for their comments, which encouraged me to continue with the work, to refine certain areas and to try to be more explicit about what I was and wasn't able to do in this book. I am very appreciative of the kind and encouraging comments made by Freya Jarman, Ros Jennings and Michael Pickering, all of whom read the complete manuscript and whose comments enabled me to undertake the final revisions with confidence. Thanks to Giles Herman and those involved in seeing the book through the final production stages.

Parts of Chapter 4 were first published in an article for a special issue of *Popular Music and Society* on Bob Dylan and place in 2009. I have presented work on the late voice at a variety of academic conferences and symposiums at Newcastle University, the University of Huddersfield, and the University of Sussex and remain grateful to participants and co-presenters who provided useful feedback or asked helpful questions.

This is the first book I have written since arriving at Sussex in 2012 and I have benefitted greatly from the welcoming and inclusive atmosphere created by colleagues there. I am particularly grateful for feedback and encouragement received from faculty in my home school of Media, Film and Music.

Thanks are due once more to my family in the United Kingdom and Portugal for constant support and for providing time and space to work on the book. Special thanks as always to Maria for support and patience during the research and writing process.

Introduction

This book had its genesis in a variety of times, places and experiences, some more easily discernible than others from the distance of the present. When choosing musical case studies for my doctoral thesis on loss, memory and nostalgia in popular song in late 2003, I became interested in exploring the work of Nina Simone, who had died earlier that year. Simone's death, and the flurry of attention her life and work received in its wake, helped to plant in my mind her potential as an artist to study further, but of equal importance was the recognition that Simone would be an ideal case study for exploring the themes of my thesis. For one thing, the obituaries invariably attested to the fact that Simone had been absent from the scene for years (not strictly true, but true enough for the kinds of life narratives and historical frameworks that obituary writers find appealing); my thesis was about absence in the form of loss, memory and nostalgia, so this seemed apt. More than this, however, was a sense of fascination that I had long held for Simone's later work. By the time of her death I had been a fan of her music for some years, during which time I had absorbed her classic material of the 1960s and had, like many others, fixed her to a particular historical moment and to a sociocultural purpose, that of spokeswoman of the civil rights movement.

But this knowledge lay in tension with other knowledge and experience I had of Simone's music. Although, like many people of my generation, I had first become aware of Simone with the reissue in the mid-1980s of her 1957 recording 'My Baby Just Cares for Me', my first serious commitment to her work came some years later with the purchase of a record, the 1977 album *Baltimore*. Because I came to know this album a few years before hearing her more explicitly political work of the 1960s, I first encountered a Simone who was twenty years into her professional recording career and who had spent much of the 1970s out of sight and sound of the record-buying public. I discovered that *Baltimore* had been a comeback album of sorts and, while it had been critically well received, was not considered canonical work. Simone remained, in the popular imagination and in the historical account, an icon of the 1960s; anything else was 'late work'. *Baltimore* was late work because, even though Simone was only forty-four at the time of recording the album, it came after a lengthy silence from the artist and seemed to delineate a before (the Simone of the late 1950s to the early 1970s, the 'long sixties') and an after that would stretch from *Baltimore* through to her death at the age of seventy. There seemed to be no 'middle period' of her career (though I later changed my mind about that).

In coming to Simone later on as an example of loss, memory and nostalgia, I was thinking of the artist who recorded the achingly sad songs 'My Father' and 'All I Want from You' for *Baltimore*. I wanted to know how those songs of late melancholy fit with the narrative of the more famous Simone of the civil rights era. Might there be a connection between the sense of weariness that I associated with *Baltimore* and the outcome of the revolutionary times in which Simone's career had burned brightest? My attempts to approach this and other questions relating to Nina Simone's work became the work of a thesis chapter and, in 2013, a book devoted to the artist.[1] During the course of my exploration of Simone's life and work, I encountered many more evocative and intriguing recordings. Among these were Simone's live recording of Sandy Denny's 'Who Knows Where the Time Goes', which appeared on the 1970 album *Black Gold*. Simone, who was thirty-six when the performance was recorded, was far from being old in any but a child's use of the term, yet there was something in her delivery that spoke to me of age, experience and time. This is partly due to the dramatic way in which Simone introduces the song to her audience. During a lengthy reflection that makes implicit reference to her celebrity and explicit reference to that of others (notably actress Faye Dunaway), Simone offers the following observations:

> Let's see what we can do with this lovely, lovely thing that goes past all racial conflict and all kinds of conflict. It is a reflective tune and some time in your life you will have occasion to say 'What is this thing called time? You know, what is that?' . . . [T]ime is a dictator, as we know it. Where does it go? What

does it do? Most of all, is it alive? Is it a thing that we cannot touch and is it alive? And then one day you look in the mirror – how old! – and you say, 'Where did the time go?'[2]

Simone's framing of the song, and her intimate, time-stopping performance, led me to consider this version as an example of what I had started to call, during my doctoral work, 'the late voice'. While my initial thoughts about the concept were mainly connected to work produced by musicians (mostly singers) in the later parts of their careers and to what has been termed, in discussion of artists more broadly, 'late style', I soon became interested in the possibility of lateness recognised at earlier stages than might be customary. In other words, while there seemed to be a fit between chronologically late work (work created by artists late in their lives and/or careers) and themes of time, age and experience, there was nothing to exclude such a connection with artists at much earlier stages in their lives. This was made even more evident by considering 'Who Knows Where the Time Goes' as a song composed by Sandy Denny at the age of nineteen or twenty.

This realisation was both enabling (in suggesting trajectories beyond those explored in my previous work) and problematic. The problem lay in my refusal to let go of the idea that to talk about age and ageing necessitated more than merely talking about later stages of life, let alone 'old age'. It might have been enough to stop at my earliest conception of late voice and to provide an account that examined the late work of a number of musicians and perhaps also their attitudes towards lateness and/or late style. Indeed, it was (and still is) tempting to do this. But critical inquiry often refuses to rest at the entry level, even for the clearing and establishing of new ground, and I was constantly drawn back to the notion of early lateness, to a more pervasive use of popular song to record experience gained and/or anticipated regardless of the age of the singer (and, as I came to realise, of the listener). This necessitated the incorporation of time into my study, because, as Denny's song so eloquently shows, we reflect on time at many stages in our lives. As a consideration of time lost, time to come and time passing, 'Who Knows Where the Time Goes' can be heard to represent a moment of transition. To place the song in its author's biography is to speculate on the thoughts of a young woman leaving behind the friends and familiars of her youth as she embarks on the rest of her life. Other such songs may spring to mind: 'Bob Dylan's Dream' (Bob Dylan), 'Meet on the Ledge' (written by Richard Thompson and sung by Sandy Denny with Fairport Convention), 'Sugar Mountain' (Neil Young), 'The Circle Game' and 'Both Sides, Now' (both Joni Mitchell).

Popular music artists, as performers in the public eye, offer a privileged site for the witnessing and analysis of ageing and its mediation. This book embarks upon such an analysis by considering issues of time, memory, innocence and experience in modern (predominantly mid- to late twentieth century) popular song and the use by singers and songwriters of a 'late voice'. Lateness, as developed in the foregoing examples and as I present it in this book, refers to five primary issues: chronology (the stage in an artist's career); the vocal act (the ability to convincingly portray experience); afterlife (posthumous careers made possible by recorded sound); retrospection (how voices 'look back' or anticipate looking back); and the writing of age, experience, lateness and loss into song texts. Supplementing theorisations of the ways that lived experience mixes with that learned from books and images, consideration of music allows us to posit the concept of 'sounded experience', a term intended to describe how music reflects upon and helps to mediate life experience over extended periods of time (indeed, over lifetimes). Connected to this is a supposition that phonography, understood as the after-effects of the revolution in experience initiated by sound recording, provides a rich site for exploring issues of memory, time, lateness and afterlife.

Recent years have witnessed a growth in research on ageing and the experience of later stages of life, focusing on physical health, lifestyle and psychology. Work in the latter field has overlapped to a certain extent with the field of memory studies. Scholars of popular music studies have also begun to explore the fertile area of age, experience and memory, although the focus to date has tended to be on the reception side, on how people use culture at later stages in their lives. My work, while embracing these fields, seeks to connect age, experience and lateness with particular performers and performance traditions via the identification and analysis of 'late voice' in singers and songwriters of mid- to late twentieth-century popular music, with a primary focus on North American and British singers at this initial stage. The recent interest in later stages of life across the arts, humanities and sciences has arguably grown as scholars react to the consequences of an ageing population. This has been reflected within popular music studies in books such as Ros Jennings and Abigail Gardner's '*Rock On': Women. Ageing and Popular Music*, Andy Bennett and Paul Hodkinson's *Ageing and Youth Cultures: Music, Style and Identity* and Bennett's *Music, Style and Aging: Growing Old Disgracefully?*[3] The first two titles, both collections of essays, intersect with my project while being distinct from it. *The Late Voice* is closer to '*Rock On*' in that the latter book examines the cultural work done by popular music performers as they reflect on issues of age, experience and public persona; it also utilises an interdisciplinary approach, highlighting the intersection of performance studies, cultural and media studies, and textual analysis. Yet '*Rock On*' differs from my project in its exclusive focus on female performers and its gender-based analyses. While issues of gender have been important to certain stages of my work, my primary focus here is on time, age and experience. My work also differs in that it explores the early attainment of 'lateness' by certain performers and also considers the 'lateness' of certain musical genres. Where Andy Bennett's monograph and the essays collected in *Ageing and Youth Cultures* dwell exclusively on audiences, my study focuses on performers, musical texts and critical discourse. Work on ageing youth cultures and popular musical audiences has proven beneficial to my project but I have not undertaken ethnographic research. One of the currents that run through my book is an emphasis on the continued importance of a textual analysis that takes performers and their texts (and the connection of the two via the late voice) as its primary material. With its suggestion of the early attainment of lateness, rather than an exclusive emphasis on older performers, *The Late Voice* shares some of the concerns of Sheila Whiteley's *Too Much Too Young: Popular Music, Age and Gender*.[4] Whiteley shows how voices have been used in popular music to give an illusion of age greater than that possessed by performers, an observation that is useful for my exploration of anticipated lateness. This focus on the voice, along with Whiteley's interest in intertextuality, provides valuable resonances with my own project. However, the overall scope of the two works is quite distinct and the focus on gender is not one which has guided the case studies or the observations in my book for the most part (though I do consider aspects of masculinity in Chapter 3).

I have attempted in *The Late Voice* to contribute towards the maintenance of popular music studies as a field in which the kind of aesthetic concerns applied to classical and art music can be explored in a rigorous and sustained manner, allowing for serious consideration of popular music texts from both musicological and sociocultural perspectives. Since Richard Leppert and George Lipsitz's landmark article on age, the body and experience in the music of Hank Williams in 1990, there has been little serious popular music research that has successfully explored the biographical, historical, cultural and geopolitical contexts in which lateness (here understood primarily as experience) is represented in musical performance, in particular that of singers and songwriters.[5] Such qualities are often recognised and highlighted in accounts of popular music in the press, but there still remains a need for scholarly, culturally and textually informed study of this area.

Ethnographic methodologies have tended to be favoured in studies of popular music and age, perhaps due to a recognition that they provide a more democratic and accurate picture of musical meaning than that allowed by the traditional musicological or critical 'expert'. This valuable insight has helped lead to the development of the disciplines of popular music studies and popular music education. Such practical considerations of musical production and consumption now arguably hold a prominent position in institutions involved in teaching and researching popular music. However, one drawback of these developments is a potential dismantling of the common ground forged between popular music studies and traditional musicology. Such a recognition of common ground enabled popular music to be valued as an aesthetically important medium, an insight that, in turn, was instrumental in allowing the space for today's popular music and music education courses. In writing this book the way I have, I wish to make a strong claim for the continued relevance of aesthetic, cultural and critical theory in the study of popular music in order to (re)assert the latter's importance in everyday life. Here, theory, far from being impractical or removed from 'the real world', is focused on constantly expanding the horizons of what it is possible to think and know about music.

Keith Negus, whose recent work provides a welcome exploration of the role of time and narrative in the interpretation of popular song, makes it clear that it is possible to combine narrative theory with phenomenological methods and to imagine, if not empirically 'prove', the relationship between the experience of an individual listener and that of a larger community. He does so partly by examining what it means to interpret songs in the first place and partly by considering the mixing of private and public listening rituals enabled by recorded music. With regard to the latter, Negus cites Richard Kearney's formulation that 'subjects, individual or communal, come to *imagine* and *know* themselves in the stories they tell about themselves'[6] and that our self-understanding develops as part of an understanding of (and learned from) others; far from being isolated from the knowledge and perspective of others, we (and this is one of the reasons I can confidently say 'we'[7]) become who we are as we become aware of others. As Negus points out, by 'emphasizing how human engagement with recorded songs can be understood as a private ritual' one is not thereby 'suggesting that this is "asocial"'; furthermore, 'notions of interiority need not be deployed to imply romantic, unmediated, essentialist qualities of artistic expression, unfiltered by or unshaped by social relationships and structures'.[8]

Classical musicology has a well-established history of associating particular stylistic characteristics to periods in the lives of composers, and theorisations of lateness and late style in the arts have invariably privileged classical music.[9] This book asks whether there is a connection between the 'seriousness' of a cultural form (the extent to which it is considered an 'art') and the acceptability of speaking about 'late style'. Does popular music only invite such consideration when it is thought of as 'art'? Furthermore, has one of the outcomes of popular music studies been to remove the 'artiness' of popular music and to reassert its social function? If so, where would that leave a seemingly artist-based theory such as the late voice? By considering artists alongside styles, and biography alongside history, I seek to examine how each sheds light on the other while revisiting the debts owed by popular music studies to cultural studies and critical theory.

One of the possibilities that can be hypothesised is that lateness in an artist's work coincides with the recognition of lateness in a style or tradition. Building on theories expounded in my previous work, I wish to ascertain the 'eventness' of contemporary popular music and argue for a theory of lateness relevant to popular music and culture..[10] While I do not intend to engage in the long-running debate initiated by Adorno's work on popular music, the seriousness which I attach to the 'late style' of popular musicians and my positing of the late voice as a concept for which popular singers and songwriters provide especially compelling case studies, is intended to serve as an argument for the aesthetic value of popular music, even as it departs from an assumption of that value rather than an attempt to justify it.

Although at some points during this project I considered testing Adorno's, Said's and Spitzer's accounts of late style against my case studies, I have ultimately – at least for this book – decided against doing so. There are a few reasons for this. Firstly, I feel there is already a lot of ground to stake out in presenting my main concepts of time, age, experience and late voice and to embark on an additional comparative process would delay even further the analytical work I wish to undertake with my case studies. Secondly, my concept of the late voice is, as already indicated, not solely (and often not even mainly) concerned with late style in the manner described by previous writers; the representation of time, age and experience alongside the ability to convincingly 'voice' such representation regardless of career-point is of more interest to me. Thirdly, it remains to be seen whether an analytical language developed with a fairly rigidly defined notion of 'music' (classical, historical, instrumental) could, or should, be transferred to the types of music under consideration here. Of these three reasons, the last is the one I remain most ambivalent about, in that I am aware that it may contradict my earlier stated desire to treat popular music as seriously as any other art form. However, I believe that by allowing my conceptualisation of the late voice to emerge from consideration of my case studies, I am following a similar process to the 'late style' theorists by allowing the musical examples to determine the conceptual framework. At the same time, those examples hopefully provide sufficient evidence to continue arguing for the seriousness of popular song.

Overview of the book

Each of my areas of interest comes with a vast literature attached to it and many concepts, theories and discoveries. The book is ambitious and impertinent enough to suggest the possibility of considering such big topics as time, age, experience and voice within a single volume that devotes most of its pages to accounts of particular singers and songwriters. But it is also, by necessity as much as inclination, modest in its realisation that it can only hope to pose certain questions, suggest some approaches, offer initial reflections and perhaps set a dialogue in motion. In Chapter 1, I provide initial thoughts about my areas of interest as they have emerged while thinking about the music that inspired the interest. I also consider my themes as encountered in other fields, including academic literature, poetry, film and fiction. The organisation of the sections according to my major themes – time, age, experience and voice – is an attempt to begin systematising the concepts in ways that are useful for the case studies which comprise the remaining chapters. Chapter 2 focuses, for the most part, on Ralph Stanley, the bluegrass or 'old-time' musician whose long career in popular music gained fresh recognition following the use of his music in the film *O Brother, Where Art Thou?* in 2000. Taking as a starting point the song 'O Death', the chapter examines discourse around Stanley's age and the ways in which age is witnessed in his voice. I provide an overview of Stanley's career, followed by a discussion of different versions of 'O Death'. I also consider the relationship between the particular and the universal and between the individual and the community. Chapter 3 offers an examination of selected work by Frank Sinatra and Leonard Cohen, analysing the ways in which age and experience are connected in popular culture to particular notions of male mastery. The era under discussion saw numerous challenges to such notions and various crises of masculinity can be determined in the work of Sinatra and Cohen, albeit that the former represents a retrospective look at an earlier, supposedly stable world, while the latter presents an arguably more progressive account of male doubt and insecurity. Both artists generated a significant amount of cultural discourse around their age, experience and relevancy at various stages of their careers and this discourse is also analysed. In Sinatra's case I am also interested in the way he functions as an authorial figure in relation to the songs he interprets. Cohen is more obviously an author in his double role as poet and singer-songwriter; the former career also delays his appearance on the music stage, earning him a reputation as a rock era performer who was always already 'old'. Chapter 4 turns to the work of Bob Dylan, an artist who claims a greater interest in 'becoming' than 'being' yet whose work also resonates with references to belonging, homeliness, stasis and the past. Dylan's work is exemplary as an analysis of lateness in twentieth-century popular and vernacular music and has followed a fascinating dialectic of belonging and distance with respect to its sociohistorical milieu. I examine Dylan's poetics of place and displacement, suggesting that his constant reiteration of themes of movement, escape and quest is tempered by a tendency to also dwell on issues of belonging, home and return. Studying these aspects of his work also contributes to an argument for establishing a coherent, singular 'self' to this most enigmatic and shape-shifting of performers. Chapter 5 explores the notion of the 'confessional' singer-songwriter via a discussion of Joni Mitchell and Neil Young, both of whom have made extensive use of innocence and experience as elements within their songwriting. Mitchell and Young make fascinating use of childlike perspectives in their work, often contrasting the depiction of youth and newness with reflections on the ageing process and on the wisdom supposedly gained through experience. Both artists' late careers are also examined to analyse the ways in which, as public figures, they have reinvented themselves and been able to reflect back on their earlier work.

Time, Age, Experience and Voice

Does some story link one sound to another?

Italo Calvino

Time

Introducing her performance of 'Who Knows Where the Time Goes' on the album *Black Gold* (1970), Nina Simone extends the question laid out in the song's title and refrain by adding further questions: 'What is this thing called time? . . . What does it do? . . . Is it a thing?'[1] Of the many things that time confirms for us, one is that, despite the remarkable endeavours of philosophy, art and science, we are only partially closer to solving the mysteries of time than those forebears who first meditated on them at length. Even to note this is to fall into the time-worn path laid out by other introductions to the topic. Paul Ricoeur, for example, begins his classic three-volume *Time and Narrative* with a direct question from Augustine's *Confessions* – 'What, then, is time?' – and devotes his first chapter to Augustine's exploration of the experience of time, before going on to connect it with Aristotle's theory of plot.[2] Augustine's question appears again in Eva Hoffman's book *Time*, at the start of a chapter on 'Time and the Mind'; here, it is immediately coupled with Augustine's own response: 'If no man ask me the question, I know; but if I pretend to explicate it to anybody, I know it not.'[3] By placing this reference at the start of my own exploration, I wish to highlight the perennial importance of mental time, the human attempt to come to terms with temporal experience. Hoffman distinguishes between time as connected to the body, to the mind and to culture, while recognising the important interconnection of all these aspects. Reflecting on the first of these, she writes that 'to be alive is to feel the passage of time, and to have time working through us in every cell, nerve ending and organ, as it takes us through its paces and plays in our bodies its mortal, vital tune'.[4] The metaphor of the tune is an apt one for my own study and I wish to retain this idea of the body as an instrument on which, and through which, the work of time, age and experience can be heard. As we pass through time and space – to put a more active stance on what we may think we are doing – so time passes through us, leaving its marks on us. We experience this passage, as Hoffman says, in all aspects of our biology. But it is as a mental exercise that we attempt to stop time, to reflect upon it. As Hoffman notes, 'If the propositions of the phenomenologists – Husserl, Bergson, Merleau-Ponty, Heidegger – still have resonance for us today, it is because they tried to analyse perceptions of time as a function of consciousness and subjectivity, rather than as an absolute, objective reality'.[5]

Mental time can be thought of, as Augustine suggested long ago, as 'expectation, attention and memory'. The future passes through the present into the past, as in Augustine's famous example of the recitation of a verse:

Suppose that I am going to recite a psalm that I know. Before I begin, my faculty of expectation is engaged by the whole of it. But once I have begun, as much of the psalm as I have removed from the province of expectation and relegated to the past now engages my memory, and the scope of the action which I am performing is divided between the two faculties of memory and expectation, the one looking back to the part which I have already recited, the other looking forward to the part which I have still to recite. But my faculty of attention is present all the while, and through it passes what was the future in the process of becoming the past. As the process continues, the province of memory is extended in proportion as that of expectation is reduced, until the whole of my expectation is absorbed. This happens when I have finished my recitation and it has passed into the province of memory.What is true of the whole psalm is also true of the parts and of each syllable. It is true of any longer action in which I may be engaged and of which the recitation of the psalm may only be a small part. It is true of a man's whole life, of which all his actions are parts. It is true of the whole history of mankind, of which each man's life is a part.[6]

That Augustine uses the examples of recitation and resonance makes appropriate the connection, if not the strict application, of his theories to music. Other thinkers have been drawn to similar analogies, such as when Husserl uses melody as an example of *retention* and *protention*, his way of explaining the flow of time through the present. For philosophers of time, there are important differences and disagreements to be highlighted in the theories of Augustine, Husserl and others, though it is not the purpose of this book to engage in those debates, nor to pick a 'winning' theory to apply to popular songs. Nor is the experience of music as time passing a primary concern here, though I do believe that an awareness of this possibility should be maintained. What can be done with a melody, and hence what can be done with time, are certainly important aspects of musical affect. Singers can play tricks with our expectations and use vocal art to alter our sense of time. Examples might include the use of *tempo rubato* ('stolen time'), rhythm and vocal phrasing, all of which affect our sense of the perception of time by opening up a long present of expectation and surprise, a dialectic engagement with song. As Philip Ward writes of Sandy Denny's vocal art, her '*rubato* elongation of a line seems to make time stand still'.[7]

Songs pass through us from future into past. Like Augustine's recited verse, they are, in one sense, fixed, bounded and knowable objects. But they are also, to adopt something closer to a Husserlian approach, examples of the open, infinite future of possible time; cloud-like they are there ahead of us and pass through us (and the present) into the past. Once they have passed, they are not simply contained in some locker room of the mind, but rather, in order to still exist, they must be replayed and pass through us again. This passing is both a process of continual loss and the promise of something regained; as such, it can be a cause of consternation and anxiety. Perhaps the desire to fix time has lain behind the many attempts to explain it, whether poetically or scientifically (or both, as in the precise, searching lines of T. S. Eliot's *Four Quartets*, to which I'll return below). The fantasy that one can fix time, or understand it as being motionless, recurs in various logical explanations from Zeno's famous paradoxes, through Newton's observations on time, space and motion to Russell's philosophical treatises and beyond. In a reflection on the passage of time and the experience of ageing, Jean Améry argues that such logical attempts to fix time are of little help when contemplating its ceaseless, unidirectional flow:

> Time has passed, flowed by, rolled on, blown away, and we pass with it . . .
> like smoke in a strong wind. We ask ourselves what time might actually be,
> about which we say that everything glides and runs by with it – ask ourselves
> with a tenacious naïveté that borders on total ridiculousness, and then are
> taught by those thinkers who are so adroit in logical play that the question,
> when asked in such a banal form, is deceptive. . . . Answers exist to many
> questions about time, and sufficiently sharp and well-trained thinkers have
> tried to find them. But what they've come away with has little to do with our
> concerns.[8]

For Améry, 'logical play . . . has little to do' with his concerns because his concerns are with the inevitability of ageing and the end of life. To stare at mortality in the stark light of this inevitability, which is what Améry wishes to do, is to find all other explanations of time – logical, illogical or paradoxical – irrelevant.

Music can be a form of escape from the realities of time or it may invite us to reflect on mortality and inevitability. The singer-songwriter Guy Clark plays on the notion of time as escape on his second album *Texas Cookin'* (1976), the back sleeve of which contains the following message for the listener: 'Once upon a good time we got together and made a record of ourselves having a good time making a record – this is it.' The album's fourth track, 'It's About Time', contains more such playfully reflexive lines, describing tunes that drift through halls 'trying to put a stop to clocks on the wall' and a record player that 'fakes it' in order for a couple to 'keep time' with each other by dancing. 'It's only time', sings Clark, 'And only time will tell.'[9] But even without this lyrical reflexivity, music can be understood to be taking us way from time, or putting us in a different configuration of time. Music, in Simon Frith's formulation, 'enables us to experience time aesthetically, intellectually, and physically in new ways. . . . [It] allows us to stop time, while we consider how it passes'.[10]

Music may be seen as a model of passing time but it is also a removal from everyday time, in which time may even be retrospectively experienced as having stood still. As Paul Virilio notes, 'At a concert, when the musical motor shuts off, not only is there a liberating violence of ovations and handclapping but also a thunderstorm of sneezing, coughing, scraping of feet – as if everyone suddenly reacquired possession of his own body.'[11] Such experiences might leave one legitimately wondering just where the time went, though it should perhaps be noted that this is only likely to occur at a performance in which one is fully engaged. We have surely all experienced concerts in which we find ourselves bored and in which time suddenly seems to drag; when this occurs, one can become all too aware of the body as one shifts uneasily in one's seat or, as is more likely in a popular music context, from one foot to another. For the drift to work, we require an engagement over time such that we lose track of time. However, while the experience of listening to music understandably provides a typical example, such moments of contemplative loss can come upon us in many other situations. Sylviane Agacinski connects the examples of a gazer on the shore and a moviegoer:

> The one whose eyes follow the flight of a gull over the sea adopts the temporality of that flight; his time becomes the gull's time. The stroller's idleness is similar to the idleness of someone at a play or a movie. Each of them yields to the rhythm of a movement that is not their own. In forgetting his own movement, and thus his own time, the stroller embraces the time of things. But the gull's time is not the departing boat's time, or the rock's time emerging from the waves, or the child's time playing on the beach. In the midst of a world that passes at such different speeds, the contemplative observer *loses time*. He no longer has his own time, and he feels the absence of absolute temporality. When we leave a movie theater, we also leave the film, and its temporality that our thoughts had so intimately embraced, to rediscover our own time and our own life. For an instant, we remain suspended between two times.[12]

That Agacinski can provide a rich variety of temporal experiences without once mentioning music or listening serves as a reminder that music, while often presented as the ultimate art of time rather than space, is not unique in its focus on temporality. Casting our eyes over a painting or sculpture is a temporal as much as a spatial experience, not only in that it takes us time to take it all in, but also in that we may discern a narrative of some kind being communicated to us in the artwork, one that, like all narratives, unfolds over time. So too with reading, as Michel de Certeau highlights:

[S]ince he is incapable of stockpiling (unless he writes or records), the reader cannot protect himself from the erosion of time (while reading, he forgets himself and he forgets what he has read) unless he buys the object (book, image) which is no more than a substitute (the spoor or promise) of moments 'lost' in reading.[13]

Leonard Cohen, the poet and singer-songwriter whose work I discuss later in this book, makes a distinction between poems and songs by saying that, whereas one can linger over a poem because of its spatial representation, reading backwards if necessary, one experiences the song as a unidirectional force in which it is impossible to go back in time. This is certainly true, and even if one attempts a thought experiment in which a combination of rewinding and replaying is made analogous to the processes of reading backwards or jumping across the space of the poem, there is a sense that the musical work falls apart more obviously during such processes. At the same time, we should recall the role of poetry as a spoken, recited or chanted medium, which also prevents such lingering, and music as a temporal flow made spatial in the process of notation or sonic visualisation. The cutting, splicing, sampling and repetition of the musical text by producers, hip hop artists and other kinds of remixers and remasterers rely on the notion of an analysis every bit as spatial as that of poetic exegesis. We might think of songs as poems voiced (and hence timed) and of poems as speech made spatial; both processes recognise a dynamic interaction of time and space.

Then there is representation. I am as interested in the ways in which texts, as well as being temporal processes – things that take time – also take time as their theme, as in the Sandy Denny and Guy Clark songs quoted earlier. Where any sentence or melody would do for a Husserlian account of temporal flow, I am interested in the signifying power, in the semantics of what is delivered in that flow. To take an example from the world of poetry, T. S. Eliot's *Four Quartets* is a work devoted to the contemplation of time, particularly in its opening poem 'Burnt Norton'. The poem contains numerous lines on the temporal flow of words and music, presenting itself as a philosophical treatise on the experience of passing time, time past and – in the religious preoccupations that come to dominate the *Four Quartets* – time to come. As a work of poetry, it is also an example of aesthetic experience and, if the distinction is necessary, the aestheticisation of experience. The famous opening lines of 'Burnt Norton', in which we read that 'Time present and time past / Are both perhaps present in time future / And time future contained in time past', strike the keynote of the poem not only in the preoccupation with the words 'time', 'present', 'past' and 'future', but also in the establishment of a twisting, riddling style that will continue through the poem. This twisting represents both the restlessness and indecision of the mind when faced with 'big issues' and the slippery nature of fixing the experience of temporal flow, echoing attempts across the centuries to account for such experience. The rest of the poem depicts a process of wandering and looking for stillness: 'the still point of the turning world'. Eliot uses speech and music as examples of things which will not stay still, just as memory will not stay still. There is a dialectic process at play: 'Except for the point, the still point, / There would be no dance, and there is only the dance.'[14] And, without the dance, there would be no desire for the still point, for the point in time and space where one might halt the dance for long enough to contemplate it fully. The *Four Quartets* constantly contrast the transient with the eternal, the latter understood via Eliot's religious beliefs. In doing so they provide an unexpected but interesting comparison with the religiously inflected old-time songs discussed in the next chapter, which often contrast the 'short life of trouble' with the eternal hereafter.[15] More pertinently for the general points I wish to make here, the poems provide an explicit example of the ways in which the contemplation of time can be represented in a form which, as Eliot shows via constant linguistic play and reference to language's incapacity to fix time, is itself subject to time.

Four Quartets highlights contemplative time, in that the poet takes a significant amount of time to get to grips with time and asks of his readers that we also take time with the poem: time to read it in the first place (it is quite long) and time to return to it, to dwell on its layers of meaning. It is also a visual device and so we are invited to let our gazes drift across the flight of words, lines and blank space, a process which opens yet another experience of time. We might choose to read the poem aloud, which will take a different amount of time again and will connect us to the type of experience essayed by Augustine in his attempt to delineate temporal flow.

Eliot provided his own recording of the poem, released as a long-playing record in the 1950s, thereby fixing a particular time to the poem's duration. In his accompanying liner note, he claims no definitive authority in his delivery, noting that 'the poem, if it is of any depth and complexity, will have meanings in it concealed from the author; and should be capable of being read in many ways, and with a variety of emotional emphases'.[16] Different emotional emphases will map on to different temporal experiences, one of the themes of the poem itself. For the listener, there is also the experience of listening to Eliot's voice and to note, beyond its now-dated pronunciation and upper-class tones, a calmness or stillness that, again, mirrors the poetic themes. We come to realise once more that the poem and the poet are still points of the turning world and that we, as listeners, are also still points. Furthermore, with the medium of sound recording now in play, we can recall the poem's preoccupation with capturing 'the dance' of word, music and time and, from a playback perspective, posit the stylus on the vinyl record as another still point of a turning world.[17]

The passing of time is rendered in numerous ways in the *Four Quartets*, from 'scientific' observation to recurring references to the passing of days, months and seasons. Diurnal and seasonal tropes are deployed via a dialectical relationship between 'plenitude' and 'vacancy' in Eliot's work, as they are in the work of numerous artists. Such representations are frequently utilised in songs, which abound with the ticking of clocks, the passing of days and nights, months and seasons, years, the feeling of time as both arrow and cycle. This has long been explicit in folk song, where songs are often about the seasons as well as being traditionally used to reflect the coming or passing of times of year. The English folk singer and writer Bob Copper sums this up in the title of one of his memoirs, *A Song for Every Season*, in which he outlines the year as experienced in the Sussex countryside and weaves in seasonal songs and reminiscences of his youth.[18] Time is narrated in various ways in songs, including desire and wishes for the future, pressing needs of the present and haunting, nostalgic or painful memories of the past. As with the folk song tradition, there are often telling associations of time to seasons, for example in Joni Mitchell's 'The Circle Game' or Frank Sinatra's 'September of My Years' (both discussed later in this book).

Keith Negus pursues a similar process of bringing temporal flow and content together. He suggests that most popular songs can be understood as being about time, as a result of being forms of narrative.[19] I would agree with this and go further by saying that most popular songs can be understood as communicating time, age and experience to listeners even when they do not take these themes as their subject matter. Nevertheless, as Negus shows by selecting the Kinks' 'Waterloo Sunset' as an example of his theories, there are certain songs that invite particular reflection on these aspects. 'Waterloo Sunset' presents a lyrical world in which the temporal reference of the song's title (and refrain), as both an appropriate time for contemplation and a moment in a diurnal cycle, is underlined by contemplative and recurring elements in the music. My own example of Sandy Denny's 'Who Knows Where the Time Goes' can be interpreted in a similar manner, and Nina Simone's version of it even more so given its additional framing context of reflection from a particular point in the life course.

If seasonal and diurnal cycles offer one ubiquitous form of temporal representation, chronological time – whether in the form of history, biography or process – has also been a mainstay of song lyrics. As well as songs that imply or metaphorise the passing of time, there are others that take time as their main subject. This may be in combination with diurnal and seasonal references, as with 'Who Knows Where the Time Goes', or it may be as a meditation on the gap opened up by time's passage, as in Willie Nelson's 'Funny How Time Slips Away'. It may be focusing on a particular time of life, as in Neil Young's 'Comes a Time'. With Bob Dylan, in whose work the word 'time' constantly reappears,[20] temporal matters have been represented in many different ways: focus on the present for political messages in 'The Times They Are A-Changin' '; historical time as narrative in 'With God on Our Side'; mythical fairy story reference in 'Like a Rolling Stone'; multidimensional, cross-cut narrative reference in 'Tangled Up in Blue'; something passing too quickly in 'Not Dark Yet'.

As is evident in much of the foregoing, to think about time is to tell stories about the passing of time, which in turn highlights the importance of narrative. As Paul Ricoeur writes, 'time becomes human time to the extent that it is organized after the manner of a narrative; narrative, in turn, is

meaningful to the extent that it portrays the features of temporal experience'.[21]
As we encounter a narrative, we engage in a temporal experience by following
action, forming expectations, having them met or challenged or sensing an
ending. Once a story or narrative structure becomes familiar the episodes are
understood as leading to a certain ending, and from this repetition 'a new
quality of time emerges', over which we feel we have some level of control.[22]
Because most stories are variations on a model we learn while still in infancy,
this sense of control is always with us. Because we recognise stories by the fact
that they have a recognisable structure, we also have a sense of the whole in
the part; we may not know the precise content of the ending, but we know that
there is an ending and so it is always present:

> [T]he repetition of a story, governed as a whole by its way of ending,
> constitutes an alternative to the representation of time as flowing from the
> past to the future, following the well-known metaphor of the 'arrow of time.'
> It is as though recollection inverted the so-called 'natural' order of time. In
> reading the ending in the beginning and the beginning in the ending, we
> also learn to read time itself backwards, as the recapitulation of the initial
> conditions of a course of action in its terminal consequences.[23]

In noting the primacy of narration, we may also be led to consider how
any work of art is a representation of something, not merely an abstract
or absolute thing. Even instrumental music, including so-called absolute
music, is 'about' something and can therefore be seen as a form of narration;
the definition of music as 'organised sound' recognises this via the notion
of organisation. Negus, in his application of Ricoeur's theories to popular
songs, has made it clear that song narrative should be understood at a
musical level as much as at a lyrical one. As is also evident from his work
on the interpretation of songs, Negus understands these aspects of textual
narrative as being in dynamic relation with other narratives, such as those
we have made of our own life experience and those we become aware that
relate to musicians' lives, which may or may not be 'explanations' for the
songs they write or perform but which get mixed up anyway in the dance of
interpretation. We can note, then, that narrative is a key part of song lyrics,
musical form (including voicing), the lives of singers and songwriters and
the narratives that are told about them.[24]

It still remains questionable whether the relationship between all these aspects is clear. To take two brief examples connected to artists discussed in this book, Andy Gill, Kevin Odegard and Nigel Williamson have produced books about Bob Dylan and Neil Young which combine interpretation of song narrative with biographical narratives and accounts of the making of records. In highlighting the inventive use of narrative employed by Dylan on his 1975 album *Blood on the Tracks*, Gill and Odegard certainly identify one of the most notable features of Dylan's writing at this point in his career.[25] Ultimately, however, one of the more important narratives for the authors to uncover seems to be the 'back story', the events in Dylan's life (particularly his marriage) that led to the creation of this album. Williamson notes Neil Young's use of narrative too, for example in the song 'Misfits' which Williamson presents as a way of narrating time shifts and even time travel.[26] At the same time Williamson spends much of the interpretive space in his book attempting to connect Young's narratives to biographical correspondences. Reading the commentary, we are constantly moving between the narrative space of the song and that of its singer's biography.[27] This is something I will return to at subsequent stages of the book; for now it is enough to note the multiplicity of narratives we may be aware of (or may be made aware of) in the 'simple' act of listening to a song.

Another type of narrative we might consider relates to music's materiality, especially the artefact in which the sound is stored. In Chapter 3, I highlight the importance of the long-playing album as a vehicle for Frank Sinatra to present a persona conducive to the representation of time, age and experience. Similar points could be made for most of the artists I discuss here, partly due to the historical moments in which they emerged as artists and partly due to an ideology of the album that extends beyond its practicality as a storage or organisational format. Bob Dylan illustrates this when recalling the challenges he faced making his first album:

> I agonized about making a record, but I wouldn't have wanted to make singles, 45s – the kind of songs they played on the radio. Folksingers, jazz artists and classical musicians made LPs, long-playing records with heaps of songs in the grooves – they forged identities and tipped the scales, gave more of the big picture. LPs were like the force of gravity. They had covers, back and front, that you could stare at for hours.[28]

Physical forces are also at play on the recording itself, such as the fading or wiping of tape and the scratching or marking of LPs and CDs. This is something else which can be woven into the tapestry of narratives already mentioned. To take an evocative example from a fan comment on Joni Mitchell's Facebook page, 'I still listen to my old albums of her. Somehow, much more endearing because every little "hiss" and scratch represents part of my life. She always had a way of doing that to us, now didn't she?'[29] Here we see the folding together of the oft-noted tendency for Joni Mitchell's songs to soundtrack moments in listeners' lives with the way in which the material object reflects the user's repeated listening. Songs also weave narratives around objects, as in Mary Chapin Carpenter's 'This Shirt', Guy Clark's 'Randall Knife' or Shel Silverstein's 'This Guitar is for Sale'. The last song presents an anthropomorphised instrument that is widely travelled but now worn and weary; on John Prine's version, an extra layer of patina is added by the singer's worn voice. In an era of pre-stressed furniture, clothes and instruments, age can be deceptive but there is no denying the effectiveness of such markers in suggesting historical narrative.[30]

Age

As we have seen, the understanding of time as something that flows from future to past in an eternal present has been contrasted with attempts to stop, measure and rationalise time in a supposedly more objective fashion. Similar conceptions can be found with reflection on age. On the one hand, the attribution of age – whether of a person, a tree, a country or a universe – is, in an objective sense, a measurement of time and an attachment of time to things to make them meaningful to humans. Age in this sense is what Proust calls 'embodied time', an aspect of a person that is objectively perceived by others such that 'people of no special perspicacity, seeing two men whom they do not know, both with black moustaches, or both clean-shaven, will say that these are two men, one of about twenty and the other of about forty years old'.[31] Age, like narrative, makes time human, or rather it helps us to understand that time, if it means anything, means in ways that can only be described as human. But wrapped up with this human understanding of age are a set of different understandings or feelings that manifest in subsets of the human race – whether at the level of a culture or an individual subject – in different ways. This becomes more evident when we move from noun to verb and consider ageing as a process which, as Mike Hepworth argues, 'is not a straightforward linear trajectory towards inevitable physical, personal and social decline but a dynamic process of highly variable change: ageing is simultaneously a collective human condition and an individualized subjective experience'.[32] When we become aware (or choose to ignore) ourselves in the process of ageing, the sense of objective measurement becomes far more confused.

As noted earlier, the study of age and ageing has expanded in recent years, partly as a result of an ageing population and partly due to an awareness that age has persisted as something of an unexplored, unacknowledged and even taboo subject within the broader identity politics developed over the past century. In a recent study of what she calls 'the pleasures and perils of ageing', but which is essentially about the politics of ageing, Lynne Segal refers to 'feminist constraints' that kept age from the agenda of feminist politics in the 1970s.[33] As she and other activists in the Women's Liberation Movement campaigned on a range of issues, they tended to take their youth for granted. Segal notes, however, that it was a feminist thinker, Simone de Beauvoir, who was writing at that time of the coming of age, albeit that this was not the aspect of her politics that was being disseminated most widely. More recently, age has featured extensively in literature related to health and well-being, though there has also been a growth in what has been termed 'critical gerontology', the study of age as social and cultural phenomenon rather than biological inevitability. This more politicised understanding of age and ageing has placed these subjects at the heart of identity politics, and age has now started to figure alongside the more familiar studies of race, class, gender and sexuality in the arts, humanities and social sciences.

As is no doubt clear from the use of 'gerontology', studies of age and ageing have predominantly focused on people in later life. This is understandable partly for reasons already mentioned – awareness of an ageing population, awareness that the 'pleasures and perils' of ageing have been neglected – and partly because a number of studies that have emerged in recent years have been undertaken as scholars take note of their own advancing age. In cultural studies, the discipline which first informed my academic interest in popular music, there has also been a recognition that the association between popular culture (and subculture) and youth was perhaps overdetermined and highly selective. Scholars such as Andrew Blaikie, Mike Featherstone and Andy Bennett have sought to address this imbalance by analysing cultural representations of later life and showing the rich variety of engagement with popular culture by ageing fans, while Ros Jennings, Abigail Gardner and others have additionally focused on creative production by older musicians.[34] In this book, I too am interested in the production, and to a certain extent the consumption, of music by older people. Nonetheless, as already noted, I am also interested in reflection on and representation of age at earlier stages in life too. In making this point, I return to the points about time and age as ongoing processes; as Mike Hepworth states, ageing should be thought of 'not simply as a matter of chronology or biology but as a complex and potentially open-ended process of interaction between the body, self and society'.[35] Segal, while focusing mostly on age as an experience of later life, is also sensitive to this open-ended aspect: 'Ageing is neither simply linear, not is it any single discrete process when, in our minds, we race around, moving seamlessly between childhood, old age and back again. There are ways in which we can, and we do, bridge different ages, psychically, all the time.'[36] Kathleen Woodward recognises this too but notes our tendency to think of age in binary terms: 'Age is a subtle continuum, but we organize this continuum into "polar opposites".'[37] This polarising of age is a process that occurs at various stages of the life course. Anyone who is old enough to have been on the receiving end of accusations by children and young people of being 'old' will be aware of the skewed reality and homogenising force of such youthful perceptions. Yet there is just as high a likelihood of older people making unbalanced assessments of the young, whether despite or because of their life experience. It can take a quite notable effort of will for either 'side' to concede ground to, and attempt to consider life as experienced by, the other. Those who show an ability to do so, whether young or old, are often seen as being in possession of valuable wisdom.

One might think that it would be possible to acquire a more balanced view from the perspective of middle age. In his reflective book on this time of life,

Christopher Hamilton alludes to such a possibility, repeatedly highlighting the Janus-like perspective available to those in middle age. Ultimately, however, Hamilton presents this period as one in which the questioning of one's place in the world, and in time, only increases. This is most obvious in the famous 'midlife crisis', the point at which one is supposed to realise that the dreams, plans or assumptions about life that one had gathered in one's youth are unlikely to materialise in the imagined form. This experience may be positive, negative or numbing, or one may equally feel indifferent towards it. Hamilton suggests that we become ever more aware of the different voices at work within us and in our relationships with others, voices we learn to put on for others so that we can live in harmony with them: 'These voices compete in us, and most of us spend a great deal of our lives trying to elevate one of them to the supreme voice, a voice that will drown out all the others, subdue them, remove them, so that we can become whole and complete.'[38] We also have a greater awareness of the complexities of life, of multiple moral, political, aesthetic and other perspectives available to us and which we have experienced. This may lead to a longing for stability – a still point in a turning world – though it could equally lead to a desire for fulfilment by adventure, distraction or some form of change. For Hamilton, 'We all find it hard to live with the tensions between these different outlooks, even though – indeed, precisely because – we can be deeply attracted to them, depending on our mood, the weather, the books we are reading and the films we are seeing, our most recent or our deepest experiences, the period of life in which we happen to find ourselves, and so on.'[39] Middle age does not allow for a perfect balance because one can never know whether one may be afflicted by the burden of the past, prey to anxiety about the future, panic about the present, a combination of these feelings or, indeed, a sense of equanimity towards past, present and/or future. It is precisely because age is a continuum that there is never a perfect moment to find a balance. It is as impossible to stand outside of age as it is to make time stand still. There can be time for reflection, though, and this has led to the wealth of meditations available to us on time, age and experience.

Simone de Beauvoir's *The Coming of Age*, published in French in 1970 when its author was 62 years old, is an example of extended reflection, one that treats its subject with the thoroughness and seriousness it deserves. Following a first half in which Beauvoir focuses on the scientific, historical and social aspects of 'the aged man as an object [described] from the outside', she turns to the internal experience of ageing, 'how he actually lives it'. Her approach, which is informative for my own study, is to accept that, although age is 'just something that happens to people who become old, and this plurality of experiences cannot possibly be confined in a concept or even a notion', we can still take readings and compare them, 'try to isolate the constants and to find the reasons for the differences'.[40] Beauvoir looks to written accounts of age, recognising that they may not be representative of all humanity. By focusing on novelists, poets, essayists and other celebrities of the written word, she is wary of paying attention to 'the privileged few'. Nevertheless, the insights gained from literature, *because* we find them insightful, are relevant to the lives of others.[41] Beauvoir's first extensive exploration of the 'being-in-the-world' of age relates to 'the discovery and assumption of old age', processes which invariably catch the perceiving subject by surprise. This may entail the surprise of feeling older or younger than one is or of having a perception of one's age that is in marked contrast to the objective truth and to how others perceive us. The result may also be a refusal to accept the symptoms of ageing when they are present or an anxiety about them when they are not. Beauvoir suggests that this aspect of the coming of age is different in adults than in children or adolescents:

> Children and adolescents are of some particular age. The mass of prohibitions and duties to which they are subjected and the behaviour of others towards them do not allow them to forget it. When we are grown up we hardly think about our age any more: we feel that the notion does not apply to us; for it is one which assumes that we look back towards the past and draw a line under the total, whereas in fact we are reaching out towards the future, gliding on imperceptibly from day to day, from year to year. Old age is particularly difficult to assume because we have always regarded it as something alien, a foreign species: 'Can I have become a different being while I still remain myself?'[42]

Our tendency to think of age as something happening to others leads us to notice age in others before we notice it in ourselves. When we do perceive our own ageing, we often do so as a realisation that others see us as old(er) and we then transfer this perception to an othering of that part of ourselves that is old. As Beauvoir writes, 'Since it is the Other within us who is old, it is natural that the revelation of our age should come to us from the outside.'[43] Beauvoir uses the example of Proust, who, in the final volume of his great novel, describes in painful but amusing detail a 'masked ball' in which his protagonist encounters friends and acquaintances he has not seen for many years. Initially perceiving the others as engaged in some kind of costume show in which they adopt different ages, he humorously describes the unpleasant aspects of their demeanour. With time he comes to realise that the only masks they are wearing are those of time and age and that the people he had once known had aged in reality but not in his mind. He then realises that the same is true for him and that he too has grown old:

> So I, having lived from one day to the next since my childhood, and having also formed definitive impressions of myself and of others, became aware for the first time, as a result of the metamorphoses that had been produced in all these people, of all the time that had passed in their lives, an idea which overwhelmed me with the revelation that it had passed equally for me.[44]

Kathleen Woodward follows Beauvoir in choosing this scene to reflect on the 'discontents' of ageing. She reads Proust's masked ball as an example of what she calls 'the mirror stage of old age', using the Lacanian theory of the mirror stage to show that the misrecognition of the self that one encounters in later life is 'the inverse of' that experienced in infancy. This process entails a separation of one's 'real self' from one's body: 'We say that our real selves – that is, our youthful selves – are hidden inside our bodies. Our *bodies* are old, *we* are not.'[45] In Lacan's formulation, the infant, recognising itself in the mirror, projects onto its mirror image a wholeness and mastery of the self that it in fact does not yet possess. Woodward argues that the mirror stage of old age reverses this process; the subject feels whole and in control of her body but perceives and projects the lack of control – the incomplete self – onto the mirror image.

The sense that, with age, one becomes more aware of time as something one carries within oneself, is evident in both Proust's 'embodied time' and Eliot's observation, in 'Burnt Norton', that 'in my end is my beginning'. Jean Améry's analysis of old age, a classic example of a polarisation of young and old, revolves around a similar idea. For Améry, the old have time within them and the young externalise time as space and world, something into which they can throw themselves or let themselves fall. 'Those who believe they have what is called "time" *in front of them*', he writes, 'know that they are truly destined to step out into *space*, to externalize themselves. Those who have life within them, i.e., authentic time, have to be internally satisfied with the deceptive magic of memory'.[46] Norberto Bobbio, having distinguished biological age from 'bureaucratic age' (defined by the age at which one might be entitled to a pension) and chronological age, describes his own experience of 'psychological or subjective age':

> Biologically, I started my old age from when I was approaching eighty years, but psychologically I have always considered myself to be a little old, even when I was young. While I felt older than my years when I was a youth, in later years I thought of myself as still young and continued to do so until a few years ago. Now I believe myself to be old in every sense of the word.[47]

Beauvoir makes similar observations, arguing that 'It is because age is not experienced in the for-itself mode and because we do not have the same lucid knowledge of it that we have of the cogito that we can say we are old early in life or think ourselves young to the very end.' She quotes Baudelaire's sense of disquiet between his own subjectivity and the objective world in which he found himself: 'I have more memories than if I were a thousand years old.'[48]

For popular music, one of the most obvious ways that age has made itself known is as a conflict between generations. To take one famous example from the 1960s, the Who's song 'My Generation' presented singer Roger Daltrey barely able to contain his frustration with the older generation as he stuttered and almost swore his way to the era-defining proclamation 'Hope I die before I get old.' As rock music discovered the possibilities of longevity, a process from which most members of the Who were able to capitalise, such a birthmark could be seen as something of a burden. Little wonder, then, that John Strausbaugh decided to target the group in *Rock 'Til You Drop*, his extended attack on 'colostomy rock'. For Strausbaugh, acts such as the Who and the Rolling Stones, although they remain immensely popular and attract new generations of fans, are betraying the rock music they helped fashion by treating the music as an exercise in nostalgia rather than as a challenge to the status quo: 'Colostomy rock is not rebellion, it's the antithesis of rebellion: it's nostalgia . . . And nostalgia is the death of rock. We were supposed to die before we got old.'[49] As I have argued elsewhere, this is a rather narrow understanding of both the political possibilities of 'the rock faithful' and of the critical potentiality of nostalgia.[50] It is also an essentially romantic view of rock music, one that fixes rock to a time and an attitude and doesn't allow for the inevitably twisted shapes that ageing subjects must adopt in trying to stay true to the events that formed them. It is not as if ageing rockers are entirely unaware of the potentially tricky situation they find themselves in, as the sixty-six-year-old Daltrey proved in a television appearance at the end of 2010. As he performed the Muddy Waters classic 'Mannish Boy' on Jools Holland's annual New Year's Eve *Hootenanny* show, there were all kinds of reasons why it shouldn't have been inspiring to see an ageing white rock star delivering a seemingly too-faithful, unoriginal take on a now-clichéd blues song. Indeed, Daltrey appeared to be going through the motions, offering little more than what one might find served up by countless other acts – amateur and professional – across the country. As 'Mannish Boy' limped on, however, something more exciting started to happen. Daltrey started to emphasise the experiential nature of the lyric, the fact that it concerns a man looking back at his boyhood even as he asserts his maturity and experience. But Daltrey took it to further, humorously self-reflexive lengths as he sang about being an old man, one whose past experience included performing the song 'My Generation' and its famous assertion about dying before he got old. Daltrey folded that experience into the text of 'Mannish Boy' in a way that was not the least bit foolish, but which was, instead, compellingly, self-deprecatingly true. Ever the butt of jokes about rock, retirement and reunions, Daltrey seemed to be doing about the most honest thing he could do in that performance space by asserting his late voice.

In recent years it has become increasingly common to hear rock musicians discussing age and ageing. This is not surprising when we consider that those who came to public attention in the rock and pop boom of the 1960s – still the canonical era for popular music of the twentieth century, for better or worse – and who are still famous have reached an age where such matters are not likely to be overlooked (Strausbaugh's critique being a notable, but far from isolated, example). Often the narratives presented are celebratory ones, as interviewers seek to find out how it feels to be a veteran in a cultural practice that was supposedly predicated against the idea of longevity. These questions are often ones that reflect back onto the artists' fans, especially those that have aged with them. As Mick Jagger told a journalist back in 1993, 'They want you to be like you were in 1969. They want you to, because otherwise their youth goes with you, you know'.[51] At the time Jagger was barely fifty years old and his band the Rolling Stones would continue performing in the following decades. Twenty years later, the Stones were the main act at Glastonbury, for years a barometer of youth culture but in recent years increasingly keen to host 'heritage' acts. Much of the press was positive, noting Jagger's ability to recreate earlier glories and guitarist Keith Richards's creaky vitality. The Stones have also been subject to a programme on BBC Radio 4's *Front Row* in which the members were interviewed to comment on the group's fiftieth anniversary; during his interview, Jagger compares being in the group to 'being a listed building'.[52]

While most of the discourse around ageing popular musicians has focused on whether or not senior stars can lay claim to youth (theirs or that of their audience), one of my concerns in this book is to consider how youth lay claim to age and experience convincingly. One way of approaching this would be to consider songs which explicitly deal with age, such as John Prine's early compositions 'Hello in There' and 'Angel from Montgomery'. Both songs bucked the trend for post-Dylan 1970s singer-songwriters to write about their own lives (the school known as 'confessional' singer-songwriters) and instead presented imagined scenarios in which the protagonists are older people reflecting on their lives. 'Hello in There' imagines old age as a time of loneliness and vulnerability, where 'all the news just repeats itself / like some forgotten dream' and where 'hollow ancient eyes' long for human engagement. 'Angel from Montgomery' tells the story of a similarly empty life, related by an 'old woman' whose 'old man is another child who's grown old'. To escape the humdrum relationship, she dreams of a rodeo cowboy who would take her away; no matter how she tries to hold on to the dream, however, 'the years just flow by like a broken down dam'.[53] Another way of approaching young artists' claim to age would be to explore the adoption by singers of vocal styles or musical genres that seem to confer age and experience upon them due to the cultural coding associated with them. In Prine's case, his youth was belied not only by the maturity of his lyrical themes, but also by the adoption of a musical style (country-inflected folk music) and a singing style (heavily regionalised, 'grainy' and 'untrained') suited to the articulation of such themes. I will return to this idea in my discussions of Ralph Stanley in Chapter 2 and Bob Dylan in Chapter 4.

The artists I devote most time to in this book are ones who attained what I refer to as early lateness (in that they were able to convincingly articulate maturity through singing and/or writing while still young) but who are old enough to allow us to witness how this early lateness develops into a 'real' lateness. But it is worth briefly considering a contemporary artist who is still young and yet engaged with the representation of age and passing time, allowing us to realise that this process can be attached to many stages in the life course. In 2012 the American singer-songwriter Taylor Swift released the song '22' as part of her fourth album *Red*. Over anthemically choppy guitar chords and ramrod-straight beats, the song extolled the virtues and the confusions of being a 22-year-old, reflecting Swift's own experience as far as anyone could tell.[54] While the verses contained barbed comments on the kind of hipsters and 'indie kids' who might routinely dismiss Swift and her mostly teenage fanbase, the explosively rhythmic, cheerleader-like chorus celebrated a perfect (if messily perfect and messily privileged) stage of life. In the words of one reviewer, '"22" is all about trying to "forget about the deadlines" and embraces only the most sugary hooks available', yet '[u]nderneath the heel-clicking positivity and shiny production sits the line "We're happy, free, confused and lonely in the best way", a rather stunning meditation on being in your early 20s that's flicked off like a piece of pre-chorus lint'.[55] As it hymned the will to party, the song rang registers of inclusivity and exclusivity, individuality and community, at once an invitation to shared experience and a reminder that those outside the song's immediate address could only look and listen with a sense of non-belonging. Not only was Swift singing about age and experience, but she was doing so while still young and with a remarkable sense of self-awareness. Even more impressive was the fact that she had already been doing this for a number of years, having gained considerable success with her first album, released in 2006 when she was 16. Prior to '22' she had already hymned youthful experience to great effect, either through explicit references in songs such as 'Fifteen', 'Dear John' and 'Place in This World', or via more general depictions of girlishness, school, first loves, summer vacations and parents. Also notable was the way in which Swift had moved from identification with country music – a genre which has traditionally placed great emphasis on time, age, experience and nostalgia – towards a more clearly pop-centred approach seemingly aimed at a teen audience and focused on the transitory pleasures and pains of youth. Swift seems to offer a message relevant to people at many different life stages, that reflection on the passing of time is something with which we are always already engaged. There is a mixture of escapism and realism that inhabits a place we all need to go to at various points in our life. This is no doubt one of the reasons her work has found praise among a number of music critics and veteran songwriters.[56]

Experience

Like age, experience can be thought as a way of measuring and feeling time. When we speak of having so many years' experience at working a job, speaking a language or living in a particular place, we are offering both a measurement of time and an authentication of our ability to do, speak or know; in such processes, time qualifies authority. As measurement, experience is presented as objective but perhaps we more frequently think of experience as being subjective and deeply felt, something that accrues inside us not so much as a measurement of ability but rather as a hardening of our being. Experience is who we are, who we have come to be. Lack of experience – which may or may not be 'innocence' – is not-yet-having-been, an incompleteness of the self, a hole yet to be filled. But, for its accrual to take place, experience also has to be immediate. In this sense, it is perception, consciousness, affect: how we take in the time and space in which we find ourselves. As perception, experience is how we become aware of time and feel time passing. As consciousness, at both private and public levels, experience is awareness of sensations both immediate and less immediate, of data bombarding us in the present or gathered over a period of time. Experience, like consciousness, is deeply entwined with memory. Walter Benjamin, who reminds us of this fact in many of his essays, was particularly interested in the relationship between *Gedächtnis* (usefully translated by Harry Zohn as 'a gathering of unconscious data') and *Erinnerung* ('an isolating of individual "memories" per se').[57] Thus we are able to remember things from our past that we might not have attached particular importance to at the time but which we find ourselves able (or unable) to focus on at a subsequent point in time. Another relationship Benjamin explores is that between *Erfahrung* ('experience over time') and *Erlebnis* ('the isolated experience of the moment').[58] Awareness gathered over time, thought of as experience and memory, can be seen, in Benjamin's formulations, to produce consciousness.

These distinctions play a prominent role in Benjamin's writing on Baudelaire and Proust, a connection I would like to use to move the consideration of experience from a very general one to the more specific field of aesthetic experience. I want to do so in order to think about how artistic statements – whether novels, plays, poems, painting, buildings or songs – can be understood as the passing on of information in such a way that it is embedded inside the perceiver of the statement, becoming part of the experience they feel they share with the artist. Benjamin is interested in the role of the story and the storyteller (a declining role as he sees it in the early twentieth century). In pursuing this interest he makes a distinction between the finding out of information from newspapers – a fragmentary, disconnected experience – and the learning of information in the form of a story:

> A story does not aim to convey an event per se, which is the purpose of information; rather, it embeds the event in the life of the storyteller in order to pass it on as experience to those listening. It thus bears the trace of the storyteller, much the way an earthen vessel bears the trace of the potter's hand.[59]

The art of the storyteller thus requires considerable skill and labour, and Benjamin is here thinking of Proust and 'the effort it took to restore the figure of the storyteller to the current [Benjamin's] generation'. Proust's great novel, of course, revolved around the relationship between voluntary and involuntary memory. The latter was most memorably (but not only) encapsulated in the tasting of the madeleine cake that, dipped in tea, sends Proust's narrator suddenly back to the lost time of his youth. Voluntary memory, meanwhile, reflects the labour necessary to reconstruct that lost time as an aesthetic experience communicable to others; not only communicable, in Benjamin's terms, as 'information', but as a richly described poetic drama bearing the 'trace' of its narrator and – for they may or may not be the same – of Proust. Furthermore, the storyteller's involuntary memory, says Benjamin, 'bears the trace of the situation that engendered it; it is part of the inventory of the individual who is isolated in various ways. Where there is experience [*Erfahrung*] in the strict sense of the word, certain contents of the individual past combine in the memory [*Gedächtnis*] with material from the collective past'.[60]

Following Proust and Benjamin, I understand accumulated experience as a necessary prerequisite for making sense of, and making something out of, isolated experiences; at the same time, experience is nothing without those isolated experiences, whether we want to relive them or not.[61] Selection and control become important here and it is through controlling purposes – selection, evasion, elision, revision and so on – that we attempt to control the narrative of our experience. As Eva Hoffman writes, 'it is tempting to see in the registration of memories, and their selection, a kind of neurological inventiveness, which, through a combination of stability and plasticity, composes the ongoing narrative or poem of our lives'.[62] Emily Keightley and Michael Pickering, while also describing the interaction of memory and experience as a kind of authorial self-fashioning, emphasise the act of editing and selecting: 'the individual subject acts not only as an authorial self, continually scripting the story of a particular life, but also as sort of editor-in-chief of the memories made to matter and cohere in the preferred version of who we think we are'.[63] One way to regain control over time is to aestheticise it and while we may not all be as adept at Proust in producing from our lives an epic novel that repays endless revisiting, we constantly encounter the potential to do so, whether in our own conversational and storytelling skills or in our recognition of those of others. We can recognise control over brief periods of time (the length of a song, say) and over much longer periods (an era, a lifetime), just as we gradually learn to control longer periods of time in our everyday lives.

All music is experience and, as we saw with the discussion of time unfolding, music is an exemplary model of experiencing, which is why it has proved so popular as a model for theories of time across the centuries, whether in Augustine's description of resonating sound and the recitation of psalms or in the work of twentieth-century novelists and phenomenologists. But if this were all that music were (and that would still be plenty), why would a significant number of songwriters write, singers sing and listeners listen to and reflect upon, a sense of time and experience that fell outside the moments of writing, singing and listening? It was those that do so that led me to thinking about the late voice in the first place and this is why, even though I find the interaction of experiences, experiencing and accumulated experience fascinating,[64] it is with the last category – accumulated experience – that I am mainly concerned. As with my preference for treating the representation of time over the temporal flow, at this preliminary exploration of the late voice, I am interested in the ways in which time, age and experience are represented both within songs and within the discourse that attends singers.

Time, age and experience are evental, by which I mean that they are understood in relation to events. Events unfold constantly, as television constantly reminds us: news programmes featuring 'current events'; dramas in which 'events occur in real time'; reality shows which feed the fantasy of a constant vigilance. But, because it is not possible to take in everything, we are inevitably selective in our positing of what makes for a significant event: in such a process, events inevitably become singular. This is clear by the way we mark time, age and experience with significant, singular markers such as birthdays, rites of passage and anniversaries. Our personal histories may not seem evental when compared with what is happening 'in the world' (i.e. to other people); indeed, they may seem like a drop in the ocean. But they are also larger than those other events because they are closer. One can feel distanced or alienated from a global historical or political event when compared to a change in one's immediate circumstances, as well as the change we make as individuals to other individuals with whom we share time. This aspect of life is beautifully and movingly hymned in Iris DeMent's song 'My Life', in which the singer, accompanied by a sad, aching piano melody, reflects on her place in the world. She sings from the perspective of a life 'half the way travelled', a classic moment for looking back. 'My life', she laments, 'don't count for nothing'; it is 'a passing September that no one will recall'.[65] The chorus brings a different perspective, however, as she recalls the joy she has given to those around her – her mother, her lover, her friends. She 'can make them feel better for a while' and this, apparently, is enough. One of the ways in which she can make people feel better is by singing and playing to them, and this seems to be one of the main points (and strengths) of the song.

Because she has recorded songs such as this, DeMent can also make other people far from her immediate experience feel better too. This is an obvious point but one I want to underline because recorded music is often criticised for its potential to de- and re-contextualise experience or for its transference of that experience to the marketplace. While one has to take such criticisms seriously, there is also a necessity to question some of the assumptions on which they rest. In a generally excellent book on country music that focuses on such 'authentic' performers as Iris DeMent, Ralph Stanley, Johnny Cash and Merle Haggard, Nicholas Dawidoff makes the following comparison between Garth Brooks (a ubiquitous 'hat act' at the time Dawidoff was writing his book) and the kinds of country artists the author admires:

> Brooks delivers his lines in a voice that is certainly pleasant, but limited in range and not especially distinctive, The real problem is, I suppose, that his songs lack both the rough edges and the feel for pressing experience that you find in the singing of people like George Jones, Merle Haggard, and Johnny Cash. Their lives really have been hard, something that's obvious from their singing. With Brooks there is often the sense that he is aping something he saw somebody else try.. . . Brooks is a pop star masquerading as a country singer, a yuppie with a lariat.[66]

I have a certain amount of sympathy with this comparison, not least because I admire the singers that Dawidoff celebrates and can understand the desire to justify their importance. However, I also find it problematic, firstly because of the need – common to music journalism – to validate those one admires by denigrating those one does not; secondly, because the notion that the hard lives of the celebrated country artists are transparently evident in their voices seems incomplete. Can it really be so straightforward? I am not saying that experience cannot be communicated in song – that is a central tenet of this book, after all – but the notion that Jones, Haggard, Cash and other 'authentic' singers are without masquerade, while Brooks is all artifice and no experience, is problematic. I believe the problem lies in the way in which we know 'their lives have been hard' from other sources and not directly from their voices. Dawidoff prefaces his comparison by reminding us that Brooks went to university where he studied marketing; it is only implied that this is unusual for a country singer but the mention is itself telling. Dawidoff's longer portraits of the other singers dwell, not surprisingly, on the aspects of their lives that were hard. As is common with much writing on country music, this is seen to lead directly to the ability to voice experience, a process that renders invisible and inaudible the various levels of mediation necessary for these singers to communicate to an audience at all. Such processes of mediation are essential for the very existence of the creative art these *artists* produce, as Keith Negus and Michael Pickering describe:

> [W]e do not have a fully formed, reflexively comprehended experience which we then reproduce in verbal or sonic form. What this experience means to us, and how we may value it, is usually only discovered in the form of utterance or figuration that is given to it. The expression not only forms the experience but also transforms it, makes it into something whose meaning changes our understanding of it. The relationship between experience and its expression is one of mutual constitution. Without its representation in words or sounds an experience often does not signify for us at all, for a feeling or an idea associated with it is made manifest through the combination of materials that characterise any particular cultural representation. It is because of this that songwriters, composers and musicians are often surprised at what they create and often only retrospectively comprehend what they were attempting to articulate.[67]

These observations resonate with John Dewey's theories of aesthetic experience. For Dewey, such experience is governed by a perception that comes after and goes beyond mere recognition of the familiar. Crucially, this perception is something that must be shared by the creator and beholder and it is in this relationship that the possibility for aesthetic experience resides. Perception, as an exploratory journey into new experience, is creative in that to perceive, a beholder must *create* his own experience. And his creation must include relations comparable to those which the original producer underwent. They are not the same in any literal sense. But with the perceiver, as with the artist, there must be an ordering of the elements of the whole that is in form, although not in details, the same as the process of organization the creator of the work consciously experienced.[68]

The kind of experience we learn from art allows and trains us to make aesthetic decisions and I would argue that these aesthetic decisions are bound up with the way we identify with and consequently authenticate art and artists. My version of Dawidoff's comparison, then, would be that I may be more convinced by the ways in which Merle Haggard has articulated experience than with the ways in which Garth Brooks has but my conviction will rest on a mixture of aesthetics and authentication.

In *Time Passing*, Sylviane Agacinski considers the way that we come to know our surroundings not only from our direct experience of passing through them, but also from the act of having previously encountered them in texts. 'The walker', she writes, 'reads many texts at once, while each of them resonates with the others. Such bookish knowledge penetrates his present perceptions.... Thus the walker's lived experience is traversed by a "second existence," the result of books, in such a way that the different types of experience merge and fade into one another'. Agacinski uses the term 'lettered experience', which she has taken from Francis Bacon, to explain this 'bookish knowledge'. Then, noting the predominance in our own era of the visual realm of photography, film and screen media, she proposes an additional term, 'imaged experience'.[69] In a previous discussion of this passage, I suggested that the term 'sounded experience' should be added to evoke the ways in which we learn about our surroundings from musical and other sonic sources.[70] While my previous work in this area was related, like Agacinski's, to the experience of the city, such sounded experience would be appropriate to other environments. I recall, for example, that the first time I encountered a real desert, I felt as if I were familiar with the landscape partly from having seen similar terrain in films (especially Westerns, as I recall) and having read about it in books, but also from having heard so many songs (especially US country and folk music) that seemed to narrate the experience of such a space (though I did not encounter my desert in the United States). I might say that a voicing of the desert had taken place before I ever arrived in it, one that did not in any way diminish the wonder of being there 'in the flesh', but of which I was aware as something feeding into my experience, feeding an intuition of déjà vu.[71]

We have already considered how music enables us to understand and create time; the same can be said for space. Writing about world music, Geoffrey O'Brien observes the following:

> There are so many invitations to lose yourself, or more properly to empty yourself of yourself. Once you succeed in clearing that personal baggage out of the way, you can wander freely through the sounds the world gives you as if wandering through the world itself, to discover at last whether you would recognize yourself once you got there. But nowhere is there any freedom from memories, stories, histories. In the very act of listening you weave a fantasy whose very groundlessness is what draws you to listening in the first place.[72]

This passage serves as a reminder that an understanding of musical experience as a losing of self must always connect to a recognition that such loss rarely if ever lasts for long and is always anyway tied up with our capacity for reflection, memory, reference and analysis: self-loss and self-understanding go hand in hand. With this in mind, I wish to retain the notion of sounded experience as essayed here and expand it to take in more than our immediate surroundings; I would like to think of it more broadly as a kind of intertextuality, a way we come to know texts (including songs) through their relationship with, and our knowledge of, other texts. In *The Pleasure of the Text*, Roland Barthes provides a connection between the kinds of experience discussed above and those that arise in the intertextual process:

> Reading a text cited by Stendhal (but not written by him) I find Proust in one minute detail.. . . Elsewhere, but in the same way, in Flaubert, it is the blossoming apple trees of Normandy which I read *according to* Proust. I savor the sway of formulas, the reversal of origins, the ease which brings the anterior text out of the subsequent one. I recognize that Proust's work, for myself at least, is *the* reference work, the mandala of the entire literary cosmogony.. . . Proust is what comes to me, not what I summon up; not an 'authority', simply a circular memory.[73]

We may be lost at times in reading, listening, watching, wandering or dreaming. But we shouldn't think that we have turned off at those points. The life of the mind continues and experience accrues. When we return to the 'real world', some of that lost time stays with us, to be reclaimed at as yet unknown moments.

Voice

To speak of the voice is to speak with the thing that is being spoken about. But in 'saying' this (in writing it), I must be immediately aware that voice is not only that which is sounded externally. For, as intimated by those quotation marks, I feel I am using a voice as I type these words; you may feel that you are discerning a voice when you read them. I make this point at this stage in order to indicate that 'voice', one of the key terms in this book, is not only related to the sound made by the speaking or singing subject, or heard by the listening subject. Although much of what follows does refer to those specific uses of voice, it is as well to understand that a wider conception of voice is operating throughout. If, therefore, I posit the sounded voice, as many have, as that which originates within my body and is then externalised to the world in which I operate, such an observation can prove equally relevant for the 'silent' voice of writing. Both these and other understandings of voice associate it with subjectivity and agency: to have a voice is to have a sense of power; to be voiceless is to lack that sense. Voice is communication of the self by a variety of mediums; it is that which mediates our innermost desire to communicate, to emote, to connect to the world beyond us. We may also direct our voices at ourselves, via a kind of internal 'conversation' (never really a monologue, for the workings of the brain are too scattered for that); even so, this is still a kind of externalisation in that we objectify ourselves by talking 'to' ourselves.

That voice is more than that sonic signal which emanates from the body of a vocalist is a point to which I will return. For now, I will stay with the sounded aspect of vocal communication. In listening to a voice, I become aware of the act of human communication, regardless of whether or not the voice is directed at me. If the voice is producing a language I understand – especially if it is a language I claim as 'mine' – then the possibility of identification with that voice increases; I find myself taking up a relative position to it and to what it is saying (or what it might be saying, if it is just out of my range of hearing or if there are other obstacles or distracting sounds intervening). If the voice is producing a language I do not know – whether speaking a foreign language or engaging in a non-semantic vocal act – I can still be aware of its communicative potential and can recognise a variety of human qualities, allowing perhaps for a different kind of identification (I can be attracted or repelled by a voice I cannot understand). In the short story 'A King Listens', Italo Calvino writes, 'A voice means this: there is a living person, throat, chest, feelings, who sends into the air this voice, different from all other voices. A voice involves the throat, saliva, infancy, the patina of experienced life, the mind's intentions, the pleasure of giving a personal form to sound waves.'[74] This is an interesting description for this book in that it suggests that a voice is always 'late'; it is the result of experience, imitation and repetition.

In Calvino's story, the king never sees the owner of the voice that leads him to these thoughts. He is presented as a paranoid, distant ruler, literally cut off from his subjects by isolation within the throne room of his palace. Everything has been carefully planned to avoid his having to leave the room (or even the throne) or to have contact with the outside world. With little to do other than retain his regal posture, he listens to the sounds of the palace: doors slamming, the shuffling of feet, stifled cries. In between these sounds, it is the silences that come to spook him the most, for they seem heavy with the threat of rebellion. He becomes obsessed with listening and finds himself able to extend his perception to the sounds of the city beyond the palace walls, 'a distant rumble at the bottom of the ear, a hum of voices, a buzz of wheels'.[75] From the anonymous buzz, he detects the voice of a woman singing and comes to the above-quoted realisation: although seemingly bodiless, this voice signifies the presence of a body and therefore of a unique person. Adriana Cavarero builds upon this realisation in her book *For More than One Voice* to argue for a philosophy of voice that does not generalise it in abstraction, but rather identifies the plurality of voices and, therefore, subjective relationships constituted through vocal communication. She posits, in response to Calvino's story, that 'the voice is the equivalent of what the unique person has that is most hidden and most genuine. This is not an unreachable treasure, or an ineffable essence, or still less, a sort of secret nucleus of the self; rather, it is a deep vitality of the unique being who takes pleasure in revealing herself through the emission of the voice'.[76] Cavarero also points out that Calvino privileges an emphasis on the vocal (on sound) over the semantic. The relationship set up between the king and the unseen and unknown female singer is one based on what Cavarero calls 'the relational valence of the vocal sphere', an arena in which mutually pleasurable relationships are established by voices and listeners.[77]

The vocal can be distinguished from the semantic but it is my contention in the examples I use in this book that we commonly listen to both together. Just as the vocal can be separated from the semantic while also being endlessly reconnected, so can the voice be separated from the body – as the singing voice is from the singer in Calvino's tale. Still, we have a tendency to provide embodied sources for 'unseen' voices, to create what Steven Connor calls a 'vocalic body'. We know that bodies produce voices but, Connor argues, the reverse is also true: 'The vocalic body is the idea – which can take the form of dream, fantasy, ideal, theological doctrine, or hallucination – of a surrogate or secondary body, a projection of a new way of having or being a body, formed and sustained out of the autonomous operations of the voice.'[78] Connor relates this process to the mental connection of hearing and seeing, and of ear and eye. Hearing a voice whose source is not immediately apparent, we create a vocalic body, either in our mind's eye or by projecting the source onto (or into) a visible, believable object. Connor's theory appears at the outset of a cultural history of ventriloquism and the ventriloquist's dummy provides an obvious example of the working of the vocalic body. But ventriloquism, as Connor shows, extends much further than the use of such props and he unearths numerous examples of the ways in which voices have been connected to 'others' through history.

The voice, as Connor repeatedly shows, is intimately connected to the perception, understanding and production of space. But the voice is also a carrier of time and of experience, a sign of the passing of time. Time passes in speaking, as speaking passes time. The same is true of singing, with which this book will be mostly engaged. Time can be measured in the length of a song, in a song's life course or in the ways in which songs revisit us through our own life course. Voices change over time and there is not much we can do to alter time's passage through the vocal cords.[79] That said, voices can also be adapted to an extent by surgical alteration or through the mechanics of vocal production. The voice in this sense is a carrier of time but it may equally be a mask of time. When we listen to Tom Waits, for example, we seem to hear a singer who has always sounded 'old' due to the depth and rasp of his voice. But it wasn't always so, and the distance travelled in his voice between his albums *Closing Time* (1973) and *Small Change* (1976) is remarkable, suggesting more than a mere three years of 'natural' vocal ageing. On earlier songs such as 'Ol' 55', Waits adopts a mid-range, occasionally high-leaning vocal that, combined with the countryish musical language, might not sound out of place on an Eagles record. When the needle drops on 'Tom Traubert's Blues', the opening song of *Small Change*, we hear Waits sing of being 'wasted and wounded' and his confession is made all the more convincing by the deep, 'wounded' grain of his voice; he sounds almost too 'wasted' to get through his tall tale.[80] On 'I Wish I Was in New Orleans', another track from *Small Change*, Waits offers a clue as to where this voice may have come from (or be directed towards) when, referencing 'St James Infirmary', he appears to channel Louis Armstrong. The attachment of a voice to a tradition, and to a bodily aesthetic associated with that tradition, is a theme that will recur in this book; here it is as if Waits has decided to ingest Armstrong's famous rasp and make it his own. Other factors must be considered of course – the effects of drink and cigarettes on Waits's voice, the demands of trumpet playing on Armstrong's – but there is also artifice at work here and in this we should be neither surprised nor disappointed. As noted earlier in the description of Calvino's story, part of vocal production is 'the pleasure of giving a personal form to sound waves'.

This sense of pleasure is central to Roland Barthes's influential essay 'The Grain of the Voice', in which Barthes distinguishes between what he calls the pheno-song and geno-song. Pheno-song includes 'all the features which derive from the structure of the sung language, from the coded form of the melisma, the idiolect, the composer, the style of interpretation: in short, everything which, in the performance, is at the service of communication, of representation, of expression'. This also includes supposedly 'subjective' qualities such as expressivity and vocal personality. Geno-song is 'the space in which the significations germinate' and 'that culmination (or depth) of production where melody actually works on language – not what it says but the voluptuous pleasure of its signifier-sounds, of its letters'.[81] Barthes uses this distinction to try and ascertain why he is more moved by one particular singer than another. It is not a matter of professional technique, for which mastery of the pheno-song (acquired typically through musical training) would be sufficient; rather, it is something in excess of (or perhaps in subtraction from) technical perfection that forms a more intimate relationship between listener and speaker/singer. For Barthes the essence of the geno-song lies in 'the grain of the voice', which he defines as

> the body in the singing voice, in the writing hand, the performing limb. If I perceive the 'grain' of this music and if I attribute to this 'grain' a theoretical value (this is the assumption of the text in the work), I cannot help making a new scheme of evaluation for myself, individual no doubt, since I am determined to listen to my relation to the body of someone who is singing or playing and since that relation is an erotic one.[82]

Adriana Cavarero is critical of Barthes's conception of the voice in that she feels it continues a long-standing philosophical tradition of privileging language over sound. Her goal is rather to account for the individuality of voices on the basis of vocal sound rather than verbal message. I find Cavarero's account compelling but, in thinking about the communication of time, age and experience in writers and singers of songs whose language I share and value, I find I have to maintain a certain allegiance to the primacy of the word. I try to do so, however, within a framework that can acknowledge the insights gained from invoking nonsemantic sound: the rasp of the voice, the rattle in the throat, the various signifiers of the passage of time through the lived body. I also continue to find Barthes's formulation of the grain of the voice useful, not least in provoking curiosity as to how grain relates to time, age and experience. As I have suggested elsewhere, I often find it useful in my listening to deploy the notion of pheno-song and geno-song alongside a range of other Barthesian concepts in which we find the irruption of one revealing mode of signifying into another.[83] This would entail, for example, thinking of moments of geno-song breaking through the pheno-song (within one song, one singer), or of the distinction made by Barthes between *plaisir* and *jouissance* and between *studium* and *punctum*. The taking over of *plaisir* by *jouissance* can be thought of simply as that of ecstasy or bliss overcoming 'mere' pleasure. The other pair of concepts was developed by Barthes to analyse visual texts (photographs) but I find myself adapting them to sonic texts too. For Barthes the *studium* is the cultural 'participat[ion] in the figures, the faces, the gestures, the settings, the actions' of a scene, while the *punctum* is the 'element which rises from the scene, shoots out of it like an arrow, and pierces me'.[84] Music texts are rife which such moments and I find resonance between *punctum* and the puncture experienced by intense sonic moments. These need not be vocal, though it is to voices I am most often drawn and I would agree with Freya Jarman when she writes that 'instrumental music has powerful effects, and is able to bring about its own set of identificatory points, but the voice, understood as being synonymous with the self, has a particular capacity in this regard'.[85]

As an example of the ways in which such notions relate to the locations of the performer within the performance, I find this description of traditional singing by the Scottish singer Dick Gaughan particularly powerful:

> People who argue that it is enough in singing traditional song to simply declaim the lyric without any involvement of the singer's personal experience are talking drivel. They are treating a repository of human experience with contempt and the approach they advocate is appropriate to stamp-collecting, not singing. Learning the words is not the job, it is merely the beginning of the preparation to do the job. The people who wrote those songs wrote them from personal experience, they have been kept alive because they say something of eternal relevence [sic] to the universality of human experience and it is the job of the singer, more than anything else, to put in the work necessary to study, understand and translate that experience so as to communicate it to the listener. Otherwise, we might as well just hand the members of the audience a printed copy of the lyric and we can all go home.[86]

While this is a powerful defence of the art of interpretation and innovation in folk song, it could still be claimed that what Gaughan is defending here is, in Barthes's terms, an effective use of pheno-song in order to communicate the message of the song. But I think it hints at more than that, especially as it forms the main paragraph of a paean to Sandy Denny, and in particular to her interpretation of 'Banks of the Nile' on the first Fotheringay album. In praising Denny's performance, Gaughan writes of 'the raw, aching, agony which she brings to her reading [and which] makes it impossible not to feel the grief and fear of the young woman at the separation from her loved one and the uncertainty of his return from the horrors of war'. This emphasis on feeling, and on pain, echoes Barthes's repeated references to the pains, as well as the pleasures, of the text (notable in his repeated use of the term *jouissance*). Similarly, Gaughan's subsequent use of the word 'tangible' to describe the way Denny offers her message to the listener strikes me as an example of the embodiment of the song language into something beyond 'mere' communication. I would also want to connect these observations to Gaughan's own extraordinary vocal art, in which his forcing of the language of folk song to his own desires leads to moments of bliss in which vocal grain takes over completely from linguistic clarity.[87] As Jarman observes, 'The (material) voice can be a mediator between body and language; it gives language meaning, in its inflections, its speed, its accent, its bodiliness, but it is also an object apart from language. It speaks more of the body than of syntax.'[88]

This aspect of mediation is an important one I believe, for it allows us to steer a course between the typically polarised concepts of Barthes's theories. For my part, I am interested in the late voice as both *pheno-text* and *geno-text* in that I am interested in how songwriters have communicated the passage of time, age and experience in the language of song texts *and* in how we as listeners may hear those qualities in voice beyond language. I am particularly engaged by moments – often, but not exclusively, found later in singers' careers – when those elements come together. To return to the example of 'Who Knows Where the Time Goes', I can say that I hear plenty of language about time, age and experience in Sandy Denny's sung words and a suitably flowing melancholy in the musical setting provided by the rest of Fairport Convention, but I hear more body, more physical weariness, in Nina Simone's version of the song. That is not to say that I cannot identify aspects of geno-song, of grain, in Denny's version; indeed, there are moments in the song where her voice becomes harsher, working against the placid beauty of the song's *studium* and bringing an edge (a *punctum*) that I read as the hardening of one's hopes and dreams in the light of experience. Yet, even with this evidence of lateness, I still hear the song as youthful; the lateness is partly attained and partly anticipated, both aspects indicative of the passage from youth to adulthood. In Simone, I hear a lateness that speaks of further experience, even of irritation at the passing of time. But more importantly for what I am trying to say here, I do not feel compelled to choose between body and language, for I find myself experiencing both a world-weary singer and a song about the ageing of the world.

For another example, I might choose, as I do in Chapter 5, an early and a late recording of 'Both Sides Now' by Joni Mitchell. Like Denny's, this is a much-covered song and there are countless fascinating versions to choose from. Most telling, perhaps, are the versions recorded by Mitchell herself, in 1969 and 2000. In the former, the pheno-song seems paramount, the clarity of the message enhanced by Mitchell's crystal-clear diction, strict poetic meter and a relative lack of adornment in voice and guitar accompaniment. It is precisely the contrast between the experience and wisdom conveyed in the song's language and the youthful 'innocence' presented by the singer that has caused so many people over the years to voice surprise that someone so young could produce such a work (such comments were also made about Judy Collins, who had a hit with the song). Mitchell's return to 'Both Sides Now' in 2000 for an album of the same title, presented a singer whose voice – noticeably aged, deeper, but also more subtly nuanced – gave body to the song in a way that underlined, and made more convincing, its claims to experience, reflection and resignation. Here the surprise came in hearing the voice 'as it really is' rather than as it was preserved on record thirty-one years earlier.

Voices age differently, though, and many remain relatively constant in comparison to other aspects of the body typically addressed in the consideration of age and change in other people (or in ourselves). Perhaps we do not expect the voice to age in the ways that other parts of the body do. Even though voices lose pitch over long periods of time, the process is not as noticeable as the changes we perceive visually. We also suffer a restriction in the frequencies we can hear as we age, making us perhaps less sensitive to changing voices. In considering ageing voices, then, it is necessary to determine to what extent there is real change, and to what extent that change is 'natural' or forced.[89] In one of the many reflections on ageing in the final volume of *In Search of Lost Time*, Proust describes a moment when, on overhearing the unchanged voice of an old friend, he is shocked to discover that its owner's looks are much altered: 'The voice seemed to be emitted by an advanced phonograph, for while it was that of my friend, it emanated from a stout, grey-haired old fellow whom I did not know.'[90] One other aspect to bear in mind when considering the 'constancy' of the voice is the possibility to alter the pitch of the voice in recording; throughout this book, I discuss the evidence found in recorded voices, so there is a heightened possibility for deception. I don't, however, believe this invalidates a listener's recognition of age or experience. What seems important here is that something is created in the sound stage of the listening experience such that the listener feels they have access to a point, or points, of identification with the voices they are listening to. Indeed, as Richard Middleton has suggested, it is in recorded music that 'we may discover – finally! – the location of that vocal "grain" which Roland Barthes so influentially identified but which neither he nor his many followers have ever satisfactorily pinned down.'[91] But just as to prove the veracity of the recorded voice is to take an extreme 'objective' position, so too is it extreme to over-emphasise 'subjective' fantasy. I would suspect that most listeners adopt a position somewhere in between these extremes. To hear a particular singer in their songs is a necessary part of identifying (with) that singer and of distinguishing them from other singers.

A recurring theme of this chapter is the question relating to location, to the possibility (or impossibility) of pinning down the aspect under consideration. Where is the time and where does it go? Where is age? Where is the voice? Where does it come from and where does it go? Can we locate the source of the voice that affects us so? Barthes's pronouncements on the grain of the voice suggest that it enables us to find the person inside; it is where they are in the song we hear. But this implies that there is a 'they' and something to be 'in', which would seem to go against the 'death of the author' announced by Barthes in another of his well-known essays. Is there a metaphysics of presence at work here? Mladen Dolar argues that Barthes's conception of the grain of the voice 'will never do' because a voice cannot be pinned to a body. 'Every emission of the voice', he writes, 'is by its very essence *ventriloquism*. Ventriloquism pertains to voice as such, to its inherently acousmatic character: the voice comes from inside the body, the belly, the stomach – from something incompatible with and irreducible to the activity of the mouth. The fact that we see the aperture does not demystify the voice; on the contrary it enhances the enigma'.[92] Dolar cites cinema as an exemplary site for witnessing this, making reference to both the work and the examples of Michel Chion.[93] This is a useful counter to Barthes but not a reason to do away with the body or the fantasy of the body; indeed, Dolar provides plenty of his own examples that connect voices to bodies and bodily functions. It could be claimed that Barthes is thinking about a vocal body in a manner analogous to the working of the text in 'The Death of the Author'. Just as the text bears the meaning rather than the biographical author who produced it, so perhaps does the vocal text bear meaning (including the conjuration of a sonorous body) independently of our knowledge of the 'real' source. This tension can serve as a reminder that the voices of age, time and experience which we encounter are both real and imaginary. They come from real sources from which we, as listeners, are forever removed. Nevertheless, we can project time, age and experience onto or into them as much as we can project other qualities. Barthes's identification of the grain might be a fantasy in Dolar's conception but, for me, it remains intriguing and believable. For if, as Dolar also says, 'listening is "always-already" incipient obedience', we might claim that one of the things to which we are obedient is an unspoken imperative to match a voice to a source.[94]

With obedience in mind, we might think of the obedience – or powerlessness – of the listener captivated by the storyteller. In Samuel Taylor Coleridge's 'The Rime of the Ancient Mariner', the mariner catches a young man on his way to a wedding and starts to tell him a story. The guest, eager to get to the festivities, protests and tries to free himself from the old man's grip – initially a physical grip ('unhand me, grey-beard loon!') but then the grip of the mariner's 'glittering eye' holds the young man in place. As the old man launches his epic tale, the guest 'cannot choose but hear'. The glittering eye is the connection to the past; it is the spark of youth and life still alive in the ancient visage. Yet so is the voice, working as it does alongside the eye to captivate the listener. As the mariner's epic tale unfolds, so experience is transferred from the teller to the listener, who leaves the listening experience 'stunned' and 'forlorn' and wakes the following morning 'a sadder and a wiser man'. But the experience has not been random, for the mariner has chosen his listener: 'I know the man that must hear me: / To him my tale I teach.' It is the tale that is important here, the carrying of the tale as burden, as something to be passed on. The tale is the witness document, the text that can be taken up by others to tap into its experience. Perhaps, then, a song seeks out the listeners who need to hear it, to learn from it.

As well as keeping pheno-song and geno-song in mind – considering them as distinct but interrelated and inter-mediated – I also wish to note the connections Barthes makes between writing and voice. In 'The Grain of the Voice', he describes the presence of the body in writing and, at the culmination of *The Pleasure of the Text*, he speculates on the notion of 'writing aloud', an aesthetic process whose 'aim is not the clarity of messages, the theatre of emotions; what it searches for (in a perspective of bliss) are the pulsional incidents, the language lined with flesh, a text where we can hear the grain of the throat, the patina of consonants, the voluptuousness of vowels, a whole carnal stereophony: the articulation of the body, of the tongue, not that of meaning, of language'.[95] The writing of time, age and experience into popular song is also, I argue, a process of knowing how to turn a phrase, provide a potent metaphor and give to these universal themes a local, specific and memorable articulation. That articulation is found, as is Barthes's 'grain' both in 'the writing hand' and 'the singing voice'. But it is also found in what the hand writes and the voice sings and these processes too I want to associate to the late voice, as the 'voicing' of time, age and experience in a variety of manifestations: the writing of songs, the construction of public persona, the reporting of the self in interview, memoir and other means.

When we talk of writers finding their voice, we are surely saying something about the identification and mastery of a voice that requires a grain, an identifying style in excess of style. In an acceptance speech he gave on receiving the Prince of Asturias Award in 2011 (a speech that is in itself a model of seductive storytelling and should be heard in its entirety), Leonard Cohen spoke of his attempts to find a voice as a young man:

Now, you know of my deep association and confraternity with the poet Federico García Lorca. I could say that when I was a young man, an adolescent, and I hungered for a voice, I studied the English poets and I knew their work well, and I copied their styles, but I could not find a voice. It was only when I read, even in translation, the works of Lorca that I understood that there was a voice. It is not that I copied his voice; I would not dare. But he gave me permission to find a voice, to locate a voice, that is to locate a self, a self that that is not fixed, a self that struggles for its own existence.[96]

Here, voice is something to be studied and also to be discovered; it is something that belongs to others but not to oneself. This understanding of voice might seem to go against more romantic interpretations of the grain of the voice as something that slips past, or sticks through, or obstructs the studied voice. But such romantic conceptions, valuable as they can be, neglect the fact that we can never escape imitation or the shadow of culture on the voice. Cohen's combination of quest, discovery and ownership, meanwhile, articulates something of the dialectic of the fixed (that which can be studied) and the unfixed (that which is concerned with coming into voice, with voice as a process). Voicing experience, whether in writing or singing, can be thought of as a way of inhabiting the world in which that experience took place, and that world is one filled with precursors. Cohen shows us this again in his compelling late composition 'Tower of Song', in which he presents himself as an inhabitant of an edifice in which one pays one's rent by turning experience into art. Others have lived and laboured there before him and their ghosts still inhabit the building; Hank Williams resides 'a hundred floors above me', at a level the struggling song-worker can only dream of achieving.[97]

As listeners in search of voices, we undertake our own quests and discoveries and come to voice in ways which are guided by exposure to other voices. With the growth of mechanical reproduction, this has increasingly become an experience in which we combine local and 'foreign' sources; many of us are not, at least, restricted to the oral culture of our immediate vicinity. Books, photographs, films, records and other promising objects offer opportunities for surrogate experiences or for a more personalised experience of learning. Rather than being a celebration of alienation, I intend this observation as a way of highlighting the importance of solitary discovery, working as it does in dialectical relationship with collective discovery and education. For example, a parent's neglected record collection might prove interesting to a child precisely because of the mystery that accumulates around its neglect (and, these days, the aura of old physical objects). Learning in isolation is an important aspect of adolescent development, and indeed of development at all stages of life. Connections made during such experience can be intense, personal and long lasting (as with Cohen's discovery of Lorca). That was certainly my experience with much of the music discussed in this book. I felt as though I had been primed for the experience but it was as if I needed to make the rest of the discovery, the intimate connection, by myself, away from other ears. That connection often had to be between the singer and myself. After that, I was content to gradually move towards a more integrated, familial and social sharing of the musical experience. This is part of the independence of growing up: leaving home, staking a claim, returning.

Living with voices

Among the many voices we live with we must include recorded voices. Listeners, like readers, inhabit texts and they do so in a manner analogous to the 'active' reading suggested by Gaston Bachelard and Michel de Certeau. While Bachelard explores the 'poetics of space' by meditating on the ways we dwell in poems and buildings, Certeau pursues the 'silent production' of the reader, in which 'a different world (the reader's) slips into the author's place':

> This mutation makes the text habitable, like a rented apartment. It transforms another person's property into a space borrowed for a moment by a transient. Renters make comparable changes in an apartment they furnish with their acts and memories; as do speakers, in the language into which they insert both the messages of their native tongue and, through their accent, through their own 'turns of phrase', etc., their own history; as do pedestrians, in the streets they fill with the forests of their desires and goals.[98]

The notion of inhabiting connects also to the taking on of another's text in the act of interpretation. If it is often said of Frank Sinatra, for example, that he 'inhabited' the songs he performed, the architectural or domestic metaphor is worth pursuing. Songs can be inhabited and adapted like houses, by decorating a part in a particular way or by making major alterations or renovations (think, for example, of the ways in which many interpreters of the Great American Songbook removed whole verses from songs and focused instead on the 32-bar refrains). A house must exist before we inhabit it and it will normally continue to exist after we do not; its inhabitant is temporary but can make lasting changes to the temporary residence (just as a modified song becomes, in its new form, a standard). Songs, like buildings, can be built upon each other; we can even imagine singers residing on different levels, as with Cohen's Tower of Song.

As listeners, we too inhabit songs and form relationships with voices, 'moving in' with them, living with them, ageing with them, perhaps leaving them. This intimate relationship between creators and perceivers of artistic products is highlighted in John Dewey's theories of aesthetic experience. There has to be a shared element of experience for such relationships to be forged, but this does not negate the possibility of novelty or originality. Of poems and pictures, for example, Dewey writes that they 'present material passed through the alembic of personal experience. They have no precedents in existence or in universal being. But, nonetheless, their material came from the public world and so has qualities in common with the material of other experiences, while the product awakens in other persons new perceptions of the meanings of the common world'.[99] I am often struck by the articulation of this experience when I read accounts of fans' and critics' relationships with the music they love, and love to analyse. Paul Williams's intense accounts of the connection he feels with the work of Neil Young and Bob Dylan are cases in point, as is Michelle Mercer's account of Joni Mitchell, which reveals, among other things, Mitchell's own awareness of this process.[100] The subjectivities that are exposed in such accounts are often telling and invite us to consider the grounds upon which our own evaluative accounts are based. In the case of Mitchell, for example, I know very well that it can be objectively argued that her 1974 album *Court & Spark* is as strong an album as *Blue* (1971), and that *Hejira* (1976) presents a poetic maturity unprecedented in Mitchell's work. But it was *Blue* that caught me first and at the right time to make an impression (I am very far from being alone or original here, as Mercer's book on Mitchell's 'Blue period' makes clear). It is often remarked that works that capture us in our youth are the ones that stay with us, but I think it goes further than this. We are subject to the recommendations of others, to canons, to what is widely or locally available, to what we can access.[101] And our personal relationships with these highly influential documents evolve as we return to them, discard them or share them with others in such ways that those first encounters get revisited and perhaps repeated.[102] 'Form', wrote Dewey, 'is the art of making clear what is involved in the organization of space and time prefigured in every course of a developing life-experience'.[103] What takes form in such a way that it can be returned to, passed on and communicated as experience is of vital importance to how we understand what the world has to offer. As Paul Williams wrote in the 1960s, in a review partly dedicated to Joni Mitchell's first album:

> [These works] are an aspect of experience, as well as the product of same; what we are today and soon is shaped by what we hear of them.. . . Our understanding of the world is daily added to, crossed out, erased, struck over, pasted together by various cyclones and breezes that blow through. If we do not listen to music, if we fail to read books or talk with each other, if we seldom look on human beauty or deep-felt expression or accidental creation, we diminish ourselves. Which somehow means there is a life-energy passed through art, through communication that is also expression (which indicates a kind of moreness or fullness).[104]

Case studies

A number of songs, albums and artists that I discuss in this book are ones I have lived with for years. It was no doubt due to that long relationship that, when I came to start formulating ideas about the late voice, I found myself thinking about these examples rather than others. Another feature common to my examples is that I recall feeling, on first encountering them, a sense of recognition, as if they were saying something I already knew but had not yet been able to articulate. Perhaps, like Leonard Cohen, I found in these voices a way of establishing a self; perhaps, like Merle Haggard, I was floored by the fact that someone could tell my story in a song.[105] These are common experiences – we all have those moments of intense *jouissance* that go by the name 'epiphanies' – and yet still intensely personal. As with songs, so with written texts: for a writer and researcher, there is something wonderful about encountering texts which seem to articulate something one had felt but had perhaps not yet put into coherent form, or which perhaps one had not yet truly perceived as being important. Reading Siegfried Zielinski's introduction to his *Deep Time of the Media* was one such experience for me and I feel drawn to quote his account of the importance of curiosities and examples in scholarship:

> [A]ttractions, sensations, events, or phenomena that create a stir and draw out attention; these demand to be portrayed in such a way that their potential to stimulate can develop and flourish. The finds must be approached with respect, care, and goodwill, not disparaged or marginalized. My [work] is written in a spirit of praise and commendation, not of critique. I am aware that this represents a break with the 'proper' approach to history that I was taught at university. At center stage, I shall put people and their works; I shall, on occasion, wander off but always remain close to them. It does not bother me that this type of historiography may be criticized as romantic. We who have chosen to teach, research, and write all have our heroes and heroines . . . The people I am concerned with here are people imbued with an enduring something that interests us passionately.[106]

I value this unembarrassed insistence on praise and commendation of people and works to whom we are drawn and which stimulate us to recognise and pass on the 'enduring something' they have revealed to us. Like Zielinski, my selections are not random but tell, I hope, a reasonably coherent story; that they are selective and partial I do not deny. As I say, this is largely a body of work that I came to as a teenager and young adult and in which I recognised the voicing of experience. One of the things that have always fascinated me with this work was how I measured my own experience (and inexperience) with what I heard in the songs. I heard and anticipated things that had not yet happened to me. But there is also much experience gained by the age of 18 and I am tempted to posit experience, in this light, as something that works like a sense. Perhaps, in encountering the representation of experiences we have not yet had, we still recognise the act, or process, of experiencing and this is initially what is meaningful; later, we fill in the gaps and identify (or not) with the specifics. It may well be that the ultimate message of this book is nothing more than that popular songs offer ideal vehicles or modes for the communication of experience, a claim which may, depending on one's perspective, be banal, modest or profound. I would still maintain that meaning can be found in the journey to reach that 'foregone' conclusion; as I have been before, I am drawn to the words of the poet Jim Harrison, who writes that 'It is not so much that I got / there from here, which is everyone's / story: but the shape / of the voyage.'[107]

Some of the examples I use are ones I came to later in the voyage and which fitted in with the general trajectory of my listening. I wanted to remain faithful to the late voice idea as it had come to me and it had done so via consideration of mainly North American and British sources, which accounted for much of my early musical experience. Having gained, over the years, a deep interest in musics from other parts of the world, I am aware that a number of themes explored in these case studies could be applied to others less canonical and/or less Anglocentric. Doing so would no doubt lead to a different set of questions and approaches, perhaps more interesting than those I have undertaken here. Yet it was equally important to me, as an initial step, to explore the case studies that had suggested themselves to me for the longest period, those songs that had invited and encouraged me to consider time, age and experience for myself and through which I had measured my own life experience. I would like this work to mark both that initial step and an invitation (to myself, to others) to consider a much wider range of musics in relation to the themes explored here.

Given the plurality of perspectives available even within my limited cultural and stylistic case studies, as well as my own insistence of anticipated lateness and the multiplicity of voices, my retention of a singular concept – *the late voice* rather than *late voices* – may seem strange. Adriana Cavarero, whom I quoted earlier, has argued against such a singular conception of the voice. Yet, following the discoveries of my original train of thought, I still believe that these various perspectives can be clustered together under a singular term, one that provocatively suggests universalism while also reserving the right to reflect different subject positions, to see lateness itself as something both achieved (an affective achievement, most prominently recognised when felt as an interference in being) and deferred (relegated to the not-yet, a not-yet that recognises lateness but sees it as something still to come).

I have said something about how I selected my examples (or rather perhaps, how they selected me). As to how I then chose to go about finding 'meaning' in them, I have, as may already be evident, allowed my cumulative experience of the songs to flavour my interpretation, while also checking the potential for distortion in such an approach by reading other accounts of the people and works I am studying. While doing so, I found recent work by Keith Negus on narrative and interpretation to be particularly resonant with some of my own experiences. In one article, Negus adopts an 'intercontextual' approach which brings in the interpreter's biography and subject position while also attempting to measure these against others' responses (e.g. those encountered in the classroom, online forums, magazines and so on).[108] This seems to me a useful strategy and, while I have not adopted such an approach in as systematic a way as Negus models, I have certainly attempted to balance my own relationship to and understanding of artists and music with those of others (critics, fans, biographers, acquaintances, students, academic colleagues and the musicians themselves). There is always a danger, in such an approach, that one finds what one wants to find in order to support one's theories, but I am not aware of an interpretive discipline for which this is not a danger; it is as likely to happen 'in the field' as it is in the classroom, the conference, the internet forum, the biography or the fabled armchair. Besides, I do not believe that, for those of us who remain faithful to the idea of intellectual curiosity, there is even a real possibility of maintaining a fixed, authoritative take on interpretation. That does not stop the questions posed and the speculations invited by interpretation from being interesting and critically productive. We should not be afraid to feel as our representative artists feel, or to project upon them the thoughts that we might have them think. As Dewey writes:

> Only the psychology that has separated things which in reality belong together holds that scientists and philosophers think while poets and painters follow their feelings. In both, and to the same extent in the degree in which they are of comparable rank, there is emotionalized thinking, and there are feelings whose substance consists of appreciated meanings or ideas.[109]

I have tended to concentrate on qualities I noticed when listening to 'my' artists and also on qualities noted by others who have written or spoken about them. It is from these observations that I have teased out patterns that might start to resemble a system for identifying aspects of the late voice. It is definitely not the case that such a system has been first devised and then applied to the case studies. In this sense I have not been systematic in my approach or my structuring, instead allowing each of the case studies to suggest certain aspects, pausing at times to systemise the patterns. Where I have tried to be systematic is in my re-testing of each case study against criteria that emerged from the case studies, especially in connection to the qualities of the late voice that I have already introduced. At no point have I sought to pin down, once and for all, the meanings of the pieces under scrutiny, for one thing experience teaches us is that meaning changes with time.

Ultimately, I believe that one's choice of examples and methods should be understood as invitations to thinking, as ways in which one particular thinker has come to have these thoughts and to communicate them. Others will have had different experiences, will have come from different backgrounds, will have inherited different bodies of work and will have negotiated the soundtracks of their lives in different ways. I hope my work can be an invitation, for those who find resonance in any of the propositions and suppositions contained in the book, to follow up on some of them and see to what extent they might relate to other contexts. Rather than critiquing what has been omitted, I would hope for others to affirm the potential of applying what has been attempted here to other situations. Some of our experiences will have been very similar, after all, for none of us escape the processes of time, age and experience.

'Won't You Spare Me Over till Another Year?': Ralph Stanley's Late Voice

We begin with death – with the promise, threat and sound of death – and with a voice pleading for more life. The voice comes to us in a scene from *O Brother, Where Art Thou?*, the film written and directed by Joel and Ethan Coen and released in 2000. The film's story takes place in Mississippi during the Great Depression of the 1930s and its principal characters are three white southerners, Ulysses Everett McGill (George Clooney), Pete Hogwallop (John Turturro) and Delmar O'Donnell (Tim Blake Nelson). Having escaped from the notorious Parchman Farm prison, the trio are on a dubious quest for treasure, a quest based loosely on Homer's *Odyssey*. The film makes numerous references to the popular culture (especially music) of the time in which the story is set. For part of their journey, the three escaped convicts are accompanied by a young black blues guitarist named Tommy Johnson (Chris Thomas King). The scene in question takes place at a point when Tommy has gone missing. The three main protagonists discover how and why when they chance upon a night-time meeting of the Ku Klux Klan; as they watch, the gathering works itself into a frenzy, feet stomping in unison and white-cloaked bodies enacting a bizarre dance before a burning wooden cross. Beneath the cross, a red-cloaked Imperial Wizard stands atop a stationary cart. A bell rings and silence descends, exacerbating the already palpable menace of the rural night. Attention shifts to the scarlet-hooded leader, who now uncrosses his arms and raises them in a kind of embrace. With a voice as old as time, he begins to sing:

Ohhh-oh-oh-oh-oh-oh-ohhhhhhhh De-uh-eth

Ohhhhh-oh-oh-oh-oh-ohhhhhhh De-uh-uh-uh-eth

Won't you spare me over till another yea-uh-uh-er?

The voice is chilling. The stretched words reverberate like a funeral bell, at once precise and out of focus, unearthly phonemes hovering around the edges of the sensible.[1] But the message is not lost and the words hang in the still air. Both voice and song sound ancient, older than anyone present in the scene, not least the spectators (the three protagonists watching the scene unfold from the relative safety of the bushes and the spectators watching from the total safety of the other side of the screen). The singer's wavering voice and the initial lack of accompaniment underline the severity of the words:

Well, what is this that I can't see
With ice cold hands takin' hold of me
Well I am Death, none can excel
I'll open the door to heaven or hell

As the singer continues, his voice is accompanied by the rough rhythm of the white-clad Klansmen marching in unison. It becomes apparent that their ritual involves a black man who they have captured and who the main characters recognise as Tommy Johnson. Following a rabble-rousing speech, the Klansmen move towards the culmination of their ritual, the murder of the black captive. In a half-serious, half-farcical scene, Ulysses, Pete and Delmar enact a rescue mission and Tommy's day of reckoning is averted. The deferral of death longed for in the song is enacted and both victim and would-be executioner are spared over until another year, or at least another day.

The Imperial Wizard, as we discover when he is unmasked, is the local gubernatorial candidate Homer Stokes, played by Wayne Duvall. But it is not Duvall's voice that we hear singing 'O Death' (sometimes 'Oh Death'; the song is also known as 'Conversation with Death' and has variants entitled 'Awful Death' and 'Money Cannot Buy Your Soul'). Watching the film, we attach an origin to the voice due to the way the camera lingers on the red hood and the body gestures emanating from the cloaked figure; yet there is no obvious vocal gesture because the head is covered. As the camera zooms in, we detect movement through a slit in the Wizard's hood, reinforcing the figure as the source of the sound we are hearing. But our desire to connect voice and body remains frustrated until the Wizard unmasks himself as Stokes/Duvall. During this process, the Grand Wizard is created as a 'vocalic body', as the entity most likely to be singing 'O Death'. As Steven Connor writes, 'the fact that an unassigned voice must always imply a body means that it will always partly supply it as well'. Furthermore,

> so strong is the embodying power of the voice, that this process occurs not only in the case of voices that seem separated from their obvious or natural sources, but also in voices . . . that have a clearly identifiable source, but seem in various ways excessive to that source. This voice then conjures for itself a different kind of body; an imaginary body which may contradict, compete with, replace, or even reshape the actual, visible body of the speaker.[2]

Although a source is presented to us in the scene I am describing, the masks of the cloak and hood obscure most traces of humanity, leaving us to fill in the gaps via the fantasy of the vocalic body. Given the inhuman figure before us and the subject matter of the song we are hearing, we might equally imagine this as a 'vocalic skeleton', as perhaps the figure of Death itself. The cloak and hood add to the suggestion, as does the subsequent assertion of this entity as one authorised to pronounce judgement on mortal subjects such as Tommy Johnson.[3]

The Wizard's subsequent unmasking is, in its way, as farcical and potentially game-changing as that in the 1939 film *The Wizard of Oz*. Mladen Dolar uses that film's Wizard as an example of the deceptive nature of the voice and of the machinery necessary to create and maintain its authority.[4] When the Wizard of Oz is revealed as a weak old man whose vocalic power is reliant on amplification, or when The Klan's Grand Wizard is revealed – in the scene already described and also later in *O Brother* – as an ineffectual leader out of touch with his community, the authority of the disembodied voice crumbles. The voice in Dolar's formulation is always already removed from the body in that we cannot locate its source or account for its power over us. The contract between speaker and listener is what Connor would call a 'ventriloquial' one in which both parties are used as puppets by the voice. This proves to be the case in *O Brother*, when neither the unmasked Homer Stokes nor the actor portraying him proves to be the real voice of 'O Death'. Just as the Wizard's song defers death in its message and obscures origin in its status as a traditional song, so we have to wait until another moment – the movie credits – to find the true origin of that chilling voice.[5]

This is the voice that I am interested in, this voice imbued with all the lateness of tradition, severity and age. It belongs to Ralph Stanley, former member of singing duo the Stanley Brothers, a pioneering figure in the world of bluegrass and old-time music, born in the Virginia mountains in 1927 and seventy-three years of age at the time of *O Brother*'s release. Because of this voice and the way it connected so effectively to this ancient, death-defying text, Stanley would go on to enjoy a revival of interest in his music, gaining a whole new audience as he approached his eightieth year. Do we follow the man, the song or the voice? Is it a matter of biography, lyrics or sound? In what follows I consider each in turn, though, not surprisingly given the subject of this book, I privilege the voice. But voice is not only sound and all the aforementioned focal points are important due to the ways in which they intersect to tell us something about lateness and the mediation of age and experience. As I do with other case studies in this book, I use biographical information where I believe it illuminates the textual material of the song, where it adds something to the exegesis, or where it makes thinkable certain issues relating to age, time or experience. In the case of Ralph Stanley, I am drawing mostly on his memoir *Man of Constant Sorrow*, a fascinating and moving account of Stanley's life and of the development of American old-time music in the twentieth century. Published in Stanley's eighty-third year, the book is also a fine example of that aspect of the late voice concerned with what we might call, after Norberto Bobbio, 'real old age', as distinct from 'imagined and feared' old age.[6] When I talk about the late voice of Ralph Stanley in his seventy-third and eighty-third years – in *O Brother* and in the memoir, respectively – I am referring not only to the timbre of voice with which he sings and speaks, but also to the writerly voice that he utilises in interviews and via the pages of the book. And when I say that we hear (and read) a late voice engaged with 'real old age', I mean that we are not encountering a voice that anticipates experience, that is older or wiser than its years, but a very real voice of experience, a voice nearer the end of its life than its beginning.

The boy with the hundred-year-old voice

Ralph Stanley packs plenty of realism into the pages of his memoir, spending much of the opening section meditating on mortality, his place in the world and the family plot where he will be buried.

> At the top of the cemetery, close by a pair of big cedar trees planted by my aunt many years ago, my grave is ready for me when it's my time to go. It's next to the graves of Carter and his wife, Mary.. . . I used to go the cemetery a lot. I don't go there as often anymore. When you get to be my age, you figure you'll be there soon enough. But it's still a place where I can spend some time and look around and linger awhile.[7]

Carter was the other half of the Stanley Brothers, the group with which Ralph found initial fame and which ended with Carter's death in 1966. Not surprisingly, much of Ralph's narrative focuses on Carter and on the brothers' shared discoveries and experiences. Carter functions for much of the text as the listener Ralph is speaking to or imagining and his ghost animates the pages, as in this early appearance, which recalls the ways in which places – not least final resting places – serve as mnemonic devices for those who pass through or linger in them.[8]

Ralph Stanley's book exemplifies a point made by Norberto Bobbio about the sharpening of long-term memory in later life:

> By remembering you rediscover yourself and your identity, in spite of the many years that have passed and the thousands of events you have experienced. You come across the years lost in time, the games played as a child, the faces, voices and gestures of your school friends, and places, especially the places of childhood, that are the most distant in time but most clearly defined in the memory.[9]

Yet, in Stanley's case, it is this rediscovery of the past that signals, early in his narrative, an aspect of himself that complicates neat teleological development towards a late voice. This revelation comes as he reflects on his earliest experience of the power of singing:

> I'm well past eighty now, but as far back as I can remember, everyone always told me I had an old-time mountain voice: what they call weathered and lived-in, like something you'd hear moaning in the woods late of a night and not from the mouth of a young'un. They called me the boy with the hundred-year-old voice. I reckon if I make it another twenty years, maybe then I'll finally get to sound like my real age. (*MCS*, 2)

This revelatory staging of lateness attained early is accompanied by the story of how, as a boy 'barely eight years old', Stanley was made to sing in the Point Truth Baptist Church of Scott County, Virginia (not his family's regular church).[10] His father had been due to lead the congregation in singing, following the Baptist practice of 'lining out' a hymn, where a leader sings a line or verse and the others repeat it. On this occasion he had forgotten the start of the hymn and pushed Ralph forward to lead in his place. Despite his nerves, the boy succeeded with his task and, in doing so, learned something of the power of song and the possibility of overcoming fear. As Stanley weaves this story into his initial reflections on singing, age, religion and his voice, he moves between remembered wonder at being 'the boy with the hundred-year-old voice' and continued attempts – his own and those of friends and critics – to map that voice onto age and history. In the passage quoted above, he writes of the increasing likelihood of sounding like his 'real age'; elsewhere he suggests that his voice has grown more mournful with life experience and the losses it has brought. There is not necessarily any disagreement here with the narratives of 'real old age' presented by Bobbio or Jean Améry and reported in Chapter 1; in many ways, Stanley asserts their claims. Yet there is still that moment, perhaps as fleeting as the passing of song itself, where something other could be imagined and a boy of eight could be heard as a man of a hundred. There are elements that once did not seem to fit – a body, a sound – but that are later seen to fit, to come into their own. Stanley here reminds us of the idea of the body as the puppet of the voice, the channel through which it is passing. 'I was too young to know what all the words really meant', he writes, 'but I can tell you now the hymn told my story, plain and simple' (*MCS*, 5).

Stanley thus appears as both boy and old man in the opening pages of his memoir, just as he will do in its moving final passages. At both points his brother is there to accompany him and it is Ralph's career in music-making, at first with Carter and then as a band leader, that fills the bulk of the narrative space between these points. Carter, born two years before Ralph in 1925, was obsessed with music from an early age. As with the fraternal relationship, Carter was very much the lead in the musical partnership and it was he who took the modernising action of getting a guitar and moving the boys away from the strict Primitive Baptist tradition of unaccompanied music. Ralph learned the banjo and followed in his brother's footsteps. The pair developed their musical style and repertoire, becoming modernisers of old-time music, Carter through his singing, guitar playing and songwriting, and Ralph through the adoption of the three-finger 'Scruggs style' of banjo playing. They started out emulating the highly popular styles of Bill Monroe and, later, Flatt & Scruggs and soon gained popularity on the radio, via the 'Farm and Fun Time' programme on Bristol-based station WCYB. They made their first recordings for the Rich-R-Tone label between 1947 and 1949, producing a number of sides featuring traditional duet singing style, with both brothers singing the same parts together. In 1949 and 1950 the Stanleys recorded for Columbia before Ralph took a short break from performing. During this time Carter played in Bill Monroe's band but the brothers reformed for further sessions with Columbia and Rich-R-Tone (their last for both labels) in 1952.

While the Rich-R-Tone recordings present a band still in thrall to standard old-time songs, the sides cut for Columbia highlight the process by which the Stanleys developed, in the words of Charles Wolfe, 'a style that at once harkened back to the mountain music of the past, and looked forward with innovative harmonies and haunting new songs'.[11] The Columbia recordings are notable for innovations in playing and songwriting, influenced by the instrumental virtuosity of Monroe, Flatt and Scruggs, Carter's desire to write songs that reflected his own experience and the development of a 'high trio' singing style that deployed harmonies in ways which were unheard of at the time, as Stanley explains:

Usually with trio harmonies, you had a lead vocal and then you had a higher tenor part and a lower baritone. We worked out a new arrangement with Carter on lead, me on tenor and then Pee Wee [Lambert] singing a high baritone way up top of all the voices. You may have heard the term 'high lonesome' to describe bluegrass singing; well, our high trio was the highest and lonesomest thing you ever heard. (*MCS*, 145)

The quality of the Stanleys' sound on the Columbia sides is also notably different from their earlier work, doubtless due to the technological resources available to them at the studio. Stanley describes the Castle Studio, located in the old ballroom of the Tulane Hotel in Nashville, as 'a dump' but the sound achieved was one that 'stood the test of time' (*MCS*, 146). One of the tests of time for recorded music of that era is how well it has been maintained or remastered. Whether the result of better original masters, format transfer or remastering, the Columbia sides compiled on CD sound richer than the Rich-R-Tone sides reissued by Revenant. The latter, as Gary Reid notes, are intimate, exciting and display 'youthful exuberance' and 'the excitement of budding talent taking shape'.[12] But there remains a thinness to the sound which, while useful for expressing urgency (as on their galloping version of Bill Monroe's 'Molly and Tenbrook'), often makes the group sound bunched-up (which they probably were) and also means that the instruments do not come through as well as they might. The Columbia recordings are not only smoother, but there is also more space and separation between voices and instruments. However, as already mentioned, the most notable development is the separation of the voices through new harmony techniques. On some songs, Carter sounds more like a country crooner than an old-time singer and even when he adopts the time-worn, 'high lonesome' style associated with Monroe's bluegrass, the harmony vocals of Ralph and mandolin player Pee Wee Lambert are always there above him, their voices sounding older and 'wilder' in comparison to his. Combined with a less rushed vocal pace on a number of the tracks, Carter's vocals resemble the contemporary honky-tonk styles of Ernest Tubb and Hank Williams but with added bluegrass elements provided by the instrumentation and harmony singing. This is particularly evident on songs such as 'A Vision of Mother', 'The Fields Have Turned Brown' and 'Gathering Flowers for the Master's Bouquet', where Carter sings the verses solo and the others harmonise on the choruses; on 'The Lonesome River' (later recorded by Ralph in duet with Bob Dylan), the opening of the verses have something of Hank Williams's blues inflections. There are still a number of songs where the brothers duet on the verses, including a re-recorded 'Little Glass of Wine' (a song originally cut for Rich-R-Tone) and these tend to sound 'older', made archaic by the new styles being tried out elsewhere.

It was during a Columbia session in 1950 that Ralph Stanley first recorded 'I'm a Man of Constant Sorrow' (later just 'Man of Constant Sorrow'), a song which would become one of his signatures. He had been performing lead vocal on the song for some time in concerts and on radio broadcasts but this was the first time he had recorded a solo vocal. In his memoir, Stanley admits that he has never been happy with the result because he can hear how scared he was. Even though the way he 'worried' his lines was just how he'd learned as a child in church, he felt he 'came up short' due to another kind of worry taking over.

> After you get seasoned and you get used to things, you can put everything you've got in there. I was holding back. When I listen to that record now, I hear how scared I was more than anything. Maybe the fear I hear in my voice fit the story of the song. I do know that the first recording I did of 'Man of Constant Sorrow' helped save the song from dying out. The record on Columbia gave it a new life, and that song has followed me ever since, and I still sing it every show I do. (*MCS*, 148)

It is true that one can detect something of a waver on the long-held notes of the song that contrasts with the confident delivery of Carter on 'The Lonesome River', with Ralph's own harmony vocals on most songs, and with Ralph's lead on 'Pretty Polly' (another song he would continue to revisit throughout his career). Yet, for all the power of the vocal on 'Pretty Polly', the song is less personal than 'Man of Constant Sorrow' and the latter contains a vulnerability that, along with its pleading, worried lyric, pins it to a confessional style somewhere in the region of contemporaneous blues and country songs such as Hank Williams's 'I'm So Lonesome I Could Cry' or 'I'll Never Get Out of this World Alive'. At the same time the wilder, 'older' singing style sees Stanley bending and dividing words in a manner that connects back to the eccentricities of old-time music.

Stanley's comments about saving 'Man of Constant Sorrow' can be affirmed by noting that both this song and 'Pretty Polly', which were released on two sides of a 78, would prove to be important songs in the folk revival of the 1950s and 1960s. Bob Dylan would include the former song on his first album and use the latter as the basis for 'The Ballad of Hollis Brown' on his third, while Judy Collins would use the female version of 'Constant Sorrow' as the title track of her debut album (*Maid of Constant Sorrow*, 1961) and perform a folk-rock version of 'Pretty Polly' on her popular *Who Knows Where the Time Goes* in 1968. 'Man of Constant Sorrow' also became the theme song of *O Brother, Where Art Thou?* in that it was featured in a number of different versions, both vocal and instrumental, in the film and on its accompanying soundtrack. The three main protagonists, along with Tommy, are seen recording the song in a remote studio in order to earn some money; later, the record becomes a regional hit and the group, going by the 'old-time' name of The Soggy Bottom Boys, become local celebrities. To a certain extent life could be seen to be imitating art when the surprisingly successful soundtrack to *O Brother* helped to make Stanley a celebrity once more; while his most obvious contribution – and the one for which he would subsequently win a Grammy – was his version of 'O Death', the Stanley Brothers song 'Angel Band' was also used in the film and it was the distinctive Stanley arrangement of 'Man of Constant Sorrow' that was used in the performance, albeit with Dan Tyminski's vocal rather than Stanley's.

Songs like 'Angel Band' and 'Man of Constant Sorrow' are among the most famous of the Stanley Brothers, but the group also produced a number of new compositions or arrangements that would become staples of the bluegrass genre, including Carter's compositions 'A Vision of Mother' and 'The Fields Have Turned Brown'. Carter's songwriting was characterised by themes of loss and regret, often articulated in songs about errant sons or departed parents. 'The Fields Have Turned Brown', a classic of the genre, describes a son who leaves home and spends 'many long years' travelling 'in sorrow'. Despite his parents' entreaties for him to not go astray – emphasised in the Stanleys' rendition by the 'highest lonesomist' harmony trios used in the chorus – the son does not return until a letter reaches him to tell him that his parents are long dead and the fields have turned brown. Such images of earthly decay contrast with the emphasis in other songs about the brightness of the life hereafter. While homecomings on Earth are often occasions for sorrow, the 'home' that awaits in Heaven is presented as a reward for the 'short life of trouble' to which mortals are sentenced. The songs of the Stanleys, not unlike those of other singing brother groups (the Monroes, the Delmores, the Louvins, the Blue Sky Boys) and of southern country music more generally, alternate tales of sin (drink, adultery, murder) with songs of Christian faith. Often this is articulated in gospel music settings and here again the Stanleys were innovators in terms of the harmony vocals they developed. On Columbia recordings such as 'Gathering Flowers for the Master's Bouquet', there is a clear template for subsequent bluegrass groups. But like the flowers hymned in that song that last for only a short while on Earth, the Stanleys' success was to be transient:

> That's how it is when you're young and never had nothing and don't know any better. When some good things finally come your way, you think it'll always be that way. Kind of like a hog under an acorn tree. The hog never looks up to see where they're coming from or how many are left. When the acorns fall, he just grabs however many he can and gobbles 'em down. Well, we felt like that old hog, and it took us a while before we realized that trees run out of acorns. (*MCS*, 119)

The acorns would become thinner on the ground as the Stanleys worked their way through the 1950s, a decade that saw them and the broader country music world sidelined by the rise of rock 'n' roll and its accompanying youth culture. From 1953 to 1958 the brothers and their accompanists, the Clinch Mountain Boys, recorded for Mercury, producing a series of recordings that are considered by many to be their best. It was not a question of quality that would prevent them becoming more famous. To a certain extent the tradition they exemplified had been anachronistic long before they began performing in the 1940s and the group would always be considered traditionalists who innovated only as far as they could go without leaving the essential style of what was called, for good reason, 'old time music'. New instrumental and vocal techniques would only take the group so far as long as the instruments and voices were still associated with the ways of the past. The songs they recorded continued to speak, in Gary Reid's words, 'of lost loves, aging parents at home, a longing for a simple life in the hills, and a love and respect for God – themes universal to the Stanleys and their rural audiences'.[13] Nicholas Dawidoff also writes of the always-already oldness of bluegrass:

> Just as the instruments are old-fashioned, the lyrical content of a bluegrass song is emphatically pre-Edison. These wistful songs of faith, family, love, loss, pain, and redemption are anchored in a distant rural past.. . . Because bluegrass songs tend to be crowded with infidels who, in fact, do stray far from home, drown their lovers in rivers, and soak themselves in moonshine, bluegrass generally features high, keening vocal harmonies that singers summon by tamping down the backs of their throats.[14]

They were not the kind of songs, messages, instruments or voices that would survive the youth culture onslaught to come. In 1954 Bill Monroe played the Stanley Brothers a recording of his song 'Blue Moon of Kentucky' that had been recorded but not yet released by Elvis Presley. Sensing the new version was going to be a hit, Monroe urged the Stanleys to record it quickly and release their version first. They did so, mimicking Presley's style and sounding quite unlike either Monroe's Bluegrass Boys or the regular Stanley Brothers. Presley's version, of course, was the hit and a strong taste of what was to come. As Colin Escott notes, 'By the time the Stanleys parted from Mercury in 1958, bluegrass was on its way to being marginalized and, later, festivalized.'[15] In his memoir Stanley puts it bluntly: 'Elvis just about starved us out' (*MCS*, 184). The brothers continued, however, and from 1958 to 1965 recorded for the connected companies King and Starday. In response to label owner Nathan King's desire for a sound like that of the earlier Delmore Brothers, the group moved the guitar to a more prominent role in place of the mandolin and fiddle; this also helped to distinguish them from Monroe and other bluegrass acts. In Stanley's words, 'We just fought to survive the best we could.. . . All we wanted to do was keep making music, and the way we made it was staying on the road. Only now we weren't so young and carefree. We were getting tired, feeling whipped. But we just kept on' (*MCS*, 182).

   If rock 'n' roll is to be thought of as a revolution, it is worth remembering that revolutionary moments do not merely do away with the old. They also bring about a level of evaluation of what went before and this can lead to 'old ways' attaining a new aura. In the case of old-time music, this entailed a re-evaluation that can partly be seen as a response to the rise of rock. This re-evaluation came in the form of the American Folk Revival, which had been gathering pace throughout the 1950s and, by the start of the new decade, was encouraging a generation of young performers and audiences to turn to folk and roots music as an alternative to commercial pop. From the perspective of the Stanley Brothers, fighting to survive as they were, what was notable was the number of young people from far away who started to seek them out. This was a fairly common feature of the time, as it was discovered that many of the musicians who young folk fans had heard on old or reissued recordings were still alive, albeit hidden away. This sense of discovery is encapsulated by the folksinger Eric Von Schmidt, who, like many of his peers, was influenced by the music to be found on the *Anthology of American Folk Music* compiled by Harry Smith and released by Moses Asch's Folkways label in 1952:

> For this music sounded like it came right out of the ground. Songs like the clods of rich dark earth, fecund, timeless. Naively we thought these Old Time Singers all dead. We assumed our Heros [sic], who had recorded these songs mostly in the late twenties and early thirties, were old even then. Actually, many were young when the records were made, as we were to realize when they started showing up – fiddles, guitars, banjos in hand – at folk festivals in the sixties. Before that we had thought only of reviving the songs, not the singers.[16]

The Stanleys do not quite belong in the category of musicians mentioned by Von Schmidt and found on Smith's Anthology, which collected recordings from the late 1920s, a generation before the brothers began performing. Furthermore, the Stanleys had been continuously performing and recording up to the time of the folk revival, unlike many of the Anthology artists who had given up professional music making before or during the Great Depression. Even so, for a band struggling to make a mark in the newly electrified world of rock 'n' roll, the Stanleys were as well placed as any to capitalise on any publicity the revival might create. As well as performing at musical festivals, they appeared on Pete Seeger's television show *Rainbow Quest* in the mid-1960s and toured Europe with other folk and old-time artists.

This brief renaissance for the group was not to last long, however. Carter Stanley, a heavy drinker, died in 1966, leaving his brother to continue alone. At first unsure whether he could make it as a solo artist, Ralph Stanley decided to continue with the job to which he was best suited and continued to perform and to record for King before moving to another independent label, Rebel. Nicholas Dawidoff suggests that, after Carter's death, Ralph 'allowed a tragic timbre to sink into his voice' and it became ever more a voice of grief. He also suggests that, in taking lead of the Clinch Mountain Boys, Ralph removed a number of Carter's innovations and moved the music back to an older-sounding format, leaving other musicians such as Monroe to appear as modernisers instead:

> Stanley went to great lengths to apply a layer of dust to his music. He sometimes played the banjo in the claw-hammer style his mother had taught him, he wrote songs notable for their lyrical austerity, and he stripped down the Clinch Mountain sound so that his voice rang clean and spare above the strings. Stanley made it seem that his was the kind of traditional string music that Bill Monroe transformed into bluegrass. And it was, except that Stanley had emphasized his connection to it in response to Monroe's discovery of bluegrass.[17]

Stanley's numerous post-Carter recordings with the Clinch Mountain Boys certainly sound like conservation projects to try and perfect and fix the classic repertoire that the group had been performing for decades. Many of the songs recorded for Rebel are 'newer' versions of those released on Columbia, Mercury, Starday and King; as with many jazz singers and instrumentalists who work with standards, the focus is on the process of making subtle changes to the material's fabric rather than cutting it into new patterns. In his memoir, Stanley is often critical of the progressive bluegrass (or 'newgrass') groups that emerged in the late 1960s and 1970s and clearly sees what he has done with his group as a preservation project.

However, as a musician, Stanley has also been imaginative and curious to see what other musicians are up to and how he might work with them. This has led to numerous collaborations over the years, even before his greatest renaissance when he was rediscovered through the Coens' film. These collaborations – sometimes his own ideas, sometimes the result of invitations or suggestions from others – have included the albums *Saturday Night and Sunday Morning*

(1992), *Clinch Mountain Country* (1997) and *Clinch Mountain Sweethearts* (2001). *Clinch Mountain Country* is a particularly successful project, teaming Stanley with a range of contemporary figures from the worlds of rock, folk, country and bluegrass such as Dwight Yoakam, George Jones, Bob Dylan, Gillian Welch, Alison Krauss and Porter Wagoner. *Clinch Mountain Sweethearts* includes a version of 'Oh Death' on which Stanley duets with Welch and which is modelled on the call-and-response duet versions recorded by the Stanley Brothers in 1964 and the Clinch Mountain Boys in 1977. The dialectic of old and new can be found in Stanley's account of how he came to record 'O Death' the way he did for the *O Brother* soundtrack. He became involved with the project after hearing from T-Bone Burnett, the musical director for the film. Although a fan of the old Stanley Brothers sounds, Burnett 'didn't want to make copies of the old records' but 'something new that had the old-time sound'; Burnett understood that Stanley had 'had to go back to go forward' (*MCS*, 425):

> [Burnett] wanted to re-create the feel of the old-time music, same as when you make a piece of antique-style furniture using all the materials and tools and techniques from bygone days: It's new but it's done the old way.. . . We talked about what songs would be right for my voice. T-Bone had already got some younger musicians like Alison Krauss and Gillian Welch to do some old country songs.. . . But something was missing. The last piece of the puzzle. What T-Bone wanted was something in the old-time lonesome style.. . . The song [he] wanted for [the big dramatic scene] was 'O Death', and he thought I was the man to do it. He wanted me to play it solo and real backwoods. Just me and my banjo, the way Dock Boggs done it back in the twenties.. . . I strapped on my banjo and played 'O Death' in the Dock Boggs style. I done two takes and it went over well.. . . [But] I didn't think the song needed a banjo. It was getting in the way of the words and the meaning. I wanted to take that song back even farther than Dock took it. I wanted to give it the old Primitive Baptist treatment.. . . I laid my banjo down and stood up to the microphone. I stuck my hands in my pockets and I sang him about three verses in the a cappella style from my church. It's where you worry out the lines so very word means something. Where you can stretch the melody out. When I don't have my banjo, I can focus more on my singing. I put my crooks and turns on the words. (*MCS*, 426–8)

The resulting recording not only played a central role in the 'big dramatic scene' described at the start of this chapter; it also won Stanley a Grammy for Best Male Country Vocal Performance. At the award ceremony in February 2002, Stanley sang the song that had made him famous again, no longer hidden behind the screen but in the full glare of the world's media. Once again, Stanley describes it best:

> I reckon I'd come a long way since I was a scared kid leading a hymn at the Point Truth Baptist Church in Nickelsville, Virginia. I was an old man with an old man's voice, and I just sang it natural and it came out just right. Bob Dylan told me it was the highlight of his career when he sang with me on 'Lonesome River.' I'd have to say the highlight of my career was singing 'O Death' on national TV. (*MCS*, 435)

O Death

Earlier I described 'O Death' as a song that could have been older than the United States. But there is compelling evidence to suggest that this is not the case. Over the years there have been various attempts to account for the origin of the song, including suggestions of broadside ballads entitled 'Death and a Lady' or 'Death and the Lady' as sources, such songs having migrated to the United States from Britain. A study carried out in the 1960s by Susan Katherine Barks concluded that 'Death and a Lady' was the source of all the versions recorded in the United States in the twentieth century, including 'O Death', 'Conversation with Death', 'Death is Awful' and others. However, in an issue of the *Journal of Folklore Research* in 2004, considerable space was given over to detailed claims that the authorship of 'Conversation with Death', and therefore of much of 'O Death', should be attributed to Lloyd Chandler, a North Carolina preacher who had composed the song around 1915 following a life-changing vision. Chandler's words are printed in the journal alongside the two articles – one by Barbara Chandler, Lloyd's daughter-in-law, the other by folklorist Carl Lindahl – as a way of acknowledging authorship and establishing copyright.[18] Lindahl's article contains a table detailing variations in a number of versions of the song. While its main purpose is to provide evidence for the claims being made for authorship, the table also provides a useful reference for anyone interested in tracing the history of the song. What remains unclear from Lindahl's account is how the song as performed by Dock Boggs, the Stanley Brothers, Nimrod Workman and others – the version on which Stanley's solo performance in *O Brother, Where Art Thou?* is based – came to be hybridised so that one of its most notable features was the refrain 'O Death, O Death / Won't you spare me over till another year'.

With the growth of digital media and the availability of such information via networks, most obviously the internet, the story becomes both more detailed and more confused. The community is wider than it was and we have to move beyond the community of song custodians that Lindahl was writing about to the recording community and the digital community. As well as having access to information about songs – whether on a Mudcat Cafe forum or a Smithsonian Folkways web archive – it has become easier in recent years to be able to get straight at the music itself via online music streaming sites. This has led to a privileging of audio recording over oral tradition, and to audio recordings that have some level of commercial release in that they are available to buy and to be included in online music services such as iTunes, Spotify or Last FM (although video sites such as YouTube are dominant music streaming services that offer possibilities for oral transmission of material in a partly 'traditional' manner). It also means that the archaeological work of uncovering a song's history becomes an invitation and a possibility for a different group of people, a new community. I am not suggesting that the access to information about multiple versions, or to the versions themselves, in itself creates a community of song scholars. Rather, it makes available the conditions of possibility for comparison, though one would still need to know of the different titles used for a song like 'O Death'. The chronology of discovery will not necessarily match the chronology of the release dates, although listeners might subsequently create a narrative based on those dates.[19]

If, following Lindahl, we take Chandler's version of the song as our original, we might wish to start with a recording of him singing, even though this is not the first available recording (that honour seems to go to Vernon

Dalhart's 1928 disc). Chandler was recorded singing 'Conversation with Death' unaccompanied in 1965 by folklorist and musician John Cohen, who released this version a decade later on a stunning collection entitled *High Atmosphere: Ballads and Banjo Tunes from Virginia and North Carolina*. The album came with a cover emphasising age (as do many old-time collections on Rounder) and a strong sense of being out of time. When the collection was reissued on CD twenty years later, it came with a note from Cohen that emphasised its importance in archiving old-time music. The original record had by then gone out of print, a reminder that the music was always in danger of slipping out of earshot. The same realisation had driven the original desire to capture the music: 'This record celebrates some of the particular riches of [the Appalachian] tradition, and asks if it also celebrates their passing.' Chandler, sixty-nine at the time of the recording, had recently suffered a stroke and was 'weakened by heart trouble', yet 'sang ["Conversation with Death"] so strongly that I could hear it echo off the surrounding hills'. Cohen suggests that recording does not do justice to the 'range of volume' and 'sheer physical force' of Chandler's singing, yet it is still a powerful reading and a quite distinct example of late voice.[20] This version is indeed presented as a conversation, albeit voiced by one man, and its main purpose seems to be to convey the religious message that a sinner is as unable to bargain with God as any mortal is with Death. Cohen had also been partly responsible for a set of recordings released on Moses Asch's Folkways label in 1964 entitled *Old Love Songs and Ballads from the Big Laurel, North Carolina*. The performances were by members of the Chandler and Wallin families. Burzilla Wallin, Lloyd Chandler's sister, was 70 years old at the time of the recording and performed a version of 'Conversation with Death' that is every bit as severe as her brother's. Singing unaccompanied, she emphasised the emotional weight of certain lines (mostly the second and fourth of each verse), furnishing the delivery with a forceful imperative.[21]

Whether or not Chandler was the source of versions of 'Conversation with Death' recorded earlier in the century, there are strong relationships between the Chandler/Wallin renditions and those of the Anglin Brothers, who recorded a version entitled 'Money Cannot Buy Your Soul' in the late 1930s, and Charlie Monroe's Boys, who recorded the song as 'Oh Death.' Neither the Anglins nor

Monroe attained the kind of severity that can be found in Chandler or Wallin, achieving what now sounds like rather light-hearted, breezy conversations with the song. The Anglins were a trio, unlike many of the more famous brother acts of the time (such as the Monroes, Dixons, Delmores and the Blue Sky Boys) and deployed trio harmonies over guitar and occasional bass. In 'Money Cannot Buy Your Soul', they sing three of Chandler's verses as verses and adapt a fourth to use as chorus after each verse: 'Oh Death, oh Death, how can it be / That I must come and go with thee / Oh Death, oh Death, how can it be / I'm unprepared (I'm unprepared) for eternity.' In the last line of the chorus, a high harmony vocal is added, echoing the words 'I'm unprepared', giving the song a gospel feel. Rhythmic guitar strumming accompanies the verses, with occasional picking on the higher guitar strings, while after each chorus there is some brief, effective blues picking on both high and bass strings in a manner that recalls the Delmore Brothers and which would also be adopted occasionally by the Stanley Brothers when they came to record for King/Starday. Chandler's song, then, undergoes a fairly radical transformation. Though the faster tempo, gospel harmony and guitar picking make it less severe, there is still a spookiness to the recording, partly due to the fact that this is another mostly discontinued style of singing, playing and recording. The themes of the Anglin Brothers, like those of the Monroes and Stanleys, were far from carefree, whatever their style might occasionally suggest; in a liner note to a 1970s reissue of the Anglins' music, Ivan Tribe noted that Jim Anglin, in later years, 'gained something of a reputation as a "grave-yard songwriter" since so many of his lyrics were so sad and mournful'.[22]

When the Stanley Brothers recorded 'Oh Death' in 1964 for the Starday label, they also provided a surprisingly uptempo rendition. But their version, which seems to have been sourced from fellow Starday artist John Reedy, is a changed song, with fewer of the 'Chandler' verses and the addition of the new refrain: 'won't you spare me over till another year', which they or Reedy may have learned from black gospel or spiritual versions. The song begins with this refrain, sung as an interesting mixture of smooth gospel harmony and rougher old-time style singing and playing. The former style is evident on the initial words 'Oh death, oh death', sung in high, blended harmony register without instrumental backing (save an initial guitar strum to establish key), with the 'oh' and the 'death' stretched out on both occasions. The words 'won't you' act as a very brief bridge to a shift to regular (non-gospel) Stanley singing (Carter low, Ralph high), the voices immediately rougher as they sing 'spare me over till another year'. At 'spare' the band (guitar, banjo mandolin, bass) enter and the speed picks up, a sudden shift from sacred to secular music making. Ralph then takes the lead on the first line ('well, what is this that I can't see . . .?'), with Carter answering as 'Death' ('well, this is Death, none can excel . . .'), the whole band then falling silent again for the gospel refrain. The pattern continues, with Ralph calling and Carter responding (though not always as Death; the pattern follows the logic of the arrangement rather than the lyric). Other notable features include a brief, startling mandolin break by Earl Taylor and the use of 'won't you spare me over till another year' as a repeated one-line refrain at the close of the song, its final message. The range of textures and styles, combined with the occasionally jarring recording style (typical 1960s stereo techniques, with clear channel separation of voices and instruments) evoke mixed moods. While the performance sounds rather stilted and gimmicky when listened to after Stanley's more famous later version or Chandler's contemporaneous recording, it has a different effect when listened to in the context of the album on which it appeared, an all-gospel set entitled *Hymns of the Cross* and which features some of Carter's most moving vocals and brilliant musicianship from all involved.[23]

By this time Dock Boggs had recorded a version of the song with the same refrain used by the Stanleys but delivered in the austere style with which it is now associated. Where the Stanleys presented a stop-start dynamic, Boggs, accompanying himself on banjo, moves more smoothly between verse and refrain and stresses the poetic quality of the lines during many parts of the song. However, the rhythm of Boggs's banjo leads the singing in most of the verses, resulting in some lines being rushed and lost. Mike Seeger, who has recorded the song a number of times, follows Boggs in style. Seeger had recorded Boggs's version in 1963, at which point Seeger was working with John Cohen in the folk revival group New Lost City Ramblers. In 1997 the group released a reunion disc, their first recordings together for twenty years. *There Ain't No Way Out* included a recording of 'Oh Death' with Seeger on fiddle and bandmate Tracy Schwarz providing vocal and guitar. Schwarz provides a liner note that details his debt to the singing of Kentucky mountain musician Roscoe Holcomb (claiming he 'would never have been able to tackle this extremely moving piece without it') and the performance certainly captures the 'high lonesome sound' associated with Holcomb.[24]

Other notable renditions of 'O Death' include those by Vera Hall and Bessie Jones, who both provide versions from the African American tradition; Hall's version is called 'Awful Death' and uses the 'spare me over till another year' refrain, as does Jones's 'O Death' (recorded by Alan Lomax and Shirley Collins on their trip to the Georgia Sea Islands in 1959).[25] Jones can also be found making reference to the song in an interview conducted by Studs Terkel in 1969, where she describes it as 'the song of the dying sinner, a person that's dying without the Lord . . . He's begging death to spare him over another year, begging death to have mercy. Also, it helps that person that is in sin to try to live up and do better . . . It's a spiritual'.[26] Jones's 'O Death', along with other songs recorded by Lomax and Collins, was sampled by the band Tangle Eye in 2004 for their CD *Alan Lomax's Southern Journey Remixed*, although Jones was not credited (another of Jones's recordings was sampled by Moby for his successful 1998 single 'Honey'). In 2000, the same year as *O Brother, Where Thou?* was released, the film *Songcatcher*, about a collector of Appalachian music, included a scene in which three singers (including the 75-year-old West Virginian bluegrass singer Hazel Dickens) perform 'Conversation with Death'. The song was also included on the *Songcatcher* soundtrack album, creating an interesting potential conversation between two film-related albums that year.[27]

Stories could be woven around other remarkable versions of this song, such as those of Kentucky-born Nimrod Workman (recorded by Mike Seeger in 1982, when Workman was in his late nineties: an exceedingly late voice); Kentucky-born singer-songwriter Sarah Ogan Gunning (on her 1965 collection *Girl of Constant Sorrow*); American folk revivalist and song collector Mike Seeger (both solo and with his group the New Lost City Ramblers); English folk singer Peter Bellamy (an unaccompanied 'Conversation with Death' on his 1983 cassette *Fair Annie*); ethnomusicologist Tim Eriksen (a startling live version with fiddle); 1960s experimental rock group Kaleidoscope; improviser Eugene Chadbourne.[28] The versions of 'O Death' that seem to work the best, that both summon the spectre of death and enact impassioned pleading and deferral, are those that emphasise starkness of arrangement. For Stanley, this is achieved by unaccompanied singing. For Mike Seeger, following Dock Boggs, it is the tone of the banjo as much as the nasal singing style. Tim Eriksen uses a nasal tone and also adds reverb to the voice and the violin to give a sense of the song going out into a void. The applause at the end of Eriksen's recording, a reminder that this is a concert performance, adds to the effect of the silent void. Eriksen also prolongs the final word of each verse and runs this into the microtonal inflections of the refrain.[29] Through his particular style of singing, Eriksen makes evident, to an even greater extent than late Ralph Stanley, that singing can be an act of deferral, of putting something off at least until the end of the song (which, in this style of singing, can often be a long time). At least while one is given a chance to plead for one's life – while one is part of a conversation – the outcome is irrelevant. Stanley and Eriksen take this deferral to extreme lengths by taking apart the words themselves, stretching their phonemes into a seemingly eternal plea.

To hear the changing versions of 'O Death' is to hear how the representation of lateness has developed over a number of decades. Through the recorded archive we bear witness to different aesthetic choices, technologies and relationships between voice, lyric and instrumentation. If we think of a dialogical model of the musical 'work', as Richard Middleton does by applying the theories of Bakhtin to popular music, we can understand these multiple versions to be conversations with each other.[30] If we think also of the work of Jacques Derrida, we might connect the deferral of death begged for in the song to the seemingly doomed search for the song's origins; each iteration brings with it another difference, another deferral of the true, theological meaning. Song, in this sense, outlasts all singers, so it is significant that the song appears as a series of traces and deferrals that make it impossible to fix to a single source. In the end, the song is the only thing that defers death, that lives on as *différance*.[31]

The presence of death in life is a notable feature of 'O Death', as it is of much American old-time, blues and religious music. On occasion, as in 'O Death', the end is something to be feared (though we should note that, in Chandler's 'Conversation with Death', this fear is the result of not having got right with

God; the extra time is only needed for the sinner to make amends in order to avoid eternity in Hell). In other songs, especially those which serve as hymns, the end of earthly life is welcomed as the beginning of the afterlife: in 'Why Should We Start and Fear to Die', a song recorded by Ralph Stanley, we hear that 'Death is a gateway to joy'. Stanley includes this performance on the religiously themed *Shine On* (2005), an album that contains a number of references to death, departure, going home, flying away and being carried off. One of the most compelling of his late performances can be found in his stark rendition of 'The Old Church Yard', which he delivers in the Primitive Baptist style.[32]

The theme of joining those who have gone before is one that Stanley also takes up at the beginning and end of his memoir; the book is framed and punctuated by reflections on the graveyard and the gone. While to a great extent the presence of such imagery can be seen as the preoccupations of a man frankly and realistically facing up to the last stage of his (earthly) life, it is also important to note that the Stanley Brothers made something of a career of such preoccupations and many of Carter Stanley's songs dwelled on images of dying mothers and children. The old-time guitarist and singer Doc Watson, a contemporary of the Stanleys from neighbouring North Carolina, put it this way:

> From the time I can remember, I was vaguely aware of death. My first memories of music, in the form of singing, unaccompanied singing, were at the church. I was sitting on my mother's lap, I must have been about two, and they were singing 'The Lone Pilgrim' and 'There's a Foundation Filled with Blood'. 'The Lone Pilgrim' speaks of death. I can remember thinking about the fellow who went to the old boy's grave and stood there in contemplation of the man's life . . . They didn't fully understand how to clarify the truths to young children. . . . But death was certainly there, very present from the time I was a little boy.[33]

Arkansas-born folk singer Almeda Riddle, a generation older than Watson and Stanley, recalled that her community 'oftimes sang songs about death. "Come Angel Band and Around Me Stand" . . . People lived within that song and they died by that. I remember in my childhood people asking me to sing it to them in their last hours'.[34] Stanley speaks in his memoir of how, as a child, the final lines of the folk song 'Barbara Allen' stuck with him more than the long, grisly story itself. These are the lines about the rose and the briar growing from the graves of the doomed lovers, who are only truly united in death, or at least in that life that comes from their death. The connection between the religious obsession with death and the life hereafter and that found in folk music is not coincidental, with both traditions feeding each other. As Sean Wilentz and Greil Marcus note in the introduction to *The Rose & the Briar: Death, Love and Liberty in the American Ballad*, 'if the work collected here is any clue, it says that our nation – dedicated to the proposition that liberty is real – is obsessed with death'.[35]

Death was central to the music of rural performers such as Dock Boggs, as Marcus highlights:

> Dock Boggs made primitive-modernist music about death. Primitive because the music was put together out of junk you could find in anyone's yard, hand-me-down melodies, folk-lyric fragments, pieces of Child ballads, mail-order instruments, and the new women's blues records they were making in the northern cities in the early years of the twenties; modernist because the music was about the choices you made in a world a disinterested God had plainly left to its own devices, where you were thrown completely back on yourself, a world where only art or revolution, the symbolic remaking of the world, could take you out of yourself.[36]

Community, politics and nostalgia

Narratives about Appalachia invariably refer to isolation. It was cultural isolation that preserved the old ways and the old songs and that projected the region onto the national imaginary as a place of backwardness. The late twentieth-century narrative was invariably about the threat to that isolation as the region became connected to the world by roads, railways, radio and subsequent broadcast media. This is one of the main themes of *Voices from the Mountains*, the 1975 publication by Guy and Candie Carawan that collected pictures, testimonies and songs of Appalachian people. The aim of the collection was not primarily to look back at the lost past in the hope of restoring it, but rather to highlight the political, economic and social challenges faced by Appalachian people in the face of poverty brought about by industry and post-industry; those whose memories were recorded had seen the area destroyed by the introduction of strip mining and then again by the decline of the mining industry. Songs played an important role in the documentation of the changing landscape and industrial relations. Those of Sarah Ogan Gunning and Nimrod Workman feature in *Voices from the Mountain*, as they do in the acclaimed 1976 documentary *Harlan County U.S.A.*

Other songs, such as 'The L & N Don't Stop Here Anymore', detail lateness at the end of industry. This body of work is a reminder of the industrial side of the *O Brother* universe, a fact made more obvious by Sarah Ogan Gunning's 'I Am a Girl of Constant Sorrow', 'Down on the Picket Line' and 'Oh, Death' (the last also recorded by mining union activist Nimrod Workman).[37] 'Girl of Constant Sorrow' is obviously related to the song recorded by the Stanley Brothers and to the female equivalent (often 'Maid of Constant Sorrow') as sung by Judy Collins and Joan Baez, but it is distinct from all of them, bearing lyrics that detail the hardships of the coal miners of Appalachia. 'Down on the Picket Line' is related to the song performed in *O Brother, Where Art Thou?* as 'Down to the River to Pray' but it replaces the Baptist-themed religious experience of that song with a report on industrial action by the miners. As performed by Alison Krauss for the Coen Brothers film (and in her own concerts), 'Down to the River to Pray' is a sublimely beautiful sound object full of emotional resonance and aesthetic permanence. Gunning's song has a different emotional register, attained through political rhetoric rather than aesthetic beauty.[38] Both songs succeed in modelling community, Krauss's via the call and response of the solo voice and choir, Gunning's by the call to solidarity. Discussing the singing of Gunning and Workman, Wilfrid Mellers wrote of a 'monody of deprivation' in which 'the flatness, the rasping tone, the lack of vocal bloom become themselves a kind of lyricism, embracing more than the mere will to endure'. Workman's singing achieves, for Mellers, the 'incantory quality of epic lament'.[39] It may also be worth noting here the description by Simon Frith of the Stanley Brothers as modelling a 'collective voice of religious submission' that results in a kind of disembodiment in which the voice is robbed of individuality.[40] This notion of submission (which might equally be applied to Alison Krauss singing with a gospel choir on 'Down to the River to Pray') exists in interesting, but sympathetic, tension with political incantation.

Where nostalgia for the pre-industrial era was voiced in the recollections, songs and images compiled in *Voices from the Mountain*, the political impetus meant that it was largely a critical one, what Svetlana Boym has termed a 'reflective' rather than 'restorative' nostalgia.[41] While such distinctions are useful as a way of critiquing the oversimplification of nostalgia as always already conservative, Boym's two modes can be said to be interdependent. Restorative nostalgias may well contain implicitly reflective, critical strands and reflective nostalgias may contain tropes of the restorative, implicit wishes not only for lost futures, but also for lost pasts.[42] Such narratives are often articulated via reference to lost things and ways of life. For example when Harriette Simpson Arnow – whose narrative is collected in the Carawans' book – is offering a critically nostalgic account of the devastation wrought by industry in eastern Kentucky, it is the detailing of lost things that provides an implicit desire for restoration:

> The hills are still there – that is most of them – though strip mining and super highways have taken their toll. Yet the life of the twenties and thirties that revolved about the communities in the shut away valleys is gone. One can walk for miles and miles through the upper reaches of the creek valleys and find only tumble-down houses, often the chimney alone, a rusted post office sign wind-lodged in a young pine tree, or a leaf-choked spring, around it scattered blocks of stone to remind the passerby that once a spring-house stood there.[43]

On the page facing this account, Mike Smathers's narrative offers a reflective perspective that desires 'to re-create a renewed and authentic form of what the mountains have always been':

> From the time that the first white settlers deliberately cut their ties with the coastal culture of colonial America to start a new life in this wilderness, the mountains have offered an alternative to mainstream America. This alternative is nearer to being absorbed today than it ever has been in the past. The task before us is to renew this alternative and endow it with the capabilities (including an adequate economic base) it will need to survive in late-twentieth-century America.[44]

But, as if conversing from her place on the opposite page, Harriette Simpson Arnow uses the evocation of lost details to suggest the impossibility of achieving such a task: 'The world I first saw in the summer of 1926 is gone; it cannot be excavated and re-created. And anyway, who can excavate a fiddle tune, the coolness of a cave now choked with the water of Lake Cumberland, or the creakings and sighing of an old log house?'[45] The Carawans' book provides numerous examples of the intangible and seemingly un-archivable as a way of marking lateness, none more evocative perhaps than one of the first entries, a narrative by Everette Tharp, born in 1899 in eastern Kentucky:

> I knew the whistle of the ground hog, the call of the crow, the songs of the birds, the cunning of the fox, and the squall of the bobcat. I knew the art and expertise of teaching an oxen [sic] to put his neck to the yoke and to kneel down low when his load was too heavy. These things that can't be taught in the classroom.[46]

Tharp refers to the region as 'a Garden of Eden', a romantic metaphor that finds a bitter echo in John Prine's song 'Paradise', also collected in *Voices from the Mountains*. Prine, a singer-songwriter born in Chicago in 1946, made frequent childhood trips to the area of Muhlenberg County in Kentucky, where his family came from. His song 'Paradise' recalls these trips via reference to Paradise, a small town in Muhlenberg that no longer exists. Prine places the cause of the town's destruction and disappearance with the Peabody coal company, whose trains 'hauled it away' through years of mining. The song mixes childhood reminiscence with a critique of destructive industrial processes which get officially written down as 'the progress of man'. Musically, Prine's song evokes rural country music, mixing straightforward narrative verses that evoke old-time ballads with a chorus that juxtaposes a pleading question – 'Daddy, won't you take me back to Muhlenberg County . . . where Paradise lay?' – with a sorrowful reply: 'Well I'm sorry my son, but you're too late in asking / Mr. Peabody's coal train has hauled it away.'[47] In the Carawans' book, the words and music of 'Paradise' are printed alongside pictures of the Peabody machinery used to strip and transport the coal ('the world's largest shovel', as memorialised in the song) and descriptions of the destruction of Paradise, KY, and the popularity of Prine's recording of the song among local coal miners and residents. The continued popularity of 'Paradise' – a song that Prine has maintained as a staple of his concerts, often performing it in duet with other artists – serves as a reminder of music's potential to bear witness to the past. The recording allows this to an even greater extent in that it has the potential to outlive the author and to inspire others to take up and renew the text. So too with the Carawans' book, which records the testimonies of a number of people born in the nineteenth century who bore witness to a different, now vanquished, world. To note this is to note once more the role of recording technologies (writing, photography, sound recording) in fixing and keeping the past.

Universal and particular

Ralph Stanley and Dock Boggs were near neighbours, though Stanley claims not to have known of Boggs or his work until the two met at the Newport Folk Festival in the 1960s. Songs such as 'O Death' and 'Pretty Polly' were in the air:

> Back in our little part of the world, singing was part of everyday living, one of the natural sounds all around us: the water running through the rocks on Big Spraddle Creek and the coon dogs barking down the hollow and the train whistle blowing as the freight cars hauled coal on the Clinchfield Railroad. Course, we didn't pay no mind to it. When you're so used to something, you don't go around making a fuss over it. (*MCS*, 2)

Such a passage clearly resonates with issues of community, geography and folklore. It is also telling in its mixture of the old and the new, and of nature and industry. Stanley seems keen to root his connection to music-making in this world, even as his career has seen him move beyond it and transfer those 'natural' sounds to what, for many, could be seen as the non-natural environment of the modern entertainment industry. It is slightly unfortunate, perhaps, that this invites an analogy between what the coal companies did with the natural resources of his homeland and what the recording industries did. The analogy, if pursued, would doubtless break down given the different kinds of 'natural resources' in question and the differences in their ultimate sustainability.[48] More pertinent for my purposes is what such a passage suggests about the universal and the particular and how we might relate that to voices, especially voices singing songs. To give a sense of what I mean, I want to briefly consider the way in which Dock Boggs has been singled out as a unique performer while also being seen as a representative of a community, whether that community is the actual homeland he shared with the Stanley Brothers or the more general, mythologised 'old, weird America' that Greil Marcus has written about.[49] Boggs is exemplary here partly because he is older than the Stanleys and therefore of the generation of Southerners who took part in the recording 'boom' of the 1920s; partly because he was included on the influential *Anthology of American Folk Music* in 1952 and subsequently rediscovered, 'revived' and reimagined to an extent that the Stanleys were not; partly, too, because he was more eccentric in his performances than Ralph Stanley, an aspect that raises interesting questions about Stanley's individuality.

In 2007, a collection of Dock Boggs' early recordings was selected by *The Guardian* as one of '1000 albums to hear before you die'. The brief accompanying text notes that 'individuality screams from his recordings, his minimal banjo playing and miserable narratives reaching beyond his Appalachian home to achieve a universal solemnity'.[50] This not untypical paean to Boggs highlights the interaction of the particular and the universal that often plays out in accounts of notable artists. Boggs is an individual and an eccentric, a performer to be singled out from among the many (including his community, which may 'explain' his background but not his genius); at the same time what he does has the possibility of speaking to – and meaning something to – anyone who can recognise 'solemnity'. Boggs can confidently take his place in another community, that of the artists who have produced the varied one thousand albums that every discerning music-lover should hear during the course of their life. Although it is only implied in the *Guardian* text, Boggs's reaching-out covers time as well as space: not just a dispatch from Appalachia, but from an Appalachia of the distant past. This is part of the territory described by Greil Marcus as 'the old, weird America' and it is no coincidence that Boggs features prominently in Marcus's essay of that name. Marcus also provides the liner notes for *The Complete Early*

Recordings, where he writes of Boggs as an individual who was unusual among his fellow Appalachians. 'Country Blues', one of the most well-known songs on the collection, was 'as commonplace as any piece in the mountains. Boggs performed it as if it were the story of his own life, as if it were coming out of his mouth for the first time anywhere'.[51]

In approaching Boggs's voice, Marcus settles on the word 'yowl', describing it as 'a smaller, fluttering presence, a creature darting out of a mouth and into the words of a song like a tiny, magical bird; it draws attention not to the singer, as a real person, but away from him, so that he too becomes a presence, a spectre, his own haunt'.[52] Here and in his influential book *Invisible Republic* (also published under the title *The Old, Weird America*), Marcus makes of Boggs something exceptional, someone both extra-terrestrial (as much out of time as out of place) and prototypically American. Boggs can thus be treated with the same combination of 'star quality' and contextual detail that had shaped the rock journalism developed by Marcus and his peers from the 1960s onwards. In treating an old-time musician as a 'star', Marcus is arguably writing against the grain of folklorists who had covered the same styles and periods. Harold Courlander, for example, had written in the liner notes to the collection of spirituals by Vera Hall Ward and Dock Reed on which 'Awful Death' was included that 'There is no question of interpretation or performance. Their singing is direct, faithful and invocative.'[53] What Courlander suggests here is surely what many collectors have sought, a direct connection to the past without 'interpretation'. This is another way of thinking about the late voice: a voice that does not interpret but that delivers its listeners 'faithfully' and 'without performance' to the past. While there is no denying the impression of directness that Courlander is expressing, it could be argued that performance and interpretation are being deliberately overlooked in such an account. And while many of us may be tempted to do this, we might want to ask ourselves why we desire such unbroken continuum.

The positions taken by Marcus and Courlander would seem to be quite distant, the former emphasising the singularity of the performer and the latter placing performers as a representative part of a larger body. But Marcus's account, on closer inspection, can actually be seen to be veering between quite different positions, at certain points marking Boggs out for individuality – a biography, a unique style, a modernist understanding of his material – and at others making a myth of Boggs that, drawn irresistibly to the non-human, actually threatens to remove agency and individuality from him. This arguably removes the humanity from the singer, making of him a channel through which time flows, with Boggs's voice becoming the voice of death (something that I also intimated earlier could be said of Stanley's singing). As conduit, the singer is subject to something other than himself. Perhaps what is missing in such narratives (my own included) is the work necessary to make the communally known notable. Here I would recall the observations made in the preceding chapter about aesthetic experience by John Dewey: 'The act of producing that is directed by intent to produce something that is enjoyed in the immediate experience of perceiving has qualities that a spontaneous or uncontrolled activity does not have. The artist embodies in himself the attitude of the perceiver while he works.'[54] There is a relationship with the perceiver of a text, for the latter must be encouraged not only to recognise what is being communicated (which, for Dewey, is merely a taking note of the familiar) but to be encouraged to perceive something new in the encounter. Carl Lindahl makes a similar argument for the effectiveness of Lloyd Chandler's singing and preaching, although he refuses to describe this as an aesthetic process. What seems to be common to these positions is what we might call the event of the encounter: what is made new about what one already (thought one) knew. As Lindahl suggests, this combination of strangeness and familiarity is what helps to make a particular text memorable.

In the preceding chapter, I also quoted the Scottish folk singer Dick Gaughan on the attachment of commitment, personal experience and individual expression to traditional songs. I want to return to Gaughan's comments, this time focusing on what he says about work:

> Learning the words is not the job, it is merely the beginning of the preparation to do the job. The people who wrote those songs wrote them from personal experience, they have been kept alive because they say something of eternal relevence [sic] to the universality of human experience and it is the job of the singer, more than anything else, to put in the work necessary to study, understand and translate that experience so as to communicate it to the listener.[55]

'The job' is, although Gaughan doesn't use the word, an act of interpretation; not a mere carrying out of banal duties but taking ownership of the work at hand, making it a part of oneself and how one operates in the world. The singer here is not a passive vessel through which melody, words and breath travel, but a *worker* manipulating the tools, technologies and techniques at one's disposal. Ralph Stanley, while he is keen to emphasise the conservative aspects of his singing style, seems to be sympathetic to the above points when, in his memoir, he emphasises his individual contributions to the tradition. He also says that 'every singer needs to find the right songs to fit his voice' which fits with the idea of appropriate tools (*MCS*, 101).

Observing this work dynamic may help us to navigate a course between the occasional excesses of the mythographer and the occasional strategic essentialism of the tradition-focused folklorist. For my part, I would simply want to rescue the humanity back from Marcus's account of Dock Boggs, while still agreeing on the individual articulation of collective experience. Indeed, I would argue that all the singers discussed in this chapter, and in the rest of the book, are simultaneously singular voices, artists and representatives of communities. In the same way that Ron Eyerman and Andrew Jamison use the terms 'movement intellectuals' and 'movement artists' to describe those public figures – singers, filmmakers, visual artists and broadcasters as much as the more traditionally understood writers and scholars – who play a fundamental role in social movements, so I would think of the singers discussed here as 'community intellectuals'.[56] I believe we can do so by taking the lead from Stanley himself, from letting him line out the song, as it were, so that we can respond. To say as much is not necessarily to return to an earlier conception of the Author as fount of all meaning. Rather, it is to be attuned to the ways in which authorial self-construction works alongside other factors such as tradition, myth, interpretation and the everyday to create symbolic meaning for cultural products such as recorded songs. As with any discussion of commodity, ownership is important. I said at the outset of the chapter that the voice that sings 'O Death' in the dramatic lynching scene of *O Brother, Where Art Thou?* belongs to Ralph Stanley. But I might equally say that, although the voice once belonged to him, it now belongs to us.

What I think is clear is that the voice of Ralph Stanley has come to many of us as both a 'real late voice' and a voice 'as old as time'. Stanley may have grown from a boy with a hundred-year-old voice to an eighty-year-old with a hundred-year-old voice but it is the latter who has become recognised 'universally' as an artist. He has done so because he presents to us a voice that is different and one that defers meaning, that opens up the space of ambiguity that all great art does. If we listen, for example, to what his voice actually does with the word 'death' in 'O Death', we may find it hard to count the number of syllables: possibly as many as ten, possibly many more given the microtonal inflections. Encountering a similar difficulty when describing Dock Boggs's voice, Greil Marcus draws a pattern in his text to try and capture his subject's wavering voice. At the start of this chapter I made my own strange transcription of what I heard when I listened to Stanley. Neither of us get it and nor would any visual transcription; it has to be heard. And when I hear it, I hear a voice and a throat and a diaphragm working at these vowels; I hear the technology of vocal production in action. And at the same time I find myself thinking that this is just the style these men and women sing in. What can be heard as singular may just be style, with its own sets of rules, community standards and ideologies. As Ralph Stanley constantly reminds his readers, his singing comes from the church.[57] But we don't put many Old Regular or Primitive Baptists on the soundtracks of films or on the stage of the Grammy Awards.

Last things and lost things

Given what has now been said about style and the labour of song, it is perhaps worth revisiting the idea of a late voice attained early in the case of Ralph Stanley. Among those texts which support this idea we might list Stanley's own account of the boy with the hundred-year-old voice, along with the many commentators over the years who have claimed to have heard something ancient in his singing. John Wright, for example, has claimed that 'Stanley's art, unlike that of, say, most modern country artists, is classic; it is no more dependent on the events of his life or the quirks of his personality than is the art of an opera singer.' The work is everything and there has been a continuum (also asserted by Stanley) that stretches from his earliest musical experiences to his latest. Age, as a matter of course, plays a part but it is a gradual evolution; Wright quotes Stanley as saying 'it took me a *long time* to reach the age of sixty'.[58] From a different perspective, we have other commentators who wish to emphasise an evolution of severity in that voice. Larry Ehrlich, for example, writes:

> I have heard people say that Ralph's voice sounded old when he was young and that he has grown into his voice. I don't think so. I think Ralph's voice has always reflected a mysterious blend of the cerebral and the instinctual that reflected his life experience at the time. Since Carter's death Ralph's voice has changed. More and more it has echoed the pain of loss, emptiness, incompleteness. More and more it is the voice of grief.[59]

Stanley himself follows up on this, by writing 'A friend of mine says he hears more grief in my singing down through the years, and I think he's right. I mourn out my songs more than I did as a young man. Like anyone my age, I've had my share of sorrows, losing people closest to me, one by one' (*MCS*, 6). This would be a more conventional description of a late voice, one that carries extra layers of experience. I wonder whether both positions might be maintained, for the voicing of lateness can play itself out in various ways including lyrical content, vocal delivery and style and the unavoidable 'real' ageing of the voice. This is how I will approach other case studies in this book, a number of whom make more obvious authorial choices than Stanley does (by which I mean that his authorial choices are more subtle and specialist). With him, we have to take into account the oldness of the music (old in terms of origin, but also mature in theme); as Ehrlich notes, what drew him to the music of the Stanley Brothers was the way 'they sang of death – before and after . . . they told us of things we already knew, and they told it in ways thrilling, beguiling and comforting'.[60]

But we also need to recognise the role of technology in bringing Stanley's voice to us. Recording and playback technology have also changed that voice, reflecting the times it lived through in ways that go beyond personal experience. When Stanley says that more grief is audible in his singing now, it is also the case that more voice is audible to us now. As we have seen with the changing versions of 'O Death' and other songs during Stanley's career, more emphasis has been placed on the voice over the other instrumental textures. For a long time those who have recorded that voice, or presented it for public performance, have realised that it is the most unique quality of Ralph Stanley and have understandably sought to foreground it before all else. This is not to deny the changing qualities of Stanley's voice and singing style, the ways he has mastered the 'worrying out' and 'mourning out' of song lines; rather, it is to say that that process has been interwoven with the technological devices that both record the wonder of the voice and allow the conditions of possibility for it to develop.

When I speak of technology, however, I am not only referring to the objects used to record, filter, focus and sustain vocal performance. The voice itself should be considered as a technology, a word that has its roots in the Greek word for art and craft (*techne*) and which shares those roots with the word 'technique'. If one useful definition of 'technology' is the manipulation of raw materials towards a particular end, then the way in which the raw materials of the body are manipulated to create vocal art affirm the voice as a process of technology/technique. Stanley, as alive to this as any professional singer, is keen to underline that the increase in vocal grief has come not only from the experience of loss, but also from the gains that a lifetime's devotion to one's art can bring:

> So many funerals. So many friends and family gone. Through the years you never stop missing them. And I wish they could hear me now, because, strange as it is and as old as I am, I believe I'm a better singer now than when I made my first records in the 1940s. I can put more into it now, not as much holding back as I used to. I'm not afraid to let all the feeling out, everything I've lived for eighty-two years. And not only the experiences I've been through, but my experience as a singer. I've worked at it more the last few years. Had to, really, because I can't lean on the banjo anymore.
>
> Now, I won't lie to you. My voice ain't what it used to be. My tenor has thinned out some. It's got more cracks in it and can get mighty rough around the edges and I can't hit all the high notes anymore. But it ain't all tore down just yet, and I know how to use my voice better. I can put a lot more feeling in now. I started adding some crooks and turns and I can worry those lines like I never could before. (*MCS*, 7)

The anxiety about decrepitude that slips out here in the reference to being 'tore down' emerges also when Stanley describes a 'famous photographer' who visited him to take pictures in his 'natural setting'. The photos, he says, 'made me look freakish, I think, more like Mr. Death than Dr. Ralph. That's maybe the way she saw me, but I don't see myself that way' (*MCS*, 13). He had a similar experience with a painter who portrayed him in his mountain landscape: 'The mountains look fine, but the banjo player don't look a bit like me. "Now, who in the world is that old fellow" I thought to myself' (*MCS*, 13). Such reactions come up again and again in the discipline of critical gerontology, whether reported by real life respondents in ethnographic research or found in texts by literary scholars. Kathleen Woodward, writing about age in Proust's work, describes this as 'the mirror stage of old age', a misrecognition of one's self in later life that offers a bookend to the Lacanian mirror stage of infancy. For Stanley, this manifests in the experience of others projecting age, time or death onto him.

In considering the 'real old age' of Stanley, it is worth considering the observations made by Robert Cantwell of older bluegrass and country stars. In his book *Bluegrass Breakdown*, Cantwell describes a gathering of stars at a music festival, among them the 65-year-old Bill Monroe:

> For people who know bluegrass, Monroe is an august, even an awesome presence in whom age figures as a moral trait, not a physical affliction. It is not only that he has ascended to eminence as the founder of a music with respectable folk ancestors, an ardent and cohesive following, and an incipient classical form, or even that he carries himself with the natural patriarchal elegance of a man who expects, by experience, to be admired. It is that he is simply a great musician and that, like all great musicians and poets, he lives in closer communion with the tyrannies of imagination than people less understanding, less reckless, or less innocent than himself.[61]

This description relates to the foregoing discussion of individuality and community in that Monroe is presented as an exceptional figure, authenticated by talent, age and experience. But there is also the notable recourse to innocence, to a different kind of authenticity that we might think of as being true to one's artistic vision. It is the kind of innocence that Bob

Dylan has described as the artist's need to become rather than to be (see Chapter 4). But Cantwell is also keen to pay tribute to experience, noting that, at his current age, 'Monroe seems closer than he has been at any other period of his life to realizing the idea of himself which has grown in him, subject to innumerable influences, over the years.' Later, Cantwell compares the voice of another veteran country singer, Roy Acuff, to that of Monroe: 'His voice . . . had, even when he was a young man, the ineffable quality of *age*: a certain angularity of tone, a quaver hidden in the recesses of pitch, a bite-like articulation that is produced somehow by a certain set of the jaw and attitude of the throat.'[62]

These observations all seem to describe Ralph Stanley, as does Cantwell's description of musicians who continue to pursue their profession in a music business that doesn't have the time, resources or inclination to support them. Wright, too, presents his profile of Stanley and other bluegrass musicians and aficionados as a process of bearing witness to tradition in a world that wants to eradicate it. He introduces his 'witnesses' in a manner which recalls the moments and memories isolated in the Carawans' *Voices from the Mountains*, while also having the quality of one of Roland Barthes's late texts:

> A band bus crawling doggedly through the night with no illumination but its parking lights; a blind prematurely aged ex-miner tending a mountain garden on two wooden legs; a small boy running away from an inhuman job at a cotton mill; a puzzled mountaineer encountering pizza for the first time; a farm wife riding an old gray mare to church; a cross-cut sawmill in Virginia; a Kentucky truck mine; a flooding creek in North Carolina; ginseng; chinquapins; fried apple pie – these images are as much a part of the music and the world that produced it as an account of a song origin or a description of a recording studio.[63]

They are also a part of the world that, for the most part, has disappeared, lending an inevitably elegiac quality to Wright's (and my) usage of such a list. At the end of his brilliant memoir, Ralph Stanley too meditates on things that have disappeared from the world (including people like Bill Monroe): 'things you don't see anymore' or, in the starker final words of the text, 'things that ain't no more'. 'When I was a boy', he writes, in one last memory of the brother who led him into a music career in the first place, 'there was chinquapin bushes all around these parts . . . I remember Carter and me roaming the hillsides, picking chinquapins and gobbling handfuls down like they was going out of style. And don't you know, they did'. As for fruit, so for people: 'We take it for granted that we'll always be around somehow, and that the world we knew, at least our memories of it, will be around, too. And then one day, it's all gone, and the mountains bury that world forever.'[64]

September of My Years: Age and Experience in the Work of Frank Sinatra and Leonard Cohen

When Frank sang ['Ebb Tide'] I could hear everything in his voice – death, God and the universe, everything.

Bob Dylan

I ache in the places where I used to play.

Leonard Cohen

In 1987, the poet and singer-songwriter Leonard Cohen gave an interview to the *NME* to mark the release of *Famous Blue Raincoat*, an album of his songs performed by his former backing-singer Jennifer Warnes. During the interview, he was asked if such a project had been suggested before. 'Well' Cohen replied, 'about a century ago Frank Sinatra talked about doing something like that . . . but it never happened. And between Frank Sinatra and Jennifer Warnes there hasn't been a murmur'.[1] The prospect of a Sinatra/Cohen album is an intriguing one and represents, for this writer at least, one of twentieth-century popular music's great lost opportunities. It is possible to imagine such a 'concept album' appearing among others released by Sinatra in the late 1960s, which may well be the era referenced by Cohen as 'a century ago'. Albums such as *Watertown* and *A Man Alone* (with lyrics by poet Rod McKuen) are far from being the most acclaimed of Sinatra's mid-period work – indeed they are reviled by certain, well-published Sinatraphiles – but they do represent telling examples of the ways in which songwriters were preparing material to present a certain image of Sinatra, that of the seasoned 'man of the world' who veered between male mastery and vulnerability. The Leonard Cohen of the same period, the poet-turned-singer whose work spoke of heartbreak, longing and a tough realism born of experience, would have been an ideal librettist – and perhaps composer – to the opera of Sinatra's life.

There is more that draws these two figures together, separated though they are by a generation (Cohen was born nineteen years after Sinatra). Both found fame young in intimate professions: Sinatra as a crooner in the big band era of the 1940s, Cohen as a popular poet in the 1950s. Both developed public personas, however, that cast them as wiser – or at least experienced – older men whose youthful ghosts would remain available to the public yet would cause a certain amount of surprise when encountered, so alien did they seem to their more familiar older counterparts. The big band crooner and the poet came to seem like skins that had been shed long ago, even though the saloon singer continued to croon and the singer-songwriter continued to publish poetry. Both were connected to 'adult' material but also made decisions in response to the new youth culture of the 1960s, attempting in their separate ways to join in and to be part of what was happening. Both seemed simultaneously out of the prevailing fashion and perennially hip. Both were masters of self-revision, though reduced this in later years to settle on a more conventional layering of the self. The time in which they most obviously coincided – the 1950s and 1960s – was one that saw notions of masculinity being challenged and starting to be changed and this is another element that can be heard in both performers' work.

For all this, there is no particular reason why Sinatra and Cohen need to share space with each other here; there is more than enough to say about each on their own merits, as a significant number of works have made clear. Yet I find it interesting to think about the two together in the bounded space of a chapter because doing so provides an opportunity to see whether one has the potential to highlight something about the other. Some of the mutually informative aspects are ones I have considered at the time of writing; others may become apparent in the space of the text and the mind of the reader. Even accepting the potential of the comparative method, it might make more sense to place together performers with more in common: Sinatra with Tony Bennett, perhaps, or Cohen with Bob Dylan.[2] But there are interesting qualities that my chosen artists share, as well as some informative differences, to which I will attend later. What follows is not a blow-by-blow comparison, for I will devote a long section to Sinatra before doing the same for Cohen. These opening comments provide an invitation to compare and the closing comments do the same. My purpose is to attempt to shed some light on the late voice and, with this in mind, I focus on aspects of age and experience that are present in the work of these two artists and the discourse surrounding them. With regard to what we know (or don't know) about these artists, I am not primarily interested here in biographical information or in a strict chronology of events, though both will surface as a result of the narrative provided. My contention is that Sinatra (especially) and Cohen (to a significant extent) are well-known public figures and it is precisely that public knowledge of them – or their personas, at least – that enables some of their material to be as effective as it is. This is particularly notable in their mid-period and late work, not surprisingly given that their publics know more of them at this stage. Celebrity speaks through their work and their late voices are the result and recognition of, and a reflexive play on, that celebrity. This is not to suggest that it is only celebrity that speaks – that these artists' work would not be artistic or would not work outside of the possibilities of fame – but rather to note that 'Frank Sinatra' and 'Leonard Cohen' increasingly become characters in the work of Frank Sinatra and Leonard Cohen. This aspect of celebrity continues a discussion initiated in the preceding chapter, where issues were raised around the relationship between the individual, the community, the particular and the universal, but moves it into an arena more pertinent to contemporary popular music. Sinatra and Cohen, as 'household names', operate in a different sphere than, say, Ralph Stanley or Bill Monroe.

Last night when we were young

To listen to 'You Make Me Feel So Young' or 'Young at Heart' – representative examples of Frank Sinatra's vocal art whose classic performances represent the ascendancy of his 'mature' style – is to hear a voice that promises to make its listeners feel young, that betrays its age (and perhaps ours) through its seductive power. Its crooning style may be aided by, and made possible by, developments in microphone technology that had revolutionised the art of singing in the years preceding these performances. But we don't hear the microphone, we hear the voice and the body it summons. As Steven Connor writes:

> the crooning voice is seductive because it appears to be at our ear, standing forward and apart from the orchestral background with which it is nevertheless integrated.. . . Such a voice promises the odours, textures, and warmth of another body.. . . Most of all, perhaps, the imaginary closeness of such voices suggest to us that they could be our own; they are the magical antidote to the grotesque and insufficient effigies of our voice returned to us by the tape-recorder. These voices – Frank Sinatra, or Billie Holiday, or Tori Amos – are loved because they are recognized.[3]

That the voice could be our own (if we could love our own voices as much as we love these) suggests that, when the voice is singing to us of youth, we may feel ourselves to be young within its presence. 'So long as the inner feeling of youth remains alive', wrote Simone de Beauvoir, 'it is the objective truth of age that seems fallacious: one has the impression of having put on a borrowed mask'.[4] Sinatra's voice offers such a subjective experience of feeling young, while also modelling a process that would be taken up by numerous other pop singers. To be sure, it is entirely possible that a person could hear this voice nowadays and find it 'old' or 'old fashioned', but that would not make the listener feel old; rather, it would be an objective assessment of a type of vocal singing that is of the past, even if it is one that seems ripe for perennial revival.

Sinatra's 1950s songs were heard as individual numbers but were also collected on extended-play singles and long-playing albums. *Songs for Swingin' Lovers!* (1956), which included 'You Make Me Feel So Young', was one of a series of concept albums that Sinatra recorded for Capitol. These albums tended to present the artist as either upbeat optimist (*A Swingin' Affair, Come Fly With Me, Come Dance With Me*) or downcast loser (*In the Wee Small Hours, Only the Lonely, Where are You?, No One Cares*). The LP, which had been introduced in the late 1940s and came of age during the following decade, was a technological event that helped to secure Sinatra's persona and was arguably as crucial to his mature art as the microphone had been to his early career. It allowed for the concept album, which in turn allowed for the crafting of time and narrative and brought cohesion to the work contained in its grooves. Such cohesion did not necessarily mean the promotion of a consistent persona or story, however; sometimes it was more important to evoke a mood as the album's concept. As Roger Gilbert observes, 'The LP proved ideal for Sinatra because, while he generally tried to give each of his albums a distinct mood, the inherent disjunctiveness of the form allowed him to explore a range of emotional tones, unfettered by the need to present a consistent persona; song followed song without the artificial glue of plot or patter.'[5] And, as Travis Elborough notes, Sinatra's parallel career as a screen actor strengthened his believability when taking on the roles suggested by his album titles and concepts, as did his listeners' awareness of his love life:

> In all these roles, he was a consummate method actor, only recording after 8 p.m. to maximise the lustre of his voice and drawing on events in his own life for sustenance. If he sounded palpably lost on 'In the Wee Small Hours' or 'Only the Lonely', then it wasn't unreasonable for audiences to assume that the recently departed Ava [Gardner] or a spat with Lauren Bacall were to blame . . . or perhaps to be credited. In many respects Sinatra accelerated and popularised this pseudo-psychological trend – to a point popular singers, much like Hollywood actors until newfangled questions of 'motivation' arose, hadn't really been expected to care about what they were saying, only to pretend and to sing the lines well.[6]

The LP was also, like many other developments in music technology, implicitly (and sometimes explicitly) gendered as a masculine artefact. Like the discourse and instructional material that had accompanied sound reproduction technology from its earliest days – notable in dedicated journals such as *The Gramophone* – the long-playing record invariably came addressed to an assumed male listener.[7] This can be discerned in the advertising of record players and records in the popular and specialist press and also in the liner notes printed on record covers. Such texts place the male listener in an idealised, isolated domestic sphere – a dedicated listening room, perhaps, equipped with the latest in high-fidelity technology – and able to reflect on life's serious issues away from the distractions of the workplace or the rest of the home. In the 1950s and 1960s, this was particularly notable in the genres of exotica, mood music and what developed into 'easy listening', but it can also be detected in the way that pop and jazz artists were presented.[8] The liner notes for *Songs for Swingin' Lovers!*, for example, present five stages, or facets, of Sinatra's career, from his early popularity as a crooner to his position over a decade later as a 'knowing' artist:

> For teen-agers, when he himself was young and frail, Frankie stood in the theater spotlight and sang with all his heart, till the throng of girls screeched their delight.. . . For adventure-loving moviegoers, he became the ill-starred soldier, private Maggio, and his spirited, sensitive performance won a coveted Academy Award.. . . For sad romantics, singing bittersweet ballads, he gently caught the mood of the wee, small hours of the morning, and created a best-selling record album.. . . For observers of the social scene, he courageously fashioned a new identity in his taut, dramatic film portrayal of the man with the golden arm.. . . And now, for swingin' lovers, he returns to what is, after all, home grounds – to the happy task of singing the most enchantedly romantic songs he knows. No one can do this with greater verve or skill than can Frank Sinatra, who is surely one of the most knowing and compelling entertainers anywhere.[9]

The distinction between the 'Sinatra for girls' and the later Sinatra(s) would become a mainstay of such texts.[10] While the first sentence of the *Swingin' Lovers* liner note is the only one that explicitly genders its audience, I would argue that a male listener is subsequently assumed partly in distinction to the screeching girls and partly through the emphasis on Sinatra's expertise and mastery, culturally coded at the time as masculine traits (or traits appreciated by men). That the 'sad romantics' he sang for were probably imagined as male is confirmed in the liner notes to *Frank Sinatra Sings for Only the Lonely* provided by lyricist Sammy Cahn and composer Jimmy Van Heusen, where 'the lonely' for whom Sinatra is singing are exemplified as 'the keeper of the lighthouse', 'the New York policeman', 'the lyricist and composer' and 'the losers'. The gender of the latter is asserted by a note that reads 'This album was nearly titled "For Losers Only," until it was decided that this could well be mistaken for a collection of songs dedicated to the gentlemen of the two-dollar window.'[11] This process of creating a Sinatra as object of admiration and identification for the male LP listener would be taken to further extremes with the launch of Sinatra's Reprise record label and Reprise executive Stan Cornyn's liner notes, to which I will return below.

While my main focus here is on the presentation of age and experience rather than gender, we can already detect some of the ways in which these issues intersect, for example in the way that the 'frail' youthful Sinatra was presented as somehow feminine in the *Swingin' Lovers* liner notes and contrasted with the mature, masterful Sinatra of multiple accomplishments and public recognition. In an article on Sinatra and masculinity in the 1950s, Roger Gilbert attends to the connections between Sinatra's maturity and the anxiety of gender that accompanied it. Gilbert places Sinatra within a cultural dynamic that includes 'Method acting, Beat writing, Confessional poetry, Action painting, and Hard Bop jazz', all aspects of what he describes as 'anxieties regarding authority, masculinity, and control played out in other aspects of both the high and popular culture of the decade'. Adapting Leo Braudy's work on 1950s Method acting, Gilbert appraises Sinatra in terms of 'permeability, inconclusiveness, and the notion of a layered self'. Arguing that the 1950s represent a greater tension in terms of gender relations than the supposedly liberated 1960s, Gilbert writes, 'The period's most representative male artists – Sinatra, Brando, Lowell, Hank Williams, Jackson Pollock – and its most enduring artifacts – *Kind of Blue*, *Vertigo*, *Catcher in the Rye* – all manifest a nearly pathological melancholia, often disguised by exaggerated sexual drive and willed nonchalance, that points to a genuine crisis of male identity.'[12] This crisis could be connected, in Sinatra's case, to a mid-life crisis:

> A striking number of Sinatra's songs of this period are based on distinctions between age and youth: 'Last Night When We Were Young', 'You Make Me Feel So Young', 'Young at Heart', 'When the World Was Young.' In all these lyrics, age is a function of psychology more than chronology, and we're reminded again of Sinatra's existential shiftiness, his propensity for slipping from one state of being to another. Entering his forties in the mid-1950s, he no longer embodied callow youth but hadn't yet earned the authority of age, and so his relation to those categories seemed to waver with his self-image from song to song.[13]

In this account, as with others which have addressed the middle-aged Sinatra, there is a sense of shifting between positions, between mastery and vulnerability, and the anxieties over lost youth and approaching age that accompany middle age. For Chris Rojek, Sinatra's position as an 'achieved celebrity' means that these traits are inevitably connected to the public's knowledge of his 'private' life. Rojek highlights the 'acting' involved in communicating experience and finds a difference between the relatively inexperienced Sinatra and the middle-aged one:

> The young Sinatra of *I Fall in Love Too Easily* (1944), *She's Funny That Way* (1944) and *I Don't Stand a Ghost of a Chance* (1945) was role-playing. He was imagining the possibilities of romantic bliss and catastrophe as all young lovers do. The classic albums of the mid to late 1950s deliberately articulate his own experience and tacitly assume that his listeners have knowledge of his love life through the media.[14]

As with other musical celebrities, Sinatra exemplifies the network of interactive knowledge whereby the listener combines experience of their own with their knowledge of the singer, of language and of musical technique, while the singer and/or songwriter do the same; in a way, they 'know' the listener. This fantasy can be seen as one of mastery and submission inasmuch as the masterful singer is able, via control of style and the manipulation of the voice as a pleasure-giving organ, to invite submission on the part of the listener. The listener becomes a 'subject' to the voice, a process also evident in the attribution of power-related titles to singers (King, Queen, Empress, Lady, High Priestess, Boss, Godfather and so on). Frank Sinatra was the recipient of at least two such authoritative titles: Chairman of the Board and The Voice.

The voice of authority is also a voice of authenticity and a voice that authenticates experience. Mladen Dolar suggests that 'there is something in the very nature of the voice that endows it with master-like authority' and that 'listening is "always-already" incipient obedience'.[15] We attempt to master our own voices even as we submit to the mastery of others' voices. In this formulation the singer can become a kind of master or dominatrix to the slave-like listener. Yet, following in the footsteps of a number of philosophers and psychoanalysts, we might posit this relationship as a dialectical one.[16] Indeed, in the dialectic of mastery and vulnerability associated with performers such as Sinatra, the roles are constantly in negotiation. A singer, exorcising a trauma through the compulsive repetition of the song, seems to enact mastery over voice, language and listening subject even as the listening subject takes up a position as the masterful analyst of the singer's condition, the subject who may, after all, have the answers – perhaps that is why audiences, critics and scholars are drawn to explanations of art that connect artists' life to their work. These voices and ears need each other: voice as mastery and the recognition of voice as mastery are prerequisites for the fantasy of authentication. Here, I am thinking of a process similar to that suggested by David Brackett in an essay on Hank Williams (one of Roger Gilbert's 'representative male artists' of the 1950s, as we have seen). Brackett is interested in the paradox of Williams as simultaneous 'man of the people' and country music star, as well as the ways Williams was able to mediate between these positions in performance:

> Williams *did* become a 'voice of the people', but only through introducing new elements, rearranging old ones, and, in short, by setting himself apart from 'the people' through the expression of a unique world view. This point only illustrates that he functioned as a star in much the same fashion as other stars function in mass culture: by becoming an object of fantasy and identification for millions of people through the projection of difference.[17]

This process is analogous to the relationship between the individual and the community discussed in the previous chapter. Where Ralph Stanley, the subject of that chapter, might seem far removed from Frank Sinatra in terms of persona, style and celebrity (and much more besides), it is worth considering that the differences in terms of artist/audience relationship are mostly ones of scale, as an 'intermediate' figure such as Hank Williams may help to show. If the notion of community and 'down home' music has been particularly strong in the old-time and country genres associated with Stanley and Williams, it was also present in the discourse surrounding pop stars such as Sinatra. Chris Rojek highlights this aspect of Sinatra's persona, while also underlining its essentially fantastic nature:

> Sinatra's early success with the Tommy Dorsey Band was predicated in [*sic*] the image of a skinny kid emerging from the anonymous ranks of the listening public. He portrayed himself as an ordinary Joe, blessed with a mellifluous singing voice but essentially no different from the other decent kids in prewar and wartime American consumer culture. This was an act of calculated affectation. Sinatra always held a high, not to say Olympian, regard for his gifts. Throughout his career he played with the motif of being an ordinary Joe, but in reality he was an unusually imperious achieved celebrity, holding most other performers and often the listening public in low esteem.[18]

A further set of connections might be made between Sinatra, Williams and Billie Holiday, another 'voice of the people' who went on to achieve a kind of stardom that removed her from the community. The connection between Williams and Holiday is made in Richard Leppert and George Lipsitz's essay on 'age, the body and experience' in Williams's work.[19] They argue that Williams became a voice of the people by reflecting the fears and uncertainties that accompanied post-war American society, especially for those in poorer rural areas. Williams was deemed authentic due to his ability to communicate these issues and in his audience's knowledge of his own rural background and his lived experience, which also included the experience of attaining stardom. Leppert and Lipsitz note the importance of Williams's physical appearance – his gaunt face, skinny frame and stooped posture – in communicating his experience. This infirmity was enhanced by Williams's lyrics and the way he voiced them, adopting a vocal style – complete with the 'vocal tear' that became a trademark of country singing[20] – that sounded older than his years. His is 'a voice of knowing, not anticipating', meaning that even lyrics that seem enthusiastic on the page are 'undercut by the doubtfulness of the delivery'. Williams was able to voice 'the sorts of failure that only age can produce' despite the fact that he was chronologically a young man (his career lasted six years, from the age of twenty-three to his death at twenty-nine).[21] Leppert and Lipsitz argue that this was due in large part to the premature ageing Williams and others of his socio-economic background (rural, working-class, poor) underwent at that particular historical moment. They make the comparison with Billie Holiday mostly to suggest that Williams's expression of vulnerability and unrequited love moved him closer to repertoire associated with black female singers like Holiday and, later, Nina Simone, though it is also worth noting that Holiday, too, was prematurely aged by the historical and social circumstances surrounding her.

I do not want to suggest that we can remove social and historical context from our consideration of singers, nor that we can easily jump from one context to another and assume that all will be equal. But I would like to return to the idea put forward in Chapter 1 that aesthetic experience – whether that of the producer or receiver of a work of art – is context plus something else. Context may provide recognition but to be truly effective an artist has to put in more than just who they are or have been. There is something in addition to the determinism of place, history, class and gender; or rather, these aspects all determine but not absolutely. Not all of these things have produced these voices and identification with a voice such as Williams goes beyond the context of his rural audience. In suggesting this, I am offering a reminder of the points made in the preceding chapter in relation to Dock Boggs and Ralph Stanley and the dialectic of the particular and universal. Something else reaches across time and space when we hear a Boggs, a Stanley or a Williams. That identification may be with the historical circumstances that allowed the music and the musicians to take the form they did but it might also be something else we hear. I would still maintain that we hear age and experience and that if we identify on these levels we do so by bridging the cultural divides rather than maintaining them.

To move to the comparison between Sinatra and Holiday, we should note that the two singers shared a large part of their repertoire and that certain Sinatra albums – *In The Wee Small Hours* being a particularly good example – evoke or sometimes pre-empt Holiday in both choice of material and mood.[22] Sinatra and Holiday were contemporaries but, as Will Friedwald writes of the generation of which these two and Ella Fitzgerald were part, 'in experience and wisdom [Holiday] was by far the oldest of them all'. Friedwald also suggests of these singers, 'As with the best of her students, including Sinatra . . . Holiday's singing was not about her mannerisms, her personal life, or even the woman herself – the only thing that mattered to her was the song and the story.'[23] This may well be the case but there are times when we hear the person rather than the song; in Holiday's late recordings, we cannot help but hear the passing of the years and the toll they have taken on her voice. This does not contradict Friedwald's point – he is talking about what matters to the singer – but it is a reminder that what the listener may hear *are* the mannerisms, the life or the person.

Blue moments

If we consider *In the Wee Small Hours* (1955) as a concept album, it is as well to start with the cover, which depicts Sinatra in suit, tie and hat, leaning nonchalantly against a building on a night-time street. We see him from the side, left profile, and he is not looking at us but at the ground in front of him, seemingly lost in thought. His preoccupation extends to the lit but neglected cigarette held between two fingers of his right hand, down by his side and almost out of the frame. Sinatra is positioned to the right of the frame and the bulk of the cover is taken up by the blue-lit, deserted street. The lettering on the cover carries Sinatra's name, further identifying him in case his familiar face and 'uniform' were not enough. The album title, meanwhile, reinforces the time of day depicted in the picture, recognisable despite the stylised buildings and lights: *in the wee small hours*, all lowercase, the last three words in much larger font than the first two. The general blueness of the cover evokes a noir world but also plays on the general sense of blueness that was a pervasive mode of melancholy by this time. As Richard Williams has noted, 'No colour has so saturated music over the last hundred years, while permitting so many shadings' and *In the Wee Small Hours*, in both title and cover imagery, is a fine example of what Williams calls 'the blue moment'.[24] As Will Friedwald observes, *In the Wee Small Hours* is a very jazzy album, with plenty of deviation from melody but also plenty of playful musical exploration. Friedwald suggests that the musical dynamism somehow contradicts the moody, static film noir aspect of the cover, though I would argue that the noir world is also a jazz world.[25] If there is a contradiction between the cover of Sinatra's album and its contents it is in the suggestion of the singer as being out in the world, in the street, whereas the mood is one of being indoors with the lights dimmed. Perhaps we should see this figure as the omnipresent Sinatra-ghost who oversees the embracing couple on the cover of *Songs for Swingin' Lovers*.

The song 'In the Wee Small Hours of the Morning' is the first on the album and is narrated in the second person throughout.[26] The 'you' who is lying awake, thinking of an absent lover, the repentant whose 'lonely heart has learned its lesson', could be the singer addressing himself or could equally be the advisor to that male addressee who, I have suggested, was the target of many (perhaps all) of Sinatra's mid-period and late albums. The realisation that the wee small hours are the 'time you miss her most of all' could be coming from immediate experience – the autopsy of a newly dead relationship – or from longer, accumulated experience, the knowledge that this happens repeatedly and that it is at this time of the night, or morning, that the feeling always comes back. The placing of 'Mood Indigo' after the title track strengthens the sense that we are hearing from an experienced loser in love; the lines 'you ain't been blue / till you've had that mood indigo' seem to speak from a place of repeated rejection and dejection, an extended blue moment. While these songs evoke disappointment in such a predicament, 'Glad to be Unhappy' – a song also memorably performed by Billie Holiday on *Lady in Satin* – finds the narrator wallowing in the pleasure of being down. He has unrequited love 'pretty bad' but feels that, 'for someone you adore, it's a pleasure to be sad'. The fourth song on the album, Hoagy Carmichael's 'I Get Along Without You Very Well' (also famously performed by Holiday), attempts another perspective on absence by using a narrator who initially tries to fool himself, and the listener, into thinking that everything is alright, that he can find balance and normality in life after the relationship. But the real truth of the song lies in the list of exceptions to this newfound ability to get along: 'except when soft rains fall', 'except when I hear your name', 'except perhaps in spring'.

These songs are just a quarter of the sixteen included on *Wee Small Hours*, and the blue mood is maintained through the others in terms of lyric and voice, even if, as Friedwald notes, the strings, horns and piano occasionally dance ahead of or between the lines, throwing in a sense of jollity that might seem at odds with the aura of doom that pervades the stories being voiced. But I believe that these sounds can be heard as the background bustle of normal life that continues apace around the singer as he narrates his tales of woe, or as the party in the bar that must go on despite the despondent man in the corner pouring out his blues, or the wedding party that is in full swing while the ancient mariner delays a guest outside in order to unburden himself of his past and his guilt. Sinatra's barroom storyteller anticipates another who will be found nearly two decades later on Joni Mitchell's album *Blue*, an old romantic who is 'cynical and drunk and boring someone in some dark café', just as the tinkling piano that plays behind Sinatra in 'Glad to Be Unhappy' anticipates the piano playing 'Jingle Bells' that lurks behind Mitchell's otherwise gloomy 'River'.[27]

As Sinatra sings these hymns to doomed love, we are made aware again of the importance of rhythm in singing. In Sinatra's case, if we think of uptempo numbers such as 'You Make Me Feel So Young', 'Young at Heart' or 'I've Got

You under My Skin', rhythm is crucial to the vocal delivery; the voice has to keep to time, to stay rhythmic as well as melodic, in order to deliver the lines effectively. What we notice on a lot of Sinatra's slower tracks, and in particular the doomier tracks of *In the Wee Small Hours, Close to You* and *Only the Lonely*, is an often severe loosening of the rhythm. The sense of losing time seems to echo the way one might lose time when drunk or depressed. There is a feeling when in such states of being liberated from time. This is something that connects Sinatra to Holiday, for this freeing of the rhythmic line can be seen as one of Holiday's legacies. From the listener's perspective, it is more difficult to follow, and to sing along with, these meandering songs. Again, comparing to the more upbeat songs, we can see that they are more upbeat because of having to stay 'on top of things' exemplified by controlling a vocal, getting it done efficiently and 'on time'. There is, of course, consummate control too in many of the doomier songs of Sinatra or Holiday, but the illusion is that there is not, that the singer has been excommunicated from the everyday time of bearing up.

Of course, Sinatra is still displaying mastery amidst the vulnerability: the mastery of his singing, control over voice which can be regulated more logically than human relationships. So, when he stretches the first word 'straying' in the line 'like a straying baby lamb' ('Glad to Be Unhappy'), when he elongates the first syllable of 'ages ago' in 'Last Night When We Were Young' or when he provides an emotional uplift to 'Oh, the night!' in 'This Love of Mine', he is escaping the vulnerability of which the lyrics speak by showcasing deft control of breath, tone and phrasing. But while this may be a 'victory' for the singer, it is not necessarily so for the listener seeking solace, reflection or identification. And it is the listener who is likely to spend the most time with this material in this particular order, merely by playing and replaying the album. The fact that there are sixteen songs on *In the Wee Small Hours* makes us feel we have spent a long time with Sinatra, that we have shared a long night of the soul.

Sinatra would ask us to spend more such nights with him, on subsequent albums *Close to You* (1957) and *Only the Lonely* (1958). When these albums are discussed together, as they are in Friedwald's book about Sinatra, they can be seen as presenting different emotional hues:

Wee Small Hours was hardly all gloom and doom, apart from 'Last Night When We Were Young' (and even that bears a pregnant-with-hope pause); it suggests a dark point that we hope will be followed by the dawn. *Close to You* depicts that sunrise, with Sinatra's protagonist refusing to wallow in self-pity but rather taking a self-deprecatingly bittersweet look at his own romantic foibles. The singer then painted what many consider his greatest ballad collection, *Frank Sinatra Sings for Only the Lonely*, in colors so pitch black that no light could possibly escape.[28]

This is partly achieved, as Friedwald records, by the loosening of the tempos of the songs recorded and by the use of rubato in places. The result is a kind of drift, reminiscent perhaps of a drunken night of maudlin self-reflection. In such times the mind goes wandering and, with some songs on *Only the Lonely*, it seems this wandering is adopted by the restless body too as it goes in search of places of escape only to find sites of painful memory. That place might be the bar (as in 'Angel Eyes') or the small café that 'only the lonely know' ('Only the Lonely'), or it might be the streets of the city that tempt one to lose oneself and with one's footsteps trace out a new map of existential despair.[29] The song 'It's a Lonesome Old Town' is one such song, presenting the singer wandering the wastelands of his town and his mind. Friedwald reads this wandering into the voice and its instrumental accompaniment: 'the two voices, Sinatra and his shadow, [trombonist] Sims, wander about this godforsaken landscape aimlessly in search of love but finding only an abyss of nothingness'.[30] This sense of nothingness is also summoned at the closing of 'Angel Eyes' when Sinatra sings 'excuse me while I disappear', a line which reflects on the protagonist in the song's lyric who has been drinking himself into oblivion (and encouraging those around him to do the same) and is also a reflexive moment for Sinatra, who does indeed disappear as his voice brings the song to a close.

In 'Good-Bye', the song that closes the first side of the *Only the Lonely* LP, the contextualising narrative tells a familiar story of lovers who swore to never forget each other. This is contrasted with the repeated moments where Sinatra almost shouts 'But that was long ago', followed by a more melodic, reflective 'You've forgotten I know'. The general situation of the song, what we might call its *studium*, is not the present in which the singer finds himself but rather the past he keeps trying to revisit; this is the world in which he is trying to live, the 'place I can go in my memory' evoked by country songwriter David Lynn Jones in his song 'When Times Were Good'.[31] This *studium* is punctured by the *punctum*, the real truth that constantly returns the rememberer to the present and to his actual solitude, a process emphasised in 'Good-Bye' by Sinatra's bellowing vocal. This rising and falling is a feature of *Only the Lonely*; throughout, Sinatra's voice rises and falls like a man attempting to rally but falling back into gloom and despondency. Writing about 'Ebb Tide', Friedwald connects the rising and falling of the orchestra to the techniques used by Debussy in *La Mer* and pursues the maritime metaphor to claim that Sinatra 'floats rhythmically as if on a life raft'.[32] For Bob Dylan, this was the song in which he felt he 'could hear everything in [Sinatra's] voice – death, God and the universe, everything'.[33]

'Spring Is Here' is one of the most melodramatic performances on *Only the Lonely*, centred on the repeated refrain 'Nobody loves me'. As in many popular songs, Spring is presented as the season of hope, a time when one should be delighted by the world. But it cannot delight Sinatra's protagonist because he is alone; the sense of rediscovery of the world that one can experience with a partner has disappeared. This mood is intensified on the following 'Gone With the Wind'. The album closes dramatically but enigmatically with 'One for My Baby', a performance described by Roger Gilbert as 'an intricate vocal dance of defensive bluster and wounded retreat':

> If Sinatra's first impulse as a young singer was to master breath control so that he could produce long, continuous, legato lines free from artificial pauses, his second impulse was to learn where to put the pauses so that they could speak as forcefully as the words. But it's the way the very grain of his voice reveals precisely how and where his contradictory selves are joined, shows us the seam or scar that connects and divides swinger and loser, that makes this record such a monumental work of expressive art.[34]

Mastery may be experience's gift but equally it may be born of a desire to overcome vulnerability and anxiety. The compulsive repetition and fetishisation of the acts of mastery, however, can lead back to a position of vulnerability. This dialectic of mastery and vulnerability is well illustrated by the figure of the man-of-experience slumped at the bar so well illustrated in the musical worlds explored by Sinatra and Hank Williams. David Brackett writes of Williams:

The very phenomenon of the 'vulnerable' male (an image circulated widely at the same time in Tin Pan Alley popular music as well), frequently perched on a bar stool in a honky-tonk, constituted one of the recurring figures of the honky-tonk style. If the expression of loss does carry with it conventional associations of femininity, then the use of those conventions by males is something of a convention itself during the period of Williams' ascendance to popularity.[35]

It is interesting to note Brackett's connection here between honky-tonk and Tin Pan Alley. And it is also worth noting that the image Brackett describes has continued to have a long history in the period since Williams's heyday. Indeed the cowboy provides a crucial mytheme for a number of popular song genres, from rock through reggae to hip hop. Cowboys and 'cowboyism' have long provided male rock (and other) musicians with a romantic role model of the loner, the outlaw or the man true to himself.[36] And while Frank Sinatra may not have obviously presented himself as such, there is something cowboyish about his late 1960s persona and his posse of Rat Packers.[37] Cowboyism, while supposedly basing itself on the image of the 'real' man, also evokes notions of play (boys' games, country and western clubs, fancy dress, the Village People) and this connection marks a paradoxical position of vulnerability in which the man becomes a child again. Vulnerability and projections back to more innocent times were staple features of a number of Sinatra's 'concept albums', such as *Where Are You?* (1957), *No One Cares* (1959), *All Alone* (1962), *September of My Years* (1965), *Cycles* (1968), *A Man Alone* (1969) and *Watertown* (1969). Chris Rojek suggests that, even though Sinatra went through a variety of stages in his career, at a certain point he seemed to remain the same man: 'Between the ages of 38 and 70, that is, during the period between 1953 and 1985, there was a sense in which Sinatra decided to put the ageing process on hold. In these years he was a sort of middle-aged adolescent.'[38] I would add to this a suggestion of a constant dialectic between the 'vulnerable' qualities associated with the youthful Sinatra and those associated with the confident mastery of his middle age. This is supported by Roger Gilbert, who writes of a similarly dialectical relationship between 'the swinger and the loser' in Sinatra's work. This is something that continues into the 1960s, by which time Sinatra seems prone to a certain amount of repetition when exploring these tensions.

Sinatra Stayeth

Will Friedwald makes much in his study of Sinatra of the connection (or lack thereof) between the man and the lyrics, especially those lyrics relating to loss and experience. *Is* it experience we are hearing – Sinatra's 'real' late voice – or is it technique, a set of skills which any competently trained and talented singer could recreate? Rather than attempt to prove or disprove either suggestion, I want to gesture towards what seems undeniably important here, namely the construction of a fantasy whereby the communication channel between singer and listener is made to seem transparent. We have already seen some of the ways this worked in the 1950s and these tropes are well in place as Sinatra entered the 1960s on his way to his fifth decade. For many commentators, the 1960s would be the point where Sinatra's art started to decline, where he became more power-hungry and arrogant, more obsessed with his 'cowboyist' public persona than with dedicating himself to great music. Some see the initial run of albums he produced for his new label Reprise as literally a 'reprise' of the work that had re-established his reputation in the previous decade. His old label Capitol clearly saw it this way too, launching legal action against Reprise for what were perceived to be almost identically themed albums to those released by the earlier label. Many of these claims are valid and Sinatra's Reprise work can be seen as a repeat of the dynamics of mastery and vulnerability essayed so powerfully on the classic Capitol albums. This does not make the later work redundant however, as these albums provide fascinating commentary both on Sinatra's continued layering of the self and on the new historical context in which he found himself. He had fairly easily survived the coming of rock 'n' roll in the 1950s, producing work that was among his strongest even as the new rockers were capturing the youth market; indeed, one way in which his music endured was precisely as an antidote to the new music, as an 'adult' alternative. We saw earlier how the Sinatra of the 1950s was contrasted with his own 'frail' and arguably feminised youthful self; now he could be contrasted with the younger generation of artists that were emerging. The 1960s proved to be a different matter, however, and by the end of the decade Sinatra was veering between continued disparagement of the new popular music and a strange attraction to it. Whereas rock 'n' roll had been fairly easy (for those who so desired) to dismiss as a fad once the seeming pioneers – Elvis Presley, Chuck Berry, Little Richard, Jerry Lee Lewis – started to disappear from sight or be absorbed into the mainstream, the pop and rock artists of the 1960s showed no such sign of fading away. Not only would some of them become labelmates of Sinatra on Reprise, many would also find The Voice recording songs they had written or with which they were associated.

One of the most obvious ways in which Sinatra's layered self developed was a continuation of the kinds of narrative written about him for promotional purposes. The following sleeve notes from Sinatra's 1966 album *Strangers in the Night*, written by Stan Cornyn, are worth quoting at length as a typical example of the way Sinatra was spoken about by hagiographers of the time:

ON SINATRA or HOW TO BE TIMELESS TONIGHT

Back in New York, where he started, where twenty thousand bobby soxers once pressed themselves against the doors of The Paramount Theatre to see him, things are different. The brilliant bronze doors are green with neglect. On one side wall, the chalk legend 'The Animals Are Loved Only By Girls Named Josephine.'

Animals may come, and they sure do go, but Sinatra stayeth. He stays to sing. Whatever it says at the top of your calendar, that's what Sinatra sings like: 66, 67, 99 . . . He isn't *with* the times. More than any other singer, he *is* the times.

If the electric guitar were disinvented tonight, a few thousand singers would be out on their amps. But not Sinatra.

He defies fad. He stayeth. He has known more and felt more about the stuff songs are made of, the words of poets. He's been a Stranger in the Night, and you have to be long rid of baby fat to be that Stranger. You can't sing the way he does until you've been belly to belly with Reality a few times.

That's what makes insight, and what's made The Sinatra. What's made him last, and get better. Allowed him to last through The Age of Anxiety and The Age of the Atom and The Age of Acne.

He's lasted. Most men would give away twenty years of life to be him, or even to have his memories.

. . .

So the man's the master of pop singing form. But that's not the big thing. What's the big thing is the way he uses form.

Sinatra, when he sings at you, doesn't look at you. He looks about six inches behind your eyes.

His eyes a little far away. A little closer to where the truth lives.[39]

There is much to note here, from the period language through the criticism of rock music to the alliance of voice and gaze. Cornyn, an executive at Reprise, was responsible for writing liner notes to sixteen of the albums Sinatra released, from 1964's *It Might as Well Be Swing* to 1984's *L.A. Is My Lady*, as well as an extended note for a 1995 collection of Reprise recordings. As Gilbert Gigliotti observes, in authoring so many liner notes, Cornyn became 'the voice of Frank Sinatra'.[40] It would be more accurate to say that Cornyn became an important part of a much larger machinery that produced this 'voice' and which would also include lyricists, composers, arrangers, musicians, engineers, producers, other label executives, promoters and critics. But Gigliotti's highlighting of Cornyn as a part of this process is an intriguing one. Gigliotti notes the mixture of New Journalism (as essayed by Tom Wolfe and others), 'hip' language, poetic devices and advertising spiel that make up this essentially hagiographic discourse. Part of Cornyn's job as a Reprise employee was to market Sinatra and so we might, as Gigliotti is aware, be suspicious of reading too much serious commentary into such texts. But it is equally important that Cornyn is shown to be a narrator of Sinatra's public life in a way that is both inclusive and exclusive; through him, we get to hear about details we might not otherwise be privy to – orchestra rehearsals, recording sessions, conversations between Sinatra and his friends and fellow musicians. More than this, Cornyn's writing reminds us, as Gigliotti notes, of the proximity between creative writing (especially poetry) and the language of marketing. Cornyn's texts become another creative component of the layered self that is Sinatra's persona. They also allow us to witness the development of Sinatra's career, replete as they invariably are with allusions to his songs and his past. This is important for a consideration of time, age and experience because these are all factors underlined by Cornyn's texts and which are used to narrate Sinatra to his audience and set the stage for listening. This sense of a narrated life becomes even clearer when the pieces are brought together, as they are in Gigliotti's analysis and in the long text 'Eye Witness', which Cornyn contributed to the boxed set *Frank Sinatra: The Complete Reprise Studio Recordings* in 1995.[41]

In returning to Steven Connor's notion of the 'vocalic body', the body projected by imagination, visual deception or fantasy as the source of a voice, we might recognise the role of these biographical and/or mythopoetic liner notes in creating such a body. In doing so we might tweak Gigliotti's suggestion that Cornyn is the voice of Sinatra and say instead that Cornyn provides the source for the vocalic body we are witness to in Sinatra's recordings. Here, Sinatra's 'existential man' returns; in hearing him sing of life, love and loss, and in seeing him portrayed on his record sleeves and in publicity material as a kind of existential hero – a graduate of the school of hard knocks, turned observer of the human condition – we simultaneously identify with his similarity to us (we too have lived, loved and lost) and marvel at his difference, his unattainable cool, his mastery of sartorial and vocal style, his success, even, Cornyn claims, his memories.

If record sleeves were one place in which Sinatra's public persona was developed to an extent that would encourage biographical readings of his song texts – something hinted at in the 1950s but never taken to quite such extremes – the material Sinatra would perform from the mid-1960s onwards would take this even further. While Sinatra had long been noted for his ability to 'own' the material he sang, now he would become more and more the explicit subject of that material as songwriters, arrangers, producers and poets lined up to create pieces specifically for Sinatra to sing. One such example, and one that explicitly addresses the themes of this chapter, is the 1965 album *September of My Years*, released as Sinatra was approaching his fiftieth birthday. The album was designed as a way of recognising and aestheticising Sinatra's 'considerable' age. The fact that fifty may not necessarily strike us as 'old' nowadays serves as a useful reminder of the relativity of age. This relativity works itself out in multiple complex ways but three pertinent points should be noted for this example: an understanding of age in the 1960s; an understanding of age in the world of pop (then and now); and an understanding of age in relation to gender. With regard to the first point, it would not have seemed as premature as it might now to refer to a 50-year-old American man as being in the autumn of his years. While there has always been a strong association between pop music and youth, Sinatra had moved on from the youth audience of his early career (1940s) to be recognised (by the 1950s) as a performer of adult contemporary material (even while pursuing the life of a 'middle-aged adolescent'). As for gender, the presentation of a 50-year-old man would have been far easier for the culture industry to handle than for a woman of the same age, due to the long-established, and still prevalent, acceptance of ageing masculinity in contrast to the disparaging of ageing femininity. Sinatra's late middle age could be noted – mournfully, elegiacally or victoriously – in ways that would not be available to female popular music performers then or more recently, as press coverage of Madonna's fiftieth birthday in 2008 proved.[42]

September of My Years is a suite of songs that present a search for lost time even as they seem to assert an acceptance of ageing.[43] Many of the references to passing time on the album are seasonal: 'one day you turn around and it's summer / the next day you turn around and it's fall' ('The September of My Years'); 'you are the summer / and I am the autumn' ('Don't Wait Too Long'); 'the autumn of my years' ('It Was a Very Good Year'); 'winter is near', 'when the wind was green at the start of the spring' ('When the Wind Was Green'). There are also references to days growing shorter, twilight nearing, lines appearing, leaves falling, colours changing, frost and snow appearing. The singer presents himself as a man for whom a life spent in 'wandering ways' has brought accumulated experience and wisdom; a man 'old enough to know', as a line in 'How Old Am I?' puts it. He is a man who has, in the words of a Borges poem, 'seen the things that men see' and he wears his experience in the lines on his face and the silver in his hair; the lines are 'well-earned souvenirs' and he notes of the silver that 'it took many lovers quarrels to put it there' ('How Old Am I?').[44] Another repeated metaphor is that of the song as a representation of passing time. In 'Don't Wait Too Long', he advises a younger person that 'your song's beginning / while mine's nearly sung', while seasons and songs are combined in 'This Is All I Ask' with the lines 'let the music play, as long there's a song to sing / then I will stay younger than spring'.

'This Is All I ask' luxuriates in the 'lingering sunsets' and the value of slowness that one may discover in later years (years which represent, for the singer, 'the prime of my life') and which, nearly five decades later, the 80-year-old Leonard Cohen would praise in his song 'Slow'.[45] This sense of lingering and luxuriating extends to Sinatra's singing, as he dwells on certain lines, syllables and sounds. While this had long been a staple of the Sinatra style, the lingering vocal has a particular relevance to the themes of passing time and spending time explored in the songs of *September of My Years*. Even as he warns younger listeners to make good use of time in 'Don't Wait Too Long', there is a sense of justification to be had in the possibility to dwell a while in the space of enunciation; this is notable as he stretches out the words 'don't', 'wait' and 'long' at the close of that song. When he reprises 'Last Night When We Were Young', the song he had recorded for *In the Wee Small Hours* over a decade before, it is not only an expression of a heartbroken lover, but also a reflection on time passing and past time. As before, Sinatra emotes most powerfully on the first syllable of 'ages ago', lingering on the first word as though he doesn't wish to let it out. This lyric now bears the additional resonance of referring to the period, 'ages ago', when Sinatra first sang the song. A similar reference to the singer's past can be read into 'Hello, Young Lovers' by thinking back to the 'lovers' albums Sinatra had recorded for Capitol: 'I've been in love like you', he sings, as though recalling the past. Of course, even back then he was often cast as the distant observer, allowing us, his listening subjects, to relegate to him the documentation of young love and the way it felt. This sense of Sinatra as the external, eternal observer is echoed in 'It Gets Lonely Early', with its references to 'every single endless day' and 'every single lovely day' and questions addressed to a general addressee: 'it gets lonely early, doesn't it?'; 'it was lovely, wasn't it?' Again, Sinatra lingers on key words, splitting 'endless' and 'lovely' into long first syllables ('end', 'love') and shorter second syllables.

'The Man in the Looking Glass' presents a classic image of ageing, that of the person looking into the mirror and not always recognising the reflection shown there. As noted in Chapter 1, Kathleen Woodward has referred to this process as 'the mirror stage of old age', a point at which the subject refuses to recognise the external signs of ageing etched on the body by time and experience; here, listening to Sinatra, we might rather think of it as a mirror stage of middle age, a time of equal anxiety for many. And, just as Woodward connects this mirror stage to the work of Marcel Proust (in particular, his extraordinary rendering, in *Le Temps Retrouvé*, of the dawning perception of age in others and in oneself), so we might detect a Proustian strategy at work here. Our singer's attempts to control the narrative of the self display mastery even as they articulate anxiety. By voicing the narrative, by modelling the promise that one could capture every moment from the past to show one hasn't lost it, the singer claims a kind of victory over time. But at the end of the song he is yet older and there is the realisation perhaps that the act of narrating involves so much time: a lifelong quest to narrate a life.

The sense of lingering extends to the running time of 'It Was a Very Good Year', which runs to nearly four and a half minutes. The song tells the story of a life in stages, with the opening and closing lines of each verse framing their contents with a reference to a particular age: 'when I was seventeen', 'when I was twenty-one', 'when I was thirty-five'. In each case the lines frame 'a very good year' and, like photographs, the verses detail a few vivid memories, what we might think of as 'biographemes', a word Roland Barthes uses to highlight the ways in which biographical writing might more helpfully evoke its subject's history through discrete fragments as much as detailed chronology:

> [W]ere I a writer, and dead, how I would love it if my life, through the pains of some friendly and detached biographer, were to reduce itself to a few details, a few preferences, a few inflections, let us say: to 'biographemes' whose distinction and mobility might go beyond any fate and come to touch, like Epicurean atoms, some future body, destined to the same dispersion; a marked life, in sum, as Proust succeeded in writing his in his work.[46]

The biographemes summoned in Sinatra's song include soft summer nights, a village green, city girls with perfumed hair and riding in limousines with 'blue-blooded girls of independent means'.[47] The fourth verse opens differently, in the present – 'But now the days are short / I'm in the autumn of the year' – and the singer considers his life in a different way, as 'vintage wine from fine old kegs'; here the 'very good year' is connected to maturity while age is seen as something to celebrate. The wine, however, like that evoked in Joni Mitchell's 'A Case of You', must be bittersweet, for the narrator seems to be lost in memories of the past even as he boasts of his achievements and his present status. The song as a whole could be heard as a bearing-up to biological destiny through a particular form of boastful masculine self-fashioning, another moment in the ongoing dialectic of the swinger and the loser, albeit that the loss hymned here is not that of a 'mere' romance, but of an unrecoverable past.

The storytelling aspect of this song, echoed on the reverse side of the LP in the song 'Once Upon a Time', calls to mind the traditional ballad, a correspondence made more explicit by the constant reference to passing years and seasons. Sean Wilentz and Greil Marcus also make this connection in their book about American ballads, *The Rose & the Briar*:

> After World War II, amid the explosion of a musical mass culture, the ballad persisted and even proliferated, not simply as folksy throwback but as a resource for telling new kinds of stories in old ways with a shifting sound and style, from the car crash in Mark Dinning's 'Teen Angel' to the changing seasons of Frank Sinatra's 'It Was a Very Good Year.'[48]

It is perhaps not surprising that we would look to the decay and renewal of the world around us to articulate our experience of time passing, as Freud showed in his essay 'On Transience', and seasonal references abound in all art forms. Such themes lend a sense of the mythical and the universal to the songs found on *September of My Years*, albeit with the caveat that its particular seasonal associations are far from being universal.[49] In 1971, Willie Nelson used a similar concept for his album *Yesterday's Wine*, which presents the life story of 'imperfect man' over the course of ten tracks. His song 'Summer Roses' dwells on the brief season of a romantic relationship, with the singer offering to bring his partner 'one springtime of Robins', 'one Summer of roses', 'one autumn of dry leaves' and 'your winter of snow'. Another song, 'December Day' relates a 'time-to-remember day' in which the singer recalls 'a spring / such a sweet tender thing / and love's summer college', the last line a reference to learned experience. As the song winds its way towards the December moment it reports how 'September wine numbed a measure of time / through the tears of October'.[50]

September of My Years found Sinatra working with songs that still held a strong connection to the lyricists and composers of the past. By the time of *Cycles* three years later, this had changed and the album found Sinatra offering readings of contemporary folk and pop songwriters associated with younger musicians of the 1960s.[51] There were two songs that had been hits for Glen Campbell (John Hartford's 'Gentle on My Mind' and Jimmy Webb's 'By the Time I Get to Phoenix') as well as a version of Joni Mitchell's 'Both Sides, Now' (listed as 'From Both Sides, Now'). The previous year Judy Collins had enjoyed a hit with her version of 'Both Sides, Now' and had included the song, along with Mitchell's 'Michael from Mountains' on her album *Wildflowers* (1967). As performed by Collins and Mitchell (who would include it on her 1969 album *Clouds*), 'Both Sides, Now' is a classic example of early lateness, the term I use to describe the seemingly precocious wisdom found in work by young singer-songwriters. While it is obvious that Mitchell (born in 1943) and Collins (born in 1939) had had ample time to accumulate lived experience by the late 1960s, it was still then, as it is now, a notable occurrence when younger singers dealt with the big questions of life with such mature balance and retrospection as found on 'Both Sides, Now'. Sinatra, however, had been cultivating precisely this image for some years prior to *Cycles*, meaning that his version of Mitchell's song ought to resound with the requisite gravitas. But the style of the song as first recorded by Collins, then imitated by Sinatra's arranger Don Costa, was jaunty, with tinkling harpsichord and 'dizzy dancing' strings: mostly devoid, in other words, of gravitas. For this reason, Sinatra's rendition does not sound particularly original and his relatively clipped delivery makes the words seem trapped in the jaunty rhythm rather than being liberated (or interrogated) by his famous phrasing. Of the early renditions, it is Mitchell's own – with its slower, deliberate guitar strumming and Mitchell's varied vocal – that provides the combination of gravitas and wonder the song calls for.

Sinatra has more success on *Cycles* with two songs written by Gayle Caldwell of the New Christy Minstrels, 'Wandering' and the title track. 'Cycles', which was also a successful single for Sinatra, presents life as a cyclical process of ups and downs: 'first there's laughter / then those tears'. As with 'Both Sides Now', the sense of having seen life from different perspectives gives the impression of accumulated experience (though it is arguably more convincing on this song) and therefore maps onto the authority invested in Sinatra as a mature purveyor of adult pop. Singing is proffered as a potential way out and as a metaphor for facing up to life's challenges, though it may not always be possible to raise one's voice; the song closes with the lines 'I'll keep on trying to sing / but please just don't ask me now'.

The 1969 album *Watertown* was another project which found contemporary pop-rock songwriters providing material for Sinatra to sing. In this case the concept of the whole album was pitched to Sinatra by Bob Gaudio and Frankie

Valli of the Four Seasons. Gaudio had previously worked with lyricist Jake Holmes on a Four Seasons record and the pair teamed up again to write the songs for *Watertown*. Over the course of the album, the songs tell the story of a rural middle-aged man whose wife has left him and their children for a new life in the city. Although the abandoned male theme was one very familiar to Sinatra and his audience, the rural setting of the story and the subject position of a father left to raise two sons alone were both new for the singer. The man can no longer run away, for it is the woman who has escaped from responsibility and who has a freedom that seems to be both criticised and envied by the subject positions adopted in the album's songs. Unlike 'One for My Baby', the song that had closed the album *Only the Lonely*, there is no road to hit after drowning one's sorrows, no endless cowboy vistas, no 'long long . . ', as the last lingering line of that song would have it, no oblivion in forgetting via drink or travel. On the contrary, the everyday domestic life is one of getting by and trying (unsuccessfully) to forget. This is hymned most poignantly on 'For a While', a song that finds the singer trying to live life as normal but being even less successful than the narrator of 'I Get Along Without You Very Well'. Days pass 'with no empty feeling' but inevitably he remembers his loss and realises that he's 'not over you for a while'. Discussing the album, Holmes says:

> I've always felt that there is that moment in your life, when you forget about something that is really terrible. For five minutes the sun is shining and everything is beautiful. Then all of a sudden you realize that the person you cared about is gone, and it all comes back. It is one of those horrible things about grief – one of those little holes in grief when it becomes even more painful.[52]

These little holes populate all the songs on the album; sometimes the singer seems in danger of plunging into them, sometimes he is able to patch them. In this, Sinatra is on familiar territory and, as with the best of his later work, the vocal mastery, in 'writing' the songs in definitive form, recalls the Proustian project of capturing the past to insulate oneself against the trauma of involuntary memory. If the singer can spin his version of the story and get it all down while still allowing time for sentiment, perhaps he may find a template to live by. One solution offered in *Watertown* is to look for the constants in the local community, the unchanging town where nothing much happens; as lines in the song 'Michael & Peter' put it, 'as far as anyone can tell / the sun will rise tomorrow'. Time is passing by ('you'll never believe how much they're growing') but many things stay the same and offer the possibility of a design for living.

Given the sense of mastery over the representation of time, age and experience that grows ever more palpable in his albums of the 1950s and 1960s, I am led to feel that Sinatra's true late voice was the voice he found in middle age rather than that he found in 'real' old age. It is not that we don't get to hear that 'real' late voice, for he continued to record and perform into his late seventies (his last full performance was in 1995 when he was seventy nine; later that year he appeared on stage at the close of a star-studded eightieth birthday celebration, singing along briefly to 'New York, New York'). We might choose, as I did with Ralph Stanley, to begin at that point, with the spectacle of the ageing singer and the sound of the wavering voice. Certainly, Sinatra's voice becomes heavier, huskier, more limited. But what I want to emphasise here, to add another layer or perspective to the late voice, is that Sinatra's greatest, most assertive presentation of lateness, when thought of as a combination of age, time and experience, is that found in his long middle period, from his comeback in 1953 to his 'retirement' in 1971. This is the time when the anticipated lateness of his early work met the response of his more experienced self in a way that led to a quite new persona (not just for Sinatra, but for popular male entertainers more generally). This may be a little too neat and I'm not suggesting these qualities can't be found earlier or later (they can), but this long middle period is a more solid representation and produces a body of work that seems to call out for a consideration of time, age and experience – and of a dialectic of mastery and submission – in a way that the early and late work does not.

How lonely does it get?

In the same way that certain Sinatra performances were clearly staged with an understanding that listeners knew about the singer and could therefore connect song to persona, so Leonard Cohen has often made a direct appeal in his songs to his listeners' knowledge about him. This is especially notable in his later work, for example that found on *I'm Your Man* onwards. The closing song of that 1988 album is 'Tower of Song', a reflexive track about the art of songwriting and, seemingly, about the singer himself; the fact that a well-known songwriter is singing makes it more likely that a process of identification will take place. The Tower of Song that is referenced at the end of each verse becomes a more tangible and believable edifice as the song progresses, moving from its initial status as a metaphor that might contain meaning – though this meaning is unclear – to a place in which we can believe the singer is resident. This process is assisted by the repetition of the metaphor and the layering of further metaphorical language, particularly notable at the point where we learn of the singer's position in the Tower relative to others. In the second verse, he asks a question of another resident in the Tower, Hank Williams: 'how lonely does it get?' He receives no reply, just the sound of Williams coughing from 'a hundred floors above me / in the Tower of Song'.[53] The implication is that there is a hierarchy: is Williams higher in the Tower because he is a better songwriter, or just because he arrived first? Is the Tower an imagined hereafter, a place for those who have gone before and upon whose work later work (such as Cohen's) is premised? Whatever the reasons, once again we see the fabled Hank Williams recognised as an advisor, one authorised to communicate the experience of loneliness.

In the same song, Cohen includes a line that makes knowing reference to the limitations of his singing. 'I can't help it', he sings, 'I had no choice / I was born with the gift of a golden voice.' In the original album version of the song, the line is already amusing and notable; in live performance it is even more so because it is invariably followed by a cheer from the audience. Cohen's audience is in on the joke, which works on more than one level. On the one hand, they know that, from the moment he began singing in public, Cohen has been categorised as a non-singer, as having a leaden rather than a golden voice. But they also know – and Cohen knows they know – that his voice has become an ever more powerful tool as he has aged and as he has found new ways to place it into musical settings. It is golden because it has endured, has become burnished in fascinating ways and, above all, has become more seductive than ever. Cohen is effectively saying to his audience that he cannot

help seducing us and we, in turn, show our willingness to be seduced. This
power and mastery, at least, he shares with Sinatra, for both men have shown
themselves to be accomplished seducers in song. But it is easy to speculate on
the disdain which some of Sinatra's critic-fans might show towards Cohen's
vocal art, given that Cohen has arguably more in common with the traditions
of French *chanson* and American country music than with the pop tradition
associated with Sinatra. As David Boucher notes, Cohen would have been
familiar with *chanson* given his background in the Montreal art scene and
this style is closer to what Cohen does than the folk or blues music popular in
the New York folk scene where his songs were first performed. Boucher writes
that Cohen 'felt much more at ease with the tradition of the *chansonnier*, where
the singer speaks the song and the aesthetic sound of the voice determines
the excellence of the work; for the *chansonnier*, it is style that matters and
not perfect pitch or polished performance'.[54] Artists like the Belgian singer-
songwriter Jacques Brel could mix romanticism with cynicism to stunning
effect and, Boucher argues, proved a more pertinent model for Cohen
than Bob Dylan. While Cohen had declared that he wished to become the
'Canadian Dylan', Boucher argues that this was not so much a declaration of
style as the desire to become 'the voice and icon of an age'.[55] This singularity –
the voice – is, of course, something that linked Cohen to Sinatra, albeit that
'voice' is being deployed in rather different ways.

'Tower of Song' is a good example of Cohen's movement between speech
and song. Cohen often uses a strict, simple meter (though he has also produced
a number of more complexly structured songs), lending his work elegance and
clarity. When used in printed collections such as *Book of Longing*, this lends
the poems a rhythmic read-out-loud quality; one hears a speaking voice.[56] In
'The Mist of Pornography', Cohen refers to 'the regular beatings / of rhyme',
highlighting the connections between writing, rigour, discipline and sacrifice.[57]
Jim Devlin writes of 'Famous Blue Raincoat' that 'it's the *inevitability* of each
successive note in Leonard's melody, notes that for the most part move up
or down only by a tone, that gives the song such a resonance'.[58] This often
deceptive simplicity should also be compared to country music, for Cohen has
long shown an interest in that genre, from his early group the Buckskin Boys,
through his ambitions to move to Nashville and become a country artist, to his

late cover of 'The Tennessee Waltz'. Cohen's biographer Sylvie Simmons brings together Cohen's fascination with cowboy culture and the Far East in a chapter entitled 'The Tao of Cowboy', which concerns Cohen's period of living in rural Tennessee.[59] One of Cohen's best-known songs, 'Bird on the Wire', can be heard as a country song, an aspect made explicit in Judy Collins's version of it and in Cohen's own late performances. Aaron Neville's cover of 'Ain't No Cure for Love', meanwhile, turns the song into a country song through its instrumental style and Neville's vocal inflections, which are especially interesting as Neville hasn't typically been associated with this type of country delivery in his other work.[60] Commenting on an interview he conducted with Cohen, the journalist Thom Jurek described Cohen's interest in Hank Williams as a master of vulnerable song: 'He called Williams's lyrics the epitome of poetry and compassion, because it was clear that the experiences Williams sang about were not only ones people could relate to but ones that the country singer had lived through.'[61]

Cohen's work, as noted at the start of this chapter, has always seemed mature and the themes of age and experience can be detected from early in his career. Sylvie Simmons observes that the contents of Cohen's first poetry collection *Let Us Compare Mythologies* (1956) seem to contradict the youthfulness of the portrait of the poet on the back cover, as well as the fact that the poems were mostly written before Cohen's twentieth birthday. In the poems the author 'appears a much older man – not just the maturity and authority of his language and his command of poetic technique, but the "raging and weeping" of the kind that suggests a man who has lived long, seen much and lost something very precious'.[62] Cohen shows an early interest in the mastery of seduction and in the role that words can play. In 'Poem' he writes of 'a man / who says words so beautifully / that if he only speaks their name / women give themselves to him'.[63] The second, final stanza of this short poem finds the poet lying awake at night beside his lover, worried that he will hear this seducer clearing his throat outside the door. It is not surprising given the themes of Cohen's work and his repeated assertions of poetry as seduction, that many have chosen to hear in the first stanza a description of the poet himself. That Cohen presents the seducer as a third party introduces a note of ambiguity that will be taken up in his song 'Famous Blue Raincoat', which on the surface describes a *ménage à trois*. But is the seducer in the song, this 'brother' or 'killer', really another person or just another aspect of the poet's persona? There is both an individual story here – the youthful poet's insecurities – and a signal of a wider context; 'Poem' and 'Famous Blue Raincoat' work as stories of threesomes because of what was becoming allowable in the discourses of art and, over the course of the 'long 1960s', of American and European society more generally.

It is interesting to recall that, while Leonard Cohen is in many ways one of the emblematic cultural figures of the 1960s, he did not release any music until late in the decade. It was through Judy Collins, another emblematic musical figure of the decade, that Cohen's songs first became widely known when she included 'Suzanne' and 'Dress Rehearsal Rag' on her sixth album *In My Life* (1966).[64] Cohen, well established as a poet by this point, had yet to record any of his songs and his first album *Songs of Leonard Cohen* appeared fourteen months after *In My Life*. While Cohen had harboured ambitions to be a musician from an early age, it appears that his move from poetry to music was also connected to the role that popular music had taken during the 1960s as the quintessential contemporary Western art form. Prior to this transition (which was never complete, for Cohen continued to publish poetry after becoming primarily known as a musician), the artist acted as a Canadian-cum-European bridge between the beat poets of the 1950s and the rock 'n' rollers of the 1960s. As a successful young poet, media figure and popular intellectual, Cohen developed a persona that exuded as much of an aura of male confidence and mastery in his world as the more mainstream Sinatra did in his. This mastery was evident not only in the way Cohen carried himself though his public engagements but also in the very material of his work, voicing as it often did a curious sense of the wonder of the poet and the *savoir faire* of the ladies' man.[65]

Songs of Leonard Cohen (1967) appeared more than a decade after *Let Us Compare Mythologies* and, for Sylvie Simmons, Cohen's maturity is evident this time from the portrait on the cover: 'Sepia-toned and with a funereal black border, it showed a solemn man in a dark jacket and white shirt, unmistakably a grown-up . . . it appeared that Leonard's bottomless eyes had seen too much in the eleven years between his first book and first LP'. As to the contents of the album, Simmons notes that they were both partly of their time, inasmuch as they 'were in keeping with the rock-music zeitgeist' but also quite unlike anything else in popular music then or since. The songs displayed experience, solemnity, maturity and poetic rigour, sounding 'both fresh and ancient, sung with the authority of a man used to being listened to'.[66] It is certainly the case that one of the ways in which Cohen has always sounded convincingly 'late' in the sense that I am trying to define and develop in this book – in his writing, recitation, composition and singing (in short, his *voicing*) of time, age and experience – is this ability to sound confident, to be understood as saying something important. At times in his career, especially in its later stages, Cohen has adopted an attitude of humility and modesty with regard to his talent and his importance, yet he has arguably been able to do so as a result of having established early in his career (and in his life, as Simmons demonstrates in her biography) a sense of importance and confidence in his mastery of the world and the word. By the time of his debut album, this sense of gravitas was enhanced by Cohen's age (thirty-four, a considerable age for a 'new' musician in the folk and rock scenes of the time) and by the fact that he was a published poet. As Anthony DeCurtis notes, this allowed Cohen to forge a musical language that was out of joint with the norms of 1967; Cohen's songs 'were entirely contemporary and strangely outside time, ancient without seeming what we would now call retro, and also visionary intimations of the future'.[67]

Songs such as 'Suzanne' and 'Master Song' introduced listeners unfamiliar with Cohen's poetry to a voice unlike any on the pop, rock or folk scenes at the time, Bob Dylan and Joni Mitchell included. The songs had the incantory quality of some of Dylan's wordier numbers, with a similar accumulation of poetic detail and vivid imagery, and the poetic rigour and sense of metaphor might call to mind some of Mitchell's work. But Cohen's incantations were unique to him, the words seeming to tumble over, under and around the minimal but compelling instrumentation. The flamenco-inspired triplets of his acoustic guitar throb with an insistent rhythmic quality that lends a ritual solemnity to the music; occasional backing vocals, percussion, bass guitar and other strings add subtle textures; but dominating all is Cohen's deep, calm voice, that of a man who is 'used to being listened to'. 'So Long, Marianne' and 'Hey, That's No Way to Say Goodbye' – the former a paean to lost youth, the latter a hymn to experience and parting – both place Cohen's 'old' voice against youthful (almost childish) female backing vocals, further maturing the singer and situating him as more bodily present than those with whom he is singing. Cohen's voice is always present in the mix but the songs often sing of absence and of being elsewhere: escape is always on the singer's lips. In a memorable metaphorical image in 'The Stranger Song', a road is glimpsed curling up like smoke behind the stranger's back, suggesting both the road behind (the map of experience) and the road of future departure. Cohen's protagonists, like Dylan's, are often looking for an escape route. Simmons picks up on this by describing the 'paradox of distance and intimacy' that runs through Cohen's life.[68]

Cohen did not hurry with his musical output, releasing his second album in 1969, his third in 1971 and continuing to publish and promote his poetry in the meantime. This meant that a number of songs continued to be heard first in versions by other singers, foremost among them Judy Collins. Collins included three Cohen songs on her popular 1967 album *Wildflowers* and two more the following year on *Who Knows Where the Time Goes*, an album that also popularised the song by Sandy Denny that provided its title and helped to establish Collins and Denny alongside Cohen and Dylan as artists focused on the distillation of expression of life experience into popular song. In late 1971 Collins released an album of concert performances recorded the previous year. The title of the album, *Living*, can be understood as both a reference to the live nature of the recordings and to a line in one of the songs included, Cohen's 'Famous Blue Raincoat': 'you're living for nothing now / I hope you're keeping some kind of record'. In this case, Collins's version of the song appeared later than Cohen's, which had been released earlier the same year on his third album *Songs of Love and Hate*. That album, as Anthony DeCurtis writes, is 'concerned with dualities', including the love and hate evoked in the title, the physical and spiritual aspects of love, the conflict of being 'righteous or damned' and, as hymned in the sung and recited lines of 'Joan of Arc', the ongoing duality of Cohen's role as poet and singer-songwriter, with his two voices 'merged and held up for comparison'.[69]

As already mentioned, there is also the duality of Cohen as narrator and character of his songs, notably evident in 'Famous Blue Raincoat'. The song manages to suggest both liberation and possession. The woman in the song, Jane, is presented as 'free', as 'nobody's wife', and simultaneously as 'my woman' or 'his woman'; seemingly less free or vocal than the two men she is involved with, she operates as an object of exchange. But are these men two separate individuals or two aspects of the narrator, who signs himself of as 'L. Cohen' at the close of the song? Bill van Dyk is not alone in wondering whether Cohen is 'addressing a duality within himself' and whether the song 'is about a failed triangle consisting of a vulnerable woman and a divided man'. Judith Fitzgerald reads the song as

> an internal dialogue, voice-over division, contrasting the better man made manifest as the slain brother relieved of his famous blue raincoat (protection against the elements) with one more thin gypsy thief that night that he 'planned to go clear' or come clean. When Cohen's voice cracks ever so slightly dropping down to the final 'go', listeners intuitively know the honeymoon's over.[70]

A number of commentators on 'Famous Blue Raincoat' mention the famous signature ('L. Cohen') at the end. The song had gone under the working title of 'The Letter' and the words are presented in the format of one man writing to another (or to himself). The signature is heard as 'unsettlingly personal' by DeCurtis, but coldly, bureaucratically impersonal by Stephen Scobie.[71] It is debatable whether this initial and surname is even the song's ultimate signature, or whether that role falls to the guitar figure that follows the final words. As important as Cohen's words are in his songs, they are often underlined – and occasionally undermined – by other vocal and musical features. There is the 'ultimately' signifying role of the nonsense phrase 'da doo dum dum' in 'Tower of Song', to which I'll return below, and the 'la la la' that ends 'Joan of Arc', a song that itself takes up a closing, signature-like role on *Songs of Love and Hate*. Of this song, DeCurtis writes that 'Words themselves have failed, only a melancholic old-world melody will do, experience has brought no wisdom, and the impassioned realms of love and hate seem no more knowable than at the album's start.'[72]

There are other ways in which the seemingly insignificant has been granted importance in Cohen's work. For Jacques Willaert, the line 'You treated my woman to a flake of your life' is the key phrase in 'Famous Blue Raincoat': 'being random, flakes cause the crucial moments of our lives. Sometimes these moments are glorious, sometimes catastrophic. The song is built up with examples of flakes: the flakes you can see immediately (a man in the station with a rose in his teeth), the flakes you remember (a lock of your hair, a famous blue raincoat)'.[73] I find this observation striking in that it identifies some of the ways in which isolated experiences become solidified into accumulated experience. Like apparently random memories, flakes serve as fragmentary moments of transcendence, as the myriad moments that make up a life, the shards that, if they could be pieced together again, might reclaim a whole experience. Flakes, fragments and shards also resonate with Roland Barthes's notion of 'biographemes' (described earlier).

The aspects of duality and the flaking of experience discussed above can be found throughout Cohen's work and are a notable aspect of 'Hallelujah', the song that went almost unnoticed at the time of its first appearance but which would go on to be Cohen's most famous song. Due to its strange history of initial neglect and gradual ascendance to ubiquity (a tale told in numerous other places and so not repeated here[74]), 'Hallelujah' can be seen as itself a 'shard' of history and memory that takes on new significance later in the life of the song itself, the singer and his audience. The song has given rise to seemingly endless interpretations, enhanced by the fact that the original mass of verses that Cohen wrote for the song (around eighty by his own account) have been edited and combined in various ways over the years, both by Cohen and by the many other singers who have performed the song. It is telling that the song first appeared on an album entitled *Various Positions* (1984), for it has been an endlessly modular and variable object for its many handlers in its three decades of existence.[75] My own understanding of the song tends to focus less on the endless search for meaning in each specific verse (though I do not decry those who have sought it) and more on the song as a series of fragments or riddles (or flakes, perhaps). I find I rarely recall most of the verses and instead become aware of this series of riddles which seem to be 'resolved' by the repeated non-explanation, 'Hallelujah'. It is not just that this wordless word resolves the riddles of the sung text, but its repetition resolves the music of the verses too. In most performances of the song, there are musical insertions at certain points that act as stabs, or shards, of expression, giving further layers of potential meaning to the song. In the recording released in 1984, this is notable at the outset, after the words 'secret chord', when a keyboard chord springs out of the musical backing; the rather obvious 'stab' is repeated at the end of the following line, providing an instrumental 'rhyme' to accompany the lyrical one. The word 'blaze' midway through the third verse ('There's a blaze of light') is also highlighted by the keyboard, while extra attack is placed on the electric guitar on the final iteration of the 'Hallelujah' refrain. At other points there is silence but these silences have been filled in various ways in subsequent performances by Cohen and others. On more recent live versions, such as that recorded for *Songs from the Road* (2010), the transition from the refrain to the verses is accompanied by a swirling organ figure that both reinforces the religious aspects of the lyrics and acts as a reference to a number of 1960s rock songs that featured organs (especially Hammonds) in prominent roles (notable examples being Bob Dylan, the Doors and Procol Harum). Neil Larsen, Cohen's keyboardist, also inserts a keyboard run in the pause before the late 'Hallelujah' refrain, adding drama and a sense of ecstasy to the song.

'Anthem' is another song which was originally recorded for *Various Positions* but only attained full exposure later. The first recorded version was shelved due to a technical error and the song subsequently appeared on Cohen's *The Future* in 1992.[76] In recent years it has become an important part of Cohen's live performances, where its simple structure, minimalist lines and stately pace provide a perfect vehicle for Cohen's luxuriously weathered voice to work in combination with gospel-style female backing vocals. The gospel feel is furthered by lines which look to the future and offer vague but inspirational advice: 'ring the bells that still can ring / forget your perfect offering'. Many of the song's lyrics express experience, not only in reported references to the past and to what the narrator has done, but also in the general sense of wisdom gained through time and imparted as guidance to others. In an interview in which he references the song, Cohen said:

> I'm the person who tries everything, and experience myself as falling apart . . . And the place where it all comes out is in the critical examination of those things – the songs. And because of this, I'm vulnerable. There's the line in 'Anthem' that says, 'There's a crack in everything / That's how the light gets in.' That sums it up; it is as close to a credo as I've come.[77]

It's been too late for years

While I have been keen to assert, as with many of the artists discussed in this book, a constant 'lateness' to Cohen's work that is evident from the outset of his career, the late voice is, with him, most evident in the accumulated, layered self that is built up across a lifetime of work. It is true that there was something 'always already' old about Cohen, yet he was never so evidently an 'old man' as when he returned from a period of exile from the music business in the 1990s to re-forge his image and career as an old master of the seductive power of song, or what the music critic Thom Jurek described as an 'elder statesman of the bedroom'.[78] This description, which actually prefaces an interview from 1993 when Cohen was fifty-eight and still in the early stages of his late resurgence, captures Cohen's continued reputation as a 'master' of romantic intrigue. Beyond this, Jurek recognises, as others have done, Cohen's ability to offer words and other sounds of wisdom on the lifelong struggle to live, love and think in a sometimes uncaring and always uncontrollable, volatile world. In the interview, Cohen reflects on the longevity of his career:

> From the very beginning, I was in it for the long haul. And the long haul for all of us is a lifetime. At fifty-eight, if I'm in my prime, I believe that's how it should be. Any artist should get better with time; there's more experience, more maturity, hopefully more vision, perhaps one even looks death a little squarer in the eye. As far as continuing relevance, I feel blessed to be part of a continuum that includes both Bob Dylan and Nick Cave. I'm gratified that I can speak to someone who is twenty-five as well – though I believe differently – as to someone who is fifty-five.[79]

In another interview the previous year, Cohen had also made reference to ageing and passion, saying 'the idea that your creative impetus is over by thirty, that you immolate yourself on this pyre of energy and sexuality and can then go back to cleaning up and doing the dishes . . . it just ain't so. The fire continues to burn fiercely as you get older'.[80] This interview, which coincided with the release of *The Future* in 1992, focused in part on the sensual aspect of Cohen's work in an attempt to alter the common myth of him as a 'miserablist' singer-songwriter. In her biography, Simmons also highlights the growing recognition of Cohen as a romancer by describing his singing on *The Future* as 'somewhere between a prophet of doom with a black sense of humour and Barry White.'[81] Another myth that was being challenged at this late point was his supposed inability to sing. Cohen had himself expressed reservations about his singing from the start of his career and the wealth of cover versions by more conventionally 'musical' artists had reinforced the idea that he was primarily a songwriter. Yet his voice has always been an integral part of his work, both as a reciter of verse and as a singer of songs; his fans had always known this but 'official' recognition seemed to be becoming a reality also when, on the back of the songs he recorded for *The Future*, Cohen was awarded Male Vocalist of the Year at the Canadian Juno Awards. Accepting the award, Cohen wryly noted that 'It's only in a country like this that I could win a Best Vocalist award.'[82] As amusing and knowing as Cohen's response is, it is also worth highlighting that this newfound acceptance of his voice is recognition of an increased gravitas that came with age.

Cohen's voice does change over the course of his career, more noticeably so than those of Bob Dylan or Neil Young. Because Dylan spent many years putting on different voices, the move from an 'early' to a 'late' vocal style is not easy to trace consistently, while Young's voice has maintained its ethereal high register throughout his career to date. Cohen also differs from Sinatra here, in that the latter was clearly more engaged in the art of singing as a process of breath control, instrumental technique and interpretation; Sinatra's skill in these areas slipped in later years, perhaps inevitably given the physical effort involved, and he subsequently appeared somehow 'less' of a singer, a 'failure' even. Cohen, perhaps because no one expected great vocal art from him for much of his career, has been able to follow a different path, turning his voice into something that can be pitched into the lyrical and musical compositions he has created with his producers, arrangers and accompanists. In some cases, this has actually made some of his earlier recorded performances sound like imperfect (perhaps 'failed') versions and his late performances as definitive versions. Describing Cohen as he sounded in his seventy-third year, Simmons writes 'His voice now was deeper than it had ever been. It was like old leather, soft and worn, a little cracked in places but for the most part supple, and hung suspended somewhere between word and song.'[83] It is also worth remembering that the art of the 'vocalist' – the category for which Cohen was recognised at the Juno Awards – can be, and often is, quite distinct from that of the 'singer'.

Simmons connects the sound of Cohen's late voice to the famous line from 'Anthem' that Cohen says is his credo; she writes that, on his 2010 tour, Cohen's voice 'sounded softer and rougher at the edges now, a little cracked, but no matter, that was how the light got in.'[84] It is a nice turn of phrase to find late in Cohen's biography and also an effective way to articulate the 'tear' that is such a crucial aspect of his vocal grain and its ability to illuminate the darkness. Like the flake of life, the shard of meaning or the *punctum* of sudden recognition that shoots out of the *studium* of a scene to pierce the senses of the beholder, so this constantly reiterated and reconfigured 'crack of light' becomes a recurring theme of Cohen's late work. It is a moment of epiphany, much like the 'Hallelujah' of Cohen's most covered song.

As he has aged, Cohen has shown a greater mastery of the self-deprecating line and the sly passing on of wisdom. On stage he makes humorous references to his age and musical abilities. He often repeats a story about setting out on tour at the age of sixty, 'just a kid with a crazy dream'. He playfully subverts the communicated wisdom of 'Tower of Song' by inserting a simple keyboard solo in the piece, then responds to the audience's applause with a comment that suggests they are being kind to him rather than applauding virtuosity. In the same song, he will occasionally suggest that the meaning of life can be found in the sentence 'da doo dum dum' (the lines sung by the backing singers). 'Lah la / lah la lah la lah la' are the first words of most late Cohen concerts as he tends to open his sets with 'Dance Me to the End of Love'; the words are sung by the (normally three) backing vocalists and later taken up by Cohen himself, an early example in each concert of how his voice will be deployed in dynamic tension with his accompanists. Such tactics play on audiences' knowledge of Cohen's image as a wise old man, and also on Cohen's knowledge of the knowledge, the expectations that come with being that person. At the same time they signal the potential for truths to be found in seemingly simple forms (perhaps the meaning of life really is 'da doo dum dum'; thinking about the possibility could certainly be beneficial).[85] This simplicity has come as a result of study in the art of entertaining and Cohen's late concerts are a fine example of how dramatic art, retrospection and entertainment can be honed into a successful, repeatable package (not unlike a successful London or Broadway show, perhaps). This has been documented in a number of live recordings and broadcasts, including the collection *Songs from the Road*. In the liner notes to that release, Leon Wieseltier reflects on the 'art of wandering' and on the road as a site of transient existence:

> If departure is the past and arrival is the future, then the road is the present, and there is nothing more spiritually difficult, or spiritually rewarding, than learning to live significantly in the present. This is accomplished by a schooling in transience, and the road is such a school. Almost as powerfully as the sea and the sky, the road is an emblem of immensity: the horizon into which it disappears is the promise of a release, which is the promise of a horizon, which is the promise of a release. From the stretch of even the most ordinary road, you may infer a suggestion of infinity.[86]

Wieseltier is using this language to illustrate both Cohen's return to touring and his eternal wandering nature, his refusal to dwell in the past; Cohen is someone who lives 'significantly in the present'. Wieseltier compares the travelling musician to the preacher and Cohen fits the bill for both, particularly on songs such as 'Hallelujah' and 'Anthem', songs he is able to wield in the way a gospel preacher might. Cohen's performance of 'Hallelujah' on this collection (recorded at the Coachella festival) inserts the word 'people' before 'I've been here before' in recognition of the assembled congregation. The territorialisation of the lyric which Cohen has introduced to the song ('I didn't come to Coachella [or London, or Dublin] just to fool you') reinforces the notion of Cohen as visiting sage, while the chorus and backing vocals lend the song its gospel register.

Old ideas

In 2012, at the age of seventy-seven, Cohen released his twelfth studio album, *Old Ideas*.[87] The title was a pun which reflected both his age and his tendency to return to core themes again and again in his work, even, in some cases, to return to ideas that had been abandoned long before (as with 'Anthem', for example). Given Cohen's interest in country and folk music, it is also tempting to read 'old' as meaning good and trustworthy, worn in and borne out by time and experience. Sylvie Simmons's comments on *Old Ideas* are typically compelling.

She underlines the combination of levity and gravity that characterises the album and makes it consistent with Cohen's previous work, especially from *I'm Your Man* onwards. She suggests that the levity of the album distinguishes it from other late-life releases such as Dylan's 'Beyond the Horizon' (a song from his 2006 album *Modern Times*), Glen Campbell's *Ghost on the Canvas* (an album released at the same time that it was announced that Campbell was suffering from Alzheimer's and would cease recording) and Johnny Cash's iconic final albums recorded with Rick Rubin. Sprinkling her text with quotations from 'Going Home', the opening song on *Old Ideas*, Simmons writes:

> Leonard Cohen, this so-called 'sage', this 'man of vision', is nothing more than a 'lazy bastard living in a suit', who wants to write about the same things he has been banging on at forever: 'a love song, an anthem of forgiving, a manual for living with defeat'. The same old ideas that were on his first album, *Songs of Leonard Cohen*, and that have been on every Leonard Cohen album since. Something as insignificant as old age was not going to change that.[88]

Unlike other singer-songwriters of the 1960s, Cohen did not have to wait to gain authority, Simmons argues, because he 'was always old'; instead, he was able to attain a 'lightness' that may have eluded others. The comparisons and contrasts do not work entirely. Johnny Cash, after all, had also always seemed old and had not required the passing of years to attain gravity; as for levity, he had experimented with it on numerous occasions (from 'A Boy Named Sue' to 'Chicken in Black'), only to find that it did not entirely suit his character or performing persona. Dylan had claimed to struggle to attain gravitas in his early career but many have noted that he did in fact seem older than his years on his debut album, in contrast to a later, learned lightness; Dylan himself, of course, had highlighted the absurdity of chronological development in 'My Back Pages' ('I was so much older then / I'm younger than that now') and continuously sprinkled his canon of 'serious' work with dashes of humorous, surreal and nonsensical songs. Campbell's case is slightly different in that the gravity he takes on in his last albums is a reflection of illness. Perhaps as an older man, he sounds more serious than at the outset of his singing career, but that early career was still built upon the sincere expression of undeniably 'adult' material.

Even with these reservations, though, it can still be said that Cohen does seem atypical inasmuch as he brings all these qualities together: the early lateness, the late lightness, the consistency in vision, the lack of an identifiably different persona in the late stage of his career. Appropriately for someone who began his professional life as a poet, his persona fits that of a writer more than a popular music entertainer, though this observation only serves to highlight the lack of acceptance of different ways to age within popular music. Reviewing *Old Ideas* for the *Chicago Tribune*, Greg Kot wrote that 'it is not another of the dreaded winter-of-my-years albums that have become a cottage industry in recent decades', suggesting Cohen's exceptionality and inviting readers to consider popular musicians who *have* engaged in such retrospective projects.[89] That said, Kot neglects to mention artists other than Cash and Dylan, who apparently only kick-started the phenomenon of 'albums about the "dying of the light" by late-period icons' which had now 'become a cliché'. Given the wording of Kot's review, it is worth returning to the example of Frank Sinatra, who could be seen as providing the template for the retrospective album with *September of My Years*. It could also be argued that Sinatra's late period, from the start of the 1970s through to his final performances, was largely retrospective in nature, featuring shows (and recorded or broadcast shows) that served to deliver the hits, the performance of a 'Frank Sinatra' character that had been honed over many years of star construction. Cohen is not immune from such a process and, while he may be exploring new old ideas on recent recordings, his stage show has taken on the form of a retrospective look at his career.

In 2014, Cohen followed *Old Ideas* with another album, *Popular Problems*, showing a level of productivity quite unusual for him.[90] The album contains a number of references to age and the passing of time, though they are once again presented in a humorous or self-deprecating manner, as in the first lines of the first song, where he says 'I'm slowing down the tune / I never liked it fast'. The song is called 'Slow' and is a poem in praise of a slowness that doesn't have to be associated with age: 'It's not because I'm old' and 'It's not the life I led' suggest a denial of art reflecting life experience. Towards the end, it becomes a song about physicality and, suggestively, physical relationships: 'Let me catch my breath / I thought we had all night.' As with many of Cohen's late songs, the tracks on *Popular Problems* use rigidly metered lines, often of less than eight syllables. There is an economy of line and language that highlights the inevitability of rhythm and rhyme that still offers unexpected insights, as if Cohen had finally mastered the art of songwriting that Hank Williams had provided the template for, the perfect miniature. The formal simplicity of Cohen's late songs calls to mind the poetic genres of *haiku* and *tanka*, promising endless variety within highly concise and bounded forms. This relationship is borne out further in the late poetry collection *Book of Longing*, which contains a number of haiku-like verses, many written during Cohen's residency at the Mount Baldy Zen Center near Los Angeles.[91] The poems describe the rigours of monastery life and provide portraits of Cohen's fellow monks, especially his teacher Kyozan Joshu Sasaki Roshi. Joshu Roshi is a fascinating character in Cohen's life story, as Simmons's biography make clear, and is notable as a long-lived senior figure in Cohen's life, a late father figure (Nathan Cohen, his father, died when Cohen was nine); as one reads *I'm Your Man*, it is fascinating to witness Joshu Roshi's ageing and his seeming immortality. He died before the release of *Popular Problems* and the liner notes include a dedication 'to our Teacher and Companion Kyozan Joshu Sasaki Roshi 1907–2014'.

The poetic simplicity of the songs on *Popular Problems* is coupled to musical forms that again suggest infinite variability within simplicity. In the case of 'Slow' this is the blues, a form which Cohen, like Bob Dylan, seems increasingly drawn to in his later years. Blues, like country, offers a musical space in which poetic message can be honed to its minimal essence while offering rich, varied and enigmatic meanings. Country and blues in their most minimal forms also demand of the voice an authority that is well suited to lateness; to sound convincing in so few words, it helps if the singer has gravity. One might think here of the absolute authority contained in Johnny Cash's voice in just the four words 'I hurt myself today' and, like Cash, Cohen has a voice that was always low, authoritative and compelling but which has attained ever more gravity with the passing of years.[92] On 'Slow', as on other performances of recent years, Cohen's voice attains a timbral depth and a huskiness which are astonishing even for those familiar with his work.

As he has always done, Cohen continues to place his voice against highly pitched female vocals. In 'Samson in New Orleans', a song which finds the poet 'blind with death and anger', his voice is accompanied by the vocals of Charlean Carmon and Dana Glover, the church organ-like keyboards of Cohen's co-writer Patrick Leonard and Alexandru Bublitchi's keening violin, a combination which lends the song a religious solemnity. This is one of Cohen's most melodic vocal contributions to the album and the resonance of his voice is particularly affective as it shifts between singing, whispering and almost speaking. Perhaps due to the labour involved in singing rather than reciting, Cohen's voice exhibits its physical limitations in compelling ways: the hiss of the whispered 'that's what I heard you say', the almost dropped second syllables of 'my friend' and 'pretend', the rasp and scrape of 'the king so kind and solemn' and 'the woman in the window'. In the blues-based 'A Street', the backing vocals offer a soothing 'mmmmmm' for the first part of the song before folding into a call-and-response articulation of Cohen's words. The song refers to a party that is over, to things that used to be and to the realisation that 'we'll never / ever be that drunk again'. In 'Did I Ever Love You', the poet notes the lemon trees blossoming and the almond trees withering, these seasonal references twinned with the observation that 'it's spring and it's summer / and it's winter forever'. As the tempo of the song switches between a gentle swing and an unnatural-seeming country canter, the backing vocals affect an almost artificial sweetness against which Cohen's voice sounds particularly harsh: the female voice blossoms, his withers. 'Nevermind', a revision of a poem from *The Book of Longing*, speaks of 'the Sweet Indifference / some call Love' and 'the High Indifference / some call Fate', of 'layers of time / you can't divide', and a sense of belonging over one's life even as others attempt to categorise or own it. While the Arabic singing that is mixed into the recording marks another meaning of the song (a commentary on the Middle East), it is easy to hear these and other lines as saying something about the poet himself. In an interview at the time of the album, the release of which coincided with his eightieth birthday, Cohen said, 'There comes a point, I think, as you get a little older, you feel that nothing represents you. You can see the value of many positions, even positions that are in savage conflict with one another. You can locate components on both sides that resonate within you.'[93] The closing song on *Popular Problems* is 'You Got Me Singing', a title and refrain which seem ironic given that, as with much of his recent work, Cohen speaks rather than sings the lyrics. It is particularly effective on this track because the song is introduced and accompanied by an exquisite string melody and supported by backing vocals which do seem, as certain lines approach their resolution, to get Cohen singing, certainly inflecting the lines with a melodic lilt. The song also refers to 'singing that Hallelujah song', a line that can be read as a self-reflexive nod to Cohen's own song or as an intimation of mortality.

Conclusion

The release of new material such as *Old Ideas* and *Popular Problems* would seem to support claims made by Cohen and a number of music critics that he is working against the kind of nostalgic retrospection that is often seen to go with late careers in the music business. Yet his highly successful stage show, which is arguably as much a part of his contemporary image as his new studio recordings, tells a slightly different story. It is a carefully planned and orchestrated affair that has been honed to perfection since Cohen's return to touring in 2008. For all its brilliance, it does not hold much in the way of variety. It is also something that can be repeatedly packaged and sold on as 'product', as is evident from the series of live albums and videos *Live in London* (2009), *Songs from the Road* (2010) and *Live in Dublin* (2014). These are fascinating documents to consume, providing lavishly produced audiovisual witnessing of Cohen's epic shows. They may not quite make up for the magic of being present at one of the concerts but they come as close as such documents can. At the same time they present Cohen's work as an ever-more canonised body of personal, critical and audience favourites, perhaps not so dissimilar from live Sinatra recordings such as *Sinatra at the Sands* (1966) or *The Main Event* (1974). Cohen arguably presents his work with greater humility than did Sinatra, suggesting a kind of anti-Sinatra. In her biography of Cohen, Sylvie Simmons refers to his song 'Bird on the Wire' as an 'anti My Way', an attempt to look back at experience and achievement in a non-bragging manner. Given this comparison, it is worth recalling that 'My Way' was adapted from a French chanson entitled 'Comme d'habitude', itself a rather humbler attempt at reflecting on the everyday rather than the exceptional; the lyrical and musical changes to the song as it became, via Paul

Anka's adaptation, a vehicle for Sinatra's star persona, say much about the ways in which such material could be presented on the French and American pop markets of the late 1960s. Cohen, closer to a *chansonnier* than to many other types of popular singer, would seem to be closer to the 'Comme d'habitude' than the 'My Way' model. Yet, despite the patina of reflection and humility that may attend Cohen's concerts, there is still something monumental about them. The musician Robert Forster touched on this when, in an interview in which he was asked to compare recent Australian concerts by Cohen and Dylan, he responded that, as brilliant as Cohen's concerts are, he would choose a Dylan concert if forced because it would be more unpredictable.[94] This sense of a lack of surprise or newness is something often associated with late work and it would appear that Cohen, in this sense, has decided to give the audience what they want. The model for late Cohen therefore becomes the tried and tested one of the 'consummate showman', exemplified by elderly peers such as Tony Bennett. Where we may go to a Dylan concert knowing that, as one of his songs says, 'things have changed', we come to Cohen in search of the reassuringly familiar. Even here, though, we find change and we learn to look for the nuances that individualise a particular performance.

Another way we might look at Cohen's late performances is as a resistance against frailty. The cover of *Popular Problems* shows him smartly dressed in suit and fedora and leaning on a cane. The image suggests elegance and a knowledge of how to present oneself. Inside, in the booklet of the CD and the inner sleeve of the LP, are pictures of Cohen sitting in various states of casual dress (and undress; in some he is in his underwear) while he polishes shoes, with the cleaning implements laid out carefully on the floor beside him. These images suggest the humility of simple labour and the importance of discipline, rigour and ritual to maintain the kind of dignity showcased in the outside world. While the outer image shows a public persona whose manicured elegance serves as a shield, the inner sleeve seems to present the intimate, inner life of the artist, showing us an almost uncomfortable vulnerability. Witnessing these unusual images as we listen to Cohen's thirteenth studio album, we may be reminded of the ways in which his work has always communicated intimacy and drawn us into a highly personal relationship with the singer. We may never have been allowed to get as close to Frank Sinatra but his work, like Cohen's, shines a light on frailty and vulnerability too. As Chris Rojek writes, 'Sinatra spent all three ages of man – youth, middle age, and old age – in the spotlight. If the core of his fame was founded in the invulnerable, insouciant persona cultivated in middle age, the beginning and end of his career are united in the admittedly calculated, nut nonetheless affecting, exhibition of human frailty.'[95]

This unflinching confrontation with frailty is a quality that links many – perhaps all – of the case studies included in this book. Whether it is through the composing of songs that face up to the realities of life, or through the attachment of voice to a tradition that does so, these singers find a way of articulating the late voice. As we saw with Ralph Stanley in the previous chapter, it is not necessary to be a songwriter to create this voice. If Stanley provides a model of someone who has stayed true to a tradition (old-time music) always already saturated in the vicissitudes of experience, Sinatra shows how it is possible to fashion a different set of shared songs (in his case those of classic American songwriting teams) into conceptual artworks that constitute, and are constituted by, a public persona. Leonard Cohen represents the figure of the poet, whose personal experience is moulded into art by his own pen and therefore more obviously reflects its author. Bob Dylan, the subject of the next chapter, provides a similar model, albeit one filtered through the lens of intense public and critical scrutiny, a combination of Sinatra's celebrity and Cohen's personal poetic message. All are subject to the processes of aesthetic experience, of adapting voices of one kind or another to an articulation that is singular (their own), seemingly stable (despite the fluctuations of persona that come with all lives) and communicable (in that it can be understood by their audiences). Leonard Cohen articulated this with customary elegance when, in a speech given at the time of accepting a Prince of Asturias Award in Oviedo in 2011, he told his audience that he owed his poetic and musical voices to Spanish culture, having been influenced at an early age by flamenco guitar and the poetry of Federico García Lorca:

> [Lorca] gave me permission to find a voice, to locate a voice, that is to locate a self, a self that that is not fixed, a self that struggles for its own existence. As I grew older, I understood that instructions came with this voice. What were these instructions? The instructions were never to lament casually. And if one is to express the great inevitable defeat that awaits us all, it must be done within the strict confines of dignity and beauty.[96]

4

Time Out of Mind: Bob Dylan, Age and Those Same Distant Places

'Twas in another lifetime

Bob Dylan

In February 2015 Bob Dylan released an album of standards associated with Frank Sinatra, the centenary of whose birth would fall later the same year. Some of the songs on *Shadows in the Night* were ones that Sinatra had recorded early in his career for Columbia (also Dylan's label), while others were numbers he had revisited or recorded for the first time in his classic middle period.[1] Pervading the selection was an emphasis on the melancholic part of Sinatra's repertoire, those songs of romantic defeat that he had turned into saloon standards. Three of the first four tracks on Dylan's album had been included on Sinatra's 1957 'concept album' *Where Are You?* and were examples of material that had reinforced Sinatra's standing as a man of the world, one who had lived and lost enough for all his audience; so too with Dylan's late renditions, which ache with the longing only a lifetime can seem to bring. A number of critics suggested that *Shadows in the Night* contained some of Dylan's finest singing in years, fine understood here as an attachment of voice to a purity of tone and a melodic ideal. This might seem only right when tackling the Great American Songbook, a set of compositions that, according to traditionalists, are most faithfully rendered when voices remain true to the written words and melodies. Some self-proclaimed long-term fans of Dylan were not so impressed by the album, however, suggesting that the singer was unable to hold a tune for long enough, or traverse melodic contours with enough skill, to do justice to the songs. Some averred that Dylan's voice was fine when paired with his own self-written material, or that it was his words that mattered, not the way he sang them.[2]

Those who made a contrast between the art of the singer-songwriter and that of the interpreter of standards were following in a long-standing tradition, one that has made occasionally crass distinctions concerning musical authorship. That tradition is exemplified by Will Friedwald when, in his *Biographical Guide to the Great Jazz and Pop Singers* (an epic work which includes Dylan among its 'extras'), he compares Dylan, the Beatles and Sinatra:

> The combined effect that Bob Dylan and the Beatles had on popular music was devastating; from about 1964 on, it was a whole new game, with whole new rules and a whole new value system.
>
> Not every change that occurs is a good thing; sometimes great music leads to a disastrous aftershock. I can only imagine that both Sinatra and Dylan had moments when they felt like Dr. Frankenstein: They had created a monster and couldn't control the damage it caused. I'm obviously glad that Frank Sinatra became the biggest thing in pop music in 1943, but the downside of his triumph was the eventual end of the big band era, which many of us still feel was the all-time high point of American popular music. Likewise, as great as Bob Dylan and the Beatles were, their arrival was, in many ways, a catastrophe for good music. As Dylan acknowledged, after the mid-1960s the age of professional songwriters was abruptly over. Suddenly, it just seemed old hat to sing songs written by people who weren't you. Nobody wanted to sing anybody else's song anymore. For the last fifty years, every musical artist has been expected to be his or her own Bob Dylan; likewise, every band is expected to have its own Lennon and McCartney.[3]

The passage is typical of Friedwald's art of exaggeration, with its insistence that individuals are solely responsible for changing history and its boisterous (and inaccurate) claim regarding the division of labour between lyricists, composers and singers in popular music.[4] But one gets the point about the superficial incompatibility between the *typical* authorial roles adopted in the Tin Pan Alley era and those which developed with the rise of rock music. And so, five years after the publication of Friedwald's Sinatra-Dylan comparison, it might have seemed strange to see Dylan surrendering his songwriting skill to become an interpreter instead.

Then again, perhaps not. By this point in his career, Dylan had performed a dialectic of reinvention and fidelity to self with such skill and naturalness that moves which might once have been portrayed in the media as somehow shocking were absorbed by that same media as if they understood all along where Dylan was going and what his plan was. No one did, of course, perhaps Dylan least of all. He would talk in late interviews of journeys set out on, roads taken, homes sought. The quest, the highway and the tour always seemed to be everything, never the destination. But the journey went both forward and back, it circled around on itself like a snake chasing its tale. It had always been so, perhaps, but it was increasingly so in Dylan's late career, where retrospection took a major role: not that of the endlessly repeating career summary, or greatest hits package, but rather a series of revisitings of the historical past – Dylan's own and that which preceded him. The title of his 'Sinatra album', emphasised by the nocturnal blues and purples of the record sleeve, once more gave the impression of autumnal reflection, of a weariness that only years can bring. The weariness can be heard in Dylan's voice, which strains at times under the weight of the melodic imperative. At times Dylan sounds less knowing than Sinatra, less knowing too than on his own self-written material, as though he is in thrall to the songs and fighting a battle to keep afloat, weariness giving way to wariness and vice versa. Yet there are also wonderful moments of vocal caress and he finishes the album with an undoubted victory over the melody and longing of 'That Lucky Old Sun', one of his most moving recent performances.

In the same month that he released *Shadows in the Night*, Dylan gave a remarkable speech at an event ahead of the Grammy Awards when he received the MusiCares 'Person of the Year' award. Reflecting on the 'long road' that his songwriting career had taken, he spent a considerable amount of time acknowledging those who had helped him, including those who had signed him to recording and publishing deals, those who had recorded his songs and those whose songs had influenced him. He also critiqued a number of industry people, critics and musicians who had not been kind to him and, in what might have come across in a less skilled orator as a rather self-pitying complaint, he even reflected on the reception of his voice:

> Some of the music critics say I can't sing. I croak. Sound like a frog. Why don't these same critics say similar things about Tom Waits? They say my voice is shot. That I have no voice. Why don't they say those things about Leonard Cohen? Why do I get special treatment? Critics say I can't carry a tune and I talk my way through a song. Really? I've never heard that said about Lou Reed. Why does he get to go scot-free? What have I done to deserve this special treatment?[5]

Dylan was presumably employing the sly wit for which he is known among his fans, for surely such things have been said on multiple occasions by critics about these artists. Dylan's comments about his songwriting 'voice' were also interesting: 'These songs didn't come out of thin air. I didn't just make them up out of whole cloth.. . . [T]here was a precedent. It all came out of traditional music: traditional folk music, traditional rock 'n' roll and traditional big-band swing orchestra music.' The interest, for me at least, is not so much that Dylan is downplaying his authorial role, but rather that he conflates these musical worlds into a single 'tradition', one that makes a mockery of the kinds of musical segregation perpetuated by critics such as Friedwald.

With *Shadows in the Night* and the MusiCares speech, Dylan offered reminders that we remember our lives as much through others as through ourselves. This recourse to collective memory and sounded experience is one part of the narrative presented in this chapter, which takes Dylan as a *sui generis* example of late voice in all the manifestations explored in this book. Time, age, memory and experience are key themes in what follows, as are place, displacement and mobility. The chapter explores Dylan's poetics of place and displacement and argues that his constant reiteration of movement, escape and quest are tempered by a tendency to also dwell on issues of belonging, home and return. While, like many before me, I stress Dylan's enigmatic qualities and his shape-shifting persona(s), I also use the poetics of place and displacement as a way of arguing for Dylan as a coherent subject. In doing so, I have in mind the argument made by Emily Keightley and Michael Pickering that, while we may be aware of the existence of a series of 'temporally successive selves' in the course of a life (our own or those of others in whom we are interested), 'most of us mange to achieve certain consistencies of attitude and aptitude, certain ways of seeing and doing' and it is 'around these relative consistencies, and what we try to hold onto in our ongoing revaluations of experience, that our sense of ourselves across the particular times in our lives hangs together and perdures'.[6] In doing so I am not at all suggesting that there is an answer to the riddle that is Bob Dylan, or that by considering his coherences we can somehow get to an ultimate 'truth' about him: not at all, for Dylan remains as enigmatic, contradictory and elusive as ever. But I am suggesting that we can consider him as a 'normal' subject too, as a man who has forged a long and fascinating artistic career and of whom, despite and because of the greatness and timelessness of his art, we should think as a person existing within a human life course, with all the normality, abnormality and revelation that that entails.

The lives and time of Bob Dylan

Dylan is an artist whose long and varied career, along with his reputation for having revolutionised the possibilities of popular song, have invited an enormous amount of critical and biographical attention. Such is the amount of commentary attached to him that it has become almost customary to refer to him as a man of many lives and personas. Among the recent works to acknowledge this multifariousness are two volumes of biography by David Bell entitled *Once Upon a Time* (2012) and *Time Out of Mind* (2013), both volumes subtitled 'The Lives of Bob Dylan'.[7] As a reference, 'once upon a time' is both a nod to the classic scene-setting gambit of the storyteller and a reminder of the opening of an iconic Dylan song, 'Like a Rolling Stone'; it also serves as an effective signifier that Bell is reaching back a long time from the twenty-first century to focus on the early part of Dylan's life and career, a familiar but still magical fable from a mythical, and potentially lost, era. 'Time out of mind' similarly refers to Dylan's work by echoing the title of his 1997 album, while providing a useful tag for the late period covered by Bell's second volume. The 'lives' of Bob Dylan are many in that he has seemed to be a variety of distinct yet related people over the course of his career: earnest folksinger, 'voice of a generation', pop star, rock surrealist, American pastoralist, born-again Christian rocker, rock has-been, elder bluesman, painter, disc jockey, chronicler of America's vernacular past and many more. This multifaceted aspect of Dylan's persona(s) was also compellingly recognised in Todd Haynes's *I'm Not There* (2007), a film inspired, as its opening credits reveal, 'by the music and the many lives of Bob Dylan'. Haynes cast six different actors to play seven aspects of Dylan's persona: Marcus Carl Franklin as 'Woody Guthrie' (named after the folk singer who provided Dylan with one of his strongest musical influences); Christian Bale in two roles, as protest singer Jack Rollins and born-again preacher Pastor John; Cate Blanchett as the 'electric' Dylan of the mid-1960s; Richard Gere as Billy the Kid, an embodiment of Dylan's interest in surreal Americana; Heath Ledger as Robbie Clark, an actor who takes on the role of Jack Rollins and whose troubled marital relationship echoes Dylan's; and Ben Whishaw as 'Arthur Rimbaud', named after the French symbolist poet who ranks among Dylan's early literary influences. At the start of the film, a voiceover by musician and actor Kris Kristofferson identifies the composite, unnamed Dylan as 'poet, prophet, outlaw, fake, [and] star of electricity'; the description serves not only to introduce the multiple personas (and actors) portrayed in *I'm Not There*, but also, in one of many intertextual references to be found in the film, to offer those in the know a reminder of the chorus of Kristofferson's 1960s song 'The Pilgrim – Chapter 33': 'He's a poet he's a picker he's a prophet he's a pusher.'[8]

Another feature to note in the title of Bell's biographies is the repeated reference to time, a concept that has played an important part in Dylan's career. For Nicholas Roe, 'Dylan's achievement as a poet, musician and singer, a "Song and Dance Man", is the resourcefulness with which he confronts, responds and plays to the passing of time.'[9] Roe mentions the number of occasions on which the word 'time' appears in Dylan's work (156 at the time of his count), noting that it appears much more than other significant words such as 'love', 'home', 'life' and 'death'. In this chapter, I pursue this fascination with time while also connecting it to space, and in particular to Dylan's poetics of displacement, which I see as returning again and again to the freewheeling processes of desire, loss, imagination and memory. The term 'time out of mind', which Dylan used for an album, Bell for a biography and which I recycle in the title of this chapter, serves as a useful summary of this conflation of the temporal ('time'), the spatial ('out') and the mental ('mind') that characterises much of Dylan's work. This conflation can also be found in Haynes's film, from its earliest scenes in which we witness 'Dylan' as an eleven-year-old boy taking on the persona of Woody Guthrie while telling his story to a pair of grizzled hobos on a freight train. The times and experiences the child narrates, and which seem absurd considering his apparent age, seem to be borne of a time out of mind, a fantasy of what Dylan might have believed he'd done before he began to sing. The details can be understood as those fleeting, resonant, telling shards of life (or myth) that Roland Barthes termed 'biographemes'. These shards, in endless recombination, form the basis for many accounts of Dylan's life, career and fame, a fact well understood by Haynes as he poetically and playfully reconfigures them once more, providing further riddles for the Dylanologists. For the study of the late voice, Haynes's 'Woody' also offers a reminder that 'real' life experience may come before its articulation in song but that it may equally include the sounded experience of hearing about life in song. This is the duality expressed by country star Merle Haggard when he says that 'The songs are written from the back of your mind and the cushion of your experience' while also claiming that 'I learned to ride a freight train because Jimmie [Rodgers] and Leftie [Frizzell] sang about it.'[10]

The narration of memory and experience provided by 'Woody' in *I'm Not There* also echoes that of the real Woody Guthrie, whose memoir *Bound for Glory* combines a mixture of biographical fact, tall tales and social and historical context. Like the scene in which Haynes's 'Woody' tells his tale, the narrative of *Bound for Glory* is framed by the conceit of Guthrie travelling on a freight train and reflecting on his life. Having described the occupants of the box car in which he finds himself, Guthrie drifts off into reflection:

> Can I remember? Remember back to where I was this morning? St. Paul. Yes. The morning before? Bismarck, North Dakota. And the morning before that? Miles City, Montana. Week ago, I was a piano player in Seattle.
>
> Who's this kid? Where's he from and where's he headed for? Will he be me when he grows up? Was I like him when I was just his size? Let me remember. Let me go back. Let me get up and walk back down the road I come. This old hard rambling and hard graveling. This old chuck-luck traveling.[11]

Looking out at the stormy night landscape passing by, Guthrie finds his mind drifting back to the past, allowing him to present his life chronologically in the chapters that follow and to close his account back in the freight car travelling towards an uncertain future. The use of the train also provides a key metaphor for Guthrie's life, shaped as it was by a constant sense of displacement and uncertainty. From a sense of abandonment experienced early in childhood to a feeling of non-belonging following the public recognition of his talent and the subsequent efforts of recording companies to market him, Guthrie places emphasis on the need for distancing throughout his life.

In *I'm Not There*, 'Woody', representing the early, imitative Dylan, is advised by one of the families who takes him in to 'Live your own time, child. Sing about your own time.' Heeding similar advice, the 'real' Dylan did indeed sing about his own time, gaining a reputation as the voice of a generation in the early 1960s; in doing so, he was influenced by Guthrie but also increasingly by the need to find his own style. He then took on the voice of another aspect of his generation as he moved towards rock and roll and onwards; he moved ahead of his time as he developed new poetic and musical forms and, when he reached the point of literally and figuratively 'crashing out', he disappeared, only to emerge as someone who seemed to be inhabiting a different time again, this one located somewhere in the past, in what Greil Marcus would later come to term the 'old, weird America'.[12] This shuttling between times and places is part of what I am alluding to by reference to a poetics of place and displacement. I am also interested in the ways in which Dylan has reflected on age at various points in his career and how age has been another riddle to add to the many he has spun (again, this is something Haynes recognises by having a young boy relate the story of a man much older than himself and be seen as a peer to the grizzled hobos with whom he is travelling). All these processes come together in Dylan's memory work, with memory operating as another kind of 'time out of mind', or mental time. Memory work, for Dylan as for most of us, never really stops, because memory is always caught up in processes of invention and reinvention (of our selves, our work, our identities). As Keightley and Pickering note, 'The remembering subject is always in a process of becoming and so always in some way changing.'[13] Yet some periods in life prove more fertile periods for the harvesting of memory than others and, in Dylan's case, the last two decades have been particularly notable for memorial projects of one kind of another. These include his albums *Time Out of Mind* (1997), *"Love and Theft"* (2001), *Modern Times* (2006), *Together through Life* (2009) and *Tempest* (2012), as well as the continuing 'Bootleg Series' of archival releases. The period has also witnessed the publication of Dylan's autobiographical *Chronicles* (2004) and two major film projects in which he was either involved or to which he gave approval, Martin Scorsese's documentary *No Direction Home: Bob Dylan* (2005) and Haynes's *I'm Not There*. Meanwhile, Dylan's reinvention of himself as a radio DJ for XM Satellite Radio (2006–9) reinforced this memory work by allowing further access to the intersection of his musical reference points with the collective memory stored in the recorded archive.

This body of work, along with a growing body of documentary material (including books, magazine and journal articles, blogs, social media sites, radio and television features) helped to fix Dylan's place in contemporary culture and, by exploring the myths which have grown around him, to question the possibility of any such fixity. In doing so, it remained faithful to, and retroactively provided constancy to, Dylan's previous work, which had always been characterised by a poetics of place and displacement. The poetics of place establishes itself in Dylan's output through recourse to repeated mentions of real and imagined places, which seem to fix many of Dylan's texts in recognisable locations and are therefore crucial to the ability of his audience to identify with the texts. These locations – actual and metaphorical – are fixed moments, or shards of experience, on which the memory can focus even as it struggles to recall other features. The poetics of displacement, meanwhile, seeks to challenge and destabilise any sense of permanence even as it simultaneously relies on a set of quilted, temporary memory sites. This poetics is enacted via recourse to a kind of 'memory theatre', peopled by real and fictitious characters representing a history of displacement. Characters that fulfil this function include Dylan's musical precursors (Woody Guthrie, Robert Johnson, Charlie Patton, Hank Williams, Jimmie Rodgers and Ralph Stanley among them) whose work simultaneously provides more of the quilting points of his narrative. Dylan's displacement techniques and refusal of a fixed identity threaten to unpick these quilting points but cannot escape the desire for stabilising moments, enacted most clearly in his continued homage to the players in the memory theatre. The often-noted ability of Dylan to continually reinvent himself is part of a poetics of displacement that cannot shed the pull of place and the desire for homely permanence. As Dylan's memory projects have shown, he is very much an artist who *does* look back.

In the wind: The poetics of place and displacement

The importance of home and displacement in Dylan's work is clearly understood by the makers of the three best-known films about Dylan, which all take their titles from lines in Dylan's songs: *Dont Look Back* (D.A. Pennebaker, 1967) quotes 'She Belongs To Me' from *Bringing It All Back Home* (1965); *No Direction Home* (Martin Scorsese, 2005) uses a line from one of Dylan's most famous songs, 'Like a Rolling Stone', from *Highway 61 Revisited* (1965); and *I'm Not There* takes its name from the title of a song recorded by Dylan with the Band in 1967 and, prior to the film's soundtrack, available only as a bootleg recording. All three films acknowledge the impossibility of capturing their subject even as they attempt to do so.[14] *No Direction Home* opens with Dylan saying the following:

> I had ambitions to set out and find like an odyssey, going home somewhere. I set out to find this home that I'd left a while back and I couldn't remember exactly where it was but I was on my way there, and encountering what I encountered on the way was how I envisioned it all. I didn't really have any ambition at all.... I was born very far from where I'm supposed to be and so I'm on my way home.[15]

This is an unusual statement because conventional quest narratives tend to present a home from which one departs to spend time out in the world, with any subsequent homecoming being a return to where one started rather than the goal of the original quest. We find this more conventional narrative in countless folk, blues and country songs, as when the Stanley Brothers sing 'Homesick and lonesome and feeling kind of blue / I'm on my long journey home.'[16] To be on the way home in such narratives suggests that one has already had experience, so Dylan's claim to being born a long way from home is an odd one also because it could be construed as saying he was born experienced (how did he know his home lay elsewhere? From where did this 'experience' come? Was it just a hunch, or was it something learned through the sounded experience of recordings by acts such as the Stanley Brothers?). This sense of being born experienced, or gaining experience at an early age, is also highlighted in Haynes's film, as already described.

In *No Direction Home*, we witness a man in his sixties make a claim to an early sense of displacement, so we need to be mindful of the autobiographical process whereby the distant past, the present and the time between – the time of accumulated experience – are conflated in the present, the site from which memory issues. Scorsese immediately follows Dylan's revelation about the quest for home with footage of his subject describing where he was born, thereby allowing a sense of constancy to the life being recalled. In doing so he is faithful to Dylan's work, which has used such projections of home and the past from early on. We can find this in the song 'I Was Young When I Left Home', recorded by Dylan in late 1961 at the age of twenty but not released at the time (it was available as a bootleg for many years and was officially released as a bonus track with certain copies of "*Love and Theft*" and again on the CD accompanying *No Direction Home*). The opening verse presents the narrator as a rambler who has been out in the world since he was young and hasn't felt the need to return home or even contact those he left behind: 'I never wrote a letter to my home' is the repeated line that resolves the verse.[17] The voice Dylan uses to sing this lyric is the heavily inflected 'Okie' accent he had adopted during his recent stay in New York, where he projected himself as a hobo traveller modelled on his hero Woody Guthrie. The husky voice belied his age and gave his singing a grain of authenticity crucial to audience identification. The sense of having been 'out there' and gained experience that only a traveller could gain is emphasised in later verses by reference to the wind, a metaphor to which Dylan would return many times in his songwriting; here the wind is something to 'make me a home out in'. But almost immediately he contradicts himself: 'I don't like it in the wind / Wanna go back home again / But I can't go home this a-way.' Suddenly, home is not something he disdains but something he is blocked from returning to. The sense of displacement is strong, especially in the dichotomy of the romantic lure of travelling when at home alongside the call of home when faced with the hardships of travelling. Accompanying this is a good deal of uncertainty, reflected in the unpredictability of the wind (a similar uncertainty would be reflected in 'Blowin' in the Wind' the following year) and in the inability of the song lyrics to properly fill their musical frame.

Despite this uncertainty, there remains a strong sense of place to 'I Was Young'. This might be due to the process outlined by Frederick Bartlett in his study *Remembering*, in which ambiguous details are filled out via an 'effort after meaning', often focused around a 'governing idea'.[18] The governing idea here is experience summoned by reference to place. The spaces, places and displacement referred to in Dylan's work are numerous but a brief survey might include song titles such as 'Rambler Gambler', 'Highway 51', 'Freight Train Blues', 'Girl from the North Country', 'Down the Highway', 'North Country Blues', 'Outlaw Blues', 'Restless Farewell', 'Like a Rolling Stone', 'Tombstone Blues', 'Highway 61 Revisited', 'Desolation Row', 'Drifter's Escape', 'Romance in Durango', 'Black Diamond Bay' and 'Where Are You Tonight?'. Such references, along with others in the lyrics of so many Dylan songs, focus our attention on place, movement and displacement and also remind us of similar references in other songs, not least those from the folk, country and blues music to which Dylan has always been attracted and which has influenced his work profoundly. Performers such as Jimmie Rodgers, Robert Johnson, Charlie Patton, Woody Guthrie, Hank Williams and Bill Monroe – all touchstones for Dylan – continued and helped create an American mythology of place that could serve as backdrop for future performances in these theatres of memory. The sense of identification with this imagined America is made explicit in a memorable section of Dylan's *Chronicles*, where he aligns himself with one of his country music contemporaries, the fiddler and bandleader Charlie Daniels: 'I felt I had a lot in common with Charlie.. . . Felt like we had dreamed the same dream with all the same distant places.'[19]

Dylan's mythology of place is strengthened through its connection to a sense of experience. It is not enough to merely list places in the manner of a litany; for their evocation to be effective, a sense of having inhabited them is crucial. Here Dylan's work can again be connected to the strategies of country, folk and blues musicians, not least in its use of verb tenses commonly used to express life experience. In 'Pretty Peggy-O', from his first album, Dylan sings

'I been around this whole country', both a claim on experience and an echo of earlier songs (the phrase, like so many in Dylan's work, is a 'floating' phrase that resurfaces in various folk, blues and country songs). In the aural road movie 'Señor (Tales of Yankee Power)', from the 1978 album *Street Legal*, the line 'feel like I been down this road before' both echoes its country precursors (Hank Williams's 'I've Been Down That Road Before' from 1951) and Dylan's own earlier work.[20] Later still, 'Driftin' Too Far from Shore' on Dylan's *Knocked Out Loaded* (1986) borrows its title, if little else, from Bill Monroe's 'Drifting Too Far from the Shore' (1936). In his MusiCares speech in 2015, Dylan made explicit reference to these kinds of influences and echoes:

> Big Bill Broonzy had a song called 'Key to the Highway'. 'I've got a key to the highway / I'm booked and I'm bound to go / Gonna leave here runnin' because walking is most too Slow'. I sang that a lot. If you sing that a lot, you just might write . . . 'He asked poor Howard where can I go / Howard said there's only one place I know / Sam said tell me quick man I got to run / Howard just pointed with his gun / And said that way down on Highway 61'. You'd have written that too if you'd sang 'Key to the Highway'.. . . If you'd listened to Robert Johnson singing, 'Better come in my kitchen, 'cause it's gonna be raining outdoors' as many times as I listened to it, sometime later you just might write 'A Hard Rain's A-Gonna Fall'.[21]

The use of the present perfect tense has often lent songs a sense of experience, as, for example, in Jimmie Rodgers's and Elsie McWilliams's 'I've Ranged, I've Roamed, I've Traveled' (1929) and this seems to be something Dylan is very aware of in songs such as 'A Hard Rain's A-Gonna Fall'. The song uses a wide variety of present perfect and past simple structures to list its protagonist's experience ('I've stumbled . . .', 'I've slept . . .', 'I've been . . .', 'I saw . . .', 'I heard . . .', 'I met . . . '), before closing with a combination of future tenses to suggest, in a Tom Joad-like monologue, that there is still agency here, and hope.[22] There is a similar combination of past and future in 'Restless Farewell' (the closing track from 1964's *The Times They Are A-Changin'*), one of Dylan's exemplary early songs of displacement, described by Paul Williams as 'a portrait of the artist in motion at the end of the evening, end of the album, end of the present myth of Bob Dylan and off into the dark towards a new one'.[23] Each verse of the song ends with a promise to say farewell and

Dylan declares at one point, 'my feet are now fast / and point away from the past'. Yet the effectiveness of this moving-on song is undermined to some extent by the repeated use of the present perfect and the clear importance to the singer of memory and experience: 'every girl that ever I've touched/ hurt', 'every foe that ever I've faced', 'every cause that ever I've fought' and 'every thought that strung a knot in my mind'. We are witnessing a lived life and there is a strong sense of looking back. From where is this 'I have' being projected if not the stability of the speaking subject 'at home' enough to reflect on past experience? The singer's feet may 'point away from the past' but it is not so clear his mind does. Indeed, there is guilt here, stealing away in the night, justification (finding reasons why he can't stay – it's closing time, it's healthy to move on) and stubbornness ('I'll . . . not give a damn'). He is trying to convince himself that moving on is the right thing to do. The vow that seals this conviction ('I'll . . . remain as I am') suggests constancy but what will be constant is the inconstant. A similar hesitancy can be found in 'One Too Many Mornings' on the same album, where, 'from the crossroads of my doorstep', the singer turns 'back to the room where my love and I have laid', and from there back to the waiting street.[24] Both songs bear comparison with Leonard Cohen's 'The Stranger Song', which is built around the ambiguous boundaries between shelter, road and railway track and around the conflicts felt by the characters (at least three but implying many more) who waver between shelter and the freedom promised by the open road: 'You tell him to come in, sit down, but something makes you turn around. The door is open. You cannot close your shelter. You try the handle of the road. It opens. Do not be afraid. It's you, my love, it's you who are the stranger.'[25]

The hesitancy in tracks such as these (heard also in the indeterminacy of 'I Was Young When I Left Home') suggests a conflict taking place within the narrator of the texts, a narrator who we may as well call 'Bob Dylan'. The conflict of this young-old figure is highlighted again in 'Bob Dylan's Dream', where the singer looks back on what he has left behind and the friends he has lost from the perspective of 'a train heading west'.[26] The song takes it melody and lyrical structure from the British ballad 'Lord Franklin', opening with a narrator who falls asleep while travelling and dreams a dream about a haunting loss. In the case of 'Lord Franklin' the dream concerns a doomed

Arctic voyage which led to the disappearance of John Franklin's ship in Baffin Bay in the 1840s. The narrator longs for the return of Franklin and the sense of wholeness such a reunion will bring. In 'Bob Dylan's Dream', the narrator mourns the loss of a past in which time could be spent easily with friends. The song thus narrates the passing of time on various levels: the passing of time in the company of friends; the passing of the years that have caused the loss of such moments; and life as a journey that separates us from home, the past, friends and family, and that threatens the impossibility of return. In 'Lord Franklin', the lover longs for the return of the beloved; in Dylan's song it is the narrator who longs to return. The differences are not great, amounting to little more, perhaps, than expressions of longing for reunion articulated from different poles.

As many have noted, Dylan sounded like an old man from early in his career, although Dylan himself would express doubt as to whether he could inhabit the material he was performing.[27] Referring to his performance of 'Don't Think Twice, It's All Right' on *The Freewheelin' Bob Dylan* (1963), he said, 'It's a hard song to sing. I can sing it sometimes, but I ain't that good yet. I don't carry myself yet the way that Big Joe Williams, Woody Guthrie, Leadbelly and Lightnin' Hopkins have carried themselves. I hope to be able to someday, but they're older people.'[28]

Dylan would subsequently mock his earlier pretensions in the 1964 song 'My Back Pages', with the claim that 'I was so much older then / I'm younger than that now.' Four decades later, in *Chronicles*, he would joke about the annoyance caused when people wanted him to be more like 'the old him', by which they invariably meant the younger him, the 'folk poet' and 'voice of a generation' that so many had projected onto him (C, 138).[29] For Mark Polizzotti, it is only on the classic mid 1960s albums, particularly *Highway 61 Revisited*, that Dylan sounds youthful: 'Earlier, Dylan had claimed to be "younger than that now," but the age-old weariness persisted, not really dissipating until he found his way back to his R&B roots.'[30] Yet for all the youthful fire and modernist challenge, these albums maintained a representation of a remembered and imagined landscape that could only have come as a projection of the past. This was particularly notable in the title of *Highway 61 Revisited*. Recalling the significance of this particular highway in *Chronicles*, Dylan writes:

Highway 61, the main thoroughfare of the country blues, begins about where I came from . . . Duluth to be exact. I always felt like I'd started on it, always had been on it and could go anywhere from it, even down into the deep Delta country. It was the same road, full of the same contradictions, the same one-horse towns, the same spiritual ancestors. The Mississippi River, the bloodstream of the blues, also starts up from my neck of the woods. I was never too far away from it. It was my place in the universe, always felt like it was in my blood. (*C*, 240–1)

Polizzotti quotes Dylan's account and emphasises *Highway 61 Revisited* as an album steeped in this mythology of place and autobiography, noting the highway's connection to the migration of jazz, blues and early rock 'n' roll:

The road trip of *Highway 61 Revisited* encompasses all of these registers, musical, mythical and autobiographical. It is a circular journey, striking out for new territory only to loop back and reconnect with old roots. It takes us from top to bottom and back again, from the frenzied urban rock of Minneapolis (en route to New York) to the midnight blues of Clarksdale, from Great Northern pretension to South of the Border dissolution.[31]

When Dylan speaks about Robert Johnson in *Chronicles*, he mentions 'Highway 61 Revisited' as an example of his attempt to claim the mythological sense of place he heard in the work of the great blues player (*C*, 288). Intriguingly, he also picks this moment to mention the effect that Arthur Rimbaud had on him, not least a key phrase of identity displacement he found in one of the poet's letters, 'Je est un autre' (I is an other). Rimbaud is added to Johnson, Guthrie and Brecht in Dylan's list of influences: '[Rimbaud's words] went right along with Johnson's dark night of the soul and Woody's hopped-up union meeting sermons and the "Pirate Jenny" framework. Everything was in transition and I was standing in the gateway' (*C*, 288). This mixture helps to explain the range of references we find in Dylan's song texts, peopling the mythological landscape in which the narratives take place. Of 'Tombstone Blues', Polizzotti observes: 'A mix of historical, fictional, mythical, and musical figures, the protagonists of "Tombstone Blues" intermingle to form a world at once recognizable and wholly alien, an outsized American landscape made up not only of our daily reality, but also of out myths, dreams, cultural archetypes, and barely formed nightmares.'[32]

For Polizzotti, Dylan's music frequently evokes place; the long songs of the mid-1960s are like 'a road stretching infinitely ahead', while the harmonica on 'It Takes A Lot To Laugh . . .' '[adds] strokes of its own to the landscape rolling by, stretching like the plains or whipping like a sudden crosswind'.[33] I would further suggest that there is a freight train-like quality to 'Most Likely You Go Your Way And I'll Go Mine' on *Blonde on Blonde*, where the instrumental blasts between some verses have a similar effect to that described by Polizzotti; here, too, Al Kooper's organ gives a sense of the eerie expanse of the plains. There are also paradoxes: in 'Desolation Row', for example, are we hearing the city or the countryside? Looking back from the perspective of November 1969, having recorded the rural-sounding *John Wesley Harding* (1968) and country-inflected *Nashville Skyline* (1969), Dylan could describe 'Desolation Row' as a 'city song', coming from 'that kind of New York period when all the songs were just "city songs"'. This was possibly due to the influence of Allen Ginsberg: 'His poetry is city poetry. Sounds like the city.'[34] Polizzotti, for his part, claims that 'Desolation Row' presents 'a city of the mind', but one nevertheless recognisable as New York. However, the sound is not nearly so 'urban', the track being notable for its lack of electric instruments or urban blues form:

> 'Desolation Row' is the soundtrack to an imaginary western, with its sepia tones, flimsy prop saloons, and corpses in the dust. . . . In [it] Dylan dredges up all the haunting visions and ghosts of childhood and adulthood, the monsters that once lived in his closet and now populated his dreams. By setting it to a musical motif so rich in resonance for those who, like him, grew up with the cowboy myths, he found a sound to match his night terrors.[35]

Perhaps these were those 'same distant places' that Dylan was to hear in Charlie Daniels's music, or the 'old, weird America' or 'undiscovered country' that Greil Marcus would write about in *Invisible Republic*. Marcus notes the mixture of familiarity and unfamiliarity in the 'basement tapes' sessions of 1967:

> The music carried an aura of familiarity, of unwritten traditions, and as deep a sense of self-recognition, the recognition of a self – the singer's? the listener's? – that was both historical and sui generis. The music was funny and comforting; at the same time it was strange, and somehow incomplete. Out of some odd displacement of art and time, the music seemed both transparent and inexplicable.[36]

Hearing the whole of the tapes, Marcus suggests, is like discovering a map: 'but if they are a map, what country, what lost mine, is it that they center and fix?'[37] Marcus is keenly attuned to the idea of positing memories in this landscape as a device for recalling the past. He describes the influence of Harry Smith's *Anthology of American Folk Music* (1952) on the folk imaginary of the time and notes the influence on his own work of Robert Cantwell's essay, 'Smith's Memory Theater'.[38] At the same time, Marcus seems suspicious of nostalgia and wants to rescue Dylan's *Basement Tapes* and early 1990s albums from any such accusations, emphasising the uncanny nature of the world to which Dylan looks back. Marcus's use of the term seems to understand nostalgia as a yearning for a *comfortable* home, which is only partly the case. Another type of nostalgia, which Svetlana Boym terms 'reflective nostalgia', is the type that connects itself to lost (or missed) causes and the imagining of alternative futures.[39] It seems to be heralded when Marcus, in the transition from Kenneth Rexroth's 'old free America' to his own 'old, weird America', speaks of 'the inevitable betrayals that stem from the infinite idealism of American democracy': there too in the 'infamy on the landscape' that Dylan mentions in the liner notes to his 1993 album *World Gone Wrong*.[40]

By the end of the 1960s, the first serious studies of rock music were appearing and Dylan's work featured prominently among them, reflecting his growing pop stardom and the value being placed on his art and his enigma. Certain themes predominated: Dylan's conversion to electric music after being the darling of the folk revival; his acceptance of what certain of his erstwhile fans saw as the vulgarity and social irresponsibility of pop music; a high exposure to mind-altering drugs; an exhausting tour schedule and hostile crowd reaction; and his disappearance from public view following a motorcycle accident. While there had been those eager to interpret Dylan's work at more than face value from almost the start of his career, it was the trilogy of albums he released in 1965–6 – *Bringing It All Back Home*, *Highway 61 Revisited* and *Blonde on Blonde* – that secured him both pop stardom and a place in an emerging rock canon that he helped show the possibility of. The silence following this high creative spurt allowed many to catch up on what he had managed to do with popular music while his subsequent re-emergence as a chronicler of religious, spiritual, mystical and emotional Americana only heightened the air of mystery around him. As he seemed forever to retreat from what he had unleashed, so many of his fans sought to reclaim it, leading to what *Rolling Stone* magazine once referred to as 'the tender madness of Dylanology'.[41] Few people who have studied Dylan's initial emergence into the world of popular music would disagree that he was able to construct himself, in a very successful manner, into the character(s) he wanted the world to see. As Stephen Scobie writes,

> If we read 'Bob Dylan' not as a person but as a textual system, it is a great advantage that Bob Dylan (or should we here say, Robert Zimmerman) has exhibited an exceptionally high degree of self-consciousness in his collaboration in that creation. Any author who adopts a pseudonym is, by that very gesture, foregrounding the writing of his life as a text. The assumed name is a kind of mask: 'It's Halloween', Dylan announced to a New York audience on October 31, 1964. 'I have my Bob Dylan mask on.'[42]

Perhaps he was no longer able to keep the mask in place by the time he 'crashed out' less than two years later. Whatever the reason, the very real, physical disappearance on Dylan's part has, I think, a parallel in the material he released and performed prior to his accident. As Dylan starts to deconstruct himself and to seemingly head towards self-destruction, so he becomes accessible in a new way to his fans. This comes about via the contrast between the collective conscience and the individual consciousness, a contrast that seems to become explicit in *Blonde on Blonde*. Dylan's protest music ('Blowin' in the Wind', 'Masters of War') and generational music ('The Times They Are A-Changin', 'Like a Rolling Stone') both appeal to a kind of collective conscience, be it association with the injustices of the world or identification with a nowness born of the pop world, the knowledge that 'something's happening' and, unlike the subject of 'Ballad of a Thin Man' you *do* know what it is. Consciousness, more evidently perhaps than conscience, can be shared – indeed it needs to be shared for a mass media product like *Blonde on Blonde* to work – but it can also involve a more individual response. It offers the possibility of a move inward and therefore sets up a number of paradoxes. For example, as Dylan's fame grows and with it his grip on the social interactive possibilities of his music, so he seems to attempt to withdraw from view, an implosion that finds a temporary conclusion with the eighteen month gap between *Blonde on Blonde* and *John Wesley Harding*, as Greil Marcus notes 'an unimaginable disappearance in the pop calculus of the time.'[43] Paralleling this is an inward direction in the lyrics and musical style. The paradox produced by this inner searching – an investigation into what can be done with lyric, voice and musical accompaniment in the rock sphere – is that the result is a music that blossoms outwards in possibilities. The more the 'message' of the whole lyrical/musical element becomes less explicit, so the possibilities for the listener open up. The 'death of the author', as Roland Barthes was to proclaim in 1968, entails the 'birth of the reader',[44] and Dylan's 'death', exacerbated by his seclusion following his accident, arguably allowed this to happen to a greater extent than hitherto witnessed; it seems no coincidence that the first serious analyses of Dylan's work start to emerge during this period. A space is opened up from *Blonde on Blonde* onwards, never completely available in Dylan's previous work, for the 'reader' to become involved in the creative process. This is a process echoed in other areas of popular music of the time such as that of the Beatles, the Beach Boys, Joni Mitchell, Van Morrison and so on, as well as in the emerging field of rock criticism where reviewing music becomes as much part of the cultural process of appreciating music as the records themselves.

In 1969 Dylan was featured in a number of the articles collected by Jonathan Eisen and published as *The Age of Rock: Sounds of the American Cultural Revolution*.[45] The collection makes explicit the seriousness with which commercial popular music was being taken in North America and Europe by this time, a seriousness that paralleled rock's growing artistic ambitions (signalled, as much as anything, by the use of the term 'rock' in distinction to 'pop') and which showcased the genre's supposed maturity. The term 'age of rock' could be seen to refer to the 'coming of age' of the genre as much as to the era in which it had become a dominant form. Included in the book were serious analyses of artists such as the Rolling Stones and the Beatles (including Richard Poirier's classic 'Learning from the Beatles'), the Doors, James Brown and Frank Zappa; essays on genres such as country, jazz, blues, folk and soul; historical and contextual accounts of the rise of the counterculture; and aesthetically focused work, such as Richard Meltzer's 'The Aesthetics of Rock'. Many of the references to Dylan emphasised his role in bringing rock to maturity and, even though he had been in the public eye for a relatively short period of time, his maturity as an artist. In a piece on *John Wesley Harding*, Jon Landau treats the album as a late work through repeated references to its distinction from early Dylan. For Landau, Dylan's first two albums had presented a singer not yet in control of the older musical and lyrical forms he was attempting but who achieves a 'vocal sophistication and honesty' on the then-new album.[46] Near the conclusion of his article, in a passage that reinforces the notion of rock as a 'serious' art form while also chiming with Barthes's contemporaneous comments on the death of the author, Landau writes:

> What we are forced to see on *JWH* is Bob Dylan growing up.. . . On this album Dylan's songs are no longer just him, they are separate identities which exist apart from their author. And we see Dylan moving toward an identity of himself as a classical artist, not as just a pop artist.. . . [W]e are also beginning to see a Dylan who is prepared more than ever to accept uncertainty, to give up the search for the finite, a Dylan who no longer feels that each of his songs must tell us everything he knows. He is prepared to look at the pieces of reality, and let the miller tell his tale.[47]

In another piece collected in *The Age of Rock*, the musicologist Wilfrid Mellers describes a similar development from early to late Dylan while also asserting a connection to 'classical' art music by comparing Dylan and the Beatles to John Cage and Morton Feldman. At one point Mellers challenges a concern that some critics had voiced about Dylan's loss of authenticity as a singer who had moved from acoustic folk protester to electric pop star:

> It's easy to say that Dylan's recent discs, employing electrically amplified guitar instead of the natural folk guitar and sometimes calling for the souped-up, big-band sound, corrupt his folk-like authenticity. Sometimes this is true, sometimes it isn't; and it is surely more, not less, 'natural' for a folk singer living in an electronic age to exploit, rather than to spurn, electronic techniques. The folk purists are also the escapists; Dylan has proved that it is possible to be a myth-hero and an artist at the same time, and to carry the integrity of the folk rural folk artist into the world of mechanization.[48]

Mellers's points relate to his larger thesis concerning renewal in American music, as detailed in his *Caliban Reborn* (1968), from which Eisen extracted this contribution. There, and in a later book on Dylan and American vernacular music, Mellers presents an artist who is often caught in a dialectic of innocence and experience that maps on to the real and mythological landscapes in which his music takes form and from which it takes its inspiration. Mellers returns frequently to the 'Edenic' in Dylan's work, hearing it as a quality in Dylan's writing and singing voice and also in his harmonica playing.[49]

To the valley below

A bewilderment of time and place can be found in Dylan's projects between the basement tapes sessions (1967) and the solo albums of the 1990s, especially in the confessional memory projects of the mid-1970s, *Blood on the Tracks* (1975), *Desire* (1976) and *Street Legal* (1978). Speaking in 1978, Dylan proffered the opinion that *Blood on the Tracks* differs from earlier work in that 'there's a code in the lyrics and also there's no sense of time. There's no respect for it: you've got yesterday, today and tomorrow all in the same room, and there's very little that you can't imagine not happening'.[50] We could shift the axes of this temporal/spatial conflation to say that here, there and everywhere are taking place at the same time. The opening song, 'Tangled up in Blue', sets the tone by roaming across time and place, suggesting that any attempt to sort the tangle of memories the singer finds himself afflicted by can only ever be provisional and temporary. The lack of fixity is emphasised by the changing personal pronouns of the verses and the tendency for Dylan to rewrite the lyrics in subsequent performances. The personal pronouns shift again in the second track of the album, 'Simple Twist of Fate', as the protagonist changes from 'he' to 'I'. The anguished cry of 'I've never gotten *used to it*' in 'If You See Her Say Hello' stresses involuntary memory while 'I replay the past' focuses on voluntary memory work. This relates to the double nature of the Proustian project whereby the unexpected flash of the past summons a desire to take control of one's history in the hope of taming the power of such flashbacks. 'Shelter from the Storm' imagines 'a place where it's always safe and warm', an appeal to the homely that contrasts with the displacement enacted elsewhere.[51]

Ian Bell, while disputing some critics' claims about the newness of fractured time and place in *Blood on the Tracks*, nevertheless recognises a new formal style emerging with the album. In the 1960s, 'words had poured out of [Dylan] in a near-spontaneous flood. Older, becoming wiser, he tried to canalise emotions by formal means, through tenses and verse structures, in order to find sense in the shapes he gave them'.[52] Dylan's new formal techniques were also noted at the time of the album's release; in his 1975 review, Michael Gray connected the changes to both Dylan's role as an ageing artist and the ageing of rock music:

> It transforms our perception of Dylan – no longer the major artist of the sixties whose decline from the end of that decade froze seminal work like *Blonde On Blonde* into a historic religious object which one chose either to put away in the attic or to revere perhaps at the expense of today's music. Instead, Dylan has legitimised his claim to a creative prowess as vital now as then – a power not, after all, bounded by the one decade he so much affected, but capable of being directed at us effectively for perhaps the next thirty years.

> Changed too must be our blueprint of how rock music moves forward. This has been that artists come and go in relatively short time-spans, with new people emerging to make the major changes. Careers are presumed to peak early and then slide into inevitable decline.[53]

Blood on the Tracks, for Gray, 'demolishes that pattern' by addressing 'our darkness within' and presenting a mature vision in a musical style that remains fresh and vigorous. As such, it can be seen, along with other albums such as Joni Mitchell's *Blue*, to signal a new way of dealing with life experience. Both these albums have become canonised over the ensuing years as among the purest examples of 'confessional' singer-songwriter work. The naturalness of the connection was exemplified in 2013 when the British rock magazine *Uncut* accompanied a cover feature on Mitchell with a list of the '50 greatest singer-songwriter albums', subtitled 'Blood on the Tracklists!'[54] Virtually all the albums featured were explained by reference to some emotional trauma in the singer-songwriter's life.

Dylan, for his part, has been widely quoted as saying that he could not understand how people could enjoy the kind of pain expressed on *Blood on the Tracks*. But the question that needs to be raised in response is whether audiences are enjoying 'his' pain or whether they are taking pleasure in the beautiful objects into which he has transformed it. As listeners we identify with the songs on various levels, including psychological and aesthetic. It is perhaps not so much that we cannot recognise the pain but that we can read it as our own; we might even feel grateful and awed that someone could articulate the pain and suffering of separation and loss so eloquently. We should also be aware of the inevitable gaps between experience, representation and perception. As Seán Burke writes, 'Even given an ideal autobiographical scenario – that of the author who is engaged in a continual and self-reflexive autobiographical writing, a perennial diarist whose only concern is with the act of diarising – there would always be a hiatus, both spatio-temporal and ontological between he who writes, and what is written.' As he goes on to note, 'this is not to say that there is no possibility of commerce between the two subjects – far from it – only that these two subjects cannot be regarded as consubstantial in space and time'.[55] And, as Keith Negus and Michael Pickering point out:

> Poets or songwriters are not simply aware of the prior meaning of what they feel in their hearts and then merely find the words and rhythms to express this feeling. This is a Romantic fallacy. What is felt is mediated by the verse, lyrics, rhythm or beat as a form of creative expression. It is realised in sounds, words and gestures. Psychological states of experience like love or anger are given form by the language and music in which they achieve expression even though they don't consist entirely of this expression. The expression itself partly forms them, in dynamic interaction with known or intuitively sensed inter-emotional states or feelings.[56]

Of course, we would not have to think that Dylan is writing about himself to enjoy the pain he is expressing, so this alone does not contradict what he has said about the enjoyment of pain. But to identify with the pain, whether of another or of oneself, is also a separable act in space and time from the 'enjoyment' of the aesthetic experience.

Blood on the Tracks is an album full of longings, imaginings and memories, peopled by a shifting but interlocking ('tangled') cast of characters. In the opening song, we meet our unreliable narrator 'heading out for the East Coast'; over the course of seven verses, we drift through New Orleans and Delacroix, settling briefly in a basement on Montague Street, only to end up where we started, 'still on the road / Headin' for another joint'. 'The only thing I knew how to do', sings Dylan through his alias, 'Was to keep on keepin' on like a bird that flew.'[57] In the words of Sean Wilentz, 'Tangled up in Blue' was a song 'that took ten years for Dylan to live and two years for him to write'.[58] This description combines a recognition that Dylan was putting himself and his pain into the song with an awareness of the craft that went into the composition both in terms of the lyrical brilliance (attributed by Dylan to new techniques he had discovered through painting) and the musical dynamism of this track and others on the album. It is possible for both performer and audience to lose their place in this music. From the performer's side, this can be witnessed by the number of live recordings in which Dylan loses his way in the lyrics; he also, it should be pointed out, battles his way out of lyrical dilemmas triumphantly and creatively, as can be heard on the alternate recordings of those *Blood on the Tracks* songs that were released on the first official *Bootleg Series* releases in 1991. This disorientation should be seen as part of the 'code' Dylan speaks of, an invitation to engage in a ritualistic setting-aside of everyday time, space and logic. Paul Williams highlights the way that the rhythmic thrust of these songs drives the listener on. Something compels us to follow Dylan into his labyrinth of words and sounds, even at the risk of losing our way. Theme and form support each other as Dylan delivers his sweeping narratives over washes of organ, driving guitar and insistent drumming. There is pleasure in the way Dylan displaces us, handing us the magical constructs of his peculiarly stressed vocals to ponder over as he moves on and away from us, leaving blood on the tracks. Nowhere is this more extravagantly achieved than on 'Idiot Wind', with its spellbinding structure. As Williams wrote of the song, 'Dylan more than ever shows himself master of juxtapositions, connections, quick dissolves and timeless freeze frames.'[59]

The sense of displacement continues on Dylan's subsequent album *Desire* (1976). 'Isis' describes a mystical place not locatable on any particular map, while 'One More Cup of Coffee' hangs its refrain around a mysterious valley, a floating device that again corresponds to no specific geography. Discussing the song, Dylan claimed that it 'wasn't about anything, so this "valley below" thing became the fixture to hang it on. But "valley below" could mean anything.'[60] There is an even more mystical geography evoked in the songs of *Street Legal* (1978), which also fixes itself around floating phrases. Interviewing Dylan shortly after the release of the album, Jonathan Cott quoted a lyric from the

closing song 'Where Are You Tonight?' – 'sacrifice is the code of the road' –
and made an analogy with Dylan's performance practice: 'To die before dying,
shedding your skin, making new songs out of old ones.' Dylan responded by
quoting an earlier song of his: 'That's my mission in life.. . . "He not busy being
born is busy dying".'[61] The Dylan speaking here seems to be the subject of 'She
Belongs to Me', the artist who 'don't look back'.

But shedding skin is a painful business and there is never any guarantee
that the old life will not continue to haunt the new. This is exemplified at
the close of *Desire*, when, after an album of wandering gypsy music and
songs that imagine distant places, we find that what is furthest away and
most impossible to reach is the past. 'Sara', Dylan's hymn of loss to his ex-
wife, is an extended piece of memory work taking in shared experiences
and imbuing the travelling life with a sense of constancy built around the
family. The longing for home and company is strong here and quite different
from the sentiments of the deliberately displaced loner. In *Chronicles*, Dylan
remembers a time at the end of the 1960s where his attempts to live the
quiet family life were constantly being interrupted by the expectations
his fame brought with it and he felt forced to escape from his fans. 'It was
tough moving around – like the Merle Haggard song, "I'm on the run, the
highway is my home." I don't know if Haggard ever had to get his family
out with him, but I know I did. It's a little different when you have to do
that. The landscape burned behind us' (*C*, 120). The song Dylan is quoting
is Haggard's 'I'm A Lonesome Fugitive' (from the 1967 album of the same
name) and suggests that this particular form of displacement is a necessarily
lonesome business: 'I'd like to settle down but they won't let me / a fugitive
must be a rolling stone', and 'he who travels fastest goes alone'. With sacrifice
the 'code of the road', the desired freedom of displacement leads inevitably
to a longing for place. As in Townes Van Zandt's 'Pancho & Lefty', a song
Dylan would occasionally perform on tour, the road's promise can turn out
to be a betrayal as the accumulated experience of displacement hardens
into resignation. Van Zandt's evocative opening verse recalls how 'living on
the road' was going to keep the song's addressee 'free and clean'; experience
changes this sense of freedom and 'Now you wear your skin like iron / and
your breath's as hard as kerosene.' This hardening of the self that is borne of

displacement recalls the sense of discovery in the Stanley Brothers' 'Long Journey Home' and in many of Dylan's songs and proclamations.[62]

The highway of regret

In a revealing passage in *Chronicles*, Dylan describes the way he felt in 1987 as he contemplated his current role in society. In his best Chandleresque, he presents the situation as a case of a missing person:

> I hadn't actually disappeared from the scene but the road had narrowed, almost was shut down and was supposed to be wide open. I hadn't gone away yet. I was lingering out on the pavement. There was a missing person inside of myself and I needed to find him.. . . I felt done for, an empty burned-out wreck. Too much static in my head and I couldn't dump the stuff. Wherever I am, I'm a '60s troubadour, a folk-rock relic, a wordsmith from bygone days, a fictitious head of state from a place nobody knows. I'm in the bottomless pit of cultural oblivion. (*C*, 147)

There was certainly a time when, for many, Dylan was the epitome of the washed-up rock star and each new album, when it eventually came, was greeted with a certain amount of anxiety and hope that this would be a return to 'classic' form. History and critical revisionism have been reasonably kind to Dylan, but many albums and live performances from this period are still seen as sub-par.[63] This, of course, is only to be expected of an artist who has been so musically active over such a long period of time. *Down in the Groove*, the album that was released in 1988 after a lengthy recording process, was critically mauled, while the next studio album *Oh Mercy* (1989) was a success with critics and fans alike, earning Dylan a respectable showing on the album charts internationally. The following year's *Under the Red Sky* disappointed many and seemed to give the lie to an artistic renaissance. Overall, the 1980s can be seen as a period where, in Lee Marshall's words, 'Dylan gradually began to lose the battle with his history.'[64]

With Dylan's public standing see-sawing as he entered his sixth decade, it seemed as though a new approach might be needed. Dylan seems to have sensed, as many of his fans had, that the much-needed fresh start might lay in his past; not as a return to past victories, but rather as a return to those musical worlds he had not felt himself entirely qualified to inhabit as a younger man. The time had come for Dylan to refashion himself as an elder statesman of American vernacular music, an old-time musician. The two solo acoustic albums Dylan released at the start of the 1990s – *Good as I Been to You* (1992) and *World Gone Wrong* (1993) – worked as a palette cleansing exercise, ushering in a 'real' late Dylan that had been suggested for many years, arguably from the very beginning of his career. Although in many ways, nothing much had changed, it suddenly became possible to see this promised elder Dylan more clearly as he took on the mantle of the blues and folk singers of whom he had spoken at the time of *The Freewheelin' Bob Dylan*, those he had seen as carrying themselves in a way he couldn't at that time muster. As Bill Flanagan writes of Dylan's version of 'Delia' (on *World Gone Wrong*), 'His world-worn voice reveals the cracks behind his stoicism in a way that this most unsentimental of singers would never allow in his lyrics. The weight of nobility and loss are as appropriate to this older Dylan's singing as anger and hunger are to the snarl of his youth.' And as Sean Wilentz writes, building on Flanagan's review, the weight and gallantry to be found on *World Gone Wrong* 'had belonged to the blues from the start; it just took Dylan a half century of living his own life for him to be able to express it this way.'[65] Near the start of this chapter I quoted Dylan claiming that he had been born a long way from where he was supposed to be and that he was therefore on his way home. The arrival at a point of expression that he had shown the possibility of so many years before might be seen as being as close to reaching this mythical place as Dylan ever gets. Making reference to the final lines sung by Dylan on *World Gone Wrong* – 'The same hand that led me through scenes most severe / Has kindly assisted me home' – Wilentz suggests that, as Dylan 'reached the end of the beginning of his own artistic reawakening', he 'reached a place that at least felt more like home.'[66]

Time Out of Mind, Dylan's critically revered 1997 album, distils many of the points raised in this chapter in a manner hitherto unseen in Dylan's work. This is partly because the album came at a late stage in Dylan's career, where the *Erfahrung*, or accumulated data, of his experience and that of his audience couldn't fail to flavour the songs with certain meanings. But it is also due to its emphasis on memory places, displacement, references to earlier work, haunting, the need to escape from ghosts and even, in the album's epic closing song 'Highlands', the refusal of memory. The opening song 'Love Sick' refers to 'streets that are dead', to a window, a meadow and the old staple 'the road'. 'Dirt Road Blues' is named after a typical vernacular memory site and also mentions a 'one room country shack' and a more ambiguous 'up above'. 'Standing in the Doorway' is a song situated, like 'One Too Many Mornings' at a site of indecision (should one leave or go back inside?) and speaks of doorways, yards, the outdoors under the moon and stars, and 'the dark land of the sun'. 'Tryin' to Get to Heaven' lists locations such as 'the skies', 'the high muddy river', 'the middle of nowhere', Heaven, Missouri, 'that lonesome valley', the road, the river, New Orleans, Baltimore, Sugartown and a world that the narrator has 'been all around'. The world is broadened to include London and Paris in 'Not Dark Yet', a song that also speaks of rivers and the sea. 'Can't Wait' includes reference to 'the lonely graveyard of my mind' and to 'somewhere back there along the line', while the album's closing song 'Highlands' mixes references to Scottish locations with others to streets, borders, lakes, home, 'the same old cage' and 'over the hills and far away'.[67]

The effect of naming so many places relies on a sense of the narrator having inhabited them and this is something Dylan achieves successfully on *Time Out of Mind*. In Greil Marcus's words, these are 'newly composed songs that . . . can sound older than Bob Dylan or the person listening will ever be'.[68] Remembering Dylan's own comments about 'the old him', it is worth considering to what extent the young-old Dylan of the early recordings has returned here, now able to carry himself in the way he earlier desired when discussing 'Don't Think Twice It's Alright'. Again, Dylan relies on the floating signifiers of experience that linger as spectral remains of earlier songs, both his and those of others. In 'Tryin' to Get to Heaven', he employs the lines 'been around the world' and 'train don't carry no gamblers', the former found in countless songs and the latter familiar from Woody Guthrie's 'This Train'. The 'highway of regret' in 'To Make You Feel My Love' not only conflates memory with place, but also sets up a contrast with the claim to move 'down the road and not give a damn' on the earlier 'Restless Farewell'. It also echoes the Stanley Brothers song 'Highway of Regret', recalls the 'lost highway' of Hank Williams's mournful 1949 song and chimes with the revisited Highway 61 of Dylan's 1965 album. Paul Williams centres his justification of *Time Out of Mind* as a song cycle on the emphasis on movement and distance. He points out the references to walking in a number of the songs, to being left behind or lost in others. The folk and blues songs Dylan quotes rely on similar notions and construct a world of movement. As Williams observes, 'It's like he's living in a garden built of folksong lyrics.'[69] Mikal Gilmore also uses a spatial metaphor when suggesting that *Time Out of Mind* is 'a trek through the unmapped frontier that lies beyond loss and disillusion'.[70]

Experience is further evoked by the sense of haunting that many of the songs carry, from the musically and lyrically stark 'Love Sick' through the claim, in ''Til I Fell in Love with You', that 'I've seen too much'. In 'Standing in the Doorway' the singer notes that 'the ghost of our old love has not gone away' and the song is haunted by fragments of past songs ('in the doorway crying', 'I'll eat when I'm hungry / drink when I'm dry'). The homecoming described in 'Cold Irons Bound' is compromised by the realisation that the 'fields have turned brown', a line that signals that the singer is haunted by the past (and the Stanley Brothers, from whose 'The Fields Have Turned Brown' the line emanates). In 'Tryin' to Get to Heaven' a different note is sounded: 'every day your memory grows dimmer / it don't haunt me like it did before'. But the song is still haunted by a history given away by the lyrics: 'walkin' that lonesome valley', 'going down the road feelin' bad', 'goin' down the river', 'been all around the world, boys', 'some trains don't pull no gamblers / no midnight ramblers', 'been to Sugartown'. The overall effect is of a weariness brought on by over-experience, hence, perhaps, why the singer is no longer haunted: to mourn is to be alive. In 'Not Dark Yet', shadows are falling and time is running away: 'there's not even room enough to be anywhere'. Again, experience is claimed ('been to London, been to gay Pa-ree'), but lessons have not been learned: 'I can't even remember what it was I came here to get away from'. As Jon Pareles noted on the release of the album, 'The voice of a generation has become a voice of experience, telling us that experience hasn't taught him anything he needs.' While the folk and blues artists to whom Dylan looked for inspiration 'offered their survival as reassurance', on this album Dylan 'refuses listeners that solace'.[71]

'Highlands' echoes a number of these themes while also presenting a kind of refusal of memory. The narrator is 'drifting from scene to scene', seeing 'big white clouds / like chariots that swing down low', and feeling 'further away than ever before': 'the party's over / and there's less and less to say / I've got new eyes / everything looks far away'. Greil Marcus compares the song to 'Like a Rolling Stone' and *Highway 61 Revisited*, suggesting that it reflects the loss of the territory that that album mapped and describing its overall mood as 'spectral'.[72] Displacement here is more to do with escaping from ghosts than witnessing them. If home in *Time Out of Mind* is often associated with memories and a lack of agency, 'Highlands' is notable for its refusal of homecoming, venturing further and further out, not unlike the outward-spiralling story emanating from the inability to remember in 'Brownsville Girl' (from the 1986 album *Knocked Out Loaded*). Yet, 'Highlands' is as contradictory as any Dylan text; in its narrator's claim not to 'do sketches from memory' even as he is providing one, it is nothing less than a refusal to be where one already is.

As Dylan's major studio work of the 1990s, *Time Out of Mind* provided more than ample evidence that he was far from being a washed-up artist. Even better, the album seemed to usher in a period of heightened creativity in the form of subsequent albums *"Love and Theft"* and *Modern Times*. When artists produce consecutive releases such as this (even when considerable time elapses between them) there is a tendency to place them into series, of which the 'trilogy' is a particularly favoured category. To a certain extent it did feel, in 2006, that Dylan had produced a classic trilogy of 'late period' albums, one worthy of comparison with the trilogies of the mid-1960s (*Bringing It All Back Home, Highway 61 Revisited, Blonde on Blonde*) and mid-1970s (*Blood on the Tracks, Desire, Street Legal*). Neat conceptualisations such as this enable us to idealise and realise our relationship with artists' *ouevres* and to apply explanatory narratives to them. Obviously, life doesn't tend to work in trilogies or neat temporal categories and so it is no surprise to find that Dylan was doing much else besides releasing these albums. By this point it had become relatively common to focus on what he was doing alongside or outside his main studio projects. Magazines, websites and fan forums by Dylanologists kept the curious up to date with Dylan's live work and contributions to other projects (collaborative albums, guest slots, film soundtrack contributions),

while Paul Williams's book trilogy *Bob Dylan: Performing Artist* provided a
compelling alternative history of Dylan's songs from the 1960s to the early
2000s (Williams would provide a similar service for fans of Neil Young by
presenting a history of the artist that relied heavily on alternative, bootlegged
performances). Curious Dylan fans had been able to access bootlegged
recordings for decades, the most collectable of all being the 'Basement Tapes',
the music Dylan made with The Band while hibernating in Woodstock in
1967. The desire for 'unofficial' Dylan was acknowledged in part by his record
company by the release, in 1985, of the *Biograph* box set, which contained a
number of then-unreleased recordings. A fuller treatment of the unreleased
catalogue came in 1991 with the multi-disc set *The Bootleg Series Volumes
1–3 [Rare & Unreleased] 1961–1991*, a collection which confirmed, for many,
the notion that some of Dylan's best work had been left off his albums. These
collections reasserted Dylan's historical importance and the length and quality
of his career. The 1991 collection provided a particularly useful narrative, with
the recordings arranged chronologically and the booklet providing a visual
biography of the artist. In the vinyl version, each of the five record sleeves
provides a snapshot of a different Dylan: the shorter-haired young folksinger
in worker's shirt; the cool, aloof subject of the 'Subterranean Homesick Blues'
film clip; the soft-bearded family man of the Woodstock years; the grizzled,
long-haired rocker of the middle years; the almost anonymous hooded man
of the late 1980s and early 1990s.[73] Here, in short, was a reminder of some of
the multiple Dylans that had been offered to the public over three decades.
Subsequent releases in the ongoing 'Bootleg Series' have offered yet more
revelations, as have the studio albums Dylan has continued to release. Each
brings with it a wave of anticipation and critical evaluation and opportunities
for retrospection. As Ian Bell writes, in a discussion of the 2012 album *Tempest*
placed near the end of his second volume of Dylan biography, the critical
discourse around Dylan can seem to have run short of available positions:

> At this stage in the game the stock of superlatives is almost exhausted.. . .
> The habit of asserting that album A is the 'best since' album B might do for a
> five-year pop career, but not for a career more than half a century long, one
> tangled up in arguments that often have nothing to do with music. In the
> case of *Tempest* the 'best since' yardstick would be extended, regardless, even

unto *Blonde on Blonde*. You would be better off talking instead of Picasso in his final years of raging turmoil, remaking Old Masters obsessively, mocking death, locked in a combat with age and libido. You will not have said much about Dylan's album, but you will have located the territory.[74]

Bell is keen to dispel the myths of the 'best since' or the culmination. Even so, the description on the back of his biography speaks of an artistic renaissance 'that culminated in 2012's acclaimed *Tempest*' and describes a book that tells 'the story of the latest, perhaps the last, of the many Bob Dylans'. It seems that many of us who write about living icons such as Dylan are drawn to the idea of culmination even as we are unable to witness it due to the simple fact that our subject's story is still unfolding (and will continue to do so for some time after he and we have gone). The sense of culmination is also a vital part of the narratives created by record companies, for whom the marketing of new releases is invariably connected to a 'best since' yardstick. When, in late 2014, Sony released a lavish 'complete edition' of the fabled 'Basement Tapes' as the latest installation of *The Bootleg Series*, the sense of teleology was as strong as ever. The Basement Tapes were where the bootlegging of Dylan had begun in earnest; perhaps the end lay, as T. S. Eliot had once claimed, in the beginning. At the same time it was obvious that this would no more be 'the end' than any other archival or new studio recording; the box set, after all, contained a flyer for the upcoming album *Shadows in the Night*.

Dylan adopted the role of DJ for XM Satellite Radio, presenting 100 shows of *Theme Time Radio Hour* between 2006 and 2009. The shows, as suggested in the title, were each based on a particular theme; indicative examples include 'Weather', 'Drinking', 'Friends & Neighbors', 'Death & Taxes' and, particularly notable for the current book, 'Young & Old' and 'Time'. *Theme Time Radio Hour* gave Dylan's fans another character, or persona, to get to know, while reinforcing his position as a living archive of old, obscure, classic or plain weird vernacular music. Dylan took on his role of curator of the old and obscure in a manner similar to predecessors such as Harry Smith and Moses Asch and peers like John Fahey, all of whom were known to mix high and low registers, applying classical philosophy to vernacular American music. Dylan's role as DJ highlights an aspect that can be found throughout his career, namely his debt to sounded experience. It is as if the American landscape and soundscape were what taught Dylan about life, after which he used that 'experience' to create and curate a vision of America back to itself and to the wider world. Here, experience equates to learning, making a mockery of those clichés which oppose the two terms ('the university of life', 'the school of hard knocks' and so on). At the same time, Dylan perpetuates some of those same clichés through his early rejection of higher education and his references to learning from real life and the road. But his is also a studied form of experience; he may have quit the University of Minnesota as a youth but be conducted plenty of research in the various documents of American folklore available to him in the early 1960s and continued to combine lettered and sounded experience throughout his career. Dylan's work is saturated in the cultural products and references available to a curious, connected North American in the mid- to late twentieth century. As he once said, 'those old songs are my lexicon'.[75]

As already discussed, Dylan's use of the past extends to his music, which has always borrowed from older, mostly American styles. This becomes ever more notable with the late albums, where folk fragments and whole lines from other texts appear in Dylan's songs. This was seemingly recognised in the quotation marks placed around the title of *"Love and Theft"*, the album with which Dylan followed *Time Out of Mind* in 2001; the title itself was borrowed (or stolen) from the title of a book by Eric Lott on blackface minstrelsy. By the release of *Modern Times* in 2006, it had become a common practice among some listeners to start posting details online of the sources Dylan had supposedly raided to write his songs. Others were merely content to appreciate the ways in which Dylan's lexicon of songs blended old and new, as when 'Ain't Talkin' continued a reference begun in 'To Make You Feel My Love' by using lines from the Stanley Brothers' 'Highway of Regret', or when 'Workingman Blues #2' tipped a hat towards the title of a Merle Haggard song. The process of combining old and new continued with subsequent albums *Together through Life* (2009) and *Tempest* (2012). With the title track of *Tempest*, Dylan approached an old staple of folk balladry, the disaster ballad, by writing an epic account of the doomed voyage of the Titanic one century earlier. As Ian Bell notes:

> Dylan's hyper-awareness of history as an active presence has been one of the distinguishing features of his 'late period'. It explains many, if not all, of his acts of alleged plagiarism. But as interesting as the awareness of the past

is the use to which he has put his understanding. Rarely does he content himself with the facts. For him everything has a mythical dimension.[76]

For Bell this makes 'Tempest' (the song) a disappointment in that it only provides 'the facts' and offers little of the mythology, strangeness and wisdom that we have come to expect from Dylan's late work. The song is 'too self-conscious, even obvious, as an excursion into the folk tradition'.[77] This is a convincing critique, though I believe we can still see 'Tempest' as an impressive example of Dylan's late voice for at least two reasons. One would be the sheer relentlessness and inevitability of the song narrative; it certainly serves as a reminder of the many previous (and often relentless) ballads and blues performed in response to the Titanic disaster, but if it doesn't go much further than its predecessors in terms of mythological detail, its sheer length seems to provide a *non plus ultra* of the doomed ship dirge.[78] Another reason would be Dylan's singing voice, which exceeds the occasionally confining narrative to take on something of the qualities of the scenes it depicts. The weathered vocal ploughs an almost straight course through the sea of instrumentation: 'almost' because it is the occasional surging and pitching of the voice in relation to the predominant gentle sway of the music that provides the emotional contact points. Or, because voice and music blend so well, we might think of Dylan's voice as the sea – constant but unpredictable – into which we as listeners are invited to submerge ourselves.[79] More than ever, Dylan's voice in later years offers both caresses and opportunities to explore the deep folds of lived experience. Michael Gray speaks of Dylan 'evoking . . . desolation by vocal caress' in his late work; following my own sea metaphor, I think here too of Hart Crane's poem 'Voyages': 'there is a line / You must not cross nor ever trust beyond it / Spry cordage of your bodies to caresses / Too lichen-faithful from too wide a breast. / The bottom of the sea is cruel.'[80] The lived experience is both Dylan's – it is the folds of his voice, after all, into which we direct our ears – and, as lettered or sounded knowledge, that of others who have gone before. 'Tempest' offers reportage on the fates of the Titanic's passengers, but also on all of those who have previously been drawn to tell those passengers' stories and to draw lessons from them. The song may attach itself closely to folk tradition and style, as other Dylan songs do to blues or rockabilly traditions and styles, but it does so in ways which still illuminate the passing of time and tell us something of the role of the narrator in late song forms, and of persistence and continuation too. Dylan's voice, at this point, can claim the sea's victory rather than the ship's defeat: it abides. Further poignancy is provided when, on *Tempest*, the title song is followed by the closing track, 'Roll on John', another tale of a doomed subject that uses a narration of sounded experience. The 'John' is John Lennon and the lyrics are taken from song lyrics and stories associated with Lennon and the Beatles; its hero is doomed but the singer's main message is the desire to 'roll on' and 'shine a light'.[81]

In addition to the now common positing of Dylan's 'love and theft' of earlier material as part of the 'folk process', it is also worth noting Robert Polito's argument that Dylan is engaged in a modernist project of rearranging fragments. Polito compares Dylan's creative use of Civil War poet Henry Timrod's work (the source of certain lines in *Modern Times*) to the 'Modernist collages' found in Ezra Pound's *Cantos*, T.S. Eliot's 'The Waste Land' and Frank Bidart's 'The Second Hour of the Night', as well as to the more recent musical practice of sampling, as found in hip hop. Polito thus suggests that a pun can be found in the title of *Modern Times* itself, connecting the work to the modernist practice of revering the past by splintering it and creating from it something that had never existed before.[82] For my part, while I agree with Polito that Dylan has used his 'conversations with his dead' to create 'daring and original' work, I also think that this perspective of Dylan as modernist can be looped back onto the 'folk process' argument to argue that those earlier folk, blues and other vernacular singers, songwriters and interpreters were also involved in modernist undertakings. This is nicely encapsulated in Greil Marcus's analysis of old-time musician Dock Boggs, already quoted in Chapter 2; Boggs's art was 'modernist because the music was about the choices you made in a world a disinterested God had plainly left to its own devices, where you were thrown completely back on yourself, a world where only art or revolution, the symbolic remaking of the world, could take you out of yourself'.[83]

The lessons of life can't be learned in a day

Dylan's connection to Henry Timrod is a reminder of Dylan's considerable interest in the American Civil War, and in history more generally. In 2002 he recorded a song for Robert Maxwell's Civil War film *Gods and Generals* (2003). Whether heard in the context of the film or not, 'Cross the Green Mountain' operates as a powerful expression of lateness and wisdom, of lessons learned after great tragedies and lived lives. It is full of striking lines, such as 'I dreamt a monstrous dream' or 'the last day's last hour / of the last happy year' and also shows Dylan's continued interest in multiple narrative perspectives.[84] It is framed by a historical narrative, told in the past tense, in which a first-person narrator tells of resting by a stream and dreaming a 'monstrous dream', recalling the opening of 'Bob Dylan's Dream' and 'Lord Franklin' in which the narrator 'dreamed a dream'.[85] Like those songs, the dream involves a person or persons absent from the narrator's life, or possibly a former self; among the numerous possible readings of the song, a tale of lovers parted by war is one possibility, a dying soldier looking back on the recent past another. Unlike the earlier songs, the bulk of the story within the dream is narrated in the present tense, providing an immediacy to the events unfolding; the narrative mostly alludes to the American Civil War (although the allusion mostly stems from the association of the song with Maxwell's film), so these events become a kind of war reportage. Narrative confusion is increased when, late in the song, the lines 'but he'll be better soon / he's in a hospital bed' are immediately followed by 'he'll never be better / he's already dead'; the narrator seems to be reporting one set of facts (the delivery of a letter in which the initially reassuring words are presented, showing the information that the letter's recipient has) and immediately contradicting them by reporting what he knows to be true, sharing this superior information with us, so that singer and listeners are able to stand outside the world of the other characters in the narrative.

Ultimately, it is not so much what the song means exactly (though there has been plenty of online activity in trying to determine that) but rather the general mood it evokes. There is an identifiable narrative, making it a clearer song than many that Dylan has previously recorded. But there are still enigmatic lines that leap out of the narrative and suggest other songs, what the jazz composer and theorist William Parker calls 'inside songs'.[86] Dylan's late work makes abundantly clear that there are practices of composition, performance and interpretation attached to his music that rely on the idea of songs within songs. This has always been the case with Dylan but the late work distils the process to the extent that it seems hardly any of his 'new old' songs should be taken as having any single 'theological' meaning; rather, they are invitations to consider multiple song narratives, mythological unfoldings and voicings of a small but infinitely variable set of fundamental stories and feelings. Following comments attributed to Dylan on his second album, it has often been pointed out that his early song 'A Hard Rain's A-Gonna Fall' was made up of the first lines of several songs he might not have time to write. Whether he has had time in subsequent years to write those songs is unclear; whether he could have, or would have ultimately wanted to, we can never know. But where that early classic (built as it was on the infinitely variable ballad 'Lord Randall') can be seen as an exercise in youthful ambition, a bringing together of epic style, litany and precocious apocalyptic vision, Dylan's later work has leant towards the infinite in a subtler, less peremptory manner. While he has recorded some notable long songs in his late career ('Highlands', 'Cross the Green Mountain', 'Tempest'), they have tended, with the notable exception of 'Highlands', to consist of simple (perhaps deceptively simple) language and meter. There are flashes of surrealism but it is often a folk surrealism (or eccentricity) with roots identifiable in traditional song rather than the new poetic language Dylan forged in the 1960s and 1970s.

Deft control of pacing was always a feature of Dylan's strongest work, whether in 'Hard Rain', 'The Lonesome Death of Hattie Carroll', 'Visions of Johanna', 'Sad-Eyed Lady of the Lowlands', 'Idiot Wind', 'Señor (Tales of Yankee Power)', 'Brownsville Girl', 'Mississippi', 'Cross the Green Mountain' or 'Roll on John'. However, while recordings have captured the 'perfection' of such tracks, they have been open to often radical reinterpretation in live performance and it has been a change of pace as much as anything that has occasionally rendered the songs unrecognisable and, for some listeners, disappointing, with Dylan seeming to be discarding the careful poise of the recorded versions. That said, there have been occasions where Dylan, in late performances, has offered versions of older songs that reinvent them as slower, stretched-out texts that suggest a world weariness (or resignation) that enhances rather than 'spoils' the power the songs already possessed. An example can be found in a 1995 performance of 'Restless Farewell' that comprised Dylan's contribution to a televised celebration of Frank Sinatra's eightieth birthday. While other performers paid tribute by covering songs associated with Sinatra, Dylan performed a song of his own that he had released on his third album in 1964. 'Restless Farewell' had been quite a long song (over five and a half minutes) even in Dylan's early reading. There it is a somewhat fragmented piece, veering between sung verses, jagged guitar picking and blasts of harmonica. In the 1995 reading, the fragmented lines are smoothed out via the application of country instrumentation and additional strings. Dylan plays the song as a slow country glide and, though a bit longer than the earlier performance, it slips by quickly. Dylan now sounds in complete control of the song and seems content to let it play out smoothly and subtly. The way the country fiddle takes off from his voice after the fifth or sixth lines of the last three verses ('but the dark does die', 'but on time you must depend', 'if the arrow is straight') is particularly affecting, as is the way his voice grows in power and volume throughout. The boyish enthusiasm with which he shouts 'Happy Birthday Mr Frank!' at the end seals the deal. The performance was placed at the end of the show, just before a star-studded 'New York New York' in which Dylan did not participate. It therefore seems to act as a farewell from one singer to another; Sinatra was not to make many more appearances in public after this and died in 1998. The knowledge of these two artists' long careers makes the performance particularly moving. Although there is a suggestion that Dylan wrote the lyrics originally in response to stories being circulated about him in the press ('the dirt of gossip' and 'the dust of rumours'), and possibly even with thoughts of giving up public performance, the lyrics attain additional meaning when projected onto Dylan's subsequent career and, through this particular performance, onto Sinatra; many more layers of gossip and rumour have accumulated over those years, after all. The song has an obvious connection to Sinatra's 'My Way', a fact not lost on online commentators.[87] Where the 22-year old Dylan had seemed to be speaking to himself, offering himself some reassurance, the 54-year-old singer seems to be cast in the role of advisor to others, both older (like Sinatra) and younger. The sagacity of the words and the delivery, backed by the quiet assurance of the country musicians, make this particularly effective.

Dylan acknowledged another debt to history in 1997 when he joined Ralph Stanley to sing 'The Lonesome River' for Stanley's collaborative album *Clinch Mountain Country*. Dylan takes on what would have been Carter Stanley's vocal role at the time of the Stanley Brothers' recording by singing the verses, with Ralph Stanley taking the higher harmony in the chorus.[88] Where the Stanleys had originally recorded the song with a trio harmony (using a high baritone to enhance the high register already provided by Ralph's high tenor), the *Clinch Mountain Country* version is sung as a vocal duo. It is fascinating to hear these two late voices – and mutual admirers of each other's work – singing together in a way that does justice to both of them. Neither really sings in a different manner than we are accustomed to hearing, yet their voices blend well together. The song is identifiably bluegrass (or 'old-time mountain music', depending whose terminology one wishes to use), which might be unusual for Dylan. But while the instrumental accompaniment, Stanley's traditional vocal and the song's old-time provenance place the recording firmly in its musical genre, Dylan does not sound like he is trying to be an old-time singer. Rather, what is audible in his vocal performance is a variety of elements that have, for the most part, always been there, albeit that they might have been understated or deployed in different ways. Most notable would be the elongation of certain words and syllables in the line, depending on the rhythm of the particular song; examples in 'The Lonesome River' include 'the *lone*some wind *blooooooooows*', 'I *hear* a voice *caaaaaaaall*', 'the *wo*man I *looooooooove*'. On the solo lines Dylan doesn't stretch the syllables quite as far as Carter Stanley or other bluegrass singers would, but the stretch is still notable; on the choruses, perhaps feeling strengthened or challenged by Stanley, the stretched words are even more obvious. Yet, while syllable stress and elongation is an obvious aspect of bluegrass and old-time singing, both have also always featured in Dylan's vocal art. It is more likely that Dylan's stretching and stressing of syllables would have been put down to 'artiness' while the equally peculiar reshaping of words that takes place in Stanley Brothers' performances would be portrayed as tradition, but both are examples of artifice, of a deliberate estranging of regularly spoken language.

Never ending

In addition to the recordings that form the bulk of the discussion in this chapter, Bob Dylan has, of course, been a prolific concert performer and this aspect of his music has gained considerable attention.[89] The label 'Never Ending Tour' (NET) has been given to the live concerts he and his band have been performing almost continuously since 1988 (the longest pause to date has been the three-month break in 1997 when Dylan was hospitalised for a chest infection). While I have focused mostly on Dylan's recorded work, sustained live performance is an obvious and important aspect of the way in which his public self – which, as Lee Marshall convincingly argues, is the only meaningful self, whether we are thinking of Dylan or ourselves – has been connected to time and history.[90] Marshall suggests that Dylan has entered a kind of timelessness in his later years, caught up as he is in the NET and in the complex recycling of tradition in his recorded work. But if it has become customary to present Dylan as an artist who confounds our sense of time and who blurs the boundaries between youth and age, past and present, Marshall argues that such practices are mainly the result of Dylan's work from *Time Out of Mind* onwards. This seems a fair point, and I have made a similar point by emphasising the late memory work undertaken by Dylan and his exegesists. However, commentary around Dylan has not ignored issues of age and dyschronia (the experience of being out of, or lost in, or having no sense of time), as evidenced by some of the older sources cited earlier in this chapter. For my part, I believe that Dylan has long provided a number of explicit references to dyschronia and that these have been noticed and made significant by fans and other commentators. At the same time I agree that the late work (including the NET, which Marshall discusses at length) has met with a far more pronounced shift towards presenting him as a 'timeless' figure, one in whom past, present and future (not only his, but those of the wider culture he represents) have folded together in stimulating and sometimes confusing ways. One of the consequences of the NET is that audiences get to witness a star both out of time (in that his fame was secured in the 'distant' past of the 1960s) and a living presence going through the labour of constant becoming. Marshall puts this well and his account is worth quoting at length:

> [T]here is some kind of rupture between the performer on stage and the person who wrote the songs. In a sense the person who wrote the songs is long gone, a myth, part of our cultural memory.... The performer we pay to

hear now bears little relation to the guy who supposedly wrote the songs – he doesn't look the same and he certainly doesn't sound the same. The singer may be in front of us, but the songwriter is from another lifetime.

The NET creates a perpetual present, never looking back to the last show, always looking forward to the next. Its past stretches back, if not to a time out of mind, then at least a long way (before some of its audience were born), and it gives the illusion that it will go on forever.

It is worth thinking about the effect of this upon Dylan's stardom. Like musical time, 'star time' also has a chronological dimension – our understanding of a star is never fixed but unfolds in time.. . . One of the effects of the NET has been to alter this experience of star time; in effect, to 'stop' star time. In becoming so firmly intertwined with tradition, Dylan's *stardom*, not just Dylan's music, has taken on this elements of timelessness. He has become, in a curious way, 'immortal'.[91]

I have also considered immortal timelessness in this chapter, though I have still found it useful (as does Marshall in his book) to consider Dylan and his music in conventional chronological terms as well. The narrative pull is still too strong and compelling to do otherwise, for unless we suffer from real dyschronia, the story makes more sense when an attempt is made to place it 'in order' even as past, present and future are blending and blurring together. There is a certain pleasure in attaching a narrative to artists who have affected us, as in the following review of Dylan's *Good as I Been to You* by the singer-songwriter John Wesley Harding which explicitly connects the narrative to the sound of Dylan's voice:

> If we once admired Dylan for his age beyond his years, now we must listen to what that kind of age *really* sounds like. What was charming and old-sounding has become old and phlegm-constricted. What sounded effortless now sounds painful. These are the facts, and they do not stand in the way of making a great record.. . . The beauty of the voice is found in the grain. The shape can tell you more than the purity of the note.. . . To listen to this album is to accept old age – Bob Dylan's and your own.[92]

As Michael Gray notes, Dylan had only recently turned fifty-one when this album was released, so Harding was exaggerating the age factor if not what he heard in the vocals. As Gray himself goes on to say, Dylan's voice had become a lot less supple by the 1990s: 'whereas once Dylan held total control of every syllable-sound he uttered, and "grain" was achieved as much by that control as by direct intensity, now this under-repaired, over-strained and coaldust-choked old steam engine might fall off the rails at any moment'.[93] Marshall, meanwhile, takes the suggestion of Barthes's 'grain of the voice' to an extreme in his own description of Dylan's voice since the 1990s: 'This voice certainly has a grain, a thick, coarse grain with a natural dignity and beauty: the grain of a 400-year-old oak tree, burning with the bark still on.'[94] In such descriptions we see a correlation between Dylan's singing voice and his writer's voice, which is similarly seen as steeped in history. Both voices will have their detractors and devotees but at least Dylan's singing voice is unlikely to be accused of plagiarism now, though it might have been once upon a time. Indeed, as Marshall highlights, it is the singing and speaking voice that seems to reveal personality and to connect those who hear it to the person producing it. As Dylan's voice ages and takes on new textures, so his authority seems to grow and he becomes even more himself. Perhaps the voyage home is the voyage towards that particular voice.

Conclusion

Bob Dylan has traced the tensions of place, displacement, time, age and experience over the course of a remarkably extensive and coherent body of work. These tensions have been enacted sometimes by an insistence on moving on and restlessness, at other times by the projection of one place from another removed but stable place. Connections are forged between highways of regret, highways to move down, lost highways, the possibility of not going back home, the world gone wrong and the feeling of overstaying one's time. Even as places are evoked, so distance from them is affirmed. The sense of displacement also extends to Dylan's response to his fame and to the expectations that come with it. Again, refusal seems to be the defining strategy: distancing himself from the folk music scene he helped to define, distancing himself from the role of 'visionary' and from any particular political stance, distancing himself from his own work and legacy through a constant reinterpretation of his songs. Like his character Alias in Sam Peckinpah's *Pat Garrett & Billy the Kid*, he is always somewhere and someone else.[95] As Greil Marcus writes of Dylan's turn to electric music in the mid-1960s, 'Dylan's performance now seemed to mean that he had never truly been where he had appeared to be only a year before, reaching for that democratic oasis of the heart – and that if he had never been there, those who had felt themselves there with him had not been there.'[96] Nicholas Roe also picks up on Dylan's use of alias, noting how one of the ways he has been himself is by evoking the ghosts of the myriad artists whose traces can be found in his work: 'Unlike nearly every other writer, for whom "finding a voice" or unique verbal identity may be an imperative, Bob Dylan is apparently most himself as a sublimely capable alias, merged into a babel of others' voices. As a performer, too, Dylan's voice is utterly unmistakable yet endlessly modulated, by turns harsh, gravelly, bawling, sneering and honey-pleading.'[97]

We might also hear a sense of distancing and displacement in Dylan's famous 'wild mercury sound', not least the feeling that any attempt to capture the sound is doomed. More generally, what might it mean to speak of 'musical displacement' in the work? We might refer to losing one's place in the music, something both performer and audience can fall prey to. There are any number of examples of left-in 'mistakes', fudged or changed words, over-wordiness, seemingly infinite alliteration, 'wrongness' of voice, unexpected vocal intonation, disorienting performance strategies, changes in musical styles and, overriding all, a stubborn wilfulness on the part of the artist not to repeat the past. As Marcus noted of the difficulty of mapping the 'undiscovered country' or 'invisible republic' of the *Basement Tapes*, and as Gilmore said of the 'unmapped frontier' explored in *Time Out of Mind*, the possibility of fixing is forever being deferred. Gilmore notes the importance of continual creation and inventiveness in Dylan's performance practice:

> Dylan . . . seems to have adopted a viewpoint similar to the one favored by jazz trumpeter and bandleader Miles Davis for most of his career: namely, that the truest vital experience of music resides in the moment of its performance, in the living act of its formation and the spontaneous yet hard-earned discoveries that those acts of creation yield. The next time the musicians play the same song, it is not really the same song. It is a new moment and creation, a new possibility, a newfound place on the map, soon to be left behind for the next place.[98]

To put it in the terms of one of Dylan's most wandering songs, 'Mr Tambourine Man', his audience have had to 'take [him] disappearing . . . with all memory and fate driven deep beneath the waves'. In that song, Dylan wanted to 'forget about today until tomorrow'.[99] Just after these lines are sounded in Scorsese's film, we hear Dylan make the following claim: 'An artist has got to be careful never really to arrive at a place where he thinks he's at somewhere. You always have to realise that you're constantly in a state of becoming.'

At the same time, these are popular songs and there is plenty of 'homecoming' in them. Dylan's numerous refrains really do bring it all back home and provide a 'round trip' that is part of the geographical quality to the songs. Blues structures suggest their resolutions right from the start, while folk ballads circle infinitely around refrains. Dylan's phrasing also brings a sense of stability even as he is 'displacing' linguistic commonplaces; examples include the role of 'idiot' in 'Idiot Wind', or feel/own/home/stone in 'Like a Rolling Stone', or, earlier still, 'pawn' in 'Only a Pawn in Their Game'. Blues is a recurring real, a music that brings the real back home, and home is the pull here. One's feet point away from the past but this says little about the temptation to turn around and look behind. Displacement derives its power from the pull of place and the two shed light on each other. As Dylan said of *Time Out of Mind*: 'I try to live within that line between despondency and hope. I'm suited to walk that line, right between the fire.. . . I see the album straight down the middle of the line, really.'[100]

5

Both Sides Now: Joni Mitchell, Neil Young and the Innocence and Experience of the Singer-Songwriter

a song so wild and blue / it scrambles time and seasons if it gets thru to you
Joni Mitchell

In a 1967 lecture entitled 'Cybernetics and Ghosts' the writer Italo Calvino put forward the proposition of a 'writing machine' capable not only of reproducing classic literature, but also of creating its own through the application of programmable rules and variants. Discussing the practical difficulties inherent in such a task, Calvino used the theoretical possibilities to illustrate various then-topical notions of the author's role in the text. Suggesting that readers could create (i.e. programme) a text, he spoke of his machine as one

> that would bring to the page all those things that we are accustomed to consider as the most jealously guarded attributes of our psychological life, of our daily experience, our unpredictable changes of mood and inner elations, despairs and moments of illumination. What are these if not so many linguistic 'fields', for which we might well succeed in establishing the vocabulary, grammar, syntax, and properties of permutation?[1]

The following year Roland Barthes was to publish his influential essay 'The Death of the Author', in which he emphasised the reader as the creative force behind the text. For Barthes, too much importance had been placed on the nontextual study of authors' works:

> [T]he image of literature to be found in contemporary culture is tyrannically centered on the author, his person, his history, his tastes, his passions; criticism still largely consists in saying that Baudelaire's oeuvre is the failure

of the man Baudelaire, Van Gogh's is his madness, Tchaikovsky's his vice: *explanation* of the work is still sought in the person of its producer, as if, through the more or less transparent allegory of fiction, it was always, ultimately, the voice of one and the same person, the *author*, which was transmitting his 'confidences'.[2]

Attractive as such declarations were (and remain), they seemed to be challenged by the contemporaneous emergence of a group of 'confessional' singer-songwriters, both in the Europe of Calvino and Barthes and in the more dominant popular music milieu of North America. These composer-lyricist-performers were seen as nothing if not authors whose work could be explained by their 'life . . . tastes . . . passions . . . failure . . . madness . . . vice' and who were, indeed 'confiding in us', their closely concentrating listeners. The work of these artists was grounded in the recognition and revelation of intimate self-knowledge with which audiences could identify; in the intimate confession of the singer-songwriter, listeners could, indeed, discern 'jealously guarded attributes of our psychological life, of our daily experience, our unpredictable changes of mood and inner elations, despairs and moments of illumination'. Those able to reveal such things to us were no machines, however, and the humanity they summoned was understood as existing in opposition to the machinery of the culture industry.

In a 1969 review of Joni Mitchell's album *Clouds*, the Guardian critic Geoffrey Cannon quoted lines from the song 'Both Sides, Now' – 'It's life's illusions I recall / I really don't know life at all' – and suggested that Mitchell 'knows herself, and fills the images of her illusion with herself'.[3] These connected ideas – knowing oneself and filling one's art with oneself – have often been seen as crucial to the work of singer-songwriters. This is especially so with the 'confessional school' of artists that emerged in the late 1960s and early 1970s, among them Mitchell, Neil Young, Leonard Cohen, Tim Hardin, Janis Ian, James Taylor, Van Morrison and Sandy Denny. As an English term, 'singer-songwriter' is most often associated with musicians from the Anglophone world, though contemporaneous forms can be found in many countries. As for the time period, the era of the confessional singer-songwriter starts in that period in which pop was seen to 'mature' into a more artistic, serious mode of representation. Bob Dylan clearly played a crucial role in this process by demonstrating new possibilities for song form in the rock era. However, while he was a singer-songwriter in the strictest sense, he was not always considered a confessional singer until later in his career, particularly around the time of *Blood on the Tracks*. The confessional singer, then, can be differentiated from the protest singer by a greater concentration on the self than on the world picture. Cannon declares Mitchell's 'The Fiddle and the Drum' (an anti-war lament) a 'failure because its metaphors don't have her living in them'. It is telling that 'Positively 4th Street', the Dylan song which Joni Mitchell has mentioned in interviews as that which showed her the possibilities of songwriting, is one that relates the feelings aroused by the breakdown of a personal relationship.[4]

This putting of the self into one's work means that the so-called confessional singer-songwriter has been understood as someone who reflects on the stages of their life. A similar process could be observed with those American poets labelled 'confessional' in the 1960s. The point where life feeds art and vice versa can be found through much of the confessional poetry of the period, an era dating by common consent from Robert Lowell's *Life Studies* (1959) through the work of W. D. Snodgrass, John Berryman, Sylvia Plath and Anne Sexton. These poets placed considerable emphasis on technical processes; it was not enough to merely prick the skin; the blood that was drawn had to be shaped into something concrete, the stripped psyche to be manipulated into art. The growing interest in psychoanalysis was a huge influence on the writing of the period. A common bond between the confessional poets – one that was greater than the stylistic similarities in their work – was the first-hand experience of analysis and hospitalisation, combined with a desire to record such experiences in their poetry. As poets they were both analysts and patients, using the discipline of the former to record the experience of the latter.

I make these observations as a way of setting up this chapter, which is concerned with the representation of time, age and experience in the work of two North American singer-songwriters, Joni Mitchell and Neil Young. While Mitchell, to her annoyance, has been regularly labelled a confessional singer-songwriter since her emergence in the 1960s, Young presents a slightly more compromised case. To borrow Barthes's words, there have been many attempts to connect the themes of Young's work to his 'life . . . tastes . . . passions . . . failure . . . madness . . . [and] vice', yet his more elliptical lyrical style has confused as often as it has clarified. As William Echard writes, 'one thing which made Young's artistic vision distinctive was the degree to which he took his own changeability and ambiguity as central themes, and this reflexive impulse, along with the generally poetic register of his language, placed Young in the singer-songwriter tradition, although his tendency toward obliqueness and abstraction generally prevent his work from seeming frankly confessional'.[5] For this reason as much as because I am not attempting here to 'explain' either artist's work via Barthes's 'list', I propose to think of Mitchell and Young mostly as 'self-analytical' rather than 'confessional' singer-songwriters. It seems to me that, whether or not they are speaking of their own lives, both artists offer exemplary instances of analysing intimate moments in the life experience, whether focused on relationships (romantic, inter-generational, platonic), the passing of time, age, nature, geography, politics, yearning, loss, memory or much else besides. Like the confessional poets, they may at times be expressing themselves as analysts or patients and so I will not completely abandon the notion of confession (and will say more on it below). Of the many themes that Mitchell and Young have tackled, I am particularly interested here in those of innocence and experience and will explore them in relation to my other core themes of time, age and the voice, the latter understood once more as both a way of writing and a way of singing.

These two artists have much in common, most notably perhaps their Canadian origins and subsequent careers in the United States (both recording for Reprise, the label Frank Sinatra had set up in 1960 and later sold to Warner Bros). Mitchell and Young came to know each other quite early in each other's careers and collaborated on a number of occasions subsequently. As writers, both make fascinating use of childlike perspectives throughout their work, often contrasting the depiction of youth and newness with reflections on the ageing process and on the wisdom supposedly gained through experience. Innocence may be evoked via naive style, childlike perspectives, the exploratory quests and questions of youth, and the adoption of an ingénue persona. Experience, meanwhile, is represented by hardened perspectives, details of journeys travelled and lives lived, commentaries on age and ageing, but also on the lateness to be found in youth. Young includes explicit references to time or age in songs such as 'I Am a Child', 'Sugar Mountain', 'Old Man' and 'Comes a Time'; even his big hit of the 1970s, 'Heart of Gold', contained in its refrain a declaration that 'I'm getting old'. Mitchell's work is less frequently about specific life stages, though these feature in songs such as 'The Circle Game', 'Woodstock', 'The Last Time I Saw Richard' and 'Chinese Cafe/Unchained Melody'; her work still presents an ongoing quest for understanding that shifts, deepens and gets blocked at various points in her protagonists' lives. Both singers are representatives of the 'time of man' (to use a term from one of Mitchell's songs) and act as cultural critics of the 1960s and its consequences.

Confession

As previously noted, one of the ways in which confession and analysis were combined in the work of the confessional poets was via the recording of the experience of psychoanalysis and, in some cases, of mental health treatments. This is not a connection I am pursuing in my discussion of Mitchell and Young but it is still worth dwelling on the kind of analysis that psychoanalysis models in that it may yield useful observations for the study of analytical songwriters. Lowell and Berryman both explored the doctor–patient dualism in their poems through a search for a self, or true voice, that results from the tension between the poet and their personas. Steven Gould Axelrod, writing on Lowell, places experience at the heart of this conflict:

> 'Experience' more truly means the sum of relations and interactions between psyche and environment. It grows from the Cartesian dualism of inner and outer, but through its interpenetrating energies abolishes the dualism. Just as experience mediates between self and world, partaking of both, so Lowell's poems mediate between himself and his world, and between his personal history and that of his readers. His poems are structures of experience. They both record his life and assume a life of their own; and as they transform the poet's life into the autonomous life of art, they reenter his life by clarifying it and completing it.[6]

This may, of course, be said for many artists and correlates to a view that the artist, more than just a mediator between the muse and the audience, is as much a part of the poem's content as its expression. As Axelrod reminds us, Emerson had held that 'the poet lives only half a life; the other half is his expression', an observation that can easily be transferred to the self-analytical singer-songwriter. In Lowell's case, the poems in *Life Studies* recognise an ongoing process – one that is necessary to engage the reader's identification – are 'still lives', frozen moments when experience is petrified. In such moments, we are offered, at the heart of the picture, amidst the supporting detail, a glimpse into the psyche of the poet.

In considering similar questions as they relate to Joni Mitchell, Michelle Mercer writes that she is 'more interested in how songwriters make their work personal than in what they get personal about'.[7] Yet she is also wise to the impossibility of ignoring the life of the author, even as one is aware of the reasons not to reduce an author's work to that life: 'I think part of the reason people see themselves in Mitchell's work is because she put so much of herself on the line. And identifying with her music does not exclude wondering about where it came from and just what she risked in making it.'[8] Mercer quotes an angry denunciation by the artist of the 'confessional songwriter' label:

> When I think of confession, two things come to mind. The swinging light and the billy club, you know, trying to get a confession out of somebody that's been captured. Confess, confess! Or a witch hunt. Or trials. Confession is somebody trying to beat something out of you externally. You're imprisoned. You're captured. They're trying to get you to admit something. Then there's the voluntary confession of Catholicism.[9]

Still, interpretation and meaning being what they are, there is no necessity to respect the artist's wish to refuse the labels placed on them, a fact that Mercer appears to be aware of in her continuation of the trope of confession even while reporting Mitchell's disavowal. As I have already indicated, confession can be a restricting term, but, like Mercer, it is not one I would entirely wish to do away with. There are other ways to understand confession, such as those suggested by the title of Pablo Neruda's memoir, *Confieso que he vivido* [I confess I have lived]. Here we get the sense of the guilt or the crime, the confession of one who has done wrong (which was Mitchell's complaint about the term). But we also get the sense of life as something to bear witness to and this loops back onto guilt in that there is a connection, via the law, between witnessing and guilt. Guilt is also an important concept to consider in relation to innocence. Guilt is something that does feature in Mitchell's work, as it does in Young's.[10]

One crucial aspect which Mercer emphasises is that, while life may provide the raw material for art, art itself is a transformation into something else such that it cannot easily be broken down into base materials or ingredients: 'Poetry is not merely recorded experience – maybe painful, maybe not – but experience transformed into insight by invention and expression.' Mitchell herself offers a description that is closer to that of Bob Dylan at the time of his album *Blood on the Tracks*:

> Art is artifice and it doesn't matter whose life I scraped to get that text. Of course, I have more access to my own. If you spend a lot of time alone, that's your major resource – your own experience.. . . You can make a good play out of anything, including yourself. But songs didn't traditionally carry these literary elements, and that's what my contribution to the songwriting form probably was, to bring songs closer to something like a good play. But I'm not making these songs out of a need to confess to anyone; it's out of a need to create a story. It works in plays; it works in movies. 'I could have been a contender . . .'. Was Brando confessing?[11]

The notion of singer-songwriter as actor and playwright is convincing to an extent, and Mitchell, like Dylan, has made great use of characterisation and narrative in her songs. But this (at least) dual role is also one of the reasons that Mitchell's comparison doesn't entirely hold up; the singer-songwriter, by taking on the role of playwright and actor, is doing more than most playwrights or actors do. Like another often quoted Mitchell comparison between painters being asked to repaint masterpieces and performing singers being asked to sing old songs, the terms of comparison, while evocative, are ultimately not close enough to be effective or convincing. To get up on stage and to sing songs one has written and which are based on one's own experience, or to go into a studio and record them in the intimate grooves of a long-playing album, is to do something rather different to the playwright, actor or painter, even if Mitchell seems unwilling to accept this. It is also not entirely convincing to claim that songs did not have these specifically literary (dramatic, story-based) qualities before; folk ballads, for example, are full of them.

But if I am suggesting that Mitchell protests too much, I am not denying her claims to art as artifice. I follow Mercer, Dewey and Negus and Pickering (quoted in previous chapters) in understanding art as experience plus extra work, work put in not only by creators but also by perceivers. In confessing to having lived and experienced, the singer-songwriter connects to an audience who have also lived and experienced. We might adapt Barthes's famous presentation of the text as a tissue of quotations by saying that it can also be a tissue of experiences, both original and shared. The aesthetic process lies in the combination and transformation of these experiences into novel and notable objects. When Michael Gray, for example, pauses to wonder at the magical complexity of a Dylan rhyme scheme in 'Idiot Wind', it is this transformed experience that is shining and meaningful, not the raw experience that led to the composition.[12] The magic of the artifice – the beautiful illusion – is what captures attention as much as anything, and is as authentic as anything found in the 'real world'. It is also to be found itself in the real world; the object has an afterlife.

Yesterday, a child

In her song 'For the Roses', Mitchell mourns the transition from being face-to-face with an audience as one becomes famous and finds 'it's just you up there / Getting them to feel like that'.[13] This sense of alienation highlights a vulnerability that should be attached also to the art of the singer-songwriter. One might even wonder if the reason for denying the confessional and for exaggerating the dramaturgical is a way of overcoming this sense of vulnerability. Vulnerability is played out in the work of Mitchell and Neil Young in the figure of the child and its dreams. Young has returned to childlike figures or visions throughout his career and his voice has maintained something of it too. It is a voice which, in the words of Emmylou Harris, 'has a real innocent quality, like a choirboy, but it's almost scary. It's very haunting, other-worldly'. Similarly, Randy Newman points to a deceptive immaturity in Young's lyrics, describing them as 'like a child grabbin' around and pickin' the first thing he finds. But between those grabs there's a high IQ at work, making it all turn out'.[14] This naivety, affected as it may be, has remained a feature of Young's work, coming into particular focus at certain points, including the late album *Psychedelic Pill* (2012). William Echard is correct in highlighting 'childhood and adolescent insecurity' as key themes in Young's early work:

In some cases this tone is simply implied in the imagery ('Helpless', 'I Am a Child'), but in others the lyrics explicitly evoke a growing responsibility and loss of innocence ('Sugar Mountain', 'Tell Me Why'). This particular feeling tone – description of a moment at once hopeful and desperate, promising and stifling – was also picked up in mood pieces not specific to childhood, sometimes in the form of a general ennui ('Everybody Knows This Is Nowhere') and sometimes as a full-blown sense of dread or disorientation ('The Loner', 'Mr. Soul').[15]

'I Am a Child' featured on the final Buffalo Springfield record; later Young was to say that, when he came to record this song, 'the group was falling apart'.[16] But if the song was born in a time of bitter experience, it exudes an air of innocence partly due to the stripped down nature of the instrumentation, partly to Young's 'other-worldly' vocal and partly to the title and refrain. 'Helpless' also evokes innocence both in its lyrical allusions to childhood and landscape, its gentle vocal and its repeated refrain of 'helpless, helpless, helpless'. At the same time, there are ominous hints of trouble in paradise, as with the 'big birds flying across the sky / throwing shadows on our eyes'. Another notable aspect of the song is the evocation of the singer's childhood home as a memory place, a location that exists in the mind as an option for the wandering imagination of the singer to visit when 'I still need a place to go'.[17] John Bauldie reads the 'big birds flying' as an evocation of time passing:

> Time throws shadows on to the world, and darkens the outlook of the child . . . With time's passing all of childhood's comforts and dreams . . . are left behind.. . . If there's to be no return, no turning away from the empty street that stretches out into the darkness, no comfort other than that of dream or memory, then all that can be embraced is despair, the oppression of the knowledge of helplessness and hopelessness . . . a despair that may only be relieved if others may be persuaded to acknowledge that same feeling of helplessness.[18]

This mixture of wonder, despair, comfort and anxiety recalls Sandy Denny's 'Who Knows Where the Time Goes', which also uses images of migrating birds in relation to transience while attempting to find ways to cope with the passing of time, and specifically of youth into adulthood. In speaking of anxiety as much as innocence, these songs call to mind an early text by Walter Benjamin:

> The mask of the adult is called 'experience.' It is expressionless, impenetrable, and ever the same. The adult has always already experienced [*erlebt*] everything: youth, ideals, hopes, woman. It was all illusion. – Often we feel intimidated or embittered. Perhaps he is right. What can our retort be? We have not yet experienced [*erfuhren*] anything.. . . More and more we are assailed by the feeling that our youth is but a brief night (fill it with rapture!); it will be followed by grand 'experience', the years of compromise, impoverishment of ideas, and lack of energy. Such is life.[19]

This observation from the young Benjamin resonates with the lyrics of 'Sugar Mountain', a song Young wrote on his nineteenth birthday as a lament for lost youth and out of concern over the cutting-off of youthful experience once one turns twenty. Even though this is one song where Young himself has been explicit about the connection between life and lyrics, the words are allusive rather than obviously biographical, the sense of distance exacerbated by the second-person delivery: 'you're finding out it's real', 'it's your first cigarette', 'you can't be twenty on Sugar Mountain'. Yet Young delivers the song with a yearning, fragile vocal, encouraging listeners to hear the 'you' as the 'I' of the singer. Performing the song in 1969, Young claimed to be ashamed of some of the lyrics but happy with some others, providing further evidence of Newman's observation about Young's intuitive and occasionally naive songwriting. Even so, he would continue to perform 'Sugar Mountain' into later years, including it in his late 1970s live retrospective *Live Rust*.

Joni Mitchell's song 'The Circle Game' was written as a response to 'Sugar Mountain' and offers a way beyond the dilemma of lost youth, looking ahead to the possibility of 'better dreams' on the horizon. As such, it speaks to the mobilisation of youthful ideals against the 'experience' of the philistine that Benjamin argued for in his early writing. The song begins with a child, who 'yesterday . . . came out to wander' and proceeds to chart the child's journey into early adulthood, using imagery connected to the seasons and the countryside. Transience and the swiftness of the passing seasons are acknowledged in reference to 'yesterday' and 'it won't be long now'. The sense in which time creeps up on us is noted in the line 'cartwheels turned to car wheels', which also cleverly combines biographical and historical development; as the vehicles we travel in or play with change in adulthood, so technological improvement and urbanisation (from cart to car) mark historical progress. But even with the onward motion of time, the emphasis is on cyclical nature; as seasons return, so do verses and refrains. The song's rhyme scheme also marks the song as something beyond the mere transcription of a narrative of life. First and third lines rhyme while placing emphasis, via slight elongation, on the first syllable of a two-syllable word or word pair: *won*der, *thun*der, *gone* now, *long* now, *twen*ty, *plen*ty. Technically, many of the verses are in trochaic pentameter, an unusual choice for a song and one which makes the overhanging syllables at the ends of the lines more noticeable. The chorus mixes the meter up, providing a sense of going 'round and round and round' while recognising different notions of time's progression: the simultaneous onward march of the ticking second hand and the recurrent circle of its physical journey. The last verse becomes more crowded syllabically, suggesting growing complexity and confusion as the life of the song (as life itself) progresses. The elegance of the rhyming lines is maintained throughout, however, giving a pull and push between formal perfection and nonconformity.

'Woodstock', another of Mitchell's early compositions, also uses the imagery of childhood, this time via the story of an encounter with a 'child of God'. The narrator tells of meeting this child on the road to the Woodstock festival and the remainder of the song is a paean to the festival and its accompanying ethos of love, peace and togetherness. The festival gathering is presented as an Edenic scene which recognises the emergence of a new generation. As such, it taps into the popular notion of the time that the youth were taking part in a new age, the 'dawning of the Age of Aquarius' as the hippie musical *Hair* would have it. But while the song may have been inspired by a real event, and told from the perspective of one who had been there, Mitchell was inspired to write it as a distant witness. Although she had been supposed to perform at the festival, she was advised to pull out of the appearance when it became unclear whether she would be able to escape the chaotic scene in time to make a scheduled television appearance. Mitchell's famous musical account of the festival, then, was a work of imagination from one who felt she should have been there but wasn't. 'Woodstock' has a double naivety in that its seemingly utopian lyrics are the product of Mitchell's etic experience. The song would become famous in a version by the new 'supergroup' Crosby, Stills, Nash & Young (who *had* been at the festival), Neil Young having joined the previous trio of Crosby, Stills & Nash shortly before. The two versions are quite distinct musically, CSNY's being an uptempo, electric guitar-driven blues rock number and Mitchell's being a slower, keyboard-based song. Vocally, the band version is distinguished by Steven Stills's raspy vocals, accompanied by the other band members' harmony vocals on the chorus, while Mitchell's high, clear voice is the only one to be heard on her version, albeit that her vocals are multi-tracked on the chorus to provide a 'Joni choir'. Her vocal has a searching quality to it, something that at this time was becoming a notable feature of her work. As well as telling the story, her voice can be heard to offer commentary and curiosity to the lines, even seeming to question the truth of what is being said. Camille Paglia, who includes 'Woodstock' among a collection of 'forty-three of the world's best poems', reads the song as imbued with cynicism towards the utopia it describes and a world weariness that contrasts sharply with the more upbeat version by CSNY. Paglia describes CSNY's version as 'a rousing anthem for the hippie counterculture . . . a stomping hoedown'; compared to this famous version, Mitchell's own recording 'is a moody and at times heartbreakingly melancholy art song [which] shows the heady visions of the sixties counterculture already receding and evaporating'.[20] Another contrast can be found in what Paglia calls the 'radical gender drama' of Mitchell's version. Where CSNY represent the all-male rock and roll band that the young man of the lyric wants to join, Mitchell's female narrator provides a levelling-out of gender relations in the song's world: 'Following Walt Whitman or Jack London, the modern woman writer takes to the road, as cloistered Emily Dickinson could never do. She and her casual companion are peers on life's journey.'[21]

Another way of looking at this is to consider Mitchell as a narrator who has the confidence to stand both outside and inside her song texts; the placing of 'Woodstock' before 'The Circle Game' on the 1970 album *Ladies of the Canyon* encourages such a reading. Here, Mitchell is the storyteller situated outside of, or above, the action, able to provide reportage but also to colour her commentary with the extra knowledge of the etic perspective. The questioning, wordless vocals that close 'Woodstock' and which seem to confirm Paglia's reading of the song as more cynical than it initially appears, veer close to screams at times; it is unclear whether they are those of one who is inside the story and terrified (of the dystopian rather than utopian possibilities of being amidst a crowd of half a million) or the horror of the one who can see what is on the horizon. In 'The Circle Game', the narrator both observes the plight of the youth ('Neil Young') and provides guidance for the future possibilities of the story. Indeed, even if the album was not written as a conceptual suite, the way it is sequenced encourages a reading based on a narrative structure that begins with the bright optimism of 'Morning Morgantown', works through the romanticism of 'For Free', 'Conversation' and 'Willie' to the possibilities and paradoxes of paradise in 'Big Yellow Taxi' ('they paved paradise / put up a parking lot') and 'Woodstock', before concluding with the learned wisdom of 'The Circle Game.'

Blueness and worldliness

If I take the time to posit such a reading of *Ladies of the Canyon* it is because I believe the songs mentioned are the ones most often plucked from the album to give a sense of its overall flavour. However, they account for only half of its songs and some of the so-far unmentioned ones might just as easily fit on the subsequent 1971 album *Blue*. This is particularly the case with 'The Arrangement', 'Rainy Night House' and 'Blue Boy', where the mood evoked via the lyrical themes, vocal approach and piano accompaniment will be instantly recognisable to a listener familiar with *Blue*.[22] These songs should be heard, as much as any, as part of what Michelle Mercer calls Mitchell's 'Blue Period', which Mercer dates from *Blue* through to *Hejira* (1976). This periodisation reflects, of course, an understanding of Mitchell's work according to the logic of the album. This is reasonable and understandable for the period, the artist and the genre under consideration (the 1970s, Joni Mitchell, singer-songwriters) and I myself have tended to use a similar logic when discussing the work of artists in this book. However, it is worth remembering that such accounts can be challenged by the singularity of songs, a singularity that is notable both in recordings made at different times (including the alternate takes that don't make 'classic albums' but then become added on in later reissues) and in ongoing evolutions made in live performances. It is interesting to know, for example, that the song 'Little Green', although first recorded for *Blue*, was written and performed by Mitchell in 1967.

But because *Blue* has achieved such canonical status as a singer-songwriter album, it is difficult not to consider it as a separate work, whatever its relationship to Mitchell's prior and subsequent output. I do not therefore intend to challenge the status of *Blue* as a standalone work but rather to note that its fame has contributed strongly to the way in which the interrelated stories of Joni Mitchell, the confessional singer-songwriter genre and the popular music of the early 1970s are told. From my own perspective, I also want to ascertain the importance of that confluence to an understanding of the possibilities of the late voice and to the representation of time and experience in popular song. *Blue* is an album of time lived, of time to come and, most notably perhaps, of time spent in contemplation (of self and others and the worlds in which they meet). Mercer suggests that the album is saturated with experience to such an extent that it even bleeds into the blue of the album cover: 'This blue was an experiential palette, a product of living. The shadow in the spotlight. Smoke's invitingly acrid edge. The ocean at dusk after you've been swimming in it.'[23] These metaphors speak to me of other references too, of the shoreline imagery of Hart Crane's poem 'Voyages', the cover of the Beach Boys' *Surf's Up* or the cover of Neil Young's *On the Beach*. I am also reminded of the meanings of blueness in mood, music and metaphor explored by Richard Williams in his book about Miles Davis, *The Blue Moment*. There is something about the darkness of the cover of *Blue* that puts us straight into the contemplative time of classic jazz photography (Blue Note album covers being an iconic example) or the hue of Frank Sinatra's *In the Wee Small Hours*. The lateness of this blue stands in marked contrast to its daylight equivalent, the innocent hope of blue skies and seas.

In reality, of course, things are never so midnight blue or baby blue. Blue skies may be obscured by clouds, as in Mitchell's song of the same name or Young's 'Helpless'. And blue seas, reflecting potentially fickle skies, may also promise a caress that is ultimately an invitation to the cruel seabed, as in Crane's

'Voyages'. But colour in general still holds suggestions of youth and innocence, as in the child's paint palette. In an early fragment entitled 'A Child's View of Colour', Walter Benjamin argued that the colour without form that one found in children's painting could be seen as a representation of a world innocent of the need to conform to the rules of representation, a world aware of colour as 'the basis from which to create the interrelated totality of the world of the imagination'.[24] I would suggest that such an understanding of blueness should hold for Mitchell's album as much as the more vaunted palette of experience. This can be perceived on the album's very first song, 'All I Want', which mixes imagery of innocent desire and experiential analysis atop a tune that dances similarly between hope and resignation.[25] As Lloyd Whitesell notes, the innocence of the song is one notably tempered by a tone of experience when the melodic arc descends to 'we both get so blue'.[26]

It is this restlessness, this impossibility to pin song narratives down that makes *Blue* such a multi-layered, mature text. Its perfection (and many listeners have found it perfect) lies in the way this restlessness exists in both lyrics and music and in the balance of narrative structures practised on the earlier albums with moments of taking flight from narrative. In the second verse of 'All I Want', the narrative is suspended on the mention of a 'juke box dive' and Mitchell seems to be channelling the song on the jukebox: 'Do you want, do you want, do you wanna dance with me.' Mitchell's voice soars out of the song as she continues the invitation – 'do you want to take a chance / On maybe finding some sweet romance?' – and it takes some rhythmic strumming of the guitar to set up a return to the narrative; when it resumes, the lyric both answers the invitation with its 'All I want' and brings the song back to something like a normal melodic pattern. In 'California', the melody rises and falls throughout, with Mitchell's voice alternating between gentle, lower tones and high, ecstatic lines that almost seem like screeches; during the lines 'All the news of home you read / Just gives you the blues' the voice drifts up and out of the song's main registers to pinpoint an emotional revelation. When, in the chorus of 'River', she sings 'I'd teach my feet to fly', the word 'fly' swoops upward for five seconds, lasting much longer than the surrounding syllables; again the effect is to pause the narrative of the lyric to dwell on the gymnastic spectacle of the voice.

Mitchell's undulating vocals do not ever mean just one thing; rather they are techniques of approach, exploration and attack that work at the lyrics to reveal additional meaning. Sometimes these techniques are in service of what Lloyd Whitesell calls Mitchell's 'ingenue' persona, at other times they support the roles of 'the mystic bard', 'the torch carrier', 'the free spirit' or 'the critic'.[27] There is evidence of all these personas on *Blue*, from the ingenue of 'All I Want' to the critic of 'The Last Time I Saw Richard'. With much of the album given over to doomed romance and 'confession', the role of the torch singer is particularly evident. As Whitesell writes of 'A Case of You':

> The idea of confessional outpouring . . . is thematized in the song: 'part of you pours out of me/In these lines from time to time'. 'These lines' refer to the song's poetic/melodic lines, of course, as the speaker is writing or performing them. But they also encompass the graphic lines of her visual art, since she identifies strongly as an artist in this poem (sketching her lover's face in verse 1, introducing herself as 'a lonely painter' in verse 2). What is being poured out is thus her unrequited emotion as well as its embodiment in art and alcohol.[28]

At one point in the song the singer is warned by another woman who once knew the song's addressed lover; the other woman tells her to 'go to him, stay with him if you can / But be prepared to bleed'. This willingness to bleed is another recognition of the outpouring of the self (of a forced confession, or opening-up, we might say) and also an awareness that the shed blood of experience might be transformed into the precious material of art. Michelle Mercer also picks up on the artistic processes at work in the song, comparing the line 'You're in my blood like holy wine' to Leonard Cohen's interest in transubstantiation and in the mixture of the divine and secular, as in the 'holy or the broken Hallelujah' of his famous song.[29]

Blue often seems to be about the disillusionment that comes with the realisation that things did not turn out the way one had dreamed they would. This mood saturates much of the album, not least its closing track 'The Last Time I Saw Richard'. Following a long, introspective piano introduction, Mitchell sings a lyric about a meeting in 1968 at which point disillusion had already set in: Richard tells the singer that 'all romantics meet the same fate someday / Cynical and drunk and boring someone in some dark café'. The singer seems immune and, after Richard starts playing songs on a jukebox (a recurring motif in Mitchell's songs), she points out to him that 'You got tombs in your eyes but the songs you punched are dreaming.' The third and final verse moves the action to the present and we learn that Richard has settled down and 'drinks at home at home now most nights with the TV on'. While he lives his (implicitly boring) domestic life, the singer can still be found in the café, alone and not wishing for company, biding her time until 'I get my gorgeous wings and fly away.' Like the night spots to be found in the songs of Billie Holiday and Frank Sinatra, these 'dark café days' offer a liminal world between day and night where the confusions of the everyday (and potentially humdrum) world can be postponed and where endless self-analysis can be undertaken. The song's verses all provide moments for Mitchell's voice to swoop up, as if tasting the air above the dark café, dreaming of a life beyond, even if it is 'only pretty lies'. 'Love can be so sweet' she sings in remembrance and hope at the close of verse 2, then, in the same upwardly soaring section of verse 3, comes the liberated vocal of 'get my gorgeous wings and fly away', quickly followed by the more down to earth 'only a phase, these dark café' days'. At the close of the song, then, and of *Blue*, Mitchell enacts the romantic dreams and self-delusions that she has been grappling with throughout the album. The question of whether she, or we, can ever escape is left hanging.

Some of the songs of experience that Mitchell, Young and others were producing by the early 1970s were a reflection on the historical moment and we witness in their work a bringing together of the personal and public. The title song of *Blue* made this clear by combining lines of personal experience ('You know, I've been to sea before') with social observation ('There's so many sinking now'). As Mercer observes:

> [I]n making *Blue* her own, Mitchell layered broader themes into the subject of love. She conflated the fall of romance with the end of the 1960s' countercultural dreams. Earlier versions of fresh-dawned towns ('Morning Morgantown') and utopian cultures ('Woodstock') were gone, traded for existential pondering and for taking a hard look at herself. When she did invoke alternative lifestyles, as on the title track, it was to decry the nihilism into which the countercultural revolution had sunk: 'Everybody's saying that hell's the hippest way to go, well, I don't think so. I'm going to take a look around it though.'[30]

Both Mitchell and Young were critical of the consequences of the 1960s and showcased this disquiet in their work. Not long after Mitchell had sung about the failures of the 1960s in 'Blue', Young made reference to the decadence of 1970s drug culture in 'The Needle and the Damage Done', a song of stark loneliness and darkness amidst the mellow vibes of his hit album *Harvest* (1972). Young wrote the song in response to the number of people in the music business that had fallen into drug addiction. Among these was Danny Whitten, one of the original members of Young's occasional band Crazy Horse. Whitten's subsequent death from heroin addiction affected Young deeply and contributed to the much darker tone of the work he released on *Time Fades Away* (1973), *On the Beach* (1974) and *Tonight's the Night* (1975); these three albums would later be christened by rock journalists as 'the doom trilogy' or 'the ditch trilogy'. *Tonight's the Night* was recorded in 1973, shortly after the deaths of Whitten and CSNY roadie Bruce Berry (also a heroin overdose), but was held back from release for two years by Young's label Reprise.

These albums have been returned to frequently by fans and rock critics due to the perception that they represent an authentic dissection of the dark fallout of the hippie dream. Allied to this has been a continued representation of Young as an authentic chronicler of the times, someone who was willing to turn his back on youthful ideals and, to an extent, on the friends, allies and audiences of his early fame, in order to follow his artistic vision. While authenticity is not my main focus here, it does relate to the representation of age and experience and to the way we relate to performers and performances. With this in mind, it is worth highlighting a few examples of the authenticity work surrounding Young's 1970s work. Hugh Barker and Yuval Taylor provide a good account of this in their book *Faking It: The Quest for Authenticity in Pop*, devoting a chapter to *Tonight's the Night*. They identify the consistency with which notions of 'realness' are attached to Young, especially in this part of his career. Barker and Taylor posit professional experience as the answer to the paradox of how Young could avoid 'thinking in music' while still producing work that stood the test of time. Young and his fellow musicians were seasoned practitioners who were able to minimise the mediation of their music by applying learned knowledge and techniques with minimum effort. This is something that also comes through in the films *Rust Never Sleeps* (1979) and

Year of the Horse (1997), both of which focus on later stages in Young's career while also reflecting back onto earlier performances. This is done explicitly in *Year of the Horse* through the mixing of footage from three different decades and implicitly in *Rust Never Sleeps* through an overview of Young's career in which early songs are placed conspicuously at the beginning. It may also explain why, with the ever-increasing longevity of the basic working unit of Crazy Horse, the music was able to become wilder, rawer and seem even more spontaneous while still being under control and repeatable.[31]

William Echard argues that, with *On the Beach*, 'Young made a conscious decision to cultivate a sort of localized anarchy which produced a specific instrumental and vocal sound.'[32] This seems right and resonates well with a description of the song 'Tonight's the Night' by Barker and Taylor:

> If James Taylor, Joni Mitchell, or John Prine had written about the life and death of Bruce Berry, it would have followed a certain logic. 'Tonight's the Night', however, follows only an internal, unknown, and probably drunken logic in its sequence of verses, and the chorus has no logical relation to the story told. Some of the verses rhyme and others don't, some of the lines scan and others run on or end too soon. 'Early in the morning at the break of day he used to sleep into the afternoon', one line runs, evading not only syntax but logic. It sounds like a strange mistake – singing the wrong line at the wrong time – that Young just decided to leave in there.
>
> And then there's the drunken performance of the song, with Young's voice wandering off-mike and off-key, the missed notes in his piano playing, the feeling that his fellow musicians, though all skilled, still don't know exactly where the song will go.[33]

The sound of the 'strange mistake' pervades *Tonight's the Night*, from raspy, worn-out vocals to untuned, broken-sounding instruments to the voyeuristic sense that we are overhearing a private, tortured and tortuous experience. In a feature on Young's 'wilderness years' of the mid-1970s in the magazine *Uncut*, Allan Jones returns to the connection between Young's 'doom trilogy' and the fallout of 1960s culture:

> Young was part of a generation that had believed it could change the world, that had championed peace, individual freedoms, sexual liberation and drugs. And for a moment in the collective euphoria that followed Woodstock in

August, 1969, everything seemed possible. The moment didn't last. In fact, it was almost immediately extinguished when Manson's hippie stormtroopers went on their murderous rampage in Beverly Hills, and at Altamont, from which CSN&Y made an undignified exit as soon as things turned ugly.[34]

As many others have done, Jones folds this historical narrative into a personal narrative centred on Young himself, bringing the mid-1970s world into the arena of confessional singer-songwriter material. Jones refers to the circumstances surrounding the recording of *Tonight's the Night* as 'some twilight zone of the soul' and describes Young's performance as a 'delivery shot through with a muted panic'. Identifying the fragility and vulnerability which echo through the album, he speaks of 'spaced out fatigue'; in 'Mellow My Mind', 'Young's voice cracks and strains, breaks, is often tuneless, off-key and by any technical terms an embarrassment. It's hard, however, to think of many vocal performances this sincerely moving.'[35]

Comes a time

In later years, Young would speak of *Tonight's the Night* as the result of a life stage: 'I was twenty-seven when we did *Tonight's the Night*, livin' down there in L.A., travelin' around . . . that's the time you start realizing, "Hey, this isn't what I thought it was gonna be." Things happen and they hit you around that age . . . but you still have enough energy to go nuts.'[36] This may well be the case, although Young's career since that album has seen him return many times to channelling his 'energy' into 'going nuts'; indeed, the process is arguably more evident than ever in his late work, to which I'll turn later. It seems more likely that he has constantly pursued a practice of alternating energies between the 'nuts' and the mellow, or what William Echard identifies as a dialectic of 'ranting' and 'drifting', marked by high and low levels of energy respectively.[37] I would relate this dialectic to another already explored in the previous chapter – that of place and displacement – and I would reconnect Young's work with Mitchell's, for both artists seem to present quests for freedom that locate it between the here and there, between home and away. Young's homeliness is best exemplified in the songs of satisfaction – 'dream comfort memory' – that contribute to some of his mellower sounding albums such as *Harvest* (1972), *Comes a Time* (1978), *Old Ways* (1985), *Harvest Moon* (1992) and *Prairie Wind* (2005). In an oft-quoted observation included in the liner notes to the 1977 compilation *Decade*, Young said of his hit single 'Heart of Gold' that it 'put me in the middle of the road. Travelling there soon became a bore so I headed for the ditch. A rougher ride but I saw more interesting people there.'[38] As many of his critics have noted, Young has spent decades veering between road and ditch. His career has indeed been something of a circle game, with the artist returning numerous times to styles he has tried before, only to move on again. The seasonal nature of Young's shifts has shown that Mitchell might have had a fairer assessment of this than Young did when, in 'Sugar Mountain', he expressed anxiety at the impossibility of returning to an earlier state. Mitchell's career has been far more linear, though its late stages have seen her circle back to the beginning to an extent.

Both artists talk about moving forward rather than looking back, but they have looked back on a number of occasions. It is interesting to view Jonathan Demme's film *Heart of Gold*, which documents Young rehabilitated into the 'home of country music' at a concert in the Ryman Auditorium in Nashville (famous as the former home of the Grand Ole Opry). Young is seen performing the songs from his *Prairie Wind* album on a homely stage set that matches the homely songs; as Sarah Berry writes, the film 'revels in a dream-like evocation of Young's pastoralism.'[39] The film also features interviews with family, friends and fellow musicians, providing a tapestry of experience via personal and collective memory. Young makes a number of references to Hank Williams during the film in both concert and non-concert footage. Williams, as Young reminds the Ryman audience, was fired from the Opry for his erratic behaviour; it's not clear whether Young is identifying with this but Williams certainly provided a model for the singer-songwriter who veered from road to ditch. As Richard Peterson points out, Williams would probably not have been thought of as an authentic country musician by the turn of the millennium, meaning that he has the paradoxical position of being an icon for the country music establishment and yet still outlawed by exclusion from mainstream playlists. The cheer that goes up the first time Young mentions Williams should therefore be heard as ironic. But Young, like Williams, is a prime example of

what Peterson called 'the dialectic of hard core and soft shell', a wild man of
rock who can charm or croon his way into people's homes with a mixture of
homely sentimentality, nostalgia, rebellion and hard-won experience.[40]

In Mitchell's case, the poetics of place and displacement can be discerned
by placing the early domesticity of 'Morning Morgantown' and 'Willie' against
the 'travelling, travelling, travelling' that permeates 'All I Want', with its
singer 'on a lonely road . . . looking for the key to set me free'. But Mitchell's
greatest exploration of space, place and travel can be found on her 1976 album
Hejira. The title of the album is adapted from an Arabic word for a journey
associated with exodus or migration and it was written while Mitchell herself
was travelling across the United States.[41] Opening track 'Coyote' presents a
mature poetic vision, not only in its air of acceptance of self and fate, but also
in its poetic language and metaphor. Coyote is the name Mitchell gives to the
man the narrator is travelling with and with whom she is engaged in a short-
term relationship. The action unfolds during days spent on and around the
freeway in liminal spaces 'where the players lick their wounds / And take their
temporary lovers'.[42] The coyote metaphor is developed throughout the song
and there is also an interlude that presents a flashback to the sighting of a real
coyote, giving the back story for the narrator's attitude towards this man and
the poet's inspiration. Life is presented as a road again, love as a set of short
journeys on that road and the hitch-hiking narrator is 'a prisoner of the white
lines on the freeway'. Here as elsewhere on the album the narrator uses transient
spaces to recall past loves, report present intrigues and imagine the return of
romance. While some commentators have been interested in who Coyote is, I
find myself more captivated by the way in which life, love and experience are
counterpoised in the song and by the way the communion promised by love
is presented as something endlessly desired but also impossible: 'how close to
the bone and the skin and the eyes / and the lips can you get / and still feel so
alone'. As songwriter and narrator, Mitchell combines the telling of a particular
story – there is detailed reportage in the verses – with the use of that story to
reflect on seemingly eternal truths. As a singer she suggests that these truths
are eternal to her; she is trapped within them, a prisoner to the pattern her life
has taken. But, as narrator, she asserts agency; she is still free enough to get on
and off the circle game at will. Life is a 'passion play', with each person playing

their role or at least taking 'their temporary lovers / and their pills and powders to get them through'.

'Coyote' sets up *Hejira* as an album about travel, freedom and independence but one always underlined by a counternarrative of attachment and longing for home. 'Amelia', one of Mitchell's most successful exercises in sustained poetic language and metaphor, folds narratives and symbols into each other, offering a phenomenology of perception played out through mental association. A vision of planes in the sky morphs into guitar strings and an imagination of flight, a narrative directed towards the pioneer aeronaut Amelia Earhart. Being in love (or not, as the case may be) is compared to living in 'clouds at icy altitudes'; the narrator wonders if she has been too cold and distant to have ever truly loved. Yet she knows that she has fallen to earth on occasion, come down to reality in the arms of lovers. She rests on 'the strange pillows of my wanderlust', an attempt to ground herself, to remain stable. The music, as it does throughout the album, rises and follows these flights of fancy. Sometimes the bass is a soft bed to fall back on, sometimes – especially on the tracks featuring exploratory bassist Jaco Pastorius – it searches for escape, swooping up and out of its supporting role in a bid for freedom. Mitchell's voice also swoops and settles, though there is less ecstasy here than on *Blue* or *For the Roses*, less wonder and more wisdom. Where before she had wished for a river to 'skate away on', now the freedom of the river and the road is both a promise and a prison. It is just what there is and the poetry comes in finding and conveying meaning from what there is. Ron Rosenbaum reflects on the mystery of the repeated lyric 'it was a false alarm' in 'Amelia':

> I'm not sure the singer *here* wants rescue. She seems in some ruefully voluptuous way to be reveling in her hejira, getting deliriously deep into her disillusion and disenchantment, exploring the unmapped territory of her newfound solitude like the eponymous aviator in the dreamy solace of long motel-punctuated drives. It occurs to me that in some way that's what 'Amelia's enigma or paradox is about: True love is far more alarming than a false alarm. True love is truly alarming. Real danger.[43]

'Hejira', the title track, presents a travelling narrator 'porous with travel fever' and pondering on love and fidelity. Putting up and settling down are equated with resignation, but resignation is not seen as being easier; life is not simple 'whether you travel the breadth of extremities / or stick to some straighter line'. Thoughts turn to life as a journey 'between the forceps and the stone', a dialectic process of 'hope and hopelessness' in which the vicissitudes of love are 'petty wars' that distract a person from the bigger picture and from some greater knowledge. Although a song about travelling, part of the narration takes place in a café, a place of waiting that acts here as a transit point between the loss of old love and the invitation of new. The café acts as a liminal space for contemplation and possible encounter, like the bar in 'A Case of You' or the recalled café days of 'The Last Time I Saw Richard'.

I've said that there is less ecstasy here than on earlier albums. But there is still longing, particularly notable towards the end of the album, in the home-seeking 'Blue Motel Room'. Here the narrator looks forward to a long journey home. Such a journey is double-edged. It is long enough for contemplation ('I've got coast to coast just to contemplate') but it is a process that is bringing her closer and closer to home, where she hopes her lover is waiting for her; hopes too that he is still in love with her. Despite their problems, old feelings haven't disappeared for her ('you think they're gone . . . they just go underground'). Contemplation has led to a proposed compromise; if he'll cease his affairs with other women, she'll cease her romance with the road ('you lay down you sneaking around . . . and I'll lay down the highway').

Hejira ends with 'Refuge of the Roads' and it's unclear whether this is a return to the romance of travel, a rumination on travel and experience as the cause of the album's 'story' or, more likely, a wide-angle view of the situation the singer is in. Where, in 'Amelia', she had imagined herself as omnipotent observer of the world from above, here the position is reversed and the album ends with an image of the world taken from space in which petty human affairs ('me here least of all') are invisible and unmeaningful in the greater scheme of things. This echoes the lines in 'Hejira' where the narrator pondered her fate in the light of the 'tributes to finality' represented by gravestones and the knowledge that 'we're only particles of change . . . orbiting around the sun'. But the tension came with the knowledge that one cannot take the bigger picture when one is anchored to the past by memory, to the present by circumstance or to the future by desire: 'how can I have that point of view / When I'm always bound and tied to someone' ('Hejira').

Mitchell's travel songs resonate with those of others, suggesting that she is writing and singing via the lettered and sounded experience of other artists. Given her interest in and knowledge of popular and elite art cultures, this does not seem an unreasonable assumption, nor does it seem perverse to hear, in the white lines and freeways of 'Coyote', an echo of country songs such as Merle Haggard's 'White Line Fever'; travelling, moving on and keeping moving are symptoms of fever for Mitchell's narrator as much as for Haggard's. Neil Young, too, has written a considerable number of road songs which owe a debt to the sounded experience of the American highway as popular myth of freedom. One of his more unusual road movies is the song 'Thrasher', which can be found on the first, acoustic side of his album *Rust Never Sleeps* (1979).[44] The song acts as a curious counterpoint to the album's opening and closing songs 'My My, Hey Hey (Out of the Blue)' and 'Hey Hey, My My (Into the Black)', which attach themselves to punk's rediscovery of an earlier rock 'n' roll death drive. 'Thrasher' asserts a break with the past but, instead of succumbing to a narrative of 'burning out' or dying a glorious rock death, it engages instead with renewal, moving on, freshness and the promise of a new day. But where such an attitude might be associated with the hippie dreams to which Young occasionally seems bound, the narrator of 'Thrasher' wishes to move on from the past. There is recourse to an Edenic vision, but it is not the vision of Woodstock (the festival) or 'Woodstock' (the song). The perspective from which the narrator sings to us is the memory of an early morning when he hit the road in an attempt to 'catch an hour on the sun'. As he makes his way through a dreamlike landscape (a place of gorges and canyons but still in sight of 'an asphalt highway bending'), he observes the enormous wheat thrashers and dreams a dream of escape from a past that threatened entrapment and cultural death: 'I was feeling like my day was just begun.' Wary of the deadening effect of material comforts, he 'knew I'd had enough, burned my credit card for fuel / Headed out to where the pavement turns to sand'. As sacrifice, he has to leave his friends behind; 'how I lost [them] I still don't understand', he sings, but it's clear that he believes it was they who did not understand. Further comforts call to him, resting places where he can get off the road awhile, but he's 'not stopping there, got my own row left to hoe / Just another line in the field of time'. A final vision of the thrashers confirms an earlier suspicion of apocalypse; they are coming to cut everyone down. He'll be stuck 'like the dinosaurs in shrines / But I'll know the time has come to give what's mine'.

'Thrasher' is one of Young's most sustained poetic visions and its affect is aided by a hypnotic acoustic guitar accompaniment and a yearning vocal melody which seeks to evade resolution. The metaphors are rich and evocative and alternate, as so often with Young, between seeming to offer 'obvious' meanings and slipping away from any firm correlation with reality. Commentators on Young's music have been quick to read the song as criticism of Young's former bandmates Crosby, Stills & Nash and to use this as evidence to authenticate Young as the only member of that fraternity to be saying anything valid in the punk era. While this offers a convincing reading of the song, there is potential for broader but still specific readings. The song's main messages could be understood as trying to cheat time ('to catch an hour on the sun') and to get ahead of the narrative that is being made of one's life. The thrashing of the past is a necessity for moving on, but this is a cyclical process of sowing, growing and harvesting (a time for everything, as another song would have it); in this reading, the friends left behind are just collateral damage. But Young, as singer and guitarist, is still connected to the past via a folk style and a rural, seasonal theme; he can be heard to be singing the first folk song of his new world, one that yet carries the baggage of the past. He may be unburdening ('better down the road without that load', he sings), but unburdening requires sharing and showing the burden; the burden is still attached to the unburdened as evidence of what he wished to leave behind. Similarly, the passing on of experience does not drain the storyteller of the experience or the story (whatever Freud might have wished for with his 'listening cure'), though it may help him to live with it (as Freud's successor Jacques Lacan might have noted). The story is his symptom; it is what remains after physical burdens have been discarded. Coleridge's mariner may lose his albatross but its ghost remains as the imperative to testify, to endlessly repeat the story.

You've changed

The 1980s were a time when many artists who had come to prominence in the 1960s seemed unsure what to do with themselves. As mentioned in the previous chapter, Bob Dylan felt he had become 'an empty burned-out wreck'. In the documentary *Woman of Heart and Mind* (2003), Joni Mitchell talks frankly about not being able to find suitably mature roles in the world of pop: 'An actress is not expected to continue to play her ingénue roles . . . I've written roles for myself to grow into gracefully, but there is no growing into gracefully in the pop world.'[45] Back in 1985, after two decades in the music business, Young had used very similar wording when he told an interviewer, 'in some ways rock n roll has let me down . . . It really doesn't leave you a way to grow old gracefully and continue to work'.[46] One of Young's responses to this feeling was to turn towards country music as a way of embracing a tradition of lateness in which age was a badge of authentication rather than a sign of non-belonging. Talking about his decision to record *Old Ways*, his most authentically country record, Young said:

> I see country music, I see people who take care of their own. You got 75 year old guys on the road. That's what I was put here to do, y'know, so I wanna make sure I surround myself with people who are gonna take care of me. 'Cos I'm in it for the long run. Willie Nelson's 54 years old and he's a happy man, doing what he loves to do. I can't think of one rock'n'roller like that.[47]

Similarly, jazz had come to be a genre that would provide Mitchell a similar acceptance of maturity; unlike Young, her musical form showed a gradual evolution rather than veering between one style and other. She has been quoted as saying that one of her ambitions was to 'grow up the American pop song into an art song' and, while such a hope would not require a particular musical form (many of her early 'folk' songs were heard by reviewers as art songs), her move towards jazz and a more layered style of writing seemed to enable the mature style she sought.[48] Her lyrics would continue to make reference to popular culture and to assert the importance of the pop life to life experience. This is exemplified in the song 'Chinese Cafe/Unchained Melody' on the 1982 album *Wild Things Run Fast*, where Mitchell offers reflections on growing older, the passing of time and the vivid memory of youth via pop culture.[49] The singer reflects on her life by comparing it to that of an old friend, a tactic used before on 'Song for Sharon' and 'The Last Time I Saw Richard'. In another repeated technique, Mitchell interweaves fragments of old, evocative pop songs into the narrative. As she reflects on being middle-aged she remembers being 'wild in the old days / birth of rock 'n' roll days' and recalls the Chinese café where she and Carol (the friend) would be 'dreamin on our dimes'. The first song recalled is the Righteous Brothers' 'Unchained Melody' and, as it is mentioned, Mitchell sings the original lyric and melody: 'Oh my love, my darling'. At the end of the second verse the café is recalled with a line from Carole King's 'Will You Still Love Me Tomorrow': 'You give your love so sweetly'. As if the past can no longer be kept at a distance, the third and final verse of the song transforms into a longer rendition of 'Unchained Melody', a miniature cover version that is used to bring the song home. These images of a youthful past are contrasted in the verses with the middle aged present, where even Carol's children are 'nearly grown and gone / Grown so fast / like the turn of a page'. With the page's turn the women 'look like our mothers did now / when we were those kids' age'. In each verse comes the repeated refrain 'nothing lasts for long' and, at the very end, after the 'Unchained Melody' cover, Mitchell sings, in fade-out, the lines 'where does the time go / I wonder where the time goes', recalling the refrain of Sandy Denny's famous song. These references all act as 'inside songs' that haunt and subvert the new song; this is emphasised musically not only by the way Mitchell changes melodies, but also the brief phrase from 'Unchained Melody' played on the piano at the start of the song before being 'suppressed' by the entry of the band. Reference to the sounded experience of the past can also be found in subtle nods to Mitchell's own recorded past: the café scene and dreaming jukebox of 'The Last Time I Saw Richard'; an observation of the changes wreaked on the singer's hometown by industry ('paving over brave little parks') that recall 'Big Yellow Taxi'; the Christmas setting that recalls 'River'; the cycle of generations that was found in 'The Circle Game'.

Both Young and Mitchell continued to record and perform in the 1980s but the work they produced met with mixed reception and is often not considered among their best, even though it includes many insightful songs. Young enjoyed a considerable renaissance in the 1990s, as albums such as

Freedom, Ragged Glory and *Weld* enjoyed critical and commercial success. Young and Crazy Horse were now cast as heroic, grizzled survivors rather than washed-up 'oldies' and their veteran status was used to forge professional and attitudinal connections with the new faces of rock authenticity such as Nirvana and Pearl Jam. Meanwhile, the growth in popularity of 'Americana' music – also marketed as 'alt.country', 'cowpunk' and 'No Depression' (after alt.country pioneers Uncle Tupelo's revision of an old Carter Family song) – shone a retrospective light on Young's similarly themed material, placing him in the role of godfather of this newly categorised genre as much as of grunge. Young would subsequently become more prolific than ever, producing hard rock albums with Crazy Horse, mellower country-flavoured works with other long-term collaborators and occasional solo projects. Like Dylan, he would eventually embark on a series of archival releases, reissues and ambitious box sets, leading to a situation where his past was constantly being worked over alongside his new work. Mitchell was far less prolific but did release new material in the 1990s, as well as allowing compilations of her work to appear under the titles *Hits* and *Misses*.

At the turn of the millennium Mitchell released *Both Sides Now*, an album that placed her voice against orchestral arrangements on a set of jazz standards and new, quite different versions of two of her early songs. As the musical director Larry Klein described the project, 'The album would be a programmatic suite documenting a relationship from initial flirtation through optimistic consummation, metamorphosing into disillusionment, ironic despair, and finally resolving in the philosophical overview of acceptance and the probability of the cycle repeating itself.'[50] As with 'The Circle Game', Mitchell was drawn to cyclical narratives that offered to show time passing while not having to abandon the hope of return and renewal. Following 'You're My Thrill' and 'At Last' – songs that speak of the anticipation, excitement and relief of new love – 'Comes Love' describes the inevitability of losing control to a new relationship; unlike other calamities that can be prepared for or avoided, 'nothing can be done' when love comes. This song inserts a note of experience, for only one who has loved can know this. Experience is at the heart of the next songs, 'You've Changed' and 'Answer Me, My Love', as love turns to disappointment and confusion. Then comes Mitchell's own

'A Case of You' and it is time to revisit that point 'just before our love got lost'. As ever with this song, infatuation and desire are the dominant themes but they are played out in a moment of lateness, a posthumous report on a love that has disappeared. The second half of the album follows the descent of the romantic arc: 'Don't Go to Strangers', 'Sometimes I'm Happy', 'Don't Worry 'Bout Me', 'Stormy Weather', 'I Wish I Were in Love Again'. The newly orchestrated version of 'Both Sides, Now' closes the suite, offering much to think about. The voice has very noticeably deepened with age and lifestyle (notably, sustained cigarette consumption) and offers a striking contrast to that heard originally delivering these songs on *Blue* and *Clouds*. This means that, assuming we know those early recordings (and many of us do), we hear Mitchell's age and implied experience in a very direct way and one which cannot help but add new layers of meaning to the lyrics being sung. More than ever these become songs of experience: ours as much as hers. For if, at first, we are mainly aware of Mitchell's voice having aged in performance, we must surely also realise that we, too, have aged with it, or will soon. The voice offers us an 'acoustic mirror' in which to witness the passing of time in our own bodies as well as in that of the singer.[51]

Another striking aspect of Mitchell's inclusion of two of her songs on this album is the implication (or perhaps assertion) that her work stands the test of time and can be placed alongside the now canonised standards of the first half of the twentieth century. The placement also works to validate Mitchell as a jazz singer (and writer), as does the inclusion of jazz veterans Wayne Shorter and Herbie Hancock on the album. These are the 'grown up' versions of the songs, we are led to understand, performed by an indisputably mature woman who is more confident than ever of her achievements. The connection to jazz singing was not lost on reviewers, several of whom made comparisons to singers of the past. In a *New York Times* review, Stephen Holden compared Mitchell's voice to those of Billie Holiday and Frank Sinatra, singers 'whose vocal deterioration brought them greater emotional depth and realism'.[52] Holiday's late voice was documented most memorably on her last two albums, *Lady in Satin* (1958) and *Billie Holiday* (1959), on which she too was accompanied by orchestral arrangements. Aspects of lateness were highlighted in Irving Townsend's original liner notes to *Lady in Satin*:

These striking performances tell a great deal about Billie Holiday's special talent. For one thing, they are the records of an artist who was making records twenty years ago (Lady Day) and who has sung with every great jazz player. The maturity this implies is there to hear, making words and phrases more meaningful, melodies of familiar sings suddenly new again. And . . . most of us know the life behind her voice. Few singers have suffered so much, paid such penalties for a career, had so few pleasant memories of fame as she. Because we know her so well, we find a more personal meaning in her songs. It's so easy to believe what she sings.[53]

Listening to *Lady in Satin* confirms the lateness in the deep, husky, 'broken' sound of Holiday's voice. For Will Friedwald, 'The dramatic contrast between [Holiday's] hoarse and passionate sound and the orchestrations . . . helps to make this one of the most moving collections of pop standards of its time – or any other.'[54] Joni Mitchell does not fit all of these criteria but there is something similar in the way we can consider *Both Sides Now*. Mitchell seems to encourage such a comparison by including two songs from Holiday's last recordings – 'You've Changed' and 'Sometimes I'm Happy' – on the album.[55] Certainly, phrases seem more meaningful in these late performances and we hear a singer with a life behind her. Where the earlier recording of 'Both Sides, Now' had found the singer, in Michelle Mercer's words, 'still young enough to be in search of settings and experiences, moorings to which she might attach the song's air of loss and nostalgia', now those moorings seem to be firmly in place.[56] 'Both Sides, Now' was never a simple binary song, despite its title. For a start, two perspectives are given in each refrain about three different areas – clouds, life and love – creating multiple perspectives when taken together. Even so, the temptation to read it as multi-faceted is greater in the late version simply because of the other matter that has worked itself into the grain of the songs in the intervening years, the folds of narrative in the lives of Mitchell and her audience are enveloped. Listening to the creases in her voice, we are drawn to the same song but a different biographical time. Hearing the repeated line at the end of the reworked 'Both Sides, Now' – 'I really don't know life at all' – we witness the sadness and resignation that come with wisdom rather than the wonder that sparked the original observation. To not know life or love in one's youth is one thing; to claim to not know it 'at all' after the bulk of a lifetime is seemingly another. Even if clouds, love and life are eternal mysteries which we can never know, we cannot easily avoid reading life experience into the new recording and recognising new wisdom in the words. From the other side of sadness and resignation, though, come happiness and acceptance and these too are gifts of wisdom.

Such observations can be attached even more forcefully to *Travelogue*, the album Mitchell released in 2002.[57] Here she repeated the experiment of placing her voice against an orchestra but this time focusing exclusively on her own songs. The long (double CD) project provides a retrospective account of her work that operates quite differently to other compilations and reissues by creating new versions of old and well-known songs. Thus we are able to hear 'The Circle Game' as it completes another circuit; the song is placed strategically at the end of the album, suggesting the artist has come full circle and may be closing down her affairs, while also hinting at another turn of the carousel of time. Throughout the album, experience is heard not only in Mitchell's deep voice, but also in the layering of the instruments, and the enriched, 'sophisticated' palette of veteran players such as Shorter and Hancock. The connections between travel, life, achievement, memory and experience are made explicit in *Travelogue*, as Mitchell revisits the past via a different route.

And the plains are endless

Neil Young's voice is notable in not having changed very noticeably over the course of his career. This places him in dramatic contrast to Joni Mitchell, whose pitch has deepened and coarsened to an extent where she has virtually retired from singing. Young has always alternated between the kind of quieter, higher, 'fragile' vocals generally found on his slower material (often, but not always, acoustic-based) and the louder, harsher 'abrasive' voice used on faster, rockier songs (often electric). William Echard argues convincingly that, while this has involved a certain dichotomy of vocal expression, Young's voice overall presents 'a single, layered persona rather than a family of distinct vocal personas'.[58] I would suggest that when considering Young's late voice, we might do as well to look to his guitar playing, understanding this instrumental voice as one which has attained added depth and patina. Where sometimes we hear of performers' later work being a shadow or imitation of earlier work, with Young it is as if the reverse were true. The later work gets wilder, longer, more epic and exploratory. The spaces opened up in the ever longer instrumental breaks that he explores with Crazy Horse become more apocalyptic and/or psychedelic, with the voice of the guitar taking over as signifier of meaning from that of the singer. Of course, Young has often performed without Crazy Horse and we should also look to his experiments and collaborations to identify aspects of artistic exploration: his vocoder work in the 1980s; the different genre experiments of his period with Geffen Records; the sharing of vocals outside of CSNY (with Nicolette Larson, Waylon Jennings and Willie Nelson in his mid-period, or the use of choirs in more recent years). But Crazy Horse is a recurring real for Young, the site to which his music always seems destined to return.

But if Young's work with Crazy Horse is in one way a return to home, it is ever more evident in their late collaborations that it is also a vehicle for extended journeys and the companionship of the epic journey where the road becomes its own kind of home. The late album *Psychedelic Pill* (2012) provides a particularly effective example of such epic journeys. The album is notably long (a double CD or triple record) and so are some of its tracks: 'Driftin' Back' is over twenty-seven minutes long and both 'Ramada Inn' and 'Walk like a Giant' are over sixteen. Young has previously used long running times to explore different paces, moods and narrative developments (e.g. in 'Down by the River', 'Cortez the Killer' and 'Change Your Mind') and there is some of that here; mostly, though, the songs seem to stretch on because the group want them to rather than because the length serves the narrative. Even so, some interesting narrative techniques are deployed. 'Driftin' Back' opens with a strummed acoustic guitar, echoing the kind of mellow work to be found on Young's *Comes a Time* (the first track of which is titled 'Goin' Back'). Then Young performs the sonic equivalent of the kind of visual flashbacks used in Jim Jarmusch's 1997 portrait of Crazy Horse, *Year of the Horse*. As he sings about drifting back, the electric guitars and drums of the band fade in and take over the acoustic music. The 'driftin' back' refrain continues as the music takes over, suggesting we are being taken back to the

endless Crazy Horse road.[59] This endless highway is embodied in startling
form by the epic length of the track, while the mellow feel of the acoustic
opening is actually maintained by the regulated, unchanging continuum of
Crazy Horse backing. With the band on cruise control, the music becomes
hypnotic, which may account for why the song does not seem as long as it is.
Listening to any song is an experience in passing time, but Young and Crazy
Horse extend this by stealing half an hour of our lives without our noticing.
Some, of course, may find such tactics incredibly boring, like a journey
without change of scenery; as if to counter this, Young judiciously inserts
verses, refrains and guitar solos. While the solos only start to approach
the incendiary qualities Crazy Horse is known for towards the end of the
track, the verses and refrains are enough to break the journey, to give it
a point. Some of the verses give up their meaning easily, while others are
more enigmatic; as with earlier work, the verses seem to be here to give a
reason for the solos to happen, with the main point of the song being the
epic music and the occasionally exploratory guitar.

This is not to say that the words are not of interest. The lyric 'I'm driftin'
back' describes and models an act of reminiscence and the recreation of
something older, while other lyrics address the discord between the present
and the past. In a bizarre act of self-reflexivity, one that virtually does away
with the normal caveat of distinguishing between singer, protagonist or other
persona, Young uses the first verse to talk about how things were different
in the past and how he 'wrote about it in my book'. He admits to worrying
'that you can't hear me now / or feel the time I took / to make you feel this
feeling'. While it is entirely possible that a listener could come to these lyrics
innocent of the information necessary to 'decode' them, it is also likely that
reasonably well-informed fans of Young will realise that he is referring to his
simultaneously released memoir *Waging Heavy Peace: A Hippie Dream*, that
he is talking about his well-publicised views on contemporary audio quality
and that he is speaking as himself (Neil Young) addressing us, his fans. Other
verses recount the singer's changed feelings towards Picasso's art now that it
appears as computer screen wallpaper, more about poor audio quality and
references to Jesus, the Maharishi and a hip hop haircut. The tone is rambling
and seemingly disconnected, as befits this wandering song; it's as if the rigidity

of the road, the unchanging nature of the musical journey has allowed for the mind to wander. This is a process mirrored in Young's book and one he seems to be well aware of, judging by the numerous remarks in the text about rambling from one thought to another. At one point he notes the usefulness of being able to write prose at a time in which he is finding it difficult to write songs: 'I am beginning to see that the rest of my life could conceivably be spent as an author, churning out books one after another . . . There is a lot of room there for me to wander, which I am very fond of doing.'[60] This songwriter's block may even account for the way in which the tracks on *Psychedelic Pill* took form as extended jams and for the choice of covering others' material on the albums *Americana* (2012) and *A Letter Home* (2014).

In a liner note for 'Driftin' Back', Young writes 'Things that bother you fade away to maybe return as a shadow, not so big.' This has resonances of being a shadow of one's former self but also serves as a way of shaking off the heavy burden of the past. In terms of age there are the parallel suggestions that things take longer as one gets older but also that there is the seemingly endless stamina of Crazy Horse and of what Echard calls Young's 'poetics of energy', an energy that appears to create its own continuum. As for the band, their purpose has always been to wander; this is less an old band taking longer to do things they used to do more economically, and more a logical extension of what they were constituted around: taking as long as it takes to explore the territory of a song. Young also uses the notion of territory in his description of music-making with Crazy Horse:

> When music is your life, there is a key that gets you to the core. I am so grateful that I still have Crazy Horse, knock on wood. You see, they are my window to the cosmic world where the muse lives and breathes. I can find myself there and go to the special area of my soul where those songs graze like buffalo. The herd is still there, and the plains are endless. Just getting there is the key thing, and Crazy Horse is my way of getting there. That is the place where music lives in my soul. It is not youth, time, or age. I dream of playing those long jams and floating over the herd like a condor. I dream of the changing wind playing on my feathers, my brothers and sisters around me, silently telling their stories and sharing their spirits with the sky. They are my life. How often can a guy make a living doing that?[61]

This is a very visual image and it is worth remembering that Young has long been interested in filmmaking. Much of his songwriting can be understood as filmic in that visual imagery and the evocation of scene often take precedence over more 'logical' narrative; the songs offer a sense of place. This connects Young once more to Mitchell, who has often described herself as a painter who makes music and whose painterly techniques can be found in the experiential palette and layering of imagery of her mature songs. In her book on the passing of time, Sylviane Agacinski writes of the experience of leaving a cinema and of transferring from the film's time to the time of the world outside: 'For an instant we remain suspended between two times.'[62] This gets at the materiality of cinema-going, or indeed of the giving over of ourselves to any activity where we are likely to be immersed in a different time world. So too with music and, while the obvious correlative would be the concert experience, we can equally think of the immersion into other listening experiences, such as listening to music at home or on a journey. With extended pieces of music, especially of the repetitive, lulling sort essayed by Crazy Horse, this sense of immersion can play tricks on our perception of time passing. For me, listening to 'Ramada Inn' or 'Walk like a Giant' rarely feels like sixteen minutes, although a more conventional LP side of four or five songs is quite likely to. This is particularly notable when I listen to *Psychedelic Pill* on vinyl, where 'Driftin' Back' has to be placed over two sides of the first record. After a little over eighteen minutes the track fades out and the listener is required to turn the record over, at which point the song fades back in and plays for a further ten minutes; this is an odd experience in the twenty-first century and also quite ironic for a song that is preoccupied at certain points with audio formats.[63]

'Ramada Inn' offers another road trip and uses its lyrical narrative to present a long-term relationship as a journey. Verses offer brief vignettes from the stages of the relationship, interspersed with epic, keening electric guitar solos. The verses emphasise continuity and the struggles, sacrifices and acceptances that come with a long relationship, while the chorus is about starting again each day and the cyclical nature of everyday life, of keeping on keeping on. 'Ramada Inn' contains some of Young's most elegantly wistful singing and playing, offering a reminder that his more fragile registers can be deployed over epic electric workout as much as his more 'folkie' or 'confessional' work on acoustic guitar and piano. Official videos for songs on *Psychedelic Pill* were released on Young's YouTube channel; the one for 'Ramada Inn' highlighted the road imagery and the notion of an endless journey while also, through the use of vintage film stock, suggesting a journey from and through the past.[64]

Conclusion

Mitchell and Young can both be seen as poets and singers of the decay of the event. The events recorded vary but two predominant themes are the 'event' of rock and roll (and its aftermath) and the 'event' of the romantic relationship. Both offer testimony in song to the failure of the dreams and ambitions of the 1960s, though this is arguably more explicit in Young's work than in Mitchell's. Mitchell's early work offers numerous examples of the hopes and disappointments of the time, while her later work offers subtler critique and reflection via the modification of a back catalogue of songs that had helped to define the times. Young also offers early examples of critique, most notably in what journalists have named his 'doom' or 'ditch' trilogy of albums. Later his music excavates, explores and repositions the back catalogue, as Mitchell's does, while also offering new visions of the past that are both utopian and dystopian. Mitchell is a more explicit chronicler of the event of the romantic relationship; this theme runs throughout her own songwriting and is later explored through the combination of that songwriting with jazz standards of the past, showcasing her contribution to a twentieth-century canon of songs of love and hate.

Decay is modelled in Mitchell's voice too, which has fallen from the high, innocent enquiry of her early performances to become a harsh chronicle of the traces life leaves on the body. Young displays his own bodily decay externally, in the sight of his body, rather than in his voice, which eerily retains much of its original 'high innocent' quality; he also displays it in the externalised force of his guitar playing and in what Jimmy McDonough calls his 'gunky distorto headache music'.[65] The rasp of Mitchell's late voice works in dynamic tension with the lush jazz-orchestral settings of her music, rough against smooth. Young often places an ethereal vocal against the high doo-wop-referencing harmonies of his band Crazy Horse and the group's devastatingly harsh sonic attack. But he also allows his voice and those of his harmony singers to roughen in places, in keeping with the particular authenticity work the band are known for: raw, energy-driven, basic (and deceptively 'amateur') guitar-bass-drums rock. His music may have its roots in, and attempt a return to, garage rock, but time, reputation and resources have ensured that the end result is more coordinated military assault than homemade bomb. Young attempts to divert such imagery by his notion of 'waging heavy peace'. But he is changeable, and much more prolific than Mitchell, giving the two artists a quite distinct presence in the popular culture of the 2000s.

Young's voice, sometimes described by detractors as a whine, is a crucial aspect of his art, its high searching tones connecting to notions of childishness, innocence and constant curiosity. This side of his art veers away from the mawkish through occasional harsh attacks on hippy ideals. He counters love and peace with a heavy peace, one that can still be waged. The dynamic of innocence and experience in his music provides its complexity and connects him to Mitchell. The 'simplicity' of her early work allows for a more clarified expression of mature themes; the music may become more complex later and the lyrics more abstract, but this speaks to a maturity of style rather than content. The content was always there, and it remains remarkable that the young singer was able to present, in such clear and simple terms, truths of great profundity and maturity. We might even say that Joni Mitchell's late voice is nowhere more apparent than in her early work and that we should more readily connect innocence to complexity. Even so, we cannot escape the real lateness of Mitchell's late voice, as displayed so movingly in her albums of the early 2000s. As the singer and songwriter Guy Garvey said when introducing Mitchell's late reading of 'A Case of You' on the programme *Desert Island Discs*, 'it's such a nostalgic song in the first place that, to hear Joni doing it as an older lady, you feel like you've been with her all that time'.[66]

Conclusion: Late Thoughts

During the writing of this book, in October 2013, I attended a relatively small and intimate concert by the American singer and songwriter Judy Collins. The show was run as a kind of autobiography in story and song, with Collins introducing most numbers with an anecdote from her long and varied career. A number of the tales were ones that have also featured in her written work, which includes volumes of memoir, theories of creativity and reflections on coping with tragedy. Some of the stories veered close to a rather solipsistic 'me and my famous friends' routine, but Collins generally managed to pull back from this potentially alienating space by reflecting thoughtfully on a long artistic career and the experience it brings. There were, perhaps not surprisingly for a performer in her seventies, a number of references to age and longevity. In revisiting the people, places, events and songs of her past, Collins also suggested the fluidity of the life course and, rather than trying to fix particular, canonical moments, she would suggest other potential trajectories. Often before singing a particular songwriter's work, she would introduce the song by singing fragments of other songs by, or associated with, that artist, intimating another possible setlist (one to play, perhaps, on another evening in another place). Before singing Leonard Cohen's 'Suzanne' (a song she made famous in 1966) she sang fragments of his 'Joan of Arc' and 'Song of Bernadette'. Stephen Sondheim's 'Send in the Clowns' (a mid-1970s hit for Collins) was prefaced by an early Sondheim song. Collins treated some parts of the concert like a folk club set, inviting participation, then singing without guitar or piano accompaniment on 'Golden Apples of the Sun', the aching song of lateness that provided the title track for her second album in 1962. She also spoke about the American folk revival of the 1950s and 1960s and emphasised the finding of songs, downplaying the role of folk singers like Pete Seeger and Woody Guthrie as authors. Of the songs she had 'found', albeit in rather different conditions than the song collectors of the past, she included Joni Mitchell's 'Chelsea

Morning' (another song and songwriter that Collins helped to introduce to the general public in the 1960s) and John Denver's 'Leaving on a Jet Plane' (which she fused with his 'Take Me Home, Country Roads' with its observation that 'life is old there'). She also included her own songs, including her early composition 'Albatross' and an epic, spellbinding rendition of her later song 'The Blizzard'.

Leaving the concert I overheard an audience member say that Collins's voice was 'not what it was'. On the one hand, this remark seemed common enough, the kind of thing we might easily say when comparing a veteran artist's work with the work that made them famous long ago. But on the other hand, it seemed a very odd thing to say. How would a voice go through life unchanged? Would this audience member say that Collins's hair (fabulously styled, but clearly that of an older woman) or any other part of her body was 'not what it was'? It led me to wonder again to what extent we expect voices to stay the same, especially, perhaps, when our main relationship to a singer is through the voice rather than the rest of their body, and through the fixed-in-amber recorded voice at that. It is perhaps customary nowadays to consider bodily image as much (if not more) than vocal ability when evaluating popular singers, especially female singers (in this sense the 'double standard of aging' has not altered much (at all?) since Susan Sontag wrote about it over four decades ago[1]). But there are still singers, and singing styles, genres and traditions, where sound is as important as sight, so the point about recording remains. Voices may not age as notably as faces (though some do, especially those engaged for long periods of time in voice-wrecking practices such as smoking, drinking or 'untamed' singing) but they do age and to expect a voice in a late-life live performance to match that of an earlier recorded (or remembered live) performance seems unreasonable. Another reason I was surprised by the comment was that my own response to Collins's vocal performance was quite positive. Although there were moments of strain in some songs (particularly transitions of register between chest and head voice), there were also moments when the voice sounded 'younger' than its owner.[2] That these moments were, for me, uncanny suggests that I at least had the expectation of hearing age in the voice. Indeed, I had gone to the concert wondering whether the voice would be up to the material. It was.

The concert encapsulated for me a number of the ideas and themes that I have tried to communicate in this book: the constant revision of the self; a self as present in the recorded past; an older self in dialogue with a younger self (and vice versa); song as a site for the presentation of last things, lost things and first loves (Collins included a beautifully nuanced version of Robin Williamson's 'First Boy I Loved'); the role of narrative in getting over, moving on from, mocking, admonishing or respecting one's younger self; the creation of new narratives from the perspective of additional lateness. Like any concert, it was a story unfolding in time and also an autobiography, a story of how that performer got to be placed in front of an audience that night, of all that had gone before in preparation for that moment of sharing.[3] Then there was the question of whether a voice was 'what it was' and if, as seemed likely, it was not, then there were other questions about whether this was cause for anxiety or celebration. As I researched the musicians discussed in this book, and read about others who I ultimately couldn't find time or space to represent, I was struck by the range of metaphors that writers use to evoke old voices. There are the descriptions that dwell on the fact that the voice is not what it was; they speak of ruins, wrecks, cracks, breaks and collapse. Then there are those which see change more positively as an inevitable process that adds rather than subtracts; they speak of vintage wines, fine old tapestries, worn leather, burnished wood, lived-in clothes, enriched palettes and patinas, the accumulation and layering of affective qualities.

These more positive accounts encourage us to witness aged objects (including voices) in the present, as things with still fascinating lives. This is how I felt about the Judy Collins concert, and how I feel when I find myself sinking into the sometimes caustic, sometimes caressing surfaces and folds of late vocal masterpieces by Bob Dylan, Merle Haggard, Willie Nelson, Lucinda Williams, Leonard Cohen, Marianne Faithful, Ralph Stanley, Joni Mitchell and many more. One of the compelling aspects of Ian Bell's second volume of Dylan biography is the way it asks us, at the outset, to consider Dylan as a septuagenarian presenting his work, his past and his life to us here and now. Even if the book then resorts to a more conventional chronological account, it nonetheless encourages this refreshingly presentist perspective. For anyone with an interest in studying and learning from history this may seem an odd thing to say, and certainly one of the challenges that those of us involved in cultural musicology face is the necessity to construct historical and social contexts for the musics we are wishing to discuss. But it is also the case that there are some examples – *Blood on the Tracks, Blue, Tonight's the Night* to name a few – where the popular discourse is already so saturated in cultural and historical context that it may occasionally be strategically necessary to remove that context and consider these artists and their work in our current context.

As I suggested in Chapter 1, such a proposition justifies a certain celebratory stance towards documenting late voice. This may lead to the possibility of positing a metaphysics of age and ageing (this is certainly something that occurs in the wider culture) and to falling back on an uncritical authentication of age and experience. I recognise this as a problem and realise that there are moments in the book where I may have let such authenticating processes go by unchallenged. If so, my critical response is not so much to remove value from the metaphysics of age but to locate it at various points in the life course. The examples I have discussed hopefully give a sense of how issues of time, age and experience, articulated by what I have been calling the late voice, are made manifest throughout life, albeit that a certain accumulation in time understandably makes 'real lateness' a particularly effective lens through which to revisit 'early lateness'.

In mentioning some examples of late voices that mean a lot to me above, I have deliberately included some names which don't otherwise make an appearance in the text. I have already spoken in the introduction about how and why I chose the examples I did for this particular exploration. Here, I just wish to note that it is a particular exploration, an experiment and a reflection of my experience. There are other experiments to undertake and I hope to be able to conduct some of them myself. Certainly there were artists, genres and musical styles I had hoped to include but ultimately could not. Among the first I considered were: Abner Jay (1921–93), the self-styled 'last ole minstrel man', who established a career as a folk-blues singer and multi-instrumentalist that drew heavily on notions of lateness, 'lastness', age and experience; Gil Scott Heron and Bobby Womack, recently deceased exponents of musical styles not discussed in these pages (rap, soul, jazz, black gospel) who recorded remarkable late works; country artists Willie Nelson, Merle Haggard, Johnny Cash, Kris Kristofferson, Guy Clark and Townes Van Zandt, all of whom make brief cameos here but of whom there is so much more to say; singer-songwriters like John Prine and Loudon Wainwright III, who moved from being 'new Dylans' (in the media, at least) to sensitive and wry chroniclers of the life course from cradle to grave; British folk/rock artists of the 1960s such as Anne Briggs, Nick Drake, Roy Harper, Richard Thompson and Shelagh McDonald, all of whose work focused interestingly on the passing of time (and of a particular time after the advent of rock music); younger performers of more recent years whose work resonates with the themes of the book, such as Amy Winehouse, Adele and Taylor Swift. And I would certainly want to say more about the people who helped me start to conceptualise *The Late Voice*, Nina Simone and Sandy Denny. Then there are the musics and musicians of other, non-Anglophone cultures, both those I have studied previously (such as fado and Latin American *nueva canción*) and those I have not. Of all the unexplored avenues mentioned here, I hope this may be the next one I can explore and that I can do so in collaboration with others perhaps more knowledgeable of and sensitive to the nuances of the cultural contexts that could be reflected.

I talk of avenues and exploration. Journeys have been a recurring theme and there is much more to be said about life as a journey. In Chapter 4, I quoted Bob Dylan speaking in the documentary *No Direction Home* about setting out to 'find . . . an odyssey' and how 'encountering what I encountered on the way was how I envisioned it all'.[4] In Chapters 1 and 3 I quoted Leonard Cohen on the journey he took towards finding a voice. Like so much that these men say, the words are both simple and profound. They are also far more effective when heard being spoken; Dylan's interview and Cohen's acceptance speech are both fine examples of the seductive power, wisdom and emotion of the singer's voice speaking outside of song. I also used the simple but effective language of the American poet Jim Harrison, who, in his masterful poem 'The Theory and Practice of Rivers', speaks of the 'shape of the voyage' being more important than the fact 'that I got there'; what is crucial and particular to each voyage, as with each river, is 'how it pushed / outward in every direction / until it stopped'.[5] The voyage as a river is central to Thomas Cole's famous series of paintings *The Voyage of Life* (1842), in which the course of a life is shown in four large canvases, each depicting a time of day, a season and a corresponding 'time of man': 'Childhood', 'Youth', 'Manhood' and Old Age'.[6] In each a figure is seen in a boat, navigating the river of life. The river exists alongside the road (or pathway) as a classic metaphor of the life journey and both are endlessly adaptable and combinable, as, for example, when Cecelia Tichi uses Cole's pictures as illustrations for her cultural study of American country music.[7] I have also used the metaphor of the road in this book, though the river is in some ways more compelling (or disturbing) in that its flow is a reminder of the unidirectionality of the life course. Like the 'carousel of time' in Joni Mitchell's 'The Circle Game', 'we can't get off we can only look / behind from where we came'. We might try to paddle upstream but, as Dylan sings in his late masterpiece 'Mississippi', 'you can always come back / but you can't come back all the way'. The river takes us one way but it also pushes 'outward in every direction', as Harrsion says. It offers escape ('I wish I had a river I could skate away on') and reflection ('there is no time but that / of convenience, time so that everything / won't happen at once') and the seduction of depth ('Have you ever gone / to the bottom of the sea?'; 'The bottom of the sea is cruel').[8] The pull is strong; we feel ourselves being taken away, drifting far from the shore. Poems and songs are part of the journey, part of the pull; they lure us away, steer us onward, have us take them up in our own voicing as we take up the tiller; they float away from us too, or wash up on shores to which we may never return. Some we leave behind, others we take with us; more wait ahead. Then there are the songs that will be sung after we're gone and that will take on new meanings in the minds, hearts and lives of others. Songs are some of the ways we experience life, and voices go before us to help plant the seeds of that experience. We live our own lives but we also live the sounded experience we gain from hearing and feeling ourselves voiced and made resonant by others.

Notes

Introduction

1 Richard Elliott, *Nina Simone* (Sheffield: Equinox, 2013).

2 Nina Simone, 'Who Knows Where The Time Goes', on *Emergency Ward / It Is Finished / Black Gold* (CD, Camden 74321924802, 2002).

3 Ros Jennings and Abigail Gardner (eds), '*Rock On': Women. Ageing and Popular Music*; Andy Bennett, *Music, Style, and Aging: Growing Old Disgracefully?* (Philadelphia: Temple University Press, 2013); Andy Bennett and Paul Hodkinson (eds), *Ageing and Youth Cultures: Music, Style and Identity* (London and New York: Berg, 2012).

4 Sheila Whiteley, *Too Much Too Young: Popular Music, Age and Gender* (London: Routledge, 2005).

5 Richard Leppert and George Lipsitz, '"Everybody's Lonesome for Somebody": Age, the Body and Experience in the Music of Hank Williams', *Popular Music* 9, no. 3 (1990): 259–74.

6 Richard Kearney, 'Narrative Imagination: Between Ethics and Poetics', quoted in Keith Negus, 'Narrative Time and the Popular Song', *Popular Music and Society* 35, no. 4 (2012): 496. See also Richard Kearney, *On Stories* (London: Routledge, 2002).

7 This 'we' does not necessarily mean you and I, but the fact that you might not be included in this 'we', that you might hold diametrically opposed views to me, does not mean that there is no shared experience; the latter comes from those whose knowledge, perspectives and explorations have helped me to shape my own. They authorise me to say 'we'.

8 Negus, 'Narrative Time', 496, 498, fn15.

9 Theodor W. Adorno, 'Late Style in Beethoven', in *Essays on Music*, ed. Richard Leppert, trans. S. H. Gillespie (Berkeley: University of California Press, 2002), 564–8; Edward W. Said, *On Late Style: Music and Literature Against the Grain* (London: Bloomsbury, 2005); Michael Spitzer, *Music as Philosophy: Adorno and Beethoven's Late Style* (Bloomington: Indiana University Press, 2006).

10   Richard Elliott, 'Popular Music and/as Event: Subjectivity, Love and Fidelity in the Aftermath of Rock 'n' Roll', *Radical Musicology* 3 (2008), http://www.radical-musicology.org.uk: 60 pars.

Chapter 1

1   Nina Simone, 'Who Knows Where The Time Goes', on *Emergency Ward / It Is Finished / Black Gold* (CD, Camden 74321924802, 2002).

2   Paul Ricoeur, *Time and Narrative*, trans. Kathleen McLaughlin and David Pellauer (Chicago: University of Chicago Press), 1: 5. The quotation from Augustine is taken from Saint Augustine, *The Confessions*, trans. R. S. Pine-Coffin (New York: Penguin, 1961).

3   Eva Hoffman, *Time* (London: Profile, 2011), 64.

4   Hoffman, *Time*, 61.

5   Hoffman, *Time*, 65.

6   Augustine, *Confessions*, 278.

7   Philip Ward, *Sandy Denny: Reflections on Her Music* (Kibworth Beauchamp: Matador, 2011), 96.

8   Jean Améry, *On Aging: Revolt and Resignation*, trans. John D. Barlow (Bloomington: Indiana University Press, 1994), 4.

9   Guy Clark, 'It's About Time', on Guy Clark, *Texas Cookin'* (LP: Edsel ED 287, 1988). All of Clark's recorded work is imbued with a strong sense of lateness. Like Leonard Cohen, he released his first album when he was already in his early thirties and, like Cohen, his songs spoke of considerable experience and reflection. Titled *Old No. 1*, his 1975 debut included the classic 'Desperados Waiting for a Train', a moving account of a boy's friendship with a much older mentor, containing evocative age-themed lines such as 'he'd sit in the kitchen and cry / and run his fingers through seventy years of livin''. The song has been covered by numerous artists, including Jerry Jeff Walker, Tom Rush, The Highwaymen (Johnny Cash, Waylon Jennings, Willie Nelson and Kris Kristofferson) and Nanci Griffith. Walker's liner note for Clark's 1975 album, written as a poem, gives a pretty good definition of the late voice: 'I think of young ones makin' it/too soon/while Tom Waits/Guy writes/of old men/and old trains/and old memories/like black & white movies . . . carved like crow's feet/in the corners of his past'. 'Desperados' and Walker's poem-note can both be found on Guy Clark, *Old No. 1* (LP: Edsel ED 285, 1988).

10 Simon Frith, *Performing Rites: On the Value of Popular Music* (Oxford: Oxford University Press, 1996), 149.

11 Paul Virilio, *The Aesthetics of Disappearance*, trans. Philip Beitchman (Los Angeles: Semiotext(e), 2009), 116.

12 Sylviane Agacinski, *Time Passing: Modernity and Nostalgia*, trans. Jody Gladding (New York: Columbia University Press, 2003), 56.

13 Michel de Certeau, *The Practice of Everyday Life*, trans. Steven Rendall (Berkeley and Los Angeles: University of California Press, 1984), xxi.

14 This and previously quoted lines from 'Burnt Norton', in T. S. Eliot, *The Complete Poems and Plays* (London: Faber and Faber, 1989), 171–6.

15 'A Short Life of Trouble' is an old-time song which circulated in the Appalachian region of the United States and is associated with the performers G. B. Grayson and Henry Whitter, who recorded it in the 1920s. The song is part of the repertoire of Ralph Stanley, the subject of the next chapter.

16 T. S. Eliot, liner note to *Four Quartets Read by the Author* (LP: His Master's Voice CLP 1115, c. 1956).

17 This last image can be transferred to other playback devices in which, whether we perceive it or not, we receive music as a flow of data passing a still point, be it the cassette head, the laser of the CD player or the line (still or moving) positioned in relation to visualised sound waves on a computer screen. As for Eliot's speaking voice, whether it can be heard as a 'late voice' is debatable but his poem is certainly a 'late' poem not only in its author's career, but also in its preoccupations, as Kathleen Woodward makes clear in her study of Eliot's late work. See Kathleen Woodward, *At Last, the Real Distinguished Thing: The Late Poems of Eliot, Pound, Stevens, and Williams* (Columbus: Ohio State University, 1980), 27–67.

18 Bob Copper, *A Song for Every Season* (Frogmore: Paladin, 1971).

19 Keith Negus, 'Narrative Time and the Popular Song', *Popular Music and Society* 35, no. 4 (2012). 483–500.

20 See Nicholas Roe, 'Playing Time', in *Do You, Mr Jones?: Bob Dylan with the Poets and Professors*, ed. Neil Corcoran (London: Chatto & Windus, 2002), 81–104.

21 Ricoeur, *Time and Narrative*, 1: 3.

22 Ricoeur, *Time and Narrative*, 1: 67.

23 Ricoeur, *Time and Narrative*, 1: 68–9.

24 Keith Negus, 'Narrative, Interpretation, and the Popular Song', *Musical Quarterly* 95, nos 2–3 (Summer–Fall 2012): 368–95.

25 Andy Gill and Kevin Odegard, *A Simple Twist of Fate: Bob Dylan and the Making of Blood and the Tracks* (Cambridge, MA: Da Capo, 2004).

26 Nigel Williamson, *Journey through the Past: The Stories behind the Classic Songs of Neil Young* (London: Carlton, 2002).

27 This conflating of biography and song text – of the latter as record of the former – seems especially notable in the case of singer-songwriters or those associated with 'confessional' music; it is also a favoured mode of much rock criticism. These two aspects often come together; to take a typical example, when the magazine *Uncut* put Joni Mitchell on its cover to celebrate her seventieth birthday in 2013, the Mitchell feature was accompanied by a list of the '50 Greatest Singer/Songwriter Albums'. Virtually all the albums featured in the list – which came with the telling subtitle 'Blood on the Tracklists!' – were explained via reference to events in their writers' lives. *Uncut* no. 199 (December 2013).

28 Bob Dylan, *Chronicles, Volume One* (London: Pocket Books, 2005), 34. Dylan would come to treat 45s in a different way in the mid-2000s, when he became a radio DJ and put them together to form a narrative.

29 Post on the Facebook page jonimitchell.com (28 August 2014), https://www.facebook.com/jonimitchellcom/posts/10152648742477436.

30 Shel Silverstein's songs make particularly good case studies for thinking about narrative in relation to experience, given as they are to building stories towards morals or lessons learned, only to twist the narrative in subversive and/or humorous ways. See for example 'A Boy Named Sue' or 'The Winner' and hear these and other Silverstein songs delivered in magnificent late voice by Johnny Cash, Marianne Faithful, Kris Kristofferson, Bobby Bare and Lucinda Williams. The latter three, and John Prine, can be heard on *Twistable, Turnable Man: A Musical Tribute to the Songs of Shel Silverstein* (LP: Sugar Hill SUG-LP-4051, 2013).

31 Marcel Proust, *In Search of Lost Time Volume 6: Finding Time Again*, trans. Ian Patterson (London: Penguin, 2002), 356.

32 Mike Hepworth, *Stories of Ageing* (Buckingham: Open University Press, 2000), 1.

33 Lynne Segal, *Out of Time: The Pleasures and Perils of Ageing* (London: Verso, 2013), 11–17.

34 See Andy Bennett, *Music, Style, and Aging: Growing Old Disgracefully?* (Philadelphia: Temple University Press, 2013); Andy Bennett and Paul Hodkinson (eds), *Ageing and Youth Cultures: Music, Style and Identity* (London and New York: Berg, 2012); Andrew Blaikie, *Ageing and Popular Culture* (Cambridge: Cambridge University Press, 1999); Mike Featherstone and Andrew Wernick (eds), *Images of Aging: Cultural Representations of Later Life* (London: Routledge, 1995); Ros Jennings and Abigail Gardner (eds), *'Rock On': Women, Ageing and Popular Music* (Farnham: Ashgate, 2012).

35 Hepworth, *Stories of Ageing*, 1.

36 Segal, *Out of Time*, 19.

37 Kathleen Woodward, *Aging and Its Discontents: Freud and Other Fictions* (Bloomington: Indiana University Press, 1991), 6. See also Woodward's *At Last, the Real Distinguished Thing*, in which she writes, 'The literature of gerontology is characterized by bipolarity: unfortunately it tends to be either flatly optimistic or pessimistic' (xi).

38 Christopher Hamilton, *Middle Age* (Stocksfield: Acumen, 2009), 71.

39 Hamilton, *Middle Age*, 72.

40 Simone de Beauvoir, *The Coming of Age*, trans. Patrick O'Brian (New York: G.P Putnam's Sons, 1972), 279.

41 I have assumed a similar justification with my musical case studies, for while the experience of reasonably successful veteran musicians may not equal that of less successful ones, or of people in other walks of life, they still offer a privileged site for the witnessing of ageing. Such will often be the case with art and artists; those nominated by any community to express the experience of that community may actually live a rather different experience but they remain meaningful to the community nonetheless. See also Kathleen Woodward's discussion of her chosen poets and their relationship to 'universal values' in Woodward, *At Last*, 20.

42 Beauvoir, *Coming of Age*, 283.

43 Beauvoir, *Coming of Age*, 288.

44 Proust, *Finding Time Again*, 235.

45 Woodward, *Aging and Its Discontents*, 62, emphasis in original.

46 Améry, *On Aging*, 15.

47 Norberto Bobbio, *Old Age and Other Essays*, trans. and ed. Allan Cameron (Cambridge, MA: Polity, 2001), 4.

48 Beauvoir, *Coming of Age*, 292–3.

49 John Strausbaugh, *Rock 'Til You Drop: The Decline from Rebellion to Nostalgia* (London: Verso, 2002), 10.

50 Richard Elliott, 'Popular Music and/as Event: Subjectivity, Love and Fidelity in the Aftermath of Rock 'n' Roll', *Radical Musicology* 3 (2008), http://www.radical-musicology.org.uk: 60 pars.

51 G. Burn, 'Jagger pushing 50', *Observer Magazine* (10 January 1993), 23, cited in Blaikie, *Ageing and Popular Culture*, 107.

52 *Front Row*, BBC Radio 4 (7 November 2012), archived at http://www.bbc.co.uk/iplayer/episode/b01nq3tc/. The same programme has conducted a series of

such heritage interviews with members of the rock 'establishment' – including Morrissey (20 April 2011), Pete Townshend (9 October 2012) and Elton John (3 July 2013) – in which ageing features prominently as a subject of conversation.

53   John Prine, 'Hello in There' and 'Angel from Montgomery', both on *John Prine* (LP: Atlantic SD 8296, 1972).

54   Taylor Swift, '22', on *Red* (LP: Big Machine/Mercury BMR3104000, 2012). The song was co-written by Swift and the album's producers Max Martin and Shellback.

55   Anonymous, 'Taylor Swift, "Red": Track-By-Track Review', *Billboard* online edition (19 October 2012), http://www.billboard.com/articles/review/1066798/taylor-swift-red-track-by-track-review (accessed 14 February 2015).

56   The well-researched and informative Wikipedia entry on Swift cites a number of veteran musicians who have praised her work, including Neil Young, Stephen Stills, James Taylor, Kris Kristofferson, Janis Ian and Stevie Nicks. 'Taylor Swift', *Wikipedia*, http://en.wikipedia.org/wiki/Taylor_Swift (accessed 14 February 2015).

57   Harry Zohn, translator's notes in Walter Benjamin, *Selected Writings Vol. 4: 1938–1940*, ed. H. Eiland and M. W. Jennings (Cambridge, MA: The Belknap Press, 2006), 344.

58   Zohn in Benjamin, *Selected Writings* 4: 345.

59   Walter Benjamin, 'On Some Motifs in Baudelaire', in Benjamin, *Selected Writings* 4: 316.

60   This and the preceding quotation from Benjamin, 'On Some Motifs', 316. For more on *Erlebnis and Erfahrung*, and on the ways in which experiences become experience via memory, see Emily Keightley and Michael Pickering, *The Mnemonic Imagination: Remembering as Creative Practice* (Basingstoke: Palgrave Macmillan, 2012), 25–31.

61   When the experience of having lost time is thought of as a condition of possibility for going in search of time and, with labour, finding it again, we are reminded of two points relating to mental life. One is that, as Eva Hoffman observes in relation to Freud's *Nachträglichkeit* (deferred action), 'We live forward and understand backward' (Hoffman, *Time*, 107). The other is that, for psychiatry, care must be taken as to how far we travel into the past and how long we dwell there.

62   Hoffman, *Time*, 78.

63   Keightley and Pickering, *Mnemonic Imagination*, 21–2.

64   We only have to think of the Jimi Hendrix Experience to see how this interaction is crucial to popular music. The group was offering 'experiences', of course, the like of which had not been heard before. The title of the group's song (and album) 'Are you Experienced?' can be interpreted in multiple ways: have you encountered the

experiences this group offers? Have you accumulated the required experience to understand what this is all about? Have you taken drugs? Are you sexually experienced? Have you experienced altered states of consciousness? Do you know what's going on?

65 Iris DeMent, *My Life* (CD: Warner Bros. 9362–45493–2, 1994).

66 Nicholas Dawidoff, *In the Country of Country* (London: Faber and Faber, 1997), 14–15.

67 Keith Negus and Michael Pickering, 'Creativity and Musical Experience', in *Popular Music Studies*, ed. David Hesmondhalgh and Keith Negus (London: Arnold, 2002), 184.

68 John Dewey, *Art as Experience* (New York: Perigee, 2005), 56, emphasis in original.

69 Agacinski, *Time Passing*, 56–7.

70 Richard Elliott, *Fado and the Place of Longing: Loss, Memory and the City* (Farnham: Ashgate, 2010), 126–30.

71 This passage, not least because I have found myself using the term 'a real desert', cannot evade an association with Jean Baudrillard's work on simulacra, simulation and 'the desert of the real' (Jean Baudrillard, *Simulacra and Simulation*, trans. Sheila Faria Glaser (Ann Arbor: The University of Michigan Press, 1994), 1).

72 Geoffrey O'Brien, *Sonata for Jukebox: Pop Music, Memory, and the Imagined Life* (New York: Counterpoint, 2004), 287.

73 Roland Barthes, *The Pleasure of the Text*, trans. Richard Miller (New York: Hill and Wang, 1975), 36.

74 Italo Calvino, *Under the Jaguar Sun*, trans. William Weaver (London: Penguin, 2002), 54.

75 Calvino, *Under the Jaguar Sun*, 50.

76 Adriana Cavarero, *For More than One Voice: Toward a Philosophy of Vocal Expression*, trans. Paul A. Kottman (Stanford: Stanford University Press, 2005), 4.

77 Cavarero, *More than One Voice*, 7. There are, of course, stereotypically gendered connotations to the use of a seductive female voice and an enraptured male listener who becomes distracted as feeling takes over from thinking. Cavarero is aware of this but argues that here the female voice, in challenging the abstract buzz of anonymous noise, 'attests to . . . the uniqueness and relationality of human beings' and does so 'against a background of sheer noise in a realm where the sounds of things and the voices of men have the same, essentially hostile, ontological status' (7).

78 Steven Connor, *Dumbstruck: A Cultural History of Ventriloquism* (Oxford: Oxford University Press, 2000), 35.

79 For more on the physiological aspects of this, see Sue Ellen Linville, *Vocal Aging* (San Diego: Singular, 2001). I decided quite early in this project that I would not follow this kind of scientific study of the voice, as fascinating as it can be. While the physical, biological changes that occur in voices clearly have a bearing on a number of my case studies, I am more interested in the cultural understanding and interpretation of the voice and of a more complex notion of what constitutes 'voice' in the representation of age (e.g. the voice of song lyrics as much as of singers). Those interested in a more conventionally scientific approach in relation to singing voices may find Linville's chapter on 'The Aging Professional Voice' useful (217–28); additionally, a number of articles in the *Journal of Voice* have studied singers.

80 Tom Waits, 'Ol' 55', on *Closing Time* (LP: Asylum AS 53030, 1973); 'Tom Traubert's Blues', on *Small Change* (LP: Asylum K53050, 1976). The 'patina of experience' is enhanced further on *Small Change* by lyrics which emphasise experience, as in the romantically epic recollections of 'Tom Traubert's Blues' or in the boast, in 'Jitterbug Boy', that 'I done it all'.

81 Roland Barthes, *The Responsibility of Forms*, trans. Richard Howard (Berkeley and Los Angeles: University of California Press, 1991), 270–1.

82 Barthes, *Responsibility of Forms*, 276.

83 See, for example, my *Fado and the Place of Longing*, 61–4.

84 Roland Barthes, *Camera Lucida: Reflections on Photography*, trans. Richard Howard (London: Vintage, 2000), 26.

85 Freya Jarman-Ivens, *Queer Voices: Technologies, Vocalities, and the Musical Flaw* (New York: Palgrave Macmillan, 2011), 2.

86 Dick Gaughan, 'Dick Gaughan's Links in the Chain: Sandy Denny', official website of Dick Gaughan, http://www.dickgaughan.co.uk/chain/sandy-denny.html (accessed 30 August 2013).

87 More or less any recording by Gaughan will provide evidence of this. A personal favourite, partly because we get to hear his voice in collaboration with two other fine but 'clearer' singers, is the version of 'Shoals of Herring' to be found on the album *Songs of Ewan MacColl* by Dave Burland, Tony Capstick and Dick Gaughan (LP: Black Crow CRO 215, 1978). The singers take turns with the verses of MacColl's song; all are moving but the song takes a notably new direction when Gaughan's voice enters, mangling the sense of the words in pursuit of the communication of emotion rather than story (rather, he reminds us forcefully that stories and narratives unfold in sonic as much as semantic form).

88 Jarman-Ivens, *Queer Voices*, 5.

89 Emily Baker's work on the 'maintained' and 'ravaged' voices of, respectively, Dolly Parton and Joni Mitchell is instructive here. Neither voice emerges from analysis as unforced, though each tells a quite different story about its owner. Emily Baker, 'Just Travelin' Thru: Ageing Voices as Queer Resistance', MA Dissertation (University of Sussex, 2013).

90 Proust, *Finding Time Again*, 252.

91 Richard Middleton, *Musical Belongings: Selected Essays* (Farnham: Ashgate, 2009), 350.

92 Mladen Dolar, *A Voice and Nothing More* (Cambridge, MA: The MIT Press, 2006), 70, emphasis in original. Dolar's comment on Barthes's essay can be found on p. 197, fn 10. See also Middleton, *Musical Belongings*, 329–52; Richard Middleton, *Voicing the Popular: On the Subjects of Popular Music* (New York: Routledge, 2006).

93 Michel Chion, *The Voice in Cinema*, ed. and trans. Claudia Gorbman (New York: Columbia University Press, 1999).

94 Dolar, *A Voice*, 76.

95 Barthes, *Pleasure of the Text*, 66–7. I gather here a suggestion of a desire within language itself to be quoted, one which Barthes seems to recognise and take pleasure in as both reader and writer, succumbing (as I do in citing him) to the bliss of the beautiful quotation.

96 Leonard Cohen, untitled acceptance speech, Prince of Asturias Awards ceremony (Oviedo, 21 October 2011). A transcription of the speech by Coco Éclair was posted at the Cohen-related website 1HeckOfAGuy.com, http://1heckofaguy. com/2011/10/25/upgraded-video-of-leonard-cohen%E2%80%99s-prince-of-asturias-awards-speech-with-no-overdubbing/.

97 Leonard Cohen, 'Tower of Song', on *I'm Your Man* (LP: CBS 4606421, 1988).

98 Certeau, *Practice*, xxi.

99 Dewey, *Art as Experience*, 86.

100 See Paul Williams, *Bob Dylan: Performing Artist 1960–1973* (London: Omnibus Press, 2004); *Bob Dylan: Performing Artist 1974–1986* (London: Omnibus Press, 2004); *Bob Dylan: Performing Artist 1986–1990 & Beyond* (London: Omnibus, 2005); *Neil Young: Love to Burn: Thirty Years of Speaking Out 1966–1996* (London: Omnibus, 1997); Michelle Mercer, *Will You Take Me As I Am: Joni Mitchell's Blue Period* (New York: Free Press, 2009).

101 Whether or not this makes it harder for such attachments to be made in a world in which so much is available in so many places so much of the time is another matter: another iteration, perhaps, of Walter Benjamin's lament for the demise

of the storyteller in modern society. See Richard Kearney, *On Stories* (London: Routledge, 2002), 125–56.

102 I could potentially plot a narrative that took in the various points at which *Blue* has come up again in my life, the new meanings it has taken on and how those meanings have joined the strata of earlier meanings, enriching the ground of my experience. For me, a geology of the self would find a *Blue* seam running long, strong and never far from the surface.

103 Dewey, *Art as Experience*, 24.

104 Paul Williams, 'The Way We Are Today', in *The Age of Rock: Sounds of the American Cultural Revolution*, ed. Jonathan Eisen (New York: Vintage, 1969), 311.

105 See Cohen's comments on Lorca, quoted above; hear Merle Haggard, 'Someone Told My Story', on *I'm a Lonesome Fugitive* (LP: Capitol ST 2702, 1967).

106 Siegfried Zielinski, *Deep Time of the Media: Toward an Archaeology of Hearing and Seeing by Technical Means*, trans. Gloria Custance (Cambridge, MA and London: The MIT Press, 2008), 34–6.

107 Jim Harrison, *The Shape of the Journey: New and Selected Poems* (Port Townsend, WA: Copper Canyon Press, 2000), 303. I have previously used this reference in my essay 'So Transported: Nina Simone, "My Sweet Lord" and the (Un)folding of Affect', in *Sound, Music, Affect: Theorizing Sonic Experience*, ed. Marie Thompson and Ian Biddle (London: Bloomsbury, 2013), 75–90; there, the attempt was to account for sonic experience as it unfolded over the course of two journeys, one physical, the other intellectual.

108 Negus, 'Narrative, Interpretation, and the Popular Song', 368–95.

109 Dewey, *Art as Experience*, 76.

Chapter 2

1 No written transcription will do justice to the sounds made in this rendition and my setting out of the lyrics is primarily intended to highlight the way in which the vocal delivery estranges and delays the understanding of the words. Only witnessing the film or listening to a recording will provide a true experience of the sound: *O Brother, Where Art Thou?*, dir. Joel and Ethan Cohn (2000); soundtrack available on CD (Mercury 170069–2, 2000).

2 Steven Connor, *Dumbstruck: A Cultural History of Ventriloquism* (Oxford: Oxford University Press, 2000), 36.

3 Issues of mortality appear earlier in the film when Tommy Johnson reveals he's been to the crossroads to sell his soul to the devil, a play on the famous blues myth; he's asked by one of the protagonists what the devil looks like and he tells them he's 'as white as you fellas'. The lynching scene can be read as the 'white devil' calling in the debt, though it should also be pointed out that this particular devil that Tommy met is identified with the lawman who is chasing the runaway prisoners and who enacts his own 'sentencing' scene later on. No doubt there were multiple instantiations of white devils for someone in Tommy's position at this time and place.

4 Mladen Dolar, *A Voice and Nothing More* (Cambridge, MA: The MIT Press, 2006), 62–9.

5 I speak of finding a true origin even though Mladen Dolar warns us such a thing is impossible (see previous chapter). I do so for the same reason my description shifts between the fantasy of presence (or these things really happening) and the deconstructive mode of Dolar and Connor; in witnessing this voice I can be both caught up in its power and aware of its falsity. The use of Ralph Stanley's voice and this particular song in the KKK scene, meanwhile, is something that has occasionally vexed me, as it has others. Stanley himself has expressed satisfaction in his performance and in the Coens' film while not only distancing himself from the Grand Wizard, but also asserting his confidence in his audience to be willing to do the same. However, viewed critically, this could be seen as an essentially solipsistic gesture which ignores the unfortunately all-too-easy connection between this 'type' of voice/singing and the racial politics of the era depicted in the film – something which the Coens explicitly play on by attaching Stanley's voice to the Klansman; they and their audience know that the voice 'fits'. It is also worth noting here the oddness of the voices of the song and the people being depicted. Why is this song even a diegetic song? Why would the Klansman be singing this when he only represents part of the conversation? Shouldn't Tommy Johnson be taking part in the 'conversation with death'? If this was non-diegetic music, we might be more likely to hear the song as a dialogue between two sides

6 Norberto Bobbio, *Old Age and Other Essays*, trans. and ed. Allan Cameron (Cambridge: Polity, 2001), 16.

7 Ralph Stanley and Eddie Dean, *Man of Constant Sorrow: My Life and Times* (New York: Gotham, 2010), 10–11. Further quotations from this text will be cited in the text as *MCS*, followed by a page number.

8 See Mark C. Taylor and Dietrich Christian Lammerts, *Grave Matters* (London: Reaktion, 2002).

9 Bobbio, *Old Age*, 13.

10 Other versions of the story age Stanley at five years old: see Nicholas Dawidoff, *In the Country of Country* (London: Faber and Faber, 1997), 90–1.

11 Charles Wolfe, liner notes to the Stanley Brothers, *The Complete Columbia Stanley Brothers* (CD: Columbia/Legacy CK 53798, 1996), 7.

12 Gary B. Reid, liner notes to Stanley Brothers, *Earliest Recordings: The Complete Rich-R-Tone 78s (1947–1952)* (CD: Rich-R-Tone/Revenant 203, 1997), 16.

13 Gary B. Reid, liner notes to Stanley Brothers, *The Stanley Brothers & The Clinch Mountain Boys: 1953–1958 & 1959* (CD: Bear Family BCD 15681 BH, 1993), 4.

14 Dawidoff, *Country of Country*, 86.

15 Colin Escott, liner notes to Stanley Brothers, *Angel Band: The Classic Mercury Recordings* (CD: Mercury/Polygram 314–528 191-2, 1995), np.

16 Eric Von Schmidt, liner note to booklet accompanying the reissue of *The Anthology of American Folk Music* (CD: Smithsonian Folkways SFW40090, 1997), 44. Von Schmidt's observation that the singers collected on the Anthology sounded 'old even then' connects to a number of observations made in this book, including the idea of a late voice attained early (due to the fact that many of the singers were young when recorded), the sound of lateness being associated with tradition and the patina of age that accrues with old recordings, however well remastered.

17 Dawidoff, *Country of Country*, 97.

18 The three texts can all be found in the *Journal of Folklore Research* 41, no. 2 (2004). They are: Lloyd Chandler, 'Conversation with Death' (125–6); Barbara Chandler, 'Why I Believe That Lloyd Chandler Wrote "Conversation with Death," also known as "O Death"' (127–32); Carl Lindahl, 'Thrills and Miracles: Legends of Lloyd Chandler' (133–71).

19 At the time of writing there were at least twenty versions of 'O Death'/'Oh Death' on Spotify and eight of 'Conversation with Death' and derivatives. A number of these overlap with Lindahl's list, though there are some that don't, suggesting the possibility of such platforms as an additional archive.

20 All quotations taken from John Cohen's liner notes to *High Atmosphere: Ballads and Banjo Tunes from Virginia and North Carolina* (CD: Rounder CD 0028, 1995). Chandler's late (and only) recording can be found on this collection.

21 Burzilla Wallin, 'Conversation with Death', *Old Love Songs & Ballads from the Big Laurel, North Carolina* (CD: Smithsonian Folkways FA2309, 2006).

22 Ivan M. Tribe, liner note to *The Anglin Brothers* (LP: Old Homestead OHCS-122, 1979); the Anglins' 'Money Cannot Buy Your Soul' is included on this record.

23 The Stanley Brothers, 'Oh Death', on *Hymns of the Cross* (LP: King 918, 1964). For

exhaustive coverage of this era of Stanley recordings, see and hear the four-disc set *The King Years: 1961–1965* (CD: King KG-09502, 2003).

24 Tracy Schwarz, liner note to New Lost City Ramblers, *There Ain't No Way Out* (CD: Smithsonian Folkways SFCD 40098, 1997). Holcomb did not record 'Oh Death' as far as I can ascertain, though anyone familiar with his style can easily imagine him singing it; hear Roscoe Holcomb, *The High Lonesome Sound* (CD: Smithsonian Folkways SFCD 40104, 1998). Boggs's 1963 recording of 'Oh Death' is on Dock Boggs, *His Folkway Years 1963–1968* (CD: Smithsonian Folkways SF 40108, 1998).

25 Hall's 'Awful Death' can be found on Dock Reed and Vera Hall, *Spirituals* (LP: Folkways 2038, 1953); Jones's 'O Death' has been compiled on a number of Folkways projects and more recently in Bessie Jones and the Georgia Sea Island Singers and Others, *Get In Union: Recordings by Alan Lomax 1959–1966* (CD: Tompkins Square TSQ 5074, 2014).

26 Bessie Jones, quoted in Studs Terkel, *Will the Circle Be Unbroken?: Reflections on Death and Dignity* (London: Granta, 2002), 263.

27 *Songcatcher*, dir, Maggie Greenwald (2000). The soundtrack CD is Vanguard 79586-2 (2001). Anne Dhu McLucas uses this performance as part of a discussion of Dickens's singing style in *The Musical Ear: Oral Tradition in the USA* (Farnham: Ashgate, 2010), 11–16.

28 At the time of writing, these versions and others could be found on the Spotify music streaming service. They could thus be placed into an online playlist and compared and contrasted. Such a process can lead to a strange flattening of the archive, where a field recording made for posterity or education ends up sitting alongside recordings made for commercial gain.

29 For another fine example of Eriksen's use of late voice as style and content, hear 'Village Churchyard', an unaccompanied song drenched in lyrics of death and burial, the words stretched out to infinity by Eriksen's formidable breath control. This performance models the kind of excessive grief found in vernacular cultures elsewhere (e.g. in fado, flamenco or rebetiko); listeners either give themselves over to it or long for resolution (much like mourning itself). Eriksen's 'O Death' can be witnessed on his *Northern Roots Live In Náměšť* (CD: Indies Scope MAM451-2, 2009); 'Village Churchyard' can be found on *Tim Eriksen* (CD: Appleseed APR CD 1053, 2001).

30 Richard Middleton, *Musical Belongings: Selected Essays* (Farnham: Ashgate, 2009), 145–74.

31 These suggestions are not proffered as an argument against the claim to authorship by Lloyd Chandler's family. Just as *différance* is just what there is, so authorial attribution also exists. If the song is Chandler's, there is no reason why his family shouldn't seek to have his name attached as author. For *différance*, see Jacques Derrida, 'Différance', in his *Margins of Philosophy*, trans. Alan Bass (Chicago: Chicago University Press, 1982), 1–28.

32 Ralph Stanley, 'Why Should We Start and Fear to Die' and 'The Old Churchyard', on *Shine On* (CD: Rebel REB-CD-1810, 2005).

33 Doc Watson, quoted in Terkel, *Will the Circle*, 236.

34 Almeda Riddle, quoted in Terkel, *Will the Circle*, 263. This account occurs in tandem with that of Bessie Jones quoted above. 'Angel Band' was another song associated with the Stanley Brothers and used in the film *O Brother, Where Art Thou?*

35 Sean Wilentz and Greil Marcus, 'Introduction', *The Rose & the Briar: Death, Love and Liberty in the American Ballad*, edited by Sean Wilentz and Greil Marcus (New York: W.W. Norton, 2005), 1.

36 Greil Marcus, liner notes to Dock Boggs, *Country Blues: Complete Early Recordings (1927–29)* (CD: Revenant 205, 1997), 5.

37 These songs can be found on Sarah Ogan Gunning, *Girl of Constant Sorrow* (CD: Folk-Legacy CD-26, 2006).

38 I am not meaning to say that these two features can't mix (as they do, for example, in the performances of many of history's more inspiring political speakers), but I don't feel they do in these particular performances of Gunning's, which, as Wilfrid Mellers argued, seem to emphasise a 'monody of deprivation' rather than 'vocal bloom'. See Wilfrid Mellers, *A Darker Shade of Pale: A Backdrop to Bob Dylan* (New York: Oxford University Press, 1985), 51.

39 Mellers, *Darker Shade of Pale*, 51–2.

40 Simon Frith, *Performing Rites: On the Value of Popular Music* (Oxford: Oxford University Press, 1996), 196.

41 Svetlana Boym, *The Future of Nostalgia* (New York: Basic Books, 2001).

42 For more on this, see Emily Keightley and Michael Pickering, *The Mnemonic Imagination: Remembering as Creative Practice* (Basingstoke: Palgrave Macmillan, 2012), 112–38.

43 Harriette Simpson Arnow, collected in Guy Carawan and Candie Carawan, *Voices from the Mountains* (New York: Alfred A. Knopf, 1975), 12.

44 In Carawan and Carawan, *Voices*, 13.

45 Simpson Arnow in Carawan and Carawan, *Voices*, 12.

46 Everette Tharp, collected in In Carawan and Carawan, *Voices*, 9.

47 Prine's recording of 'Paradise can be found on *John Prine* (LP: Atlantic DS8296, 1972). Prine's vocal style also connects to its subject matter and to rural music more generally by its use of what critic Roger Ebert referred to, at the time of Prine's first performances, as a 'ghost of a Kentucky accent' and his tendency, especially on this song, to affect the 'high lonesome' tone of classic bluegrass and old-time music. (Ebert is quoted in vintage press materials included in John Prine, *The Singing Mailman Delivers* (CD: Oh Boy OBR-040, 2011).) That Prine was only 23 at the time he first started performing 'Paradise' and other self-written songs was, as Ebert noted, remarkable. This early attainment of a late voice (whether by the voicing of 'late' lyrics, by the attachment of a singing/writing style to 'old' music formats, or a combination of these and other factors) is a theme which recurs throughout this book.

48 Patrick Huber's work on the creation of country music among millworkers in the heavily industrialised and urbanised Piedmont area is illuminating here in that it invites a comparison between the textile and music industries. As Huber observes, 'the commercial broadcasting and recording of hillbilly music between 1922 and 1942 marked the first time that the southern white working class played a central role in shaping American popular music and mass culture'. Patrick Huber, *Linthead Stomp: The Creation of Country Music in the Piedmont South* (Chapel Hill: The University of North Carolina Press, 2008), 22.

49 Greil Marcus, *Invisible Republic: Bob Dylan's Basement Tapes* (London: Picador, 1997), 87–126.

50 '1000 Albums to Hear before You Die', *The Guardian* supplement (17 November 2007), 11. The collection, cited earlier, is Boggs, *Country Blues*.

51 Greil Marcus, liner notes to Boggs, *Country Blues*, 12.

52 Marcus, liner notes to Boggs, *Country Blues*, 21.

53 Harold Courlander, liner notes to Reed and Hall, *Spirituals*.

54 John Dewey, *Art as Experience* (New York: Perigee, 2005), 50.

55 Dick Gaughan on Sandy Denny's 'Banks of the Nile', official website of Dick Gaughan, http://www.dickgaughan.co.uk/chain/sandy-denny.html (accessed 30 August 2013).

56 Ron Eyerman and Andrew Jamison, *Music and Social Movements: Mobilizing Traditions in the Twentieth Century* (Cambridge: Cambridge University Press, 1998), 164.

57   For a good overview of the kind of lined-out singing style that Stanley bases much of his vocal work on, see Jeff Todd Titon's liner notes to – and hear the Old Regular Baptists of Defeated Creek Church, Linefork, Kentucky, sing on – *Songs of the Old Regular Baptists: Lined-out Hymnody from Southeastern Kentucky* (CD: Smithsonian Folkways SFCD 40106, 1997).

58   John Wright, *Traveling the High Way Home: Ralph Stanley and the World of Traditional Bluegrass Music* (Urbana: University of Illinois Press, 1993), xii, 21. Wright also uses the example of song as labour when he writes that 'For over two decades Stanley's Works and Days have been as predictable and unchanging as those of a farmer' (xii). This is somewhat different to the emphasis I have placed on aesthetic labour and individuality, which, in my presentation, make Stanley seem unpredictable. I wonder whether Wright and I are really so far apart, though; I'm sure his account is spot on in terms of how Stanley goes about his job; perhaps what I have been trying to get at is the different way this comes over to a perceiver of the sounds.

59   Larry Ehrlich, liner notes to the Stanley Brothers, *An Evening Long Ago* (CD: Columbia/DMZ/Legacy CK 86747, 2004).

60   Ehrlich, liner notes, *An Evening*.

61   Robert Cantwell, *Bluegrass Breakdown: The Making of the Old Southern Sound* (New York: Da Capo, 1992), 6.

62   Cantwell, *Bluegrass Breakdown*, 15, 79.

63   Wright, *Traveling the High Way Home*, xiv. In making a comparison to Barthes, I am anticipating my use of his concept of the 'biographeme' later in this book.

64   These quotations all come from the final two pages of Stanley's memoir (*MCS*, 451–2) but I have changed the order in which they appear in his text. On a final note, it was announced in the summer of 2013 that Ralph Stanley would embark on a year-long, 80-date 'farewell tour', to culminate in December 2014.

Chapter 3

1   Biba Kopf, 'Lenny and *Jenny Sings Lenny*', *New Musical Express* (14 March 1987), archived at *Rock's Backpages*, http://www.rocksbackpages.com/Library/Article/lenny-and-jenny-sings-lenny (accessed 28 February 2015).

2   For an example of the latter, see David Boucher, *Dylan and Cohen: Poets of Rock and Roll* (New York: Continuum, 2004).

3 Steven Connor, *Dumbstruck: A Cultural History of Ventriloquism* (Oxford: Oxford University Press, 2000), 38.

4 Simone de Beauvoir, *The Coming of Age*, trans. Patrick O'Brian (New York: G.P Putnam's Sons, 1972), 296.

5 Roger Gilbert, 'The Swinger and the Loser: Sinatra, Masculinity, and Fifties Culture', in *Frank Sinatra and Popular Culture: Essays on an American Icon*, ed. Leonard Mustazza (Westport, CT: Praeger, 1998), 43.

6 Travis Elborough, *The Long-Player Goodbye: The Album from Vinyl to iPod and Back Again* (London: Sceptre, 2009), 141.

7 For a sample of the 'gender wars' of early phonography, see Timothy D. Taylor, Mark Katz and Tony Grajeda (eds), *Music, Sound and Technology in America: A Documentary History of Early Phonograph, Cinema, and Radio* (Durham, NC: Duke University Press, 2012), 70–8.

8 For more on the assumed male listeners of exotica and related genres, see Timothy D. Taylor, *Strange Sounds: Music, Technology, and Culture* (New York: Routledge, 2001); Joseph Lanza, *Elevator Music: A Surreal History of Muzak, Easy-Listening and other Moodsong* (London: Quartet, 2004).

9 Uncredited liner notes to Frank Sinatra, *Songs for Swingin' Lovers!* (LP: Capitol W653, 1957).

10 Sometimes a distinction is made between the teenage female audience and an older female audience, as on the (uncredited) liner notes to Frank Sinatra, *Someone to Watch over Me* (LP: CBS/Hallmark HM592, 1968), where we are told that '*all* the females swoon from sixteen to sixty' (emphasis in original). The same liner notes that 'Even men like him for his unequaled way with a song; and they admire him, perhaps grudgingly, for his prowess as a Casanova.' Far from contradicting my suggestion that an implied male fan is addressed in most of the liner notes, I feel this only confirms it; it speaks to the male listener between the lines, as it were.

11 Sammy Cahn and James Van Heusen, liner notes to *Frank Sinatra Sings for Only the Lonely* (LP: Capitol W1053, c. 1962).

12 Gilbert, 'Swinger and the Loser', 39–40.

13 Gilbert, 'Swinger and the Loser', 45.

14 Chris Rojek, *Frank Sinatra* (Cambridge: Polity, 2004), 44.

15 Mladen Dolar, *A Voice and Nothing More* (Cambridge, MA and London: The MIT Press, 2006), 76.

16 I am thinking here of an intellectual trajectory that takes in Hegel's master and slave dialectic, Freud's observations on the 'fort-da' game, Lacan's reworking of

Freud and Žižek's reworking of all these thinkers. This history has informed my thinking, though I do not explore it in detail in this work.

17   David Brackett, *Interpreting Popular Music* (Berkeley: University of California Press, 2000), 106.

18   Rojek, *Frank Sinatra*, 41.

19   Richard Leppert and George Lipsitz, '"Everybody's Lonesome for Somebody": Age, the Body and Experience in the Music of Hank Williams', *Popular Music* 9, no. 3 (1990): 259–74.

20   Leppert and Lipsitz play on the double meaning of 'tear' in 'vocal tear' to refer to both 'weeping and pulling apart' as trademarks of emotionality in Williams's voice. They note the use of the vocal tear in the work of Patsy Cline too and I would argue that such a device can be heard in many country artists, even among those singing long after Williams's vocal style supposedly went out of fashion. It seems as good a term as any, for example, to describe those moments in Merle Haggard's singing when his voice drops out of or down from the song's main register. These moments are usually timed to coincide with particularly emotional words in the song text, providing further layers of meaning, or even subverting the meaning of the lyrics. At these points the singer sounds 'choked up', unable to communicate, while actually communicating very effectively. Such moments also 'tear' the song line, messing with the continuity of semantics, melody and rhythm. In terms borrowed from Roland Barthes, each such tear/drop offers a *punctum* in contrast to the *studium* of the surrounding performance. Nicholas Dawidoff, meanwhile, describes such moments in Merle Haggard's art as 'the unexpected wrinkles of feeling that put the ache in his sad songs'. Nicholas Dawidoff, *In the Country of Country* (London: Faber and Faber, 1997), 250.

21   Leppert and Lipsitz, 'Everybody's Lonesome', 265.

22   Holiday would include three of the tracks from *Wee Small Hours* on her penultimate album *Lady in Satin*.

23   Will Friedwald, *A Biographical Guide to the Great Jazz and Pop Singers* (New York: Pantheon, 2010), 233, 232.

24   Richard Williams, *The Blue Moment: Miles Davis's* Kind of Blue *and the Remaking of Modern Music* (London: Faber and Faber, 2009), 37–8.

25   Will Friedwald, *Sinatra! The Song Is You: A Singer's Art* (New York: Da Capo Press, 1997), 238. A similar combination of noir-style cover and noir-style jazz can be found on Tom Waits's *The Heart of Saturday Night* (LP: Asylum AS 53035, 1974) and it is interesting to compare the depiction of Waits on the cover of that album to that of Sinatra two decades earlier on *In The Wee Small Hours*.

26 This song and the subsequently discussed 'Mood Indigo', 'Glad to Be Unhappy', 'I Get Along without You Very Well', 'Last Night When We Were Young' and 'This Love of Mine' are all on Frank Sinatra, *In the Wee Small Hours* (LP: Capitol W581, 1955).

27 Joni Mitchell, 'The Last Time I Saw Richard' and 'River', both on *Blue* (LP: Reprise K44128, 1971). Another point of comparison would be the way Nina Simone weaves the melody of 'Good King Wenceslas' into her version of 'Little Girl Blue', another classic, multilayered blue moment. Nina Simone, 'Little Girl Blue', on *Jazz as Played in an Exclusive Side Street Club* (CD: Charly SNAP 216CD, 2002).

28 Friedwald, *The Song Is You*, 244–5.

29 These songs and the subsequently discussed 'It's a Lonesome Old Town', 'Good-Bye', 'Ebb Tide', 'Spring Is Here', 'Gone With the Wind' and 'One for My Baby' are on Frank Sinatra, *Frank Sinatra Sings for Only the Lonely* (LP: Capitol W1053, 1958).

30 Friedwald, *The Song is You*, 205.

31 David Lynn Jones, 'When Times Were Good', on *Wood, Wind and Stone* (CD: Mercury 836951–2, 1990).

32 Friedwald, *The Song Is You*, 247.

33 Bob Dylan, *Chronicles, Volume One* (London: Pocket Books, 2005), 81.

34 Gilbert, 'Swinger and the Loser', 48–9.

35 Brackett, *Interpreting Popular Music*, 95.

36 For a fuller discussion of cowboys and cowboyism, see Cecelia Tichi, *High Lonesome: The American Culture of Country Music* (Chapel Hill: University of North Carolina Press, 1994), 103–30.

37 Similarly, for Barbara Ching, there is something Sinatra-ish about the group of country singers who went under the name The Outlaws in the 1970s (Willie Nelson, Waylon Jennings, Tompall Glaser and Kris Kristofferson): 'While their battles with record companies lacked silver-screen drama, their success did seem to validate the American worship of wild and woolly entrepreneurship. Like Frank Sinatra or William Randolph Hearst, the Outlaws made a lot of noise about doing it their way.' Barbara Ching, *Wrong's What I Do Best: Hard Country Music and Contemporary Culture* (Oxford and New York: Oxford University Press, 2001), 120. See also Michael Streissguth, *Outlaw: Waylon, Willie, Kris, and the Renegades of Nashville* (New York: It Books, 2013).

38 Rojek, *Frank Sinatra*, 107.

39 Stan Cornyn, liner notes to Frank Sinatra, *Strangers in the Night* (CD: Reprise 7599–27034–2, 1990).

40 Gilbert L. Gigliotti, 'The Composition of Celebrity: Sinatra as Text in the Liner Notes of Stan Cornyn', in *Frank Sinatra and Popular Culture: Essays on an American Icon*, ed. Leonard Mustazza (Westport, CT: Praeger, 1998), 69. This essay also appears in Gigliotti's *A Storied Singer: Frank Sinatra as Literary Conceit* (Westport, CT: Greenwood Press, 2002), which explores in greater detail the extent to which Sinatra was invented as a 'text' by artists and critics.

41 Stan Cornyn' 'Eye Witness', in *Frank Sinatra and Popular Culture: Essays on an American Icon*, ed. Leonard Mustazza (Westport, CT: Praeger, 1998), 213–22.

42 See Lucy O'Brien, 'Like a Crone', in *'Rock On': Women, Ageing and Popular Music*, ed. Ros Jennings and Abigail Gardner (Farnham: Ashgate, 2012), 19–33. See also, from a period closer to the period under discussion here, Susan Sontag, 'The Double Standard of Aging', *Saturday Review* (23 September 1972): 29–38; Simone de Beauvoir, *The Coming of Age*, trans. Patrick O'Brian (New York: G.P Putnam's Sons, 1972). Beauvoir argues that 'Some "handsome old men" may be admired, but the male is not a quarry; neither bloom, gentleness nor grace are required of him, but rather the strength and intelligence of the conquering subject: white hair and wrinkles are not in conflict with this manly ideal' (297).

43 Frank Sinatra, *September of My Years* (LP: Reprise R 1014, 1965).

44 Jorge Luis Borges, 'Elegy', trans. Donald A. Yates, in *Labyrinths*, ed. Donald A. Yates and James E. Irby (Harmondsworth: Penguin, 1985), 287. Borges goes on to list the things he has seen, including 'death, the sluggish dawn, the plains, / and the delicate stars'. There is notably little sense of death in Sinatra's work, despite repeated mentions of autumns and winters (and leaves falling to the ground), proof perhaps that the focus was very much on life. This unlikely connection between the North American crooner and the South American poet is perhaps on firmer ground when Borges contrasts his having 'seen the things men see' with having 'seen nothing, or almost nothing / except the face of a girl from Buenos Aires / a face that does not want you to remember it'; Sinatra would surely have recognised, and lingered on, such a situation.

45 'I like to take my time / I like to linger as it flies / A weekend on your lips / A lifetime in your eyes.' Leonard Cohen, 'Slow', on *Popular Problems* (CD: Columbia 88875014292, 2014).

46 Roland Barthes, *Sade, Fourier, Loyola*, trans. Richard Miller (London: Jonathan Cape, 1977), 9.

47 Following the logic of the biographeme, Stan Cornyn channels the imagery of the album's themes into his liner notes: 'He sings of the penny days. Of the rose-lipt

girls and candy apple times. Of green winds, of a first lass who had perfumed hair. . . . He has lived enough for two lives, and can sing now of September. Of the bruising days. Of the rouged lips and bourbon times. Of chill winds, of forgotten ladies who ride in limousines' (liner notes to Sinatra, *September of My Years*).

48 Sean Wilentz and Greil Marcus, 'Introduction', in *The Rose & the Briar: Death, Love and Liberty in the American Ballad*, ed. Sean Wilentz and Greil Marcus (New York: W. W. Norton, 2005), 2.

49 Seasons are geographically and culturally specific, a point worth noting when, as in the song that gives this chapter its title, months are used metonymically to stand in for seasons and stages in a life course. This book is primarily focused on music of the United States, Canada and United Kingdom, so we can read the seasonal references with a certain amount of consistency while remembering that they are not universal understandings.

50 Willie Nelson, *Yesterday's Wine* (LP: RCA Victor LSP-4568, 1971).

51 Frank Sinatra, *Cycles* (LP: Reprise RSLP 1027, 1968).

52 Jake Holmes quoted in liner notes to Frank Sinatra, *Watertown* (CD: Reprise 9362–45689–2, c. 1990).

53 Leonard Cohen', Tower of Song', on *I'm Your Man* (LP: CBS 4606421, 1988).

54 Boucher, *Dylan and Cohen*, 137.

55 Boucher, *Dylan and Cohen*, 137.

56 Occasionally this can lead to tedium, as is arguably the case on the song version of 'Death of a Ladies' Man', where the music and the vocal delivery never really change until the closing section.

57 Leonard Cohen, *Book of Longing* (Toronto: McClelland & Stewart, 2006), 98.

58 Jim Devlin, 'Reflections on "Famous Blue Raincoat"', in *Intricate Preparations: Writing Leonard Cohen*, ed. Stephen Scobie (Toronto: ECW Press, 2000), 101. At the same time, there is also great variety in this song compared to others, as Devlin goes on to note; following the minor key verses and bridges, the chorus brings the 'brought' modulation to the major, both an example of 'the minor fall, the major lift' that Cohen would hymn in his song 'Hallelujah' and, as Devlin picks up on, of the crack that lets the light in, a metaphor which Cohen would memorably introduce in another song, 'Anthem', and which would become one of the most-quoted lines in descriptions of his work.

59 Sylvie Simmons, *I'm Your Man: The Life of Leonard Cohen* (London: Vintage, 2013).

60 Aaron Neville, 'Ain't No Cure for Love', on Various Artists, *Tower of Song: The Songs of Leonard Cohen* (CD: A&M 540, 1995), 259–2. The same album features

further country music connections in Willie Nelson's 'Bird on a Wire' [*sic*] and Trisha Yearwood's 'Coming Back to You'.

61   Thom Jurek cited in Jeff Burger, *Leonard Cohen on Leonard Cohen: Interviews and Encounters* (Chicago: Chicago Review Press, 2014), 362.

62   Simmons, *Leonard Cohen*, 53.

63   Leonard Cohen, 'Poem', in *Stranger Music: Selected Poems and Songs* (London: Jonathan Cape, 1993), 3.

64   As should be apparent by now, Judy Collins acts as an important enabling and connecting presence to many of the musicians discussed in this book: Ralph Stanley (via well-known versions of 'Maid of Constant Sorrow' and 'Pretty Polly'); Bob Dylan (numerous cover versions); Leonard Cohen (first cover versions of his material and mutual encouragement as artists); Frank Sinatra (taking Sondheim's 'Send in the Clowns' to even greater success in 1975 than Sinatra had in 1973); Joni Mitchell (first cover versions of Mitchell's work, including a hit version of 'Both Sides, Now'). For the connections between Collins, Sandy Denny and Nina Simone (most notably via 'Who Knows Where the Time Goes'), see Richard Elliott, '"Across the Evening Sky": The Late Voices of Sandy Denny, Judy Collins and Nina Simone', in *Gender, Age and Musical Creativity*, ed. Lisa Colton and Rachel Haworth (Farnham: Ashgate, 2015), 141–53.

65   A 1977 album by Cohen was entitled *Death of a Ladies' Man*. The second song on *Songs of Leonard Cohen*, meanwhile, is entitled 'Master Song'. For a fascinating, if dated, account of the young master-poet, see the 1965 documentary *Ladies and Gentlemen, Mr Leonard Cohen*, dir. Donald Brittain and Don Owen (DVD: WinStar 720917305028, 1998).

66   Simmons, *Leonard Cohen*, 183–4.

67   Anthony DeCurtis, liner notes to Leonard Cohen, *Songs of Leonard Cohen* (CD: Columbia/Legacy 88697093892, 2007).

68   Simmons, *Leonard Cohen*, 349.

69   Anthony DeCurtis, liner notes to Leonard Cohen, *Songs of Love and Hate* (CD: Columbia/Legacy 88697093872, 2007).

70   Both Judith Fitzgerald's and Bill van Dyk's analyses form part of the collective discussion compiled as Douglas Barbour, George Bowering, Jim Devlin, Bill van Dyk, Judith Fitzgerald, Christoph Herold, Drew Mildon, Christopher Rollason, Stephen Scobie and Jacques Willaert, 'Famous Blue Raincoat: A Symposium', in *Intricate Preparations*, ed. Scobie, 100–116.

71   DeCurtis, liner notes to *Songs of Love and Hate*; Scobie in Barbour et al., 'Famous Blue Raincoat', 114.

72 DeCurtis, liner notes to *Songs of Love and Hate*.

73 Jacques Willaert in Barbour et al., 'Famous Blue Raincoat', 116–17.

74 The best book-length study to date of the phenomenon is Alan Light, *The Holy or the Broken: Leonard Cohen, Jeff Buckley, and the Unlikely Ascent of 'Hallelujah'* (New York: Atria, 2012). Babette Babich's *The Hallelujah Effect: Philosophical Reflections on Music, Performance Practice, and Technology* (Farnham: Ashgate, 2013) relates many aspects of the song's strange career in a more fragmentary and freewheeling fashion, weaving in numerous deviations into philosophy and cultural theory. The song is also discussed in Sylvie Simmons's biography (cited above) and there have been numerous features in the media (print, broadcast and online) about the song, including a 2008 BBC radio documentary, *The Fourth, the Fifth, The Minor Fall*, presented by Guy Garvey of the British rock group Elbow.

75 Leonard Cohen, *Various Positions* (LP: CBS S-26222, 1984).

76 Leonard Cohen, *The Future* (LP: Columbia 4724981, 1992).

77 Quoted in Burger, *Leonard Cohen*, 366.

78 Jurek in Burger, *Leonard Cohen*, 363.

79 Quoted in Burger, *Leonard Cohen*, 364.

80 Quoted in Burger, *Leonard Cohen*, 307.

81 Simmons, *Leonard Cohen*, 368.

82 Simmons, *Leonard Cohen*, 367.

83 Simmons, *Leonard Cohen*, 445.

84 Simmons, *Leonard Cohen*, 477.

85 Perhaps Cohen can also be seen to be communicating his years of Buddhist study when he offers his 'beginner's' keyboard solos. The concept of *shoshin*, or 'beginner's mind', might be useful here; see Shunryu Suzuki, *Zen Mind, Beginner's Mind*, ed. Trudy Dixon (Boston: Shambhala, 2011).

86 Leon Wieseltier, 'The Art of Wandering', liner note to Leonard Cohen, *Songs from the Road* (CD/DVD: Columbia/Legacy 88697768392, 2010).

87 Leonard Cohen, *Old Ideas* (CD: Columbia 88697986712, 2012).

88 Simmons, *Leonard Cohen*, 494.

89 Greg Kot, 'Album Review: Leonard Cohen, "Old Ideas"', *Chicago Tribune*, online edition (24 January 2012), http://articles.chicagotribune.com/2012–01–24/entertainment/chi-leonard-cohen-album-review-old-ideas-reviewed-20120124_1_leonard-cohen-album-review-12th-studio-album (accessed 12 December 2014).

90 Leonard Cohen, Popular Problems (CD: Columbia 88875014292, 2014).

91   Cohen, *Book of Longing*.

92   Johnny Cash, 'Hurt', on *American IV: The Man Comes Around* (CD: American/ Lost Highway 063339–2, 2002).

93   Cohen quoted in Neil McCormick, 'Leonard Cohen at 80: "The Other Side of the Hill Is No Time to Tarry"', *The Telegraph*, online edition (20 September 2014), http://www.telegraph.co.uk/culture/music/rockandpopfeatures/11110223/ Leonard-Cohen-at-80-The-other-side-of-the-hill-is-no-time-to-tarry.html. The subtitle of the feature, a quotation from Cohen, resonates with the themes of Sinatra's *September of My Years*, notably 'Don't Wait Too Long' (accessed 12 December 2014).

94   Robert Forster, interviewed on *Drive*, 612 ABC Brisbane (28 August 2014).

95   Rojek, *Frank Sinatra*, 56.

96   Leonard Cohen, untitled acceptance speech, Prince of Asturias Awards ceremony (Oviedo, 21 October 2011). A transcription of the speech by Coco Éclair was posted at the Cohen-related website 1HeckOfAGuy.com, http://1heckofaguy. com/2011/10/25/upgraded-video-of-leonard-cohen%E2%80%99s-prince-of- asturias-awards-speech-with-no-overdubbing/.

Chapter 4

1   Bob Dylan, *Shadows in the Night* (LP: Columbia/Sony 88875057961, 2015).

2   This summary is based on the negative commentary left online by users of retail sites such as Amazon in the month following the release of *Shadows in the Night*. Of the 200 reviews reported on Amazon.co.uk as of 8 March 2015, 102 were five star (the highest rank available), 25 four star, 17 three star, 11 two star and 45 one star (the lowest available); the statistics at the American site Amazon.com were similarly divided, with both sites reporting an overall score of three and a half stars. The album fared better with the (mostly professional) music critics whose reviews were listed at Metacritic.com on the same date, with the album scoring an average of 83 per cent based on thirty published reviews. http://www.metacritic. com/music/shadows-in-the-night/bob-dylan/critic-reviews.

3   Will Friedwald, *A Biographical Guide to the Great Jazz and Pop Singers* (New York: Pantheon, 2010), 781.

4   Friedwald conveniently ignores the traditions of folk, blues and country music that fed the development of rock, even though he includes the singer-songwriter

Hank Williams among his handful of non-jazz-and-pop 'extras'. Williams, Huddie Ledbetter and Woody Guthrie represent just some of the other authorship models operated in popular music prior to the advent of rock and roll.

5 Bob Dylan, untitled acceptance speech, MusiCares Person of the Year ceremony (Los Angeles, 6 February 2015). At the time of writing Dylan's speech had not been broadcast in full but had appeared in transcriptions on various news sites following the event, with many commentators marvelling at Dylan's openness concerning his art and his fellow artists. I am quoting from the transcription provided by the Grammys website at http://www.grammy.org/files/pages/bob-dylan-speech-transcription.pdf (accessed 1 March 2015).

6 Emily Keightley and Michael Pickering, *The Mnemonic Imagination: Remembering as Creative Practice* (Basingstoke: Palgrave Macmillan, 2012), 16.

7 Ian Bell, *Once Upon a Time: The Lives of Bob Dylan* (Edinburgh: Mainstream, 2013); Ian Bell, *Time Out of Mind: The Lives of Bob Dylan* (Edinburgh: Mainstream, 2014).

8 Kris Kristofferson, 'The Pilgrim-Chapter 33', on *The Silver Tongued Devil and I* (LP: Monument 64636, 1971). The song continues 'He's a walking contradiction / partly truth and partly fiction', lines which relate to the issues of persona discussed in this chapter. Further, the reference to making wrong decisions 'on his lonely way back home' resonates with those other homeward-bound imaginings mentioned here.

9 Nicholas Roe, 'Playing Time', in *Do You, Mr Jones?: Bob Dylan with the Poets and Professors*, ed. Neil Corcoran (London: Chatto & Windus, 2002), 82.

10 The first Haggard quotation is from Nicholas Dawidoff, *In the Country of Country* (London: Faber and Faber, 1997), 257; the second is from Merle Haggard and Tom Carter, *My House of Memories* (New York: Cliff Street Books, 1999), 18. Like Haggard, Dylan mixes the sounded experience of the fan who learns about life through other people's songs with the articulation of his own experience (and/or that of his protagonists) through his own songs.

11 Woody Guthrie, *Bound for Glory* (New York: Plume, 1983), 36.

12 Greil Marcus, *Invisible Republic: Bob Dylan's Basement Tapes* (London: Picador, 1997).

13 Keightley and Pickering, *Mnemonic Imagination*, 24.

14 This is a practice we can also observe among the numerous books written about Dylan such as Robert Shelton's *No Direction Home*, Greil Marcus's *Invisible Republic* and *Like a Rolling Stone: Bob Dylan at the Crossroads*, and Howard Sounes's *Down the Highway*.

15   Bob Dylan in *No Direction Home: Bob Dylan*, dir. Martin Scorsese (2005).

16   The Stanley Brothers, 'Long Journey Home', on *Long Journey Home* (CD: Rebel Records REB-CD-1110, 1990).

17   Bob Dylan, 'I Was Young When I Left Home', on bonus disc issued with *"Love and Theft"* (CD: Columbia COL 5043649, 2001).

18   Cited in James Fentress and Chris Wickham, *Social Memory* (Oxford: Blackwell, 1992), 32–6.

19   Bob Dylan, *Chronicles, Volume One* (London: Pocket Books, 2005), 136. Subsequent reference to this work will be cited in the text as *C*, followed by a page number.

20   Bob Dylan, 'Señor (Tales of Yankee Power)', on *Street Legal* (LP: CBS 86067, 1978). Williams's song was released under his alter-ego Luke the Drifter. Dylan and the Band recorded another Luke the Drifter song, 'Stones That You Throw', as part of the 'basement tapes' sessions, with Dylan emulating Luke's trademark spoken delivery. The group also recorded Williams's 'You Win Again' during the same sessions.

21   Dylan, MusiCares speech, adapted from the Grammys.org transcription cited above. In the first comparison, Dylan is quoting a verse of his song 'Highway 61 Revisited', on (*Highway 61 Revisited*. LP: CBS 4609531, 1965).

22   Bob Dylan, 'A Hard Rain's A-Gonna Fall', on *The Freewheelin' Bob Dylan* (LP: CBS 62193, 1963).

23   Paul Williams, *Bob Dylan: Performing Artist 1960–1973* (London: Omnibus Press, 2004), 95.

24   Bob Dylan, 'Restless Farewell' and 'One Too Many Mornings', both on *The Times They Are A-Changin'* (LP: CBS 62251, 1964).

25   Leonard Cohen, 'The Stranger Song', on *Songs of Leonard Cohen* (CD: Columbia/Legacy 88697093892, 2007). I have used the text format provided by Cohen in his *Stranger Music: Selected Poems and Songs* (London: Jonathan Cape, 1993), which makes explicit the story form of the song and the indecision and shifting roles of the protagonists.

26   Bob Dylan, 'Bob Dylan's Dream', on *Freewheelin' Bob Dylan*.

27   See, for example, Williams, *Performing Artist 1960*, 75, and Greil Marcus, *Like a Rolling Stone: Bob Dylan at the Crossroads* (London: Faber, 2005), 21, but references to early oldness abound in the literature on Dylan.

28   Bob Dylan, liner notes to *Freewheelin' Bob Dylan*.

29   This different use of the word 'old' only confuses the issue further, suggesting that the 'young him' was the 'old him'!

30 Mark Polizzotti, *Bob Dylan's Highway 61 Revisited* (New York: Continuum, 2006), 20.

31 Polizzotti, *Highway 61*, 25.

32 Polizzotti, *Highway 61*, 74.

33 Polizzotti, *Highway 61*, 55, 86.

34 Quoted in Jonathan Cott (ed.), *Dylan on Dylan: The Essential Interviews* (London: Hodder & Stoughton, 2006), 148.

35 Polizzotti, *Highway 61*, 133, 140.

36 Marcus, *Invisible Republic*, xv.

37 Marcus, *Invisible Republic*, xv.

38 Robert Cantwell, 'Smith's Memory Theater', *New England Review* 12, nos 1–2 (1991): 364–97. Cantwell's essay reappears as a chapter in his *When We Were Good: The Folk Revival* (Cambridge, MA: Harvard University Press, 1996). Marcus discusses Cantwell's conception in *Invisible Republic*, 113.

39 Svetlana Boym, *The Future of Nostalgia* (New York: Basic Books, 2001), xvi.

40 Marcus, *Invisible Republic*, 89; Bob Dylan, liner notes to *World Gone Wrong* (CD: Columbia 4748572, 1993).

41 Mark Jacobson, 'Tangled Up in Bob', *Rolling Stone* no. 866, (12 April 2001): 64–74, 151.

42 Stephen Scobie, *Alias Bob Dylan* (Alberta: Red Deer College Press, 1991), 21.

43 Marcus, *Invisible Republic*, 265. For a brilliant extended discussion of Dylan's fame see Lee Marshall, *Bob Dylan: The Never Ending Star* (Cambridge, UK: Polity, 2007).

44 Roland Barthes, 'The Death of the Author', in *The Rustle of Language*, trans. Richard Howard (Berkeley: University of California Press, 1989), 49–55.

45 Jonathan Eisen (ed.), *The Age of Rock: Sounds of the American Cultural Revolution* (New York: Vintage, 1969).

46 Jon Landau, 'John Wesley Harding', in *The Age of Rock: Sounds of the American Cultural Revolution*, ed. Eisen (New York: Vintage, 1969), 226.

47 Landau, 'John Wesley Harding', 229. Of course, Landau is still referring to Dylan as an author in these comments but he is suggesting that we don't need to look to Dylan himself for an explanation of the work, which was really Barthes's point. Barthes, after all, remained fascinated by author figures throughout his writing and was keen to assert that his repeated appeal to 'the pleasure of the text' was one that allowed 'the amicable return of the author' (Roland Barthes, *Sade, Fourier, Loyola*, trans. Richard Miller (London: Jonathan Cape, 1977), 8). See also Seán

Burke, *The Death and Return of the Author: Criticism and Subjectivity in Barthes, Foucault and Derrida*, 2nd edn (Edinburgh: Edinburgh University Press), 1998.

48   Wilfrid Mellers, 'New Music in a New World', in *The Age of Rock: Sounds of the American Cultural Revolution*, ed. Eisen (New York: Vintage, 1969), 187.

49   Wilfrid Mellers, *A Darker Shade of Pale: A Backdrop to Bob Dylan* (New York: Oxford University Press, 1985).

50   Quoted in Cott, *Dylan on Dylan*, 260.

51   All the songs cited in this paragraph are on Bob Dylan, *Blood on the Tracks* (LP: CBS 69097, 1974).

52   Bell, *Time Out of Mind*, 38.

53   Michael Gray, 'Signs of Life', *Let It Rock* (April 1975), 34.

54   *Uncut* no. 199 (December 2013), cover. Dylan's album only placed number 17 on the list of 50; *Blue* was at 10 and the top three were the debut albums by Tim Hardin and Leonard Cohen (1 and 2 respectively), followed by Laura Nyro's *New York Tendaberry*.

55   Burke, *Death and Return*, 55.

56   Keith Negus and Michael Pickering, *Creativity, Communication and Cultural Value* (London: Sage, 2004), 25.

57   Bob Dylan, 'Tangled Up in Blue', on *Blood on the Tracks*.

58   Sean Wilentz, *Bob Dylan in America* (London: Vintage, 2011), 140.

59   Paul Williams, *Bob Dylan: Performing Artist 1974–1986* (London: Omnibus Press, 2004), 31–2.

60   Quoted in Cott, *Dylan on Dylan*, 387.

61   Cott, *Dylan on Dylan*, 264.

62   Merle Haggard, 'I'm a Lonesome Fugitive', on *I'm a Lonesome Fugitive* (LP: Capitol ST 2702. 1967); Townes Van Zandt, 'Pancho & Lefty', on *The Late Great Townes Van Zandt* (LP: Tomato/Charly LIK49, 1988).

63   For a fascinating revisionist example, see the tribute album *Bob Dylan in the 80s: Volume One* (LP: ATO 0224, 2014), on which a variety of contemporary artists cover Dylan's 1980s songs and for which Jonathan Lethem provides an essay in which he claims that 'the earlier Dylan belonged to our parents, while '80s Dylan was our Dylan'. I can personally attest to this and, much as Lethem recalls first hearing Dylan on the radio in 1979 ('Gotta Serve Somebody', from *Slow Train Coming*), I vividly recall the 1981 album *Shot of Love*. That said, that album was still my parents' Dylan: it was their cassette I recall!

64   Marshall, *Never Ending Star*, 152.

65 Bill Flanagan, quoted in Wilentz, *Dylan in America*, 235.

66 Wilentz, *Dylan in America*, 253. The lyrics are from the album's final track, 'Lone Pilgrim'.

67 All the songs cited in this paragraph are on Bob Dylan, *Time Out of Mind* (LP: Columbia/Music on Vinyl MOVLP1049, 1997).

68 Marcus, *Invisible Republic*, 21.

69 Paul Williams, *Bob Dylan: Performing Artist 1986–1990 & Beyond* (London: Omnibus, 2005), 314.

70 In Cott, *Dylan on Dylan*, 412.

71 In Cott, *Dylan on Dylan*, 398.

72 Marcus, *Like a Rolling Stone*, 199–201, 232.

73 Bob Dylan, *The Bootleg Series Volumes 1–3: Rare & Unreleased 1961–1991* (LP: Columbia 4680861, 1991).

74 Bell, *Time Out of Mind*, 520.

75 In Cott, *Dylan on Dylan*, 396.

76 Bell, *Time Out of Mind*, 526.

77 Bell, *Time Out of Mind*, 526.

78 For earlier songs written in response to the Titanic disaster, see *People Take Warning! Murder Ballads & Disaster Songs, 1913–1938* (CD/book: Tomkins Square TSQ 1875, 2007).

79 This music-as-sea analogy is also used by Michael Gray when he describes his engagement with *Time Out of Mind* as 'communing with a real Bob Dylan album – the inward thrill, the continuous inner dialogue, the repeated playing, cross-referencing, laughing aloud, floating on the moving sea of it and finding within it a cohesion of sound and purpose'. Michael Gray, *Song & Dance Man III: The Art of Bob Dylan* (London: Continuum, 2000), 791.

80 Gray, *Song & Dance Man III*, 713; Hart Crane, 'Voyages', in *The Collected Poems of Hart Crane*, ed. Waldo Frank (New York: Liveright, 1933).

81 Bob Dylan, 'Tempest' and 'Roll on John', both on *Tempest* (LP: Columbia 88725457601, 2012).

82 Robert Polito, 'Bob Dylan: Henry Timrod Revisited', Poetry Foundation website (6 October 2006), http://www.poetryfoundation.org/article/178703.

83 Greil Marcus, liner notes to Dock Boggs, *Country Blues: Complete Early Recordings (1927–29)* (CD: Revenant 205, 1997), 5.

84 Bob Dylan, 'Cross the Green Mountain', on *Tell Tale Signs: Rare and Unreleased 1989–2006* (CD: Columbia/Legacy 8869774610, 2010).

85 The song may also recall 'I Dreamed a Dream', the much-covered song from the English adaptation of the musical *Les Misérables*. Well-known since the mid-1980s, the song became ubiquitous in 2009 when the then-unknown Susan Boyle performed it on the television show *Britain's Got Talent*. Always a song of lateness and regret, 'I Dreamed a Dream' became an anthem for Boyle's 'lost' life prior to her breakthrough success at the age of forty-eight and, through audience identification with the singer, to the missed opportunities that populate every life.

86 'Every song has an inside song which lives in the shadows, in-between the sounds and silences and behind the words, pulsating, waiting to be reborn as a new song.' William Parker, liner notes to his album *I Plan to Stay a Believer: The Inside Songs of Curtis Mayfield* (CD, AUM Fidelity AUM062/63, 2010).

87 A thread archived at the fan website expectingrain.com shows online discussion occurring around the time of the US broadcast, in which the full performance was cut from five verses to three. Among the commentators, veteran Dylanologist Stephen Scobie wrote: 'what we got was only 3 out of 5 verses. Magnificently sung, though, and with a wonderful scowl into the camera on the "every foe I've ever fought" line. In the midst of an evening of surpassing banality and falseness, this performance stood out as moment [*sic*] of uncompromising sincerity. No wonder the audience looked stunned'. http://expectingrain.com/dok/set/95/9511/951119. html (accessed 1 December 2014).

88 Ralph Stanley and Friends, *Clinch Mountain Country* (CD: Rebel REB-5001, 1997). The Stanley Brothers recorded the song in 1950 during a session which also provided the classic Columbia recording of 'I'm a Man of Constant Sorrow'. Both songs are available on *The Complete Columbia Stanley Brothers* (CD: Columbia/Legacy CK 53798, 1996).

89 In addition to the already cited works by Paul Williams and Lee Marshall, see Andrew Muir, *The Razor's Edge: Bob Dylan and the Never-Ending Tour* (London: Helter Skelter, 2000).

90 Marshall, *Never Ending Star*.

91 Marshall, *Never Ending Star*, 261, 264–5.

92 John Wesley Harding, 'Good as He's Been to Us', quoted in Gray, *Song & Dance Man III*, 712. Harding – real name Wesley Stace – takes his pseudonym, of course, from Dylan's 1967 album.

93 Gray, *Song & Dance Man III*, 712.

94 Marshall, *Never Ending Star*, 236–7. Marshall puts the change in Dylan's voice during this period to the lack of rest it has received during the NET.

95   See Scobie, *Alias Bob Dylan*.

96   Marcus, *Invisible Republic*, 31.

97   Roe, 'Playing Time', 85–6.

98   In Cott, *Dylan on Dylan*, 412–3.

99   Bob Dylan, 'Mr Tambourine Man', on *Bringing It All Back Home* (LP: CBS 32344, 1965).

100 In Cott, *Dylan on Dylan*, 399.

Chapter 5

1   Italo Calvino, *The Literature Machine: Essays*, trans. Patrick Creagh (London: Secker & Warburg, 1987), 12.

2   Roland Barthes, *The Rustle of Language*, trans. Richard Howard (Berkeley: University of California Press, 1989), 50.

3   Geoffrey Cannon, review of Joni Mitchell's *Clouds*, *The Guardian* (1969), archived at *Rock's Backpages*, http://www.rocksbackpages.com/Library/Article/joni-mitchell-iclouds) (accessed 15 December 2014).

4   The definitions and distinctions are, of course, problematic. Wasn't Nina Simone a confessional singer-songwriter when she vented her feelings in 'Mississippi Goddam', a song often invoked as one of the great 'protest anthems' of the 1960s?

5   William Echard, *Neil Young and the Poetics of Energy* (Bloomington: Indiana University Press, 2005), 14.

6   Steven Gould Axelrod, *Robert Lowell: Life and Art* (Princeton, NJ: Princeton University Press, 1978), 4–5.

7   Michelle Mercer, *Will You Take Me as I Am: Joni Mitchell's* Blue *Period* (New York: Free Press, 2009), 12.

8   Mercer, *Will You Take Me*, 7.

9   Mercer, *Will You Take Me*, 42–3. In her song 'For the Roses', Mitchell sings about record companies offering slices of life, a lovely (if sinister) metaphor for the record; perhaps these are the confessions that are extracted?

10 Mitchell herself said she started writing songs when she gave up her daughter and stopped when her daughter returned, which might be a connection between guilt and confession. But I don't really want to psychoanalyse Mitchell; I merely offer this as evidence of the complexity of work, life, intention and interpretation.

11 This and the previous quotation both from Mercer, *Will You Take Me*, 46.

12   See Michael Gray, 'Signs of Life', *Let It Rock* (April 1975), 34.

13   Joni Mitchell, 'For the Roses', on *For the Roses* (LP: Elektra/Asylum K53007, 1976).

14   Emmylou Harris and Randy Newman both quoted in Jimmy McDonough, *Shakey: Neil Young's Biography* (London: Vintage, 2003), 302, 340.

15   Echard, *Poetics of Energy*, 15.

16   Neil Young, liner notes to Neil Young, *Decade* (LP: Reprise, 64037, 1977).

17   Neil Young, 'Helpless', on *Decade*. Young's line 'In my mind I still need a place to go' finds an echo in David Lynn Jones's country song with 'When Times Were Good', which opens with reference to 'a place I can go in my memory'. The song has also been recorded by Merle Haggard and Willie Nelson in a particularly moving version, a model of how memory places can also be created in the folds of singers' voices. David Lynn Jones, 'When Times Were Good', on *Wood, Wind and Stone* (CD: Mercury 836951-2, 1990); Merle Haggard and Willie Nelson, 'When Times Were Good', on *Seashores of Old Mexico* (CD: Epic EK 40293, 1987).

18   John Bauldie, 'Helpless', in *Neil Young and Broken Arrow: On a Journey through the Past*, ed. Alan Jenkins (Bridgend: Neil Young Appreciation Society, 1994), 56.

19   Walter Benjamin, 'Experience', in *Selected Writing Vol. 1:1913-1926*, ed. Marcus Bullock and Michael W. Jennings, trans. Lloyd Spencer and Stefan Jos (Cambridge, MA: Belknap Press, 2004), 3. Parenthetical translations in original.

20   Camille Paglia, *Break, Blow, Burn* (New York: Pantheon, 2005), 227.

21   Paglia, *Break, Blow, Burn*, 228.

22   Is it necessary to make the obvious point here that the phenomenology of listening to recordings makes it as likely as not that a listener will encounter the later album before the earlier? In this case the probability of a listener hearing *Blue* first is enhanced by the album's canonical status and the very high likelihood of devoted or 'converted' listeners recommending it to others.

23   Mercer, *Will You Take Me*, 1.

24   Benjamin, 'Experience', 50-1.

25   Joni Mitchell, *Blue* (LP: Reprise K44128, 1971).

26   Lloyd Whitesell, *The Music of Joni Mitchell* (Oxford: Oxford University Press, 2008), 66-7.

27   Whitesell, *Music of Joni Mitchell*, 66-77.

28   Whitesell, *Music of Joni Mitchell*, 71.

29   Mercer, *Will You Take Me*, 104.

30   Mercer, *Will You Take Me*, 175.

31 Hugh Barker and Yuval Taylor, *Faking It: The Quest for Authenticity in Popular Music* (London: Faber, 2007), 221–3. Barker and Taylor make an analogy with the improvisatory practice of Keith Jarrett, while a number of critics have compared Young's guitar explorations with the work of John Coltrane.

32 Echard, *Poetics of Energy*, 191.

33 Barker and Taylor, *Faking It*, 219–20.

34 Allan Jones, 'The Edge of Darkness', *Uncut* no. 16 (September 1998), 58.

35 Jones, 'Edge of Darkness', 61–4.

36 Neil Young, quoted in McDonough, *Shakey*, 415.

37 Echard, *Poetics of Energy*, 165–8.

38 Young, liner notes to *Decade*.

39 Sarah Berry, 'Hank Williams Will Never Die: I'm Your Man and Heart of Gold', *Studies in Documentary Film* 2, no. 3, (2008): 248.

40 Richard A. Peterson, *Creating Country Music: Fabricating Authenticity* (Chicago: University of Chicago Press, 1997); Richard A. Peterson, 'The Dialectic of Hard-Core and Soft-Shell Country Music', in *Reading Country Music: Steel Guitars, Opry Stars and Honky-Tonk Bars*, ed. Cecilia Tichi (Durham, NC: Duke University Press, 1998), 234–55.

41 Karen O'Brien, *Joni Mitchell: Shadows and Light* (London: Virgin Books, 2002), 178–80.

42 Joni Mitchell, 'Coyote', on *Hejira* (LP: Elektra/Asylum K53053, 1976).

43 Ron Rosenbaum, 'The Best Joni Mitchell Song Ever: An Ode to Obsessive Listening', *The Slate*, online edition (14 December 2007), http://www.slate.com/articles/life/the_spectator/2007/12/the_best_jonI_mitchell_song_Ever.single.html (accessed 1 November 2014).

44 Neil Young, 'Thrasher', on *Rust Never Sleeps* (LP: Reprise K54105, 1979).

45 Mitchell interviewed in *Woman of Heart and Mind*, dir. Susan Lacey (2003).

46 Neil Young quoted in Adam Sweeting, 'Legend of a Loner', *Melody Maker* (7 September 1985), archived at *Rock's Backpages*, http://www.rocksbackpages.com/Library/Article/neil-young-legend-of-a-loner-part-1 (accessed 1 November 2014).

47 Young quoted in Sweeting, 'Legend of a Loner'. Bob Dylan would also compare himself to Willie Nelson when complaining about the way people referred to his age in connection to his continued touring; see Ian Bell, *Time Out of Mind: The Lives of Bob Dylan* (Edinburgh: Mainstream, 2014), 14. Country music comes freighted with this assumption of age.

48   Mercer, *Will You Take Me*, 97.

49   Joni Mitchell, 'Chinese Cafe/Unchained Melody', on *Wild Things Run Fast* (LP: Geffen GEF25102, 1982).

50   Larry Klein, liner note to Joni Mitchell, *Both Sides Now* (CD: Reprise 9362–47620–2, 2000).

51   I am referring here to the concept of the 'acoustic mirror' developed by Kaja Silverman. Following Guy Rosolato, Silverman takes Jacques Lacan's account of the process by which the infant develops an illusion of itself as a whole being in possession of a mastery it does not yet possess and analyses the role of sound in this process. Here, voice replaces gaze as the primary channel by which the attempt to claim mastery over oneself is enacted. As discussed in Chapter 1, Kathleen Woodward has also adapted Lacan's mirror stage to reflect on the disconnection being self-image and mirror image encountered by the ageing subject. Here I propose a sonicised version, via Rosolato and Silverman, of Woodward's 'mirror stage of old age'. See Kaja Silverman, *The Acoustic Mirror: The Female Voice in Psychoanalysis and Cinema* (Bloomington: Indiana University Press, 1988); Kathleen Woodward, *Aging and Its Discontents: Freud and Other Fictions* (Bloomington: Indiana University Press, 1991).

52   Quoted in O'Brien, *Shadows and Light*, 284.

53   Irving Townsend, liner notes to Billie Holiday, *Lady in Satin* (CD: Columbia/ Legacy CK65144, 1997).

54   Will Friedwald, *A Biographical Guide to the Great Jazz and Pop Singers* (New York: Pantheon, 2010), 232.

55   Billie Holiday's late recording of 'You've Changed' can be found on *Lady in Satin*; 'Sometimes I'm Happy' can be found on *Billie Holiday* (LP: MGM SE3764, 1959).

56   Mercer, *Will You Take Me*, 50.

57   Joni Mitchell, *Travelogue* (CD: Nonesuch 79817–2, 2002).

58   Echard, *Poetics of Energy*, 190.

59   Neil Young, 'Driftin' Back', on *Psychedelic Pill* (LP: Reprise 9362–49486–0, 2012).

60   Neil Young, *Waging Heavy Peace: A Hippie Dream* (London: Viking, 2012), 140. It is worth noting that Joni Mitchell has frequently made similar observations about switching between painting and music.

61   Young, *Waging Heavy Peace*, 137.

62   Sylviane Agacinski, *Time Passing: Modernity and Nostalgia*, trans. Jody Gladding (New York: Columbia University Press, 2003), 56.

63 Young's extended jams with Crazy Horse are often reminiscent of the late work of John Coltrane, who made ever longer explorations, many hard to capture adequately in the vinyl era. The band Swans are also notable as an example of trying to capture the epic, intense rock songs explored in live performance onto commercial releases; like Young and Crazy Horse, they have also had to break songs over sides of their vinyl records. For an interesting description of the subjective experience of time while listening to Bob Dylan's *Time Out of Mind*, see Lee Marshall, *Bob Dylan: The Never Ending Star* (Cambridge, UK: Polity, 2007), 243–7.

64 Around the same time, it was becoming increasingly common for users of video sharing websites to post entire sets by Young and Crazy Horse on YouTube. These videos attested to the heaviness being waged by the band around the world, with epic running times for many songs being the norm. They show the band as a seemingly unstoppable juggernaut, gaining ever greater solidity and heaviness as it travels on.

65 McDonough, *Shakey*, 539.

66 Guy Garvey, interviewed by Kirsty Young on *Desert Island Discs*, BBC Radio 4 (8 August 2014). Garvey also describes the late version of the song in a feature on 'The 30 Greatest Songs of Joni Mitchell' in *Uncut* no. 215 (April 2015), 41. In the same feature, Philip Selway of Radiohead makes similar comments about the early and late versions of 'Both Sides, Now' (32), while singer-songwriter Jimmy Webb describes Mitchell as 'an interesting combination of world-weary and totally innocent' (36).

Conclusion

1 Susan Sontag, 'The Double Standard of Aging', *Saturday Review* (23 September 1972): 29–38.

2 Collins has had quite extensive voice training, although she only began this training some years after her early career had already established her as a singer of great clarity and emotion. She discusses this, and much else, in Judy Collins, *Sweet Judy Blue Eyes: My Life in Music* (New York: Three Rivers Press, 2011).

3 I do not mean only rehearsal or previous musical experience; even an improviser on her first ever attempt to share publicly is presenting some form of 'back story'.

4 Bob Dylan in *No Direction Home: Bob Dylan*, dir. Martin Scorsese (2005).

5 Jim Harrison, 'The Theory and Practice of Rivers', in *The Shape of the Journey: New and Selected Poems* (Port Townsend: Copper Canyon Press, 2000), 303.

6 For an interesting discussion of Cole's work in relation to ageing, see chapter 6 of the book by his namesake, Thomas R. Cole, *The Journey of Life: A Cultural History of Aging in America* (Cambridge: Cambridge University Press, 1992), 110–38,

7 Cecelia Tichi, *The American Culture of Country Music* (Chapel Hill: University of North Carolina Press, 1994).

8 The quotations in this sentence are taken from, in order: Joni Mitchell, 'River' (from her album *Blue*); Harrison, 'Theory and Practice', 304; Hart Crane, 'Voyages', in *The Collected Poems of Hart Crane*, ed. Waldo Frank (New York: Liveright, 1933).

Bibliography

Adorno, Theodor W. 'Late Style in Beethoven'. In *Essays on Music*, edited by Richard Leppert. Translated by S. H. Gillespie. Berkeley: University of California Press, 2002, 564–8.

Agacinski, Sylviane. *Time Passing: Modernity and Nostalgia*. Translated by Jody Gladding. New York: Columbia University Press, 2003.

Améry, Jean. *On Aging: Revolt and Resignation*. Translated by John D. Barlow. Bloomington: Indiana University Press, 1994.

Augustine. *Confessions*. Translated by R. S. Pine-Coffin. London: Penguin, 1961.

Axelrod, Steven Gould. *Robert Lowell: Life and Art*. Princeton, NJ: Princeton University Press, 1978.

Babich, Babette. *The Hallelujah Effect: Philosophical Reflections on Music, Performance Practice, and Technology*. Farnham: Ashgate, 2013.

Baker, Emily. 'Just Travelin' Thru: Ageing Voices as Queer Resistance'. MA Dissertation. University of Sussex, 2013.

Barbour, Douglas, George Bowering, Jim Devlin, Bill van Dyk, Judith Fitzgerald, Christoph Herold, Drew Mildon, Christopher Rollason, Stephen Scobie and Jacques Willaert. 'Famous Blue Raincoat: A Symposium'. In *Intricate Preparations: Writing Leonard Cohen*, edited by Stephen Scobie. Toronto: ECW Press, 2000, 100–16.

Barker, Hugh and Yuval Taylor. *Faking It: The Quest for Authenticity in Popular Music*. London: Faber, 2007.

Barthes, Roland. *Camera Lucida: Reflections on Photography*. Translated by Richard Howard. London: Vintage, 2000.

Barthes, Roland. *The Pleasure of the Text*. Translated by Richard Miller. New York: Hill and Wang, 1975.

Barthes, Roland. *The Responsibility of Forms*. Translated by Richard Howard. Berkeley and Los Angeles: University of California Press, 1991.

Barthes, Roland. *The Rustle of Language*. Translated by Richard Howard. Berkeley: University of California Press, 1989.

Barthes, Roland. *Sade, Fourier, Loyola*. Translated by Richard Miller. London: Jonathan Cape, 1977.

Baudrillard, Jean. *Simulacra and Simulation*. Translated by Sheila Faria Glaser. Ann Arbor: The University of Michigan Press, 1994.

Bauldie, John. 'Helpless'. In *Neil Young and Broken Arrow: On a Journey through the Past*, edited by Alan Jenkins. Bridgend: Neil Young Appreciation Society, 1994, 53–6.

Beauvoir, Simone de. *The Coming of Age*. Translated by Patrick O'Brian. New York: G.P Putnam's Sons, 1972.

Bell, Ian. *Once Upon a Time: The Lives of Bob Dylan*. Edinburgh: Mainstream, 2013.

Bell, Ian. *Time Out of Mind: The Lives of Bob Dylan*. Edinburgh: Mainstream, 2014.

Benjamin, Walter. *Selected Writing Vol. 1: 1913-1926*. Edited by Marcus Bullock and Michael W. Jennings. Translated by Rodney Livingstone et al. Cambridge: The Belknap Press, 2004.

Benjamin, Walter. *Selected Writings Vol. 4: 1938-1940*. Edited by Howard Eiland and Michael W. Jennings. Translated by Edmund Jephcott et al. Cambridge: The Belknap Press, 2006.

Bennett, Andy. *Music, Style, and Aging: Growing Old Disgracefully?* Philadelphia: Temple University Press, 2013.

Bennett, Andy and Paul Hodkinson, eds. *Ageing and Youth Cultures: Music, Style and Identity*. London and New York: Berg, 2012.

Berry, Sarah. 'Hank Williams Will Never Die: I'm Your Man and Heart of Gold'. *Studies in Documentary Film* 2, no. 3, (2008): 247–55.

Blaikie, Andrew. *Ageing and Popular Culture*. Cambridge: Cambridge University Press, 1999.

Bobbio, Norberto. *Old Age and Other Essays*. Translated and edited by Allan Cameron. Cambridge: Polity, 2001.

Borges, Jorge Luis. *Labyrinths*. Edited by Donald A. Yates and James E. Irby. Penguin: Harmondsworth, 1985.

Boucher, David. *Dylan and Cohen: Poets of Rock and Roll*. New York: Continuum, 2004.

Boym, Svetlana. *The Future of Nostalgia*. New York: Basic Books, 2001.

Brackett, David. *Interpreting Popular Music*. Berkeley: University of California Press, 2000.

Burger, Jeff, ed. *Leonard Cohen on Leonard Cohen: Interviews and Encounters*. Chicago: Chicago Review Press, 2014.

Burke, Seán. *The Death and Return of the Author: Criticism and Subjectivity in Barthes, Foucault and Derrida*, 2nd edn. Edinburgh: Edinburgh University Press, 1998.

Calvino, Italo. *The Literature Machine: Essays*. Translated by Patrick Creagh. London: Secker & Warburg, 1987.

Calvino, Italo. *Under the Jaguar Sun*. Translated by William Weaver. London: Penguin, 2002.

Cannon, Geoffrey. Review of Joni Mitchell's *Clouds*. *The Guardian* (1969). Archived at *Rock's Backpages*, http://www.rocksbackpages.com/Library/Article/joni-mitchell-icloudsi. Accessed 15 December 2014.

Cantwell, Robert. *Bluegrass Breakdown: The Making of the Old Southern Sound*. New York: Da Capo, 1992.

Cantwell, Robert. 'Smith's Memory Theater'. *New England Review* 12, nos 1–2 (1991): 364–97.

Cantwell, Robert. *When We Were Good: The Folk Revival*. Cambridge, MA: Harvard University Press, 1996.

Carawan, Guy and Candie Carawan. *Voices from the Mountains*. New York: Alfred A. Knopf, 1975.

Cavarero, Adriana. *For More than One Voice: Toward a Philosophy of Vocal Expression*. Translated by Paul A. Kottman. Stanford: Stanford University Press, 2005.

Certeau, Michel de. *The Practice of Everyday Life*. Translated by Steven Rendall. Berkeley: University of California Press, 1984.

Chandler, Barbara. 'Why I Believe That Lloyd Chandler Wrote "Conversation with Death," also Known as "O Death"'. *Journal of Folklore Research* 41, nos 2/3 (2004): 127–32.

Chandler, Lloyd. 'Conversation with Death'. *Journal of Folklore Research* 41, nos 2/3 (2004): 125–6.

Ching, Barbara. *Wrong's What I Do Best: Hard Country Music and Contemporary Culture*. Oxford: Oxford University Press, 2001.

Chion, Michel. *The Voice in Cinema*. Edited and translated by Claudia Gorbman. New York: Columbia University Press, 1999.

Cohen, Leonard. *Book of Longing*. Toronto: McClelland & Stewart, 2006.

Cohen, Leonard. *Stranger Music: Selected Poems and Songs*. London: Jonathan Cape, 1993.

Cohen, Leonard. Untitled Acceptance Speech. Prince of Asturias Awards Ceremony. Oviedo, 21 October 2011.

Cole, Thomas R. *The Journey of Life: A Cultural History of Aging in America*. Cambridge: Cambridge University Press, 1992.

Collins, Judy. *Sweet Judy Blue Eyes: My Life in Music*. New York: Three Rivers Press, 2011.

Connor, Steven. *Dumbstruck: A Cultural History of Ventriloquism*. Oxford: Oxford University Press, 2000.

Copper, Bob. *A Song for Every Season*. Frogmore: Paladin, 1971.

Corcoran, Neil, ed. *Do You, Mr Jones?: Bob Dylan with the Poets and Professors*. London: Chatto & Windus, 2002.

Cornyn, Stan. 'Eye Witness'. In *Frank Sinatra and Popular Culture: Essays on an American Icon*, edited by Leonard Mustazza. Westport, CT: Praeger, 1998, 213–22.

Cott, Jonathan, ed. *Dylan on Dylan: The Essential Interviews*. London: Hodder & Stoughton, 2006.

Crane, Hart. *The Collected Poems of Hart Crane*. Edited by Waldo Frank. New York: Liveright Publishing Corporation, 1933.

Dawidoff, Nicholas. *In the Country of Country*. London: Faber and Faber, 1997.

Derrida, Jacques. *Margins of Philosophy*. Translated by Alan Bass. Chicago: Chicago University Press, 1982.

Devlin, Jim. 'Reflections on "Famous Blue Raincoat"'. In *Intricate Preparations: Writing Leonard Cohen*, edited by Stephen Scobie. Toronto: ECW Press, 2000, 101–3.

Dewey, John. *Art as Experience*. New York: Perigee, 2005.

Dolar, Mladen. *A Voice and Nothing More*. Cambridge, MA: The MIT Press, 2006.

Dylan, Bob. *Chronicles, Volume One*. London: Pocket Books, 2005.

Dylan, Bob. Untitled Acceptance Speech. MusiCares Person of the Year Ceremony. Los Angeles, 6 February 2015.

Echard, William. *Neil Young and the Poetics of Energy*. Bloomington: Indiana University Press, 2005.

Eisen, Jonathan, ed. *The Age of Rock: Sounds of the American Cultural Revolution*. New York: Vintage, 1969.

Elborough, Travis. *The Long-Player Goodbye: The Album from Vinyl to iPod and Back Again*. London: Sceptre, 2009.

Eliot, T. S. *The Complete Poems and Plays*. London: Faber and Faber, 1989.

Elliott, Richard. '"Across the Evening Sky": The Late Voices of Sandy Denny, Judy Collins and Nina Simone'. In *Gender, Age and Musical Creativity*, edited by Lisa Colton and Rachel Haworth. Farnham: Ashgate, 2015, 141–53.

Elliott, Richard. *Fado and the Place of Longing: Loss, Memory and the City*. Farnham: Ashgate, 2010.

Elliott, Richard. *Nina Simone*. Sheffield: Equinox, 2013.

Elliott, Richard. 'Popular Music and/as Event: Subjectivity, Love and Fidelity in the Aftermath of Rock 'n' Roll'. *Radical Musicology* 3 (2008), http://www.radical-musicology.org.uk: 60 pars.

Elliott, Richard. 'So Transported: Nina Simone, "My Sweet Lord" and the (Un)folding of Affect'. In *Sound, Music, Affect: Theorizing Sonic Experience*, edited by Marie Thompson and Ian Biddle. London: Bloomsbury, 2013, 75–90.

Eyerman, Ron and Andrew Jamison. *Music and Social Movements: Mobilizing Traditions in the Twentieth Century*. Cambridge: Cambridge University Press, 1998.

Featherstone, Mike and Andrew Wernick, eds. *Images of Aging: Cultural Representations of Later Life*. London: Routledge, 1995.

Fentress, James and Chris Wickham. *Social Memory*. Oxford: Blackwell, 1992.

Friedwald, Will. *A Biographical Guide to the Great Jazz and Pop Singers*. New York: Pantheon, 2010.

Friedwald, Will. *Sinatra! The Song Is You: A Singer's Art*. New York: Da Capo Press, 1997.

Frith, Simon. *Performing Rites: On the Value of Popular Music*. Oxford: Oxford University Press, 1996.

Gaughan, Dick. 'Dick Gaughan's Links in the Chain: Sandy Denny'. Official Website of Dick Gaughan. http://www.dickgaughan.co.uk/chain/sandy-denny.html. Accessed 30 August 2013.

Gigliotti, Gilbert L. 'The Composition of Celebrity: Sinatra as Text in the Liner Notes of Stan Cornyn'. In *Frank Sinatra and Popular Culture: Essays on an American Icon*, edited by Leonard Mustazza. Westport, CT: Praeger, 1998, 69–82.

Gigliotti, Gilbert L. *A Storied Singer: Frank Sinatra as Literary Conceit*. Westport, CT: Greenwood Press, 2002.

Gilbert, Roger. 'The Swinger and the Loser: Sinatra, Masculinity, and Fifties Culture'. In *Frank Sinatra and Popular Culture: Essays on an American Icon*, edited by Leonard Mustazza. Westport, CT: Praeger, 1998, 38–49.

Gill, Andy and Kevin Odegard. *A Simple Twist of Fate: Bob Dylan and the Making of Blood and the Tracks*. Cambridge, MA: Da Capo, 2004.

Gray, Michael. 'Signs of Life'. *Let It Rock* (April 1975): 34–5.

Gray, Michael. *Song & Dance Man III: The Art of Bob Dylan*. London: Continuum, 2000.

Guthrie, Woody. *Bound for Glory*. New York: Plume, 1983.

Haggard, Merle and Tom Carter. *My House of Memories*. New York: Cliff Street Books, 1999.

Hamilton, Christopher. *Middle Age*. Stocksfield: Acumen, 2009.

Harrison, Jim. *The Shape of the Journey: New and Selected Poems*. Port Townsend, WA: Copper Canyon Press, 2000.

Hepworth, Mike. *Stories of Ageing*. Buckingham: Open University Press, 2000.

Hoffman, Eva. *Time*. London: Profile, 2011.

Huber, Patrick. *Linthead Stomp: The Creation of Country Music in the Piedmont South*. Chapel Hill: The University of North Carolina Press, 2008.

Jacobson, Mark. 'Tangled Up In Bob'. In *Rolling Stone*, no. 866 (12 April 2001): 64–74, 151.

Jarman-Ivens, Freya. *Queer Voices: Technologies, Vocalities, and the Musical Flaw.* New York: Palgrave Macmillan, 2011.

Jennings, Ros and Abigail Gardner, eds. *'Rock On': Women, Ageing and Popular Music.* Farnham: Ashgate, 2012.

Jones, Allan. 'The Edge of Darkness'. *Uncut*, no. 16 (September 1998): 54–64.

Kearney, Richard. *On Stories.* London: Routledge, 2002.

Keightley, Emily and Michael Pickering. *The Mnemonic Imagination: Remembering as Creative Practice.* Basingstoke: Palgrave Macmillan, 2012.

Kopf, Biba. 'Lenny and *Jenny Sings Lenny*'. *New Musical Express* (14 March 1987). Archived at *Rock's Backpages*. http://www.rocksbackpages.com/Library/Article/lenny-and-jenny-sings-lenny. Accessed 28 February 2015.

Kot, Greg. 'Album Review: Leonard Cohen, "Old Ideas"'. *Chicago Tribune*, online edition (24 January 2012). http://articles.chicagotribune.com/2012–01–24/entertainment/chi-leonard-cohen-album-review-old-ideas-reviewed-20120124_1_leonard-cohen-album-review-12th-studio-album. Accessed 12 December 2014.

Lanza, Joseph. *Elevator Music: A Surreal History of Muzak, Easy-Listening and Other Moodsong.* London: Quartet, 2004.

Leppert, Richard and George Lipsitz. '"Everybody's Lonesome for Somebody": Age, the Body and Experience in the Music of Hank Williams'. *Popular Music* 9, no. 3 (1990): 259–74.

Light, Alan. *The Holy or the Broken: Leonard Cohen, Jeff Buckley, and the Unlikely Ascent of 'Hallelujah'.* New York: Atria, 2012.

Lindahl, Carl. 'Thrills and Miracles: Legends of Lloyd Chandler'. *Journal of Folklore Research* 41, nos 2/3 (2004): 133–71.

Linville, Sue Ellen. *Vocal Aging.* San Diego: Singular, 2001.

Marcus, Greil. *Invisible Republic: Bob Dylan's Basement Tapes.* London: Picador, 1997.

Marcus, Greil. *Like a Rolling Stone: Bob Dylan at the Crossroads.* London: Faber, 2005.

Marshall, Lee. *Bob Dylan: The Never Ending Star.* Cambridge: Polity, 2007.

McCormick, Neil. 'Leonard Cohen at 80: "The Other Side of the Hill Is No Time to Tarry"'. *The Telegraph*, online edition (20 September 2014). http://www.telegraph.co.uk/culture/music/rockandpopfeatures/11110223/Leonard-Cohen-at-80-The-other-side-of-the-hill-is-no-time-to-tarry.html. Accessed 12 December 2014.

McDonough, Jimmy. *Shakey: Neil Young's Biography.* London: Vintage, 2003.

McLucas, Anne Dhu. *The Musical Ear: Oral Tradition in the USA.* Farnham: Ashgate, 2010.

Mellers, Wilfrid. *A Darker Shade of Pale: A Backdrop to Bob Dylan.* New York: Oxford University Press, 1985.

Mercer, Michelle. *Will You Take Me As I Am: Joni Mitchell's* Blue *Period*. New York: Free Press, 2009.

Middleton, Richard. *Musical Belongings: Selected Essays*. Farnham: Ashgate, 2009.

Middleton, Richard. *Voicing the Popular: On the Subjects of Popular Music*. New York: Routledge, 2006.

Muir, Andrew. *The Razor's Edge: Bob Dylan and the Never-Ending Tour*. London: Helter Skelter, 2000.

Mustazza, Leonard, ed. *Frank Sinatra and Popular Culture: Essays on an American Icon*. Westport, CT: Praeger, 1998.

Nadel, Ira B. *Various Positions: A Life of Leonard Cohen*. Austin: University of West Texas Press, 2007.

Negus, Keith. 'Narrative, Interpretation, and the Popular Song'. *Musical Quarterly* 95, nos 2–3 (Summer–Fall 2012): 368–95.

Negus, Keith. 'Narrative Time and the Popular Song'. *Popular Music and Society* 35, no. 4 (2012): 483–500.

Negus, Keith and Michael Pickering. 'Creativity and Musical Experience'. In *Popular Music Studies*, edited by David Hesmondhalgh and Keith Negus. London: Arnold, 2002, 178–90.

Negus, Keith and Michael Pickering. *Creativity, Communication and Cultural Value*. London: Sage, 2004.

O'Brien, Geoffrey. *Sonata for Jukebox: Pop Music, Memory, and the Imagined Life*. New York: Counterpoint, 2004.

O'Brien, Karen. *Joni Mitchell: Shadows and Light*. London: Virgin Books, 2002.

O'Brien, Lucy. 'Like a Crone'. In *'Rock On': Women, Ageing and Popular Music*, edited by Ros Jennings and Abigail Gardner. Farnham: Ashgate, 2012, 19–33.

Paglia, Camille. *Break, Blow, Burn*. New York: Pantheon, 2005.

Peterson, Richard A. *Creating Country Music: Fabricating Authenticity*. Chicago: University of Chicago Press, 1997.

Peterson, Richard A. 'The Dialectic of Hard-Core and Soft-Shell Country Music'. In *Reading Country Music: Steel Guitars, Opry Stars and Honky-Tonk Bars*, edited by Cecilia Tichi. Durham, NC: Duke University Press, 1998, 234–55.

Polito, Robert. 'Bob Dylan: Henry Timrod Revisited'. Poetry Foundation Website (6 October 2006), http://www.poetryfoundation.org/article/178703.

Polizzotti, Mark. *Bob Dylan's Highway 61 Revisited*. New York: Continuum, 2006.

Proust, Marcel. *In Search of Lost Time Volume 6: Finding Time Again*. Translated by Ian Patterson. London: Penguin, 2002.

Ricoeur, Paul. *Time and Narrative*. Translated by Kathleen McLaughlin/Blamey and David Pellauer, 3 vols. Chicago: University of Chicago Press, 1984–8.

Roe, Nicholas. 'Playing Time'. In *Do You, Mr Jones?: Bob Dylan with the Poets and Professors*, edited by Neil Corcoran. London: Chatto & Windus, 2002, 81–104.

Rojek, Chris. *Frank Sinatra*. Cambridge: Polity, 2004.

Rosenbaum, Ron. 'The Best Joni Mitchell Song Ever: An Ode to Obsessive Listening'. *The Slate*, online edition (14 December 2007). http://www.slate.com/articles/life/the_spectator/2007/12/the_best_jonI_mitchell_song_Ever.single.html. Accessed 1 November 2014.

Said, Edward W. *On Late Style: Music and Literature Against the Grain*. London: Bloomsbury, 2005.

Scobie, Stephen. *Alias Bob Dylan*. Alberta: Red Deer College Press, 1991.

Scobie, Stephen, ed. *Intricate Preparations: Writing Leonard Cohen*. Toronto: ECW Press, 2000.

Segal, Lynne. *Out of Time: The Pleasures and Perils of Ageing*. London: Verso, 2013.

Shank, Barry. *Dissonant Identities: The Rock 'n' Roll Scene in Austin, Texas*. Hanover: Wesleyan University Press, 1994.

Silverman, Kaja. *The Acoustic Mirror: The Female Voice in Psychoanalysis and Cinema*. Bloomington and Indianapolis: Indiana University Press, 1988.

Simmons, Sylvie. *I'm Your Man: The Life of Leonard Cohen*. London: Vintage, 2013.

Simone, Nina and Stephen Cleary. *I Put a Spell On You: The Autobiography of Nina Simone*. New York: Da Capo Press, 2003.

Sontag, Susan. 'The Double Standard of Aging'. *Saturday Review* (23 September 1972): 29–38.

Spitzer, Michael. *Music as Philosophy: Adorno and Beethoven's Late Style*. Bloomington: Indiana University Press, 2006.

Stanley, Ralph and Eddie Dean. *Man of Constant Sorrow: My Life and Times*. New York: Gotham, 2010.

Strausbaugh, John. *Rock 'Til You Drop: The Decline from Rebellion to Nostalgia*. London: Verso, 2002.

Streissguth, Michael. *Outlaw: Waylon, Willie, Kris, and the Renegades of Nashville*. New York: It Books, 2013.

Suzuki, Shunryu. *Zen Mind, Beginner's Mind*. Edited by Trudy Dixon. Boston: Shambhala, 2011.

Sweeting, Adam. 'Legend of a Loner'. *Melody Maker* (7 September 1985). Archived at *Rock's Backpages*. http://www.rocksbackpages.com/Library/Article/neil-young-legend-of-a-loner-part-1. Accessed 1 November 2014.

Taylor, Mark C. and Dietrich Christian Lammerts. *Grave Matters*. London: Reaktion, 2002.

Taylor, Timothy D. *Strange Sounds: Music, Technology, and Culture*. New York: Routledge, 2001.

Taylor, Timothy D., Mark Katz and Tony Grajeda, eds. *Music, Sound and Technology in America: A Documentary History of Early Phonograph, Cinema, and Radio*. Durham, NC: Duke University Press, 2012.

Terkel, Studs. *Will the Circle Be Unbroken?: Reflections on Death and Dignity*. London: Granta, 2002.

Tichi, Cecelia. *High Lonesome: The American Culture of Country Music*. Chapel Hill: University of North Carolina Press, 1994.

Virilio, Paul. *The Aesthetics of Disappearance*. Translated by Philip Beitchman. Los Angeles: Semiotext(e), 2009.

Ward, Philip. *Sandy Denny: Reflections on Her Music*. Kibworth Beauchamp: Matador, 2011.

Whiteley, Sheila. *Too Much Too Young: Popular Music, Age and Gender*. London: Routledge, 2005.

Whitesell, Lloyd. *The Music of Joni Mitchell*. Oxford: Oxford University Press, 2008.

Wilentz, Sean. *Bob Dylan in America*. London: Vintage, 2011.

Wilentz, Sean and Greil Marcus, eds. *The Rose & the Briar: Death, Love and Liberty in the American Ballad*. New York: W.W. Norton, 2005.

Williams, Paul. *Bob Dylan: Performing Artist 1960–1973*. London: Omnibus Press, 2004.

Williams, Paul. *Bob Dylan: Performing Artist 1974–1986*. London: Omnibus Press, 2004.

Williams, Paul. *Bob Dylan: Performing Artist 1986–1990 & Beyond*. London: Omnibus, 2005.

Williams, Paul. *Neil Young: Love to Burn: Thirty Years of Speaking Out 1966–1996*. London: Omnibus, 1997.

Williams, Paul. 'The Way We Are Today'. In *The Age of Rock: Sounds of the American Cultural Revolution*, edited by Jonathan Eisen. New York: Vintage, 1969, 307–14.

Williams, Richard. *The Blue Moment: Miles Davis's* Kind of Blue *and the Remaking of Modern Music*. London: Faber and Faber, 2009.

Williamson, Nigel. *Journey through the Past: The Stories behind the Classic Songs of Neil Young*. London: Carlton, 2002.

Woodward, Kathleen. *Aging and Its Discontents: Freud and Other Fictions*. Bloomington: Indiana University Press, 1991.

Woodward, Kathleen. *At Last, the Real Distinguished Thing: The Late Poems of Eliot, Pound, Stevens, and Williams*. Columbus: Ohio State University Press, 1980.

Wright, John. *Traveling the High Way Home: Ralph Stanley and the World of Traditional Bluegrass Music*. Urbana: University of Illinois Press, 1993.

Young, Neil. *Waging Heavy Peace: A Hippie Dream*. London: Viking, 2012.

Zielinski, Siegfried. *Deep Time of the Media: Toward an Archaeology of Hearing and Seeing by Technical Means*. Translated by Gloria Custance. Cambridge: The MIT Press, 2008.

Discography

Rather than considering which format may be most convenient for the reader (which is often the case with discographies whose main purpose is to recommend listening), I have listed the formats I used when listening to the music. In most cases, this has also been the version that I own and through which I originally experienced the music. This reflects a discussion initiated in Chapter 1 regarding the materiality of music and histories and autobiographies of listening, while also making a case for musical recordings to be taken as seriously as literary ones in scholarly work – not just 'recommended listening', but the source of ideas and information.

Anglin Brothers, The. *The Anglin Brothers*. LP. Old Homestead OHCS-122, 1979.

Boggs, Dock. *Country Blues: Complete Early Recordings (1927–29)*. CD. Revenant 205, 1997.

Boggs, Dock. *His Folkway Years 1963–1968*. CD. Smithsonian Folkways SF 40108, 1998.

Burland, Dave. Tony Capstick and Dick Gaughan. *Songs of Ewan MacColl*. LP. Black Crow CRO 215, 1978.

Cash, Johnny. *American IV: The Man Comes Around*. CD. American/Lost Highway 063339–2, 2002.

Clark, Guy. *Old No. 1*. LP. Edsel ED 285, 1988.

Clark, Guy. *Texas Cookin'*. LP. Edsel ED 287, 1988.

Cohen, Leonard. *The Future*. LP. Columbia 4724981, 1992.

Cohen, Leonard. *I'm Your Man*. LP. CBS 4606421, 1988.

Cohen, Leonard. *Live in Dublin*. CD/DVD. Sony 88875035582, 2014.

Cohen, Leonard. *Old Ideas*. CD. Columbia 88697986712, 2012.

Cohen, Leonard. *Popular Problems*. CD. Columbia 88875014292, 2014.

Cohen, Leonard. *Songs from the Road*. CD/DVD. Columbia/Legacy 88697768392, 2010.

Cohen, Leonard. *Songs of Leonard Cohen*. CD. Columbia/Legacy 88697093892, 2007.

Cohen, Leonard. *Songs of Love and Hate*. CD. Columbia/Legacy 88697093872, 2007.

Cohen, Leonard. *Various Positions*. LP. CBS S-26222, 1984.

DeMent, Iris. *My Life*. CD. Warner Bros. 9362–45493–2, 1994.

Dylan, Bob. *Blood on the Tracks*. LP. CBS 69097, 1974.

Dylan, Bob. *The Bootleg Series Volumes 1–3: Rare & Unreleased 1961–1991*. LP. Columbia 4680861, 1991.

Dylan, Bob. *Bringing It All Back Home*. LP. CBS 32344, 1965.

Dylan, Bob. *Desire*. LP. CBS 86003, 1975.

Dylan, Bob. *The Freewheelin' Bob Dylan*. LP. CBS 62193, 1963.

Dylan, Bob. *Highway 61 Revisited*. LP. CBS 4609531, 1965.

Dylan, Bob. *"Love and Theft"*. CD. Columbia COL 5043649, 2001.

Dylan, Bob. *Modern Times*. Columbia 82876876061, 2006.

Dylan, Bob. *Shadows in the Night*. LP. Columbia/Sony 88875057961, 2015.

Dylan, Bob. *Street Legal*. LP. CBS 86067, 1978.

Dylan, Bob. *Tell Tale Signs: Rare and Unreleased 1989–2006*. CD. Columbia/Legacy 8869774610, 2010.

Dylan, Bob. *Tempest*. LP. Columbia 88725457601, 2012.

Dylan, Bob. *Time Out of Mind*. LP. Columbia/Music on Vinyl MOVLP1049, 1997.

Dylan, Bob. *The Times They Are A-Changin'*. LP. CBS 62251, 1964.

Dylan, Bob. *World Gone Wrong*. CD. Columbia 4748572, 1993.

Eliot, T. S. *Four Quartets Read by the Author*. LP. His Master's Voice CLP 1115, c. 1956.

Eriksen, Tim. *Northern Roots Live In Náměšť*. CD. Indies Scope MAM451–2, 2009.

Eriksen, Tim. *Tim Eriksen*. CD. Appleseed APR CD 1053, 2001.

Gunning, Sarah Ogan. *Girl of Constant Sorrow*. CD. Folk-Legacy CD-26, 2006.

Haggard, Merle. *I'm a Lonesome Fugitive*. LP. Capitol ST 2702. 1967.

Haggard, Merle and Willie Nelson. *Seashores of Old Mexico*. CD. Epic EK 40293, 1987.

Holcomb, Roscoe. *The High Lonesome Sound*. CD. Smithsonian Folkways SFCD 40104, 1998.

Holiday, Billie. *Billie Holiday*. LP. MGM SE3764, 1959.

Holiday, Billie. *Lady in Satin*. CD. Columbia/Legacy CK65144, 1997.

Jones, Bessie with the Georgia Sea Island Singers and Others. CD. *Get In Union: Recordings by Alan Lomax 1959–1966*. Tompkins Square TSQ 5074, 2014.

Jones, David Lynn. *Wood, Wind and Stone*. CD. Mercury 836951–2, 1990.

Kristofferson, Kris. *The Silver Tongued Devil and I*. LP. Monument 64636, 1971.

Mitchell, Joni. *Blue*. LP. Reprise K44128, 1971.

Mitchell, Joni. *Both Sides Now*. CD Reprise 9362–47620–2, 2000.

Mitchell, Joni. *Court and Spark*. LP. Asylum SYLA8756, 1974.

Mitchell, Joni. *For the Roses*. LP. Elektra/Asylum K53007, 1976.

Mitchell, Joni. *Hejira*. LP. Elektra/Asylum K53053, 1976.

Mitchell, Joni. *Travelogue*. CD. Nonesuch 79817–2, 2002.

Mitchell, Joni. *Wild Things Run Fast*. LP. Geffen GEF25102, 1982.

Nelson, Willie. *Yesterday's Wine*. LP. RCA Victor LSP-4568, 1971.

New Lost City Ramblers. *There Ain't No Way Out*. CD. Smithsonian Folkways SFCD
    40098, 1997).

Parker, William. *I Plan to Stay a Believer: The Inside Songs of Curtis Mayfield*. CD,
    AUM Fidelity AUM062/63, 2010.

Prine, John. *John Prine*. LP. Atlantic SD 8296, 1972.

Prine, John. *The Singing Mailman Delivers*. CD. Oh Boy OBR-040, 2011.

Reed, Dock and Vera Hall. *Spirituals*. LP. Folkways 2038, 1953.

Simone, Nina. *Emergency Ward / It Is Finished / Black Gold*. CD. Camden
    74321924802, 2002.

Simone, Nina. *Jazz as Played in an Exclusive Side Street Club*. CD. Charly SNAP
    216CD, 2002.

Sinatra, Frank. *Cycles*. LP. Reprise RSLP 1027, 1968.

Sinatra, Frank. *Frank Sinatra Sings for Only the Lonely*. LP. Capitol W1053, 1958.

Sinatra, Frank. *In the Wee Small Hours*. LP. Capitol W581, 1955.

Sinatra, Frank. *September of My Years*. LP. Reprise R 1014, 1965.

Sinatra, Frank. *Someone to Watch Over Me*. LP. CBS/Hallmark HM592, 1968.

Sinatra, Frank. *Songs for Swingin' Lovers!*. LP. Capitol W653, 1957.

Sinatra, Frank. *Strangers in the Night*. CD. Reprise 7599–27034–2, 1990.

Sinatra, Frank. *Watertown*. CD. Reprise 9362–45689–2, c. 1990.

Stanley, Ralph. *Clinch Mountain Country*. CD. Rebel REB-5001, 1997.

Stanley, Ralph. *Shine On*. CD. Rebel REB-CD-1810, 2005.

Stanley Brothers, The. *Angel Band: The Classic Mercury Recordings*. CD. Mercury/
    Polygram 314–528 191–2, 1995.

Stanley Brothers, The. *The Complete Columbia Stanley Brothers*. CD. Columbia/
    Legacy CK 53798, 1996.

Stanley Brothers, The. *Earliest Recordings: The Complete Rich-R-Tone 78s (1947–
    1952)*. CD. Rich-R-Tone/Revenant 203, 1997.

Stanley Brothers, The. *An Evening Long Ago*. CD. Columbia/DMZ/Legacy CK 86747,
    2004.

Stanley Brothers, The. *Hymns of the Cross*. LP. King 918, 1964.

Stanley Brothers, The. *The King Years: 1961–1965*. CD. King KG-09502, 2003.

Stanley Brothers, The. *Long Journey Home*. CD. Rebel Records REB-CD-1110, 1990.

Stanley Brothers, The. *The Stanley Brothers & The Clinch Mountain Boys: 1953–1958 & 1959*. CD. Bear Family BCD 15681 BH, 1993.

Swift, Taylor. *Red*. LP. Big Machine/Mercury BMR3104000, 2012.

Van Zandt, Townes. *The Late Great Townes Van Zandt*. LP. Tomato/Charly LIK49, 1988.

Various. *The Anthology of American Folk Music*. CD. Smithsonian Folkways SFW40090, 1997.

Various. *Bob Dylan in the 80s: Volume One*. LP. ATO 0224, 2014.

Various. *High Atmosphere: Ballads and Banjo Tunes from Virginia and North Carolina*. CD. Rounder CD 0028, 1995.

Various. *Music from the Motion Picture O Brother, Where Art Thou?* CD. Mercury 170069–2, 2000.

Various. *Old Love Songs & Ballads from the Big Laurel, North Carolina*. CD. Smithsonian Folkways FA2309, 2006.

Various. *People Take Warning! Murder Ballads & Disaster Songs, 1913–1938*. CD/book. Tomkins Square TSQ 1875, 2007.

Various. *Songcatcher* (Music From And Inspired By The Motion Picture). CD. Vanguard 79586–2, 2001.

Various. *Songs of the Old Regular Baptists: Lined-out Hymnody from Southeastern Kentucky*. CD. Smithsonian Folkways SFCD 40106, 1997.

Various. *Tower of Song: The Songs of Leonard Cohen*. CD. A&M 540 259–2, 1995.

Various. *Twistable, Turnable Man: A Musical Tribute to the Songs of Shel Silverstein*. LP. Sugar Hill SUG-LP-4051, 2013.

Waits, Tom. *Closing Time*. LP. Asylum AS 53030, 1973.

Waits, Tom. *The Heart of Saturday Night*. LP. Asylum AS 53035, 1974.

Waits, Tom. *Small Change*. LP. Asylum K53050, 1976

Workman, Nimrod. *I Want to Go Where Things Are Beautiful*. CD. Twos & Fews/Drag City DC379CD, 2008.

Young, Neil. *Americana*. LP. Reprise 9362–49508–6, 2012. *Decade*. LP. Reprise REP64037, 1977.

Young, Neil. *Comes a Time*. LP. Reprise K 54099, 1978.

Young, Neil. *Decade*. LP. Reprise 64037, 1977.

Young, Neil. *Harvest*. LP. Reprise K 54005, 1972.

Young, Neil. *A Letter Home*. Third Man. TMR 245, 2014.

Young, Neil. *Live Rust*. LP. Reprise REP 64041, 1979.

Young, Neil. *Old Ways*. LP. Geffen GEF 26377, 1985.

Young, Neil. *Psychedelic Pill*. LP. Reprise 9362–49486–0, 2012.

Young, Neil. *Rust Never Sleeps*. LP. Reprise K54105, 1979.

Young, Neil. *Tonight's the Night*. LP. Reprise MS222, 1975.

Young, Neil. *Weld*. LP. Reprise 7599–26671–1, 1991.

Filmography

Dont Look Back. Directed by D. A. Pennebaker, 1967.

Down from the Mountain. Directed by Nick Doob, Chris Hegedus and D. A. Pennebaker, 2000.

God and Generals. Directed by Robert Maxwell, 2003.

Harlan County U.S.A. Directed by Barbara Kopple, 1976.

I'm Not There. Directed by Todd Haynes, 2007.

Ladies and Gentlemen, Mr Leonard Cohen. Directed by Donald Brittain and Don Owen, 1965.

Leonard Cohen: I'm Your Man. Directed by Lian Lunson, 2005.

Neil Young: Heart of Gold. Directed by Jonathan Demme, 2006.

No Direction Home: Bob Dylan. Directed by Martin Scorsese, 2005.

O Brother, Where Art Thou? Directed by Joel and Ethan Cohn, 2000.

Rust Never Sleeps. Directed by Neil Young, 1979.

Songcatcher. Directed by Maggie Greenwald, 2000.

Woman of Heart and Mind. Directed by Susan Lacey, 2003.

Year of the Horse. Directed by Jim Jarmusch, 1997.

Index

Lightning Source UK Ltd.
Milton Keynes UK
UKOW06f0840230517
301806UK00011B/242/P

9 781501 332142